GEORGE ELIOT AND HERBERT SPENCER

GEORGE ELIOT AND
HERBERT SPENCER

FEMINISM, EVOLUTIONISM, AND THE
RECONSTRUCTION OF GENDER

Nancy L. Paxton

PRINCETON UNIVERSITY PRESS   PRINCETON, NEW JERSEY

Library of Congress Cataloging-in-Publication Data

Paxton, Nancy L., 1949–
George Eliot and Herbert Spencer : feminism, evolutionism,
and the reconstruction of gender / Nancy L. Paxton.
p. cm.
Includes bibliographical references and index.
ISBN 0-691-06841-0 (alk. paper)
1. Eliot George, 1819–1880—Political and social views.
2. Spencer, Herbert, 1820–1903. 3. Feminism and literature—Great Britain—
History—19th century. 4. Literature and science—Great Britain—History—
19th century. 5. Evolution in literature. 6. Sex role in literature.
7. Women in literature. I. Title.
PR4692.F45P39   1991
823'.8—dc20   90-44942   CIP

This book has been composed in Adobe Baskerville

Printed in the United States of America by
Princeton University Press,
Princeton, New Jersey

10   9   8   7   6   5   4   3   2   1

For my mother and father

Contents

Acknowledgments ———————————————————

Had it not been for the generous intellectual, moral, and financial support of many people, this book might have suffered the same fate as Edward Casaubon's *Key to All Mythologies*. This study was inspired, first of all, by George Levine, whose dedicated teaching and scholarly work on George Eliot offered profound insights into Victorian culture and Eliot's place in it as an intellectual and as a woman. Likewise, I am deeply indebted to Elaine Showalter for her guidance in formulating this study, for our many conversations about feminist literary criticism, and for her important scholarship on Victorian women. Finally, I wish to express my warmest appreciation to Catharine Stimpson for her ongoing interest in this project, for her unfailing generosity, and for her sympathetic support.

While it is impossible to thank all the people who have sustained me while I completed the research for and writing of this manuscript, there are several individuals whose assistance has been essential. I wish to thank Nancy K. Miller for offering a stimulating seminar on feminist literary criticism, sponsored by the National Endowment for the Humanities in 1987. She and the other members of the seminar offered brilliant criticism and valuable bibliographical suggestions that were instrumental in redefining the theoretical framework for this study. Ellen Graham, of Yale University Press, also offered valuable practical advice and reassurance. Finally, I wish to express deepest appreciation to Barry Qualls for his astute, thorough, and extraordinarily generous reading of this manuscript. His advice helped me immeasurably in transforming this study into its final form. Thanks also go to Bob Brown and Jane Low, at Princeton University Press, and to my copyeditor, Victoria Wilson-Schwartz; each has offered personal attention and assistance with the countless and sometimes arcane details of the publication process.

I would also not have been able to complete this book without the help of many friends, colleagues, and students whose interest in my work on George Eliot has encouraged me over more than ten years. This book simply would not have been written without the support of Joe Boles, who never lost faith in the importance of this project, who helped me master the mysteries of word processing, and who proofread endless earlier drafts. Vicky Anderson-Schiff offered much appreciated help by editing a recent draft of this manuscript. Special thanks for theoretical and bibliographical suggestions and for dependable and enthusiastic interest go to Susan Jacobs, Marie Logue, Helen Cooper, Diane Marting, Susan Nash, Kate Ellis, Ann Snitow, Laura Quinn, Becky Hogan, and Julia Watson. Susan Squire, Shoshana Knapp, Dena Goodman, Johanna Drucker, Mary Berg, Deb Nord, and Virginia Davidson have also provided sound critical advice.

To my colleagues and students at Northern Arizona University, I also owe a deep debt of gratitude. Bryan Short, Sharon Crowley, and Susan Foster, in particular, have shared their critical insights and have offered both sympathy and timely support when it was needed most. Thanks, too, to Paul Ferlazzo, Karl Webb, Henry Hooper, and to members of the Northern Arizona University Organized Research Council for providing the released time and financial support over several summers that allowed me to complete the research for this project.

I am also grateful to several organizations which awarded me the fellowships and grants that provided the time and money that allowed this project to come at last to fruition. Initial research for this project was supported by the Louis J. Bevier Fellowship at Rutgers University and by the Charlotte Newcombe Foundation. Heartfelt thanks also go to Richard M. Hunt and to the Andrew W. Mellon Faculty Fellowship Program at Harvard University for the award in 1988–1989 that provided the time that allowed me to complete this book at last.

GEORGE ELIOT AND HERBERT SPENCER

1 ——————————————————————

Introduction

Now we think it an immense mistake to maintain that there is no sex in literature. Science
has no sex: the mere knowing and reasoning
faculties, if they act correctly, must go through
the same process, and arrive at the same result.
But in art and literature, which imply the action of the entire being, in which every fibre of
the nature is engaged, in which every peculiar
modification of the individual makes itself felt,
woman has something to contribute. Under
every imaginable social condition, she will necessarily have a class of sensations and emotions—the maternal ones—which must remain
unknown to man; and the fact of her comparative physical weakness, which, however it may
have been exaggerated by a vicious civilization,
can never be cancelled, introduces a distinc-
tively feminine condition into the wondrous
chemistry of the affections and sentiments,
which inevitably gives rise to distinctive forms
and combinations.
   —George Eliot,
      "Woman in France: Madame de Sablé"

GEORGE ELIOT is still frequently regarded as a sort of Victorian Athena,
the self-created, motherless, and mother-denying daughter who sprang
full-grown and fully armed, with a pen at least, from the head of a paternal and magisterial George Henry Lewes. Henry James may have initiated this critical tradition when he complained that Eliot always pro-
ceeded "from the abstract to the concrete," and his assessment of Eliot
as an overly intellectual novelist has been elaborated by some of her most
celebrated critics.[1] Most of Eliot's more recent readers, however, no
longer regard her intellectualism as necessarily a defect, and they have
produced many excellent studies in the last twenty years describing her
response to the philosophical and scientific traditions of her day. Yet the

habit of seeing Eliot as the overly intellectual creation of the men she knew, or read, persists. She is portrayed, for example, in major biographical studies, as well as in a number of otherwise successful analyses of her thought, as a passive vessel into which the ideas of Darwin, Spencer, Lewes, Comte, Bain, and others were poured.[2]

Gordon Haight cautions against taking this approach when he writes that "every main bias of Eliot's mind" had been established before she met Lewes.[3] Eliot's letters show that she insisted on her own intellectual independence when her friends or contemporaries presumed that Lewes—or, indeed, any one else—spoke for her. In 1860, for example, she wrote a bristling letter to Sara Hennell, in which she complained: "Let me say for once for all that you must not impute my opinions to him nor vice versa. The intense happiness of our union is derived in a high degree from the perfect freedom with which we each follow and declare our own impressions" (*GEL* 3: 358). Eliot's correspondence and biography demonstrate repeatedly her effort to establish and protect her identity as a strong-minded woman.

Several recent studies of Eliot's response to Victorian science have avoided this condescending depiction of Eliot as Lewes's creature by revealing her penetrating criticism of Darwinian science, but they nonetheless misrepresent the extent of Eliot's feminist resistance to evolutionary theory by ignoring the prior and more pervasive role that Herbert Spencer played in Eliot's life and writing throughout her career.[4]

Spencer's contributions to evolutionary theory are typically ignored by most recent historians of science who retrospectively see Charles Darwin as the only true spokesman of evolution. Robert M. Young, for example, contends that the "significance of the writings of Robert Chambers, Herbert Spencer, and A. R. Wallace was far greater than has been reflected in writings about the debate."[5] This exclusive focus on Darwin not only distorts our understanding of the history of Victorian science but also reifies the authority of modern science by suppressing the history of its mistakes. In describing Spencer's contributions to Victorian science, in particular, Young contends:

> The problem about Spencer is . . . to get historians to see how central his work and influence were to the nineteenth-century debate, both among scientists and the broader public. His reputation has suffered most among the leaders of thought in the period because subsequent scientists (followed dutifully by historians) have anachronistically dismissed him for holding a "Lamarckian" theory of the mechanism of evolution. Two things should be noticed about this position. First, that it was a theory which, though embattled, was taken seriously throughout the nineteenth century and indeed, was given increasing weight by Darwin (just as Spencer allowed the increasing role for natural selection). This point should lend perspective to the dismissal of Spencer as a seri-

ous figure. Second, he was unequivocal in pointing out that he attached great weight to the question of the mechanism of evolution precisely because of its ethical, educational, social, and political consequences. Throughout his mature life he was seeking a scientific basis for a doctrine of inevitable progress which would justify his belief in an extreme of laissez-faire economics and social theory. ("Historiographic" 382–83)

Spencer's role in establishing evolutionary science as a master discourse defining sexuality, knowledge, and power in the second half of the nineteenth century can best be seen when we consider the matrix of ideas suggested by the broad term evolutionism, which spans the uncertain and shifting territory defined by his interpretations of biogenetic law, natural and sexual selection, adaptation, equilibrium, and decadence.[6]

The primary objective of this study is to disclose Eliot's ongoing dialogue with Spencer throughout her career, and to demonstrate her resolute feminist resistance to many aspects of Spencer's biological determinism, especially as it found expression in his developing analysis of female sexuality and motherhood. Moreover, by understanding Eliot's acceptance of some tenets of Spencerian—as opposed to Darwinian—evolutionism, we can begin to understand the conservative force that Victorian science and evolutionary theory exerted in containing the debate on what Victorians called the Woman Question. Indeed, in an era when Darwin could simply dismiss J. S. Mill's arguments for women's emancipation in *The Subjection of Women* as "unscientific" (Russett 13-14), we must recognize the monumental challenge that evolutionary theory posed for feminist intellectuals who, like Eliot, saw Victorian science as promoting a more accurate view of the natural world.

Of course, the problem of defining the origins of ideas—evolutionary or otherwise—is a complex and humbling one, as Eliot reminds us in *Daniel Deronda*.Instructed by this novel, I do not propose to argue that Spencer influenced Eliot more profoundly than Darwin did. Instead, I wish to trace those parallels in their lives and in their ideas about evolution, nature, women, sex, and gender that have not been recognized sufficiently by critics of Eliot's work. Many biographical similarities invite this approach, for Eliot and Spencer were born only a year apart and both grew up in the Midlands. Early in life, both were exposed to this region's Dissenting traditions of evangelicalism and socialism. Both were largely self-educated and both earned their livelihoods, for a time, as editors of serious intellectual periodicals. And both won fame among the ranks of the most prolific and ambitious thinkers of their time. But this comparison also exposes the profound impact of gender on their lives and in the positions they take, revealing how Eliot's gender limited her agency and means of resistance as an intellectual woman in Victorian England.

The following chapters show that when Eliot and Spencer began their lifelong friendship in 1851, they agreed in endorsing several of the goals espoused by Victorian feminists in the 1840s and 1850s. However, by the time Eliot's *Adam Bede* appeared in 1859, Spencer had already begun his dramatic repudiation of the feminist causes he originally supported. How Spencer's feminism transformed itself into passionate antifeminism under the pressure of his evolutionary ideas, and how Eliot retained what has seemed to most modern readers an ambivalent feminism at best, is part of the story I wish to relate in the pages that follow.

This study presents an analysis of the anxiety of influence that existed between George Eliot and Herbert Spencer rather than an argument about the direction of influence.[7] The extant biographical record is too incomplete on several important questions to allow the dynamics of influence to be determined more precisely, for John Cross destroyed many of Eliot's letters, especially from the crucial early years of her friendship with Spencer, and many of Spencer's letters from this period have also been lost (Haight, *George Eliot* 71, 112). While the letters that remain do show that Eliot initially responded to Spencer's work with enthusiasm, they also reveal how her appreciation for his developing evolutionary analysis turned to an angry criticism which, by 1861, prompted her refusal to discuss with him its implications for art, literature, education, social reform, and feminism. This criticism is inscribed in all of her novels. By the time *Middlemarch* (1871–1872) had established Eliot's reputation as a serious novelist, however, she had achieved a more good-humored perspective on Spencer and regarded her friend's intellectual crotchets with more indulgence. Perhaps this is why Darwinism appears to be more influential in her last two novels.

In Eliot's own time and after her death, however, she was regarded as a disciple of Spencer rather than Darwin. A few months after Eliot's death in 1880, Spencer himself tried to correct what he saw as an overestimation of his influence on her. To one journalist he wrote:

> It may be, and probably is as you say, that she was influenced all along by my books. In fact, accepting their general views as she did, it could hardly be otherwise; and it may be that the *Principles of Psychology* was a help to her in the respect of her analysis. But it never occurred to me to consider the effect so great as you suppose. Her powers in respect of introspection and sympathetic insight into others were naturally extremely great; and I think her achievements in the way of delineation of character are almost wholly due to spontaneous intuition.[8]

Because many of Eliot's readers apparently continued to have difficulty imagining that she possessed a mind of her own, Spencer's ambivalent efforts to correct presumptions about her debts to him went unheeded until his own reputation suffered a precipitous decline in the early years of this century.

Spencer's debts to Eliot have been even more difficult to recognize, because, first of all, he seemed incapable of acknowledging intellectual influences of any kind. His refutation of the obvious influence of Comte on his social theories is, perhaps, the best known example.[9] While he did not, and probably could not, admit that Eliot had also profoundly influenced his thought, he describes numerous meetings and conversations with her in his *Autobiography*.

The most persuasive evidence that Spencer felt an anxiety of influence in his relation to Eliot can be seen in his efforts to suppress most of the passages in his writing that reveal Eliot's role in his personal and intellectual life, especially in the 1850s. After Eliot's death in 1880, Spencer obliterated or distorted the record of his early position on feminism by erasing most of the chapter on "The Rights of Women" and rewriting many other passages about women in his *Social Statics* and in the first editions of the earlier volumes of his *Synthetic Philosophy*. None of his modern editors has commented on the significance of these changes.[10] Similarly, his depiction of Eliot—and his comments and silences about women more generally in his *Autobiography*—expose, but do not acknowledge or justify, the astonishing reversal in his assessment of feminism and women's evolutionary potential.

In fact, Spencer's failure to reconcile his ideas about evolutionism with his attitudes about Victorian feminism, and his subsequent repudiation and erasure of his inconsistencies, especially in his evaluation of gender roles and motherhood, give us insight into how post-Darwinian science and medicine received and subsequently reinscribed traditional interpretations of biological differences in what I call the "reconstruction of gender" that followed Darwin's revolution. Unlike most Victorians, who began to discern the profound implications of evolutionary theory only after the publication of *On the Origin of Species* and *The Descent of Man*, Spencer and Eliot recognized the challenge that evolutionary theory posed for feminism and other social reforms in the early 1850s. They both realized that as orthodox Christianity came under attack by evolutionary theory, a reassessment of the "biopolitics" of Victorian society would follow, requiring a reevaluation, for example, of the elements Michel Foucault has identified as central to it: "health, progeny, race, the future of the species, [and] the vitality of the social body."[11] These issues were most sharply confronted, as we shall see, when they considered the subject of motherhood and the language, symbols, and ideology that defined it.

Another consequence of Spencer's habit of revising himself is that it is difficult to reconstruct and document a clear chronology of the development of his ideas by consulting standard editions of his *Synthetic Philosophy*. Nearly all of the prose that appears in the *Synthetic Philosophy* was published at least twice, appearing first in contemporary periodicals or in serial form available in installments to individual private subscribers. These "numbers" were later consolidated, usually without further editing, and reissued as complete volumes. In the analysis that follows, I cite whenever possible from the first editions of these volumes rather than from the earlier ephemeral serial versions, though this sometimes may create the impression that Eliot was responding to ideas that Spencer had not yet published.

Eliot's letters show, however, that she and George Henry Lewes helped Spencer develop his plan for the serial publication of the *Synthetic Philosophy*, kept in close contact with him over the years, and often read his essays, sometimes in draft form and frequently before their publication as numbers. Moreover, it was not difficult to anticipate the general direction that Spencer's evolutionary analysis would take after 1860 when he published a detailed outline for his projected series of volumes, later called the *Synthetic Philosophy*. Over the next twelve years, Spencer doggedly organized his research and writing according to this schedule. It was not until February 1872, when Eliot was writing Book 5 of *Middlemarch*, that Spencer interrupted his research for the first volume of *The Principles of Sociology* in order to write *The Study of Sociology*, first published in *Contemporary Review* between April 1872 and October 1873. Thus, for most of Eliot's writing career, Spencer's evolutionary ideas developed in very predictable patterns. My reading of her novels indicates that Eliot often responded to and sometimes anticipated Spencer's most sexist and racist evolutionary arguments.

Eliot's intellectualism and her contributions to the Victorian novel and to Victorian thought no longer need to be defended, but Spencer's work still demands reassessment. Like Eliot, he too occupies a unique place in the intellectual history of the Victorian period because he acted as an interpreter, promoting the dialogue between what Foucault has described as two distinct orders of knowledge in nineteenth-century discourse about sex: "a biology of reproduction which developed continuously according to a general scientific normativity" and "a medicine of sex conforming to quite different rules of formulation" (54). Foucault argues that there was no real exchange between these two orders of knowledge, but Spencer's writing belies this assertion. Moreover, Spencer's work facilitated this exchange and profoundly influenced scientists and doctors on both sides of the Atlantic, helping to change permanently the ways Victorians wrote about women, gender, sex, and motherhood.

My second goal in this study is more theoretical, for in my analysis of the dialogue between Eliot and Spencer, I offer readings that demonstrate how much contemporary feminist criticism has contributed to the "new historicism."[12] This analysis of the writings of Eliot and Spencer is an archeological effort, then, designed to recover a lost chapter in the history of sexuality by articulating the voice of feminist resistance as it finds expression in Eliot's sometimes problematic treatment of nature, women, gender, female sexuality, motherhood, feminist ambition, and desire. This lost voice becomes audible in Eliot's writing when we attend to what Elaine Showalter has called the "double voiced" discourse of women's writing.[13] Women have access to what Showalter calls a "wild zone":

> We can think of the "wild zone" of women's culture spatially, experientially, or metaphysically. Spatially it stands for an area which is literally no-man's land, which corresponds to the zone . . . which is off limits to women. Experientially it stands for the aspects of the female life-style which are outside of and unlike those of men; again, there is a corresponding zone of male experience alien to women. But if we think of the wild zone metaphysically, or in terms of consciousness, it has no corresponding male space since all of male consciousness is within the circle of the dominant structure and thus accessible to or structured by language. ("Feminist" 200)

The second voice in Eliot's novels finds expression, I would argue, when she asserts her privileged access to aspects of female experience that lie outside male experience and are unmapped by language. In her essay, "Woman in France: Madame de Sablé" (1854), Eliot identifies a "class of sensations and emotions—the maternal ones—which must remain unknown to man,"[14] and her novels assert her experiential and metaphysical authority as a woman writer when she describes these elemental female experiences.

Twenty years ago, many of Eliot's critics ignored or even suppressed this "other half" of her discourse. The following example from W. J. Harvey provides perhaps the most dramatic illustration. In order to demonstrate Eliot's debt to Wordsworth and to Herbert Spencer, Harvey cites the following passage from *Adam Bede*, but he omits without comment all of Eliot's references to the maternal in this passage. Because it is revealing to see what Harvey removed from the original passage, I present what was omitted in italics:

> Nature, that great tragic dramatist, knits us together by bone and muscle, and divides us by the subtler web of our brains; blends yearning and repulsion; and ties us by our heart strings to the beings that jar us at every moment. [*We hear a voice with the very cadence of our own uttering the thoughts we despise; we see eyes— ah! so like our mother's—averted from us in cold alienation; and our last darling child startles us with the air and gestures of the sister we parted from in bitterness long years ago.*] The father to whom we owe our best heritage—the mechanical instinct,

the keen sensibility to harmony, the unconscious skill of the modelling hand—galls us, and puts us to shame by his daily errors, [*the long-lost mother whose face we begin to see in the glass as our own wrinkles come, once fettered our young soul with her anxious humors and irrational persistence*].[15]

The pioneering work of many feminist scholars has made it possible to identify and interpret this second voice in Eliot's fiction, and I hope this work, too, will advance our understanding of the conditions of women's lives and authorship in Victorian England.[16]

Many of Eliot's critics have continued to regard her as a sort of literary hermaphrodite who uncritically worshiped the patriarchal values of Victorian culture and society. Critics who take this view generally see Eliot as a skillful ventriloquist who, despite her sex, "wrote like a man." This view of Eliot is so pervasive that we seldom register the incongruity of the pronoun reference when we read "George Eliot . . . she." In many feminist analyses as well, Eliot appears as "the intellectual woman of the non-feminine type" who, according to Helene Deutch, has "no mother in the psychological sense of the term. She is . . . like Pallas Athena, the woman born out of her father's head."[17]

In the following pages, I will argue that Eliot has appeared as this false Athena to many of her readers in part because of her complex response to Victorian feminism. Most critics who have discussed Eliot's feminism at all have not discriminated between the rhetoric and goals of nineteenth- and twentieth-century feminist thought.[18] As Deirdre David has noted, when Eliot's sexual politics are evaluated in these terms, they "disappoint" because her extraordinary success "leads us to expect more from her than we do from other Victorian women intellectuals" (164). Thus, many readers conclude by seeing Eliot, anachronistically, as a "feminine anti-feminist," as Sandra M. Gilbert and Susan Gubar have argued in their influential study, *The Madwoman in the Attic.* Feminist critics have generally tried to fit Eliot into one of two categories. Those who use political activism in the public sphere as a touchstone regard Eliot as a failed feminist, while others, who read her description of women's places in Victorian society as a conservative prescription, see her as an antifeminist "intellectual." Eliot is inadequately described by either definition.

Eliot's biography and letters do pose several obstacles to seeing her as an unambiguous feminist. In her letters in the 1850s, she expresses somewhat enigmatic support for feminist legal and educational reforms. By the 1860s, however, Eliot had assumed an "Epicurean" aloofness (*GEL* 2: 396) on the question of the vote for women and refused to sign Barbara Bodichon's petition for women's suffrage in 1867. Some of Eliot's ambivalence can be understood when we see the limits of the

agency that she claimed as an intellectual woman who wished to participate in a "world of disinterested reason, a world to which [she] was
thought not to belong in the first place" (David 3). Eliot understandably
saw herself as a contradiction in terms.

Spencer's evolutionary reading of the division of labor encouraged
Eliot to regard herself as one of the few women fitted for the intellectual
work she had chosen for herself (Russett 139). Eliot's desire to preserve
her "disinterestedness" may have prevented her from participating more
actively in the political canvassing and agitations that many of her closest
friends undertook in support of women's suffrage. Nonetheless, Eliot's
writing shows a sensitivity to all the feminist issues of the time and discloses her persistent "resistance" to the androcentric premises of her
society and culture.

Eliot recognized that she was perhaps uniquely qualified to participate
in the scientific debates of the time that, as Mary Poovey argues in *Uneven
Developments: The Ideological Work of Gender in Mid-Victorian England*, admitted so few feminist voices. Poovey explains, "the right to write about
the body belonged to men at midcentury and to the medical expert in
particular" (43). Because women were excluded from the formal education that would allow them to speak with equal authority as scientists or
medical practitioners and because women were silenced as "patients"
(43–44), their voice, and their resistance, was rarely heard. Eliot, because of her work as editor of the *Westminster Review* and because of her
understanding of contemporary science, was able to speak with familiarity and authority not only to Spencer but to and about most of the important scientific theorists of her time.

Critics who assert Eliot's antifeminism also frequently cite her notori-
ously unsisterly assessment of the work of other women writers as proof
that she accepted, without qualification, the androcentric literary prejudices of her age. To be sure, Eliot writes wickedly about other women
writers in her letters, calling Hannah More, for example, that "most disagreeable of monsters, a blue stocking" (*GEL* 1: 245). Likewise, in her
essay "Silly Novels by Lady Novelists," for example, Eliot indicts many
women writers for their amazing ignorance, both of science and of life,
and criticizes their "silly novels" for suggesting that such ignorance is
regarded as the "best possible qualification for forming an opinion on
the knottiest moral and speculative questions" (*Essays* 310).

Yet, even as she condemns these novels as a "nuisance" because they
"tend to confirm the popular prejudice against the more solid education
of women" (*Essays* 316), Eliot registers her own appreciation of feminist
educational reforms and her recognition of the difficulties facing all serious women writers in a culture where the literary means of production
are controlled by men and where the critical judgments passed on all

women's writings betray a pernicious sexual double standard. Eliot protests the peculiar chivalry practiced by male reviewers, commenting in
this same essay, for example, that:

> By a peculiar theometric adjustment, when a woman's writing talent is at zero,
> journalistic approbation is at the boiling pitch; when she attains mediocrity, it
> is already no more than summer heat; and if ever she reaches excellence,
> critical enthusiasm drops to the freezing point. Harriet Martineau, Currer
> Bell, and Mrs. Gaskell have been treated as cavalierly as if they had been men.
> (*Essays* 322)

In light of these remarks, Eliot's decision to assume a male pseudonym
should not be seen simply as a betrayal of feminist solidarity, for in
choosing a male pseudonym, she was consciously following the examples
of the female writers she most admired: Charlotte Brontë and George
Sand. Moreover, in taking her pseudonym, as Margaret Homans argues,
George Eliot "thematized" the position of women's language in a culture
that does not admit it (*Bearing* 20).

My ultimate goal in this analysis is to penetrate beyond the myth of
Eliot as Athena by disclosing the conflicts in her writing between her
feminism, on the one hand, and her evolutionism, on the other. Some
of Eliot's most sophisticated feminist critics, including Sandra M.
Gilbert, Susan Gubar, and Margaret Homans, have assumed a psychoanalytic perspective in order to focus on Eliot's struggles with her literary
fathers or with the patriarchal word. As a result, they have provided psychoanalytic explanations for Eliot's ambivalent feminism. This approach, however, tends to represent Eliot as a victim of a universal lo-
gocentric culture and to obscure the particular historical grounds of her
resistance and success.

In the 1850s, Eliot's contemporaries regarded "base Science" as revealing a "greater epic" than the *Iliad*, as Edward Fitzgerald wrote; and in
accepting many of the insights of evolutionary science, Eliot claimed a
literary authority that she saw as equal to that of many of her favorite epic
poets, including Milton, Wordsworth, Shakespeare, Dante, and Aeschylus. Because Eliot saw culture, like biological life, as moving through
gradual evolutionary changes, she recognized that some literary produc-
tions became obsolete, making room for new fictions and forms. Thus,
Eliot's acceptance of the theory of evolution freed her from much of
what Susan Gubar and Sandra Gilbert describe as that special anxiety of
influence experienced by women writers when they confront their poetic fathers.

As a student of Greek literature, Eliot knew that the myth of Athena
submerged an older creation myth about the destruction of Metis, the
mother goddess who was swallowed alive by Zeus in order to prevent his

own overthrow. Eliot's understanding of this myth informs her effort to establish a legitimate basis for her resistance to Spencer's conclusions about women's nature and capacities. Her struggles are outlined in the following chapters, beginning with her effort to counter Spencer's interpretation of woman's place in the natural world (chapters 2 and 3) and detailing her resistance to his conclusions about gender in his analysis of education and authority (chapter 4), psychology (chapter 5), history and religion (chapter 6), political change (chapter 7), marriage (chapter 8), and race and national culture (chapter 9).

In seeking to return Eliot to this historical context, in attempting to define what was at stake in Eliot's "compulsion to speak about the unspeakable" (Biddy Martin 9) by establishing an alternative interpretation of the meaning of gender in her novels, I demonstrate the feminist resistance that finds expression in her intellectual struggle to defend what she identified as "maternal" values from degradation. This study, then, focuses on Eliot's representation of acts of resistance which help to define what she meant by "the maternal." It presents readings of the moments when mothers instruct daughters about the relationship between sexuality and power as it is institutionalized in the family and in the laws of church and state; when sisters confess to sisters about the nature of their desires and their wish to transcend the limits of woman's proper sphere; and when daughters assert their desire for the men they love, often in defiance of the social conventions that a new evolutionary science would normalize.[19]

In appropriating some of the insights and methods of Michel Foucault and other "new historicists" in my reading of Eliot's and Spencer's works, I hope to demonstrate, as Judith Newton has argued, that the "new historicism" is not "new" at all but rather has its "mother roots" in "the women's movement and the feminist theory and feminist scholarship which grew from it" ("History" 90). Because Foucault ignores who speaks, he offers what Frances Bartkowski calls "another patriarchal history of sexuality" (45). The objective in this present study is to represent the impact of gender in the writings of Eliot and Spencer and to establish the grounds of Eliot's resistance to evolutionary interpretations of biological difference. By particularizing and historicizing the relation between power and resistance in their writing, I hope to demystify the ubiquitous force of power, knowledge, and pleasure that Foucault describes as always, already at work.

The comparison of Eliot's beautiful and sonorous prose and elegant novelistic form with Spencer's utilitarian and often ugly scientific language and repetitive argumentation, may seem to demonstrate, finally, why contemporary historians of science have rightly avoided detailed textual analysis of Spencer's writing, but this contrast also emphasizes important differences in Eliot's and Spencer's epistemologies. Eliot's choice of the novel as a vehicle for her philosophical meditations on feminism and evolutionism expresses her belief that feeling must join rationality if truth is to be named. It also allows her insights to be presented in terms more accessible to a general audience, which included women as well as men.

Spencer, in contrast to both Eliot and Darwin, constructed a philosophical discourse that rigorously excluded emotion—and indeed, nearly all playfulness, wit, nuance, metaphor, and allusion—and thus he chose a style that expressed his extraordinarily dogmatic and unquestioning belief in the self-evident and enduring nature of fact. He makes no rhetorical concessions to his audience. In comparing the development and formal qualities of the discourses that Eliot and Spencer produced, we can observe not only the development of two new and opposing interpretations of men's and women's place in nature and the meaning of gender differences and human sexuality but also the emergence of that great separation between the discourses of literature and modern science.

Thus, by comparing the writing of Eliot and Spencer, I hope finally to add my own contribution to the study of realism by illuminating the "horizon" between the worlds of art and science, that contiguous space where science "passes over into art," for, as Avrom Fleishman has explained, such comparisons enhance our understanding of both art and science:

> the scientifically described world is no longer left standing in its own realm but confronts other ranges of experience and becomes illuminated by that confrontation; facts are still facts but show a new side when placed with fictions—sometimes revealing their own fictional elements in the process. A novel is, then, a field of differences between fact and fiction, art and science, and among the sciences severally: it is constituted neither by being purely representational nor purely imaginary but by its associative and differentiating processes. If fiction has this peculiarly differential working, it can make a special claim to stand as the supplement of the human sciences. It is, as it were, their horizon, the space where they pass over into what is beyond science.[20]

2

Feminism, Evolutionism, and the Reconstruction of Gender

GEORGE ELIOT met Herbert Spencer in 1851, at the beginning of that catastrophic decade when Victorian sex roles became a problem of truth. When their lifelong friendship began, both agreed in endorsing at least three of the tenets of mid-Victorian feminism, though this agreement is astonishing in light of Spencer's vehement antifeminism in the last four decades of his life. Nonetheless, in 1851 both agreed on the need for the reform of marriage and divorce laws, on the value of women's social emancipation, and on the right of women to better education and vocational opportunities. We can begin to establish how, when, and why Spencer began his dramatic repudiation of his early support for these feminist causes by reviewing the few biographical details about his relationship with Eliot that appear in the surviving letters of each and by examining the essays each produced in the 1850s. By reconstructing the relationship between Eliot and Spencer in these years, we can see how the theory of evolution directly challenged the feminism of each and observe some of the compromises Eliot developed in order to reconcile her feminism with Spencerian evolutionism, while Spencer himself began his dramatic repudiation of these same causes.

By 1859, when George Eliot read *On the Origin of Species*, she was so familiar with the theory of evolution that she commented about the importance of Darwin's discoveries with stunning nonchalance in a letter to her beloved friend Barbara Smith Bodichon, the feminist activist:

> We have just been reading Darwin's book on the "Origin of Species" just now: it makes an epoch, as the expression of his thorough adhesion, after long years of study, to the Doctrine of Development—and not the adhesion of an anonym like the author of the "Vestiges," but of a long-celebrated naturalist. The book is ill-written and sadly wanting in illustrative facts, of which he has collected a vast number, but reserves them for a future book of which this smaller one is the *avant-courier*. This will prevent the work from becoming popular as the "Vestiges" did, but it will have a great effect in the scientific world, causing a thorough and open discussion of a question about which people have hitherto felt timid. So the world gets on step by step towards brave clearness and honesty! But to me the Development theory and all other explanations of

process by which things came to be, produce a feeble impression compared with the mystery that lies under the process. (*GEL* 3:227)[1]

This letter should remind us that it was in Spencer's early essays, and not in the *Origin*, that Eliot first encountered the "developmental theory" and recognized its power to redefine the place of men and women in nature and society.[2]

It is in the decade of the 1850s, then, that Eliot began her lifelong debate with Herbert Spencer and the issues he raised. In fact, since Eliot met Spencer in August 1851, a year before he published his seminal essay, "The Developmental Hypothesis," she had had the opportunity to hear, firsthand, how he initially articulated his evolutionary theories (Haight, *George Eliot* 112). Moreover, she helped Spencer adjust the language of these early essays, on occasion, and remained an astute and attentive critic of Spencer's thought, witnessing how these ideas developed and later found expression in his encyclopedic *Synthetic Philosophy* (*GEL* 2:145; Haight, *George Eliot* 116–17).[3]

In the course of this first decade of his friendship with Eliot, Spencer took up an even more ambitious task than articulating the truth about sexual identity and practices. Indeed, in that revolutionary decade when the traditional Christian interpretation of Genesis, which justifed the subordination of women by men, was undermined by Lyell's geology and Darwin's biology, Spencer, with characteristic self-confidence, began to formulate a philosophy which was to redefine men's and women's place "in nature" by prescribing their biologically "necessary" relation as authorized by "natural laws" derived from evolutionary science. While Darwin remained reticent about the implications of evolutionary theory for human beings, especially in these early years, Spencer, as early as 1852, began to speculate and write about the impact of evolution on Victorian gender roles.

While Spencer focuses on the problem of male and female gender roles in his essays on education and other occasional pieces written between 1852 and 1864, he did not incorporate these views into his *Synthetic Philosophy* until he began to write his *Principles of Biology* (1864–1867). Nonetheless, his view of male and female sex differences profoundly influenced the direction of his theory of evolution, as did the unacknowledged residue of his evangelicalism and his Lamarckian racism (Peel 135–36,145), even before they found a scientific basis and justification in this later work. In watching the progress of Spencer's thinking from the 1850s to the 1880s, and in observing his silences as well as his arguments about how he established a "scientific" authority for his theories about gender differences, we can see how, in his case, science interacted with ideology and how his sexual chauvinism, like his racial prejudices, were born in their "modern biologizing statist form" in his writing (Foucault 149).

Though many important documents about Eliot's relationship with Spencer in the 1850s have been lost, we can piece together some of the details of their friendship from their published correspondence and from Spencer's *Autobiography*. In May 1852, nine months after her first meeting with Spencer, George Eliot wrote in a letter to Sara Hennell: "My brightest spot next to my love of *old* friends is the deliciously calm new friendship that Herbert Spencer gives me. We see each other every day and have a delightful *camaraderie* in everything. But for him my life would be desolate enough . . . " (*GEL* 2:29). As early as June 1852, Eliot was humorously voicing the criticism that Huxley was to assert repeatedly about Spencer's method in the 1860s and 1870s. To Sara Hennell, she wrote: "I went to Kew yesterday on a scientific expedition with Herbert Spencer, who has all sorts of theories about plants—I should have said a *proof*-hunting expedition. Of course, if the flowers didn't correspond to the theories, we said '*tant pis pour les fleurs*' " (*GEL* 2:40). Though Eliot was willing at this point in her relation with Spencer to join him in dismissing natural facts when they failed to correspond to theory, she did not long remain so compliant.

Spencer also records his early impressions of Eliot in his *Autobiography*, where he cites a letter, written nine months after their first meeting, to his friend Edward Lott, describing her as "the translatress of Strauss and as the most admirable woman, mentally, I ever met. We have been for some time on intimate terms. I am very frequently at Chapman's and the greatness of her intellect conjoined with her womanly qualities and manner, generally keep me by her side most of the evening" (1:394–95). Spencer goes on in his *Autobiography* to depict Eliot retrospectively as a sort of hermaphrodite, calling her intellect "masculine," as if he could not imagine her large and powerful mind to be feminine like the rest of her. Characteristically, he begins his portrait of her by describing her physical self, remarking that in her "physique there was, perhaps, a trace of that masculinity characterizing her intellect; for though of but ordinary feminine height, she was strongly built" (1:395).

Despite his difficulties in fitting Eliot retrospectively into the evolutionary scheme he subsequently developed in the 1870s and 1880s, Spencer struggled to do justice to her "large intellect" in the only extended description of her in his autobiography. Recognizing her "extraordinarily good memory" and "great quickness of apprehension which made acquisition of every kind easy," Spencer goes on to provide a description that reveals his thinly veiled competition with her and his concern to valorize his own "synthetic" imagination as superior to Eliot's "analytical" capacity:

> Even as it was, however, her psychological powers were remarkable. I have
> known but few men with whom I could discuss a question in philosophy
> with more satisfaction. Capacity for abstract thinking is rarely found along
> with capacity for concrete representation, even in men: and among women,
> such a union as existed in her, has, I should think, never been paralleled.
> (*Autobiography* 1:397)

Following this portrait of Eliot, Spencer goes on to discuss their personal
relationship in 1852 and 1853, but he suppresses more details about it
than he does about any other event in his *Autobiography*. Spencer's defensiveness about Eliot, even years after her death, suggests not only the
intellectual but also the psychological dimensions of the conflict between them.

In discussing the intellectual influences Eliot exerted over him, Spencer notes that it was she who urged him to read Auguste Comte's *Cours
de philosophie positive*. He reports that he skimmed it, but since he was
unable to read French very well, he absorbed very little. Quite abruptly,
then, he changes the subject, and comments about his personal relationship with Eliot: "Of course, we were frequently seen together, people
drew inferences. . . . There were reports that I was in love with her, and
that we were about to be married. But neither of these reports was true"
(*Autobiography* 1:399; Haight, *George Eliot* 117–22).

Spencer's remaining letters reveal some of what he suppressed in his
description of his relationship with Eliot in these years, since he keeps
silence in his *Autobiography*. In a letter to E. L. Youmans that does not
appear in his autobiography, Spencer gives a much more complete record of the personal as well as the intellectual "intimacy" that existed
between him and George Eliot from 1851 to 1853. By 1852, Spencer
explains, Eliot's feelings became "involved and mine did not. The lack of
physical attraction was fatal. Strongly as my judgment prompted, my instincts would not respond" (*GEL* 9:43). He goes on to explain:

> It was a most painful affair, continuing through the summer of '52 on through
> autumn, and, I think, into the beginning of '53. She was very desponding and
> I passed the most miserable time that has occurred in my experience; for,
> hopeless as the relation was, she would not agree that we should cease to
> see one another. So much did I feel the evil that I had done involuntarily,
> or rather, against my will, that I hinted at the possibility of marriage, even
> without positive affection on my part; but this, she saw at once would lead to
> unhappiness. (*GEL* 8:43)

Eliot's own letters also help fill in the gaps in Spencer's narrative of these
years, revealing, as well, her pain and bitterness during the summer of
1852.

In one letter in particular Eliot makes clear the degree to which Spencer's evolutionary theories apparently provided him with a vocabulary for, and a justification of, his feelings toward her. In a letter written in July 1852 after one of Spencer's visits with her at Broadstairs, she explains the state of her feelings and mind, using evolutionary examples and Spencer's characteristic vocabulary:

> I fancy I should soon be on equality, in point of sensibility, with the star-fish and sea-egg—perhaps you will wickedly say I want little of being a *Medusa*. I have a loathing for books. . . . You see I am sinking fast toward "homogeniety" and my brain will soon be a mere pulp unless you come to arrest the downward process. (*GEL* 8:51)

This letter reveals, of course, Eliot's prickly self-consciousness about her lack of conventional good looks as well as her mockery of Spencer's fastidiousness in her playful suggestion that he may regard her as a repulsive "*Medusa*." More importantly, however, it also indicates how Eliot served as Spencer's first problematic example upon which to test his developing theory that beauty was a sign of "heterogeneity" in women and the lack of it a mark of "homogeneity." In "A Theory of Population" (1852), Spencer cites the egg-producing Medusa as demonstrating the "antagonism of individuation and reproduction."[4] Eliot's letter thus shows that she recognized the sexist assumptions underlying Spencer's theory about women's biological inferiority, which is later elaborated in *The Principles of Biology*.[5]

When Spencer did come to visit Eliot a second time at Broadstairs, she wrote him an extraordinary letter, remarking that "no woman ever wrote such a letter as this":

> I want to know if you can assure me that you will not forsake me, that you will always be with me as much as you can and share your thoughts and feelings with me. If you become attached to someone else, then I must die, but until then, I could gather courage to work and make life valuable, if only I had you near me. I do not ask you to sacrifice anything—I would be very good and cheerful and never annoy you. But I find it impossible to contemplate life under any other conditions. (*GEL* 8:57)

It could be argued that Spencer was being both generously chivalrous toward Eliot and appropriately circumspect in his *Autobiography* in not revealing her humiliating desire for his love and companionship, even outside marriage. But Spencer's decision to omit these details reveals, as well, his desire to mask any evidence of the personal motives that are later justified and intellectualized by the scientific arguments he developed to identify womanly beauty as the female's primary contribution to biological progress. What would his analysis of the evolutionary process have been if he had entered into this intimacy with Eliot, we might ask?

Such a question, of course, cannot be answered, and if we are to move beyond these sketchy biographical details and achieve a more complete intellectual portrait of Eliot's and Spencer's responses to evolutionism and feminism, we must begin by establishing their perspectives on both subjects in the 1840s and 1850s. Eliot's letters show her increasing skepticism about any system of natural philosophy which depended upon the conventional Biblical interpretations of Genesis. After 1842, when she liberated herself from what she called the "wretched giant's bed of dogmas" (*GEL* 1:162), Eliot was free to develop an analysis of the source and meaning of gender differences, human sexuality, and reproduction that challenged the scriptural authority by which patriarchal interpretations of humanity's relation to Nature and God were justified.

In contrast to most of her feminist contemporaries, Eliot accepted the "doctrine of development" so calmly and readily in the 1850s because she had already assumed a position as a freethinker. Though Eliot had been influenced in her school years by the evangelicalism of her teacher, Maria Lewis, she returned to a more orthodox Christianity and then renounced her faith entirely in 1842, shortly after she read Charles Hennell's *Inquiry into the Origins of Christianity* (Haight, *George Eliot* 38). Her religious doubts nearly caused a permanent rupture with her father when she refused to accompany him to church. In the "holy wars" which followed, Sara Hennell and Charles and Cara Bray supported Eliot and remained her close friends throughout her life. Though Eliot and her father were ultimately reconciled, the break with him allowed her to recognize the economic marginality of women in Victorian society, as she contemplated the "doleful lodgings and scanty meals" that would be the consequence of living alone and supporting herself (*GEL* 1:131). Eliot's resistance to patriarchal religion was not quenched when she agreed to return to her assigned place in the family pew; it was simply channeled into more subversive intellectual activities.

In 1844, Eliot began translating David Friedrich Strauss's *Das Leben Jesu*, a work of German higher criticism that helped to undermine literalist readings of the Bible for many intellectuals. Eliot's reading of the German higher criticism gave her a sophisticated understanding of the theological and philosophical debates over the Genesis account of creation. Thus, she was in advance of most of her contemporaries in recognizing the teleological shift that, according to Michael Timko,[6] prevented later Victorians from seeing Nature in Romantic terms:

> No longer was it a question of man's divine strivings pitted against his bestial predisposition, a struggle that always took for granted God's concern for man

and assumed that man's bestiality was an aberration that could be overcome with time, effort, and faith. On the contrary, in the Darwinian context, the old assumptions were swept away and the struggle became a far more desperate one. The questions were now strictly Victorian in the sense that the old problem was exactly reversed. No longer was man attempting to explain his bestiality in the face of his divine nature; he had to define and assert his humanness in the face of his demonstrated participation in the bestial nature. (615)

This reversal made the idealization of motherhood untenable because it redefined motherhood as a sign of woman's participation in a "bestial" natural world; but most Victorians, including evolutionary scientists, were loath to recognize this change.

Even before she met Spencer, Eliot was skeptical about the Romantic literary conventions that idealized motherhood by linking mothers with the Divine in Nature. On her twenty-eighth birthday in 1848, Eliot wrote a witty letter to the Hennells which included a playful description of her own genesis and presented a pastiche of several philosophical and literary traditions that have defined the interpretation of mankind's genesis. Eliot writes:

Mother Nature—who by the bye is an old lady with some bad habits of her own—like other great names does her work by deputy and so gets both credit and discredit that don't properly belong to her. The vulgar may not know it, but she in fact leaves the creation of her plants and her animals and her homunculi to a whole herd of sprites and genii some of whom make but laughing work of it. Now over a quarter of a century ago there was a very young sprite who forsooth having turned out some respectable toads and a few indifferent lemurs and marmosets must fain try his hand on a human article and one 22nd of November he presented to Dame Nature at her evening levee a rough though unmistakeable sketch of a human baby. The Old Mother had been rollicking all the autumn in the vintage and wanted no less than a winter's sleep to sober her. Being rather cross-grained in her cups she was in no humour to make the best of a bad business so she said, What have we here? in such a snappish tone, flourishing a bunch of nettles all the while, that the poor little Prometheus of a sprite began to look very snubbed. "A Pretty piece of work I should have to patch up this thing into a human soul and body that should hang together! Here," she called to one of her Vishnu-sprites, "smother it at once to save further harm." Thereupon the poor little spriteling fell a crying that his first Homunculus was to be sent to limbo without having one chance given it. So some of his brother genii who were bringing in their day's work were touched with pity, and began to intercede for him and his Homonculus. . . . And so Dame Nature heard the intercession and the brother-sprites kept their word. For the poor sketch of a soul was found by the

dark eyed maiden and those other bright and good mortals and they pitied
and helped it, so that at last it grew to think and to love. (*GEL* 1:272-73)

In Eliot's irreverent parody of Genesis, Dame Nature contrasts dramatically, for example, with the essentially Romantic image of a nurturant
Mother Nature in Darwin's *The Origin of Species.*

Darwin, as Gillian Beer argues, realized that he must put "something
in the space left by God" in *The Origin of Species*, and to fill this gap he
constructed a maternal figure which ameliorates the harshness of the
biological contest he described. Beer explains: "Natural selection appears as an aspect or avatar of the more general 'Nature,' whose maternal ordering is contrasted with the egocentric one of man. She tends and
nurses with scrupulous concern for human betterment" (*Darwin's Plots*
70). Eliot, in contrast, found it far less difficult to imagine the violent and
destructive aspects of Nature; in fact, as this letter indicates, she was inclined to imagine Dame Nature in more human terms: as a mother who
could be inattentive or violent, who was as liable to "smother" as to nurture human life.

Eliot's personal experience as a daughter suggests several sources for
her resistance to the idealization of motherhood that finds expression in
Darwin's personification of Mother Nature and in Victorian literature
more generally. Eliot lost her own mother when she was only sixteen,
and Ruby Redinger argues that the negative depiction of mothers in
Eliot's fiction reflects her deep psychological ambivalence about this
loss.[7] Indeed, in this fantasy of her own genesis, Eliot identifies neither
Mother Nature nor her own mother as the caregiver who nurtures the
"rough sketch of a human baby"; "other bright and good mortals" teach
the child "to think and to love." Thus, Eliot exposes the painful antagonism in Victorian families between unconventional and ambitious intellectual daughters and conventional mothers; Eliot's personal insight
into the conflict-ridden relationship between such mothers and daughters is perhaps most eloquently articulated in *The Mill on the Floss.*

Eliot's depiction of Dame Nature in this letter may also be seen to
express her uneasy relation to her own physical self and to her "feminine
nature." Eliot was, we are too often reminded, morbidly sensitive about
her appearance; Henry James unkindly called her "magnificently ugly"
and "deliciously hideous" and few commentators, then or now, have
been able to resist repeating this *bon mot* (Haight, *George Eliot* 416–17).
Moreover, Spencer's rejection of Eliot because he found she lacked appropriate feminine charms could hardly have enhanced her self-image.
Eliot came to see herself as having a "large" nature, one in which, as the
Victorians would say, her unusually strong "animal" sensibilities were
kept somewhat precariously in check only by her correspondingly large

capacity for "moral emotion." Throughout her life, Eliot felt her body to be as ill-constructed as "the human article" described in her genesis story, and her letters are thick with her complaints about the physical weakness she suffered and the countless illnesses she endured. Like many Victorian women, Eliot seems to have regarded many of her physical infirmities as arising from what Victorians called woman's particular "subjection" to nature, and her novels express her sense of the special betrayals of the body that women experience because of their biology.

Moreover, Eliot's birthday letter to the Hennells also suggests her insight into the ways that the Biblical account of Genesis operated to prevent Victorians, including men of science, from constructing a new and more biologically accurate version of the father's and mother's roles in reproduction, as her mocking use of the "homunculus" in this letter shows. Victorian scientists apparently found it difficult to surrender the Aristotelian view of human reproduction, whereby men provided the active force and women acted as passive vessels for the fetus. Aristotle's view of reproduction was reiterated in the "homunculus theory" of human genesis that influenced Milton's *Paradise Lost* and prevailed in British thought during the eighteenth century. Though the ovary's production of eggs was first observed in 1827 and the spontaneous periodic production of the ovum in mammals was recognized in 1845, "the fantasy that the child originates in and belongs to the father and that the mother provides merely the environment in which the child grows, persisted," retarding scientific investigations of human reproduction throughout Eliot's lifetime (Homans, *Bearing* 155). In 1852, Spencer reinscribed this traditional view of human reproduction in "A Theory of Population," when he explained that the "sperm cell . . . contains co-ordinating matter; and the germ cell . . . contains matter to be co-ordinated" (490). Eliot, in contrast, lampoons similar "scientific" theories about the role of the homunculus in human reproduction in this birthday letter. Likewise, her allusions to Vishnu and to Eastern as well as Western myths of creation demonstrate some of the sources of her skepticism about traditional readings of Genesis. Eliot's understanding of contemporary theology and biology thus informed her assertion in "Woman in France: Madame de Sablé" (1854), that the "maternal" sensations and emotions were "unknown to men" (*Essays* 53).

By the time Eliot wrote this letter to the Hennells, she had already transgressed against one of the major cultural prohibitions that defined Victorian gender roles: the notion that "men produced, women reproduced" (Russett 12). By remaining unmarried and by taking up her work as a translator of profoundly subversive texts, Eliot enacted her resistance to the gender arrangements that Spencer and Darwin later normalized. Moreover, in moving beyond the private sphere and beyond her self-effacing position as translator and silent editor of the *Westminster Review*, Eliot enlarged both her authority and the ground of her resistance when she found her métier as a novelist and took her place in the glare of publicity that followed her triumphant success. Before she began to write fiction, Eliot tried to convert "femininity" from a liability into an advantage by locating woman's special authority as writer in what Elaine Showalter has described as the "wild zone" of female experience ("Feminist" 200), and her novels show her careful exploration of this uncharted territory. Yet, Eliot's identification of the "maternal" as the fountainhead of woman's creative insight also reveals her audacity, since she could not herself claim the authority of experience in her representation of biological motherhood as could other Victorian women writers who bore children. For this reason too, I would argue, Eliot chose to valorize the "maternal" sensations and emotions that might be felt by all women rather than to idealize the bonds of biological motherhood.[8]

In this respect, Eliot's representation of motherhood in her novels differs from that of many female, as well as most male, novelists of the period because she turned to evolutionary science rather than to experience to extend the daughter's view of motherhood. Several Victorian women who wrote novels and were also mothers reinscribed the compelling—and flattering—phallocentric literary conventions that idealized motherhood. Mrs. Gaskell, in *Ruth*, for example, reproduced these conventions when she described her heroine's transformation from a "woman into a mother." Even Elizabeth Barrett Browning, in *Aurora Leigh*, remained more conventional than Eliot in her depiction of the unwed motherhood of Marian Earle. Though Eliot sometimes felt that her own "passionate nature" made her something of an anomaly among the members of her sex, she nevertheless persisted, in the face of severe criticism from the Mrs. Grundys in her society, to describe the relationship between erotic and maternal love and to define the power of both in the lives of the women she represented in her novels. Motherhood became in Eliot's novels, then, not an emblem of the repression or denial of female sexuality, as it is, for example, in Dickens and Thackeray, but an expression of it.[9]

Yet, Eliot's turn to science was not without its difficulties and, for all the reasons described above, the "maternal" remained uncertain and contested ground upon which to erect a defense of her own authority as a writer and a feminist critic of evolutionary thought. In the 1850s Spencer focused on the problem of female fertility and later reasserted the traditional confusion of women with Nature in his unexamined assumptions about woman's nature and "instinct," especially after the publication of *First Principles* in 1862. Eliot, in contrast, tried in *Adam Bede* and subsequent novels to demystify maternal "instinct" by exposing the gap between the physical capacity for reproduction and the readiness for motherhood that may come when a woman achieves emotional maturity. Thus, Eliot's enterprise in her fiction in some ways parallels the work of contemporary feminist theorists who have tried to discriminate differences between sex and gender.[10] The most "maternal" heroines in Eliot's novels are not those who conceive and bring forth children in the course of the narrative, as do Hetty Sorrel, Tessa, and Lydia Glasher, but rather those women who give birth to a self that is fully responsive to the demands of mutual and passionate love and capable of genuine, spontaneous, and heroic acts of altruism, emotions that Eliot identified as "maternal." Though Maggie Tulliver and Romola de'Bardi have no children, they demonstrate the "maternal" ideal, as do Dinah Morris, Eppie Marner, Esther Lyon, and Dorothea Brooke, who actually become mothers at the end of the novels in which they appear. In keeping children out of the picture in most of her novels, Eliot is better able to challenge Spencer's—and Darwin's—unexamined assumption that all women "naturally" become mothers and that biological instinct qualifies them all equally for motherhood.

By 1857, Eliot wrote in a letter to Sara Hennell that she, Herbert Spencer, and George Henry Lewes all agreed in seeing "the conception of creative design to be untenable" (*GEL* 2:306). In the analysis of an extract of Hennell's work that appears in this letter, we can see just how sensitive Eliot was to the difficulties that faced writers who wanted to argue against "natural theology" in a language encumbered by the very traditions they wished to reject. She writes, for example: "According to your definition of science, there can be no true knowledge of things, except in their *evolution*—their dependence on observed antecedents, yet you directly fly off from that position into an anthropomorphic assumption as to the origin of things" (*GEL* 2:271). It is no wonder, then, that Eliot was not particularly impressed with the writing in *On the Origin of Species* since Darwin, as Beer so convincingly demonstrates, employed similar anthropomorphic language about Mother Nature, design, and selection (Beer, *Darwin's Plots* 53).

Spencer's struggle to surrender Deism is far more ambivalent and complex than Eliot's, and indeed, many modern critics of Spencer's evolutionary ideas argue that, despite his protests to the contrary, Spencer never actually surrendered his belief in a moral law which directs and controls natural evolutionary processes. Only in *Social Statics* (1850) does Spencer mention God as Creator, and this work remains the only book in his *oeuvre* where he acknowledges a consistently Deist perspective.[11] In this work he asserts that a "moral law" sanctioned by the Creator moved civilization naturally toward perfection. Thus, "progress," he wrote, "is not an accident but a necessity. Instead of civilization being artificial, it

is a part of Nature; all of a piece with the development of the embryo or
the unfolding of a flower. The modifications mankind has undergone
result from a law underlying the whole organic creation" (*Social Statics*
65). This organic "moral law" would ultimately bring to fruition a perfect
society where "all despotism, whether political or religious, whether of
sex, of caste, or of custom" would cease (*Social Statics* 435).

By 1852, however, Spencer saw how profoundly the theory of evolution challenged the teleology of his age. In his essay, "The Developmental Hypothesis" (1852), he attacks the Biblical authority of the "Mosaic
account of creation" and rejects the doctrine of "special creation"
whereby many Victorians temporarily reconciled their reading of Genesis with the discoveries of Lyell, Chambers, Spencer, and Darwin. He
writes:

> Ask one of our leading geologists or physiologists whether he believes in the
> Mosaic account of creation, and he will take the question as next to an insult.
> Either he rejects the narrative entirely, or understands it in some vague non-
> natural sense. Yet one part of it he unconsciously adopts; and that, too, liter-
> ally. From whence he got this notion of "special creation" which he thinks so
> reasonable, and fights for so vigorously. Evidently he can trace it back to no
> other source than this myth which he repudiates.[12]

In the essays that followed in the 1850s, Spencer tried to cleanse his own
evolutionary theory of the false assumptions promoted by the "Mosaic
account of creation," but in this effort he was not entirely successful.

Spencer, in contrast to Darwin in *Origin*, consistently avoids the traditional association of Nature with a nurturing maternal presence when he
begins to formulate his development theory. In his "Theory of Population Deduced from the General Law of Animal Fertility" (1852),[13] for
example, Spencer presents Nature as a remote and impersonal force. In
a rare passage in this otherwise severely unmetaphorical discourse, he
personifies Nature as a strict disciplinarian, a figure reminiscent of
Eliot's Dame Nature rather than Darwin's nurturing Mother:

> Nature secures each step in advance by a succession of trials, which are perpet-
> ually repeated and cannot fail to be repeated, until success is achieved. All
> mankind in turn subject themselves more or less to the discipline described;
> they either may or may not advance under it; but, in the nature of things, only
> those who do advance under it eventually survive. . . . It unavoidably follows
> that those left behind to continue the race, are those in whom the power of
> self-preservation is the greatest—the select of their generation. (499–500)

Though Spencer, like Darwin, drew inspiration from Malthus, as is evident in this passage, he did not at the time see that the process of selection that he described here "must hold, not of mankind only, but of all

animals" (*Autobiography* 1:389) because he was so preoccupied, personally as well as intellectually, with the problem of human fertility. Thus, he lamented in his *Autobiography*, he failed to anticipate Darwin's analysis of "natural selection" in his great work, though by 1859 Spencer had developed a theory of "sexual selection" that he applied to humans with far less hesitation than Darwin does in the fourth chapter of *Origin*.

In appropriating Malthusian ideas, Spencer, like Darwin, found a reason for optimism in the "excess of fertility," because it insured diverse variations and thus contributed to the development of successful adaptions to the environment. Since Spencer began by applying his theory of evolution to humans, he found it difficult to regard human fertility as similarly benevolent. Positing a self-regulating force that restrained human fertility and protected the existing social hierarchy, Spencer argued that there is an "*a priori* law of maintenance of race" which causes the "necessary antagonism of individuation and reproduction" and results in an "inverse relation between intelligence and fertility" ("Theory" 478). By 1852, Spencer had formulated the concept of a self-regulating "law of equilibrium," which he used to explain the low fertility rates of the most intellectually developed, or "heterogeneous," members of the human race, a theory which, incidentally, justified his own chosen place as a celibate in the evolutionary order.[14]

Spencer, in contrast to Darwin, constructed an evolutionary analysis that identified universal laws that embraced not only mankind and all forms of biological life but also the inorganic and "superorganic" realms. In "Progress: Its Law and Cause" (1852), Spencer writes:

> Whether it be in the development of the Earth, in the development of Life upon its surface, in the development of society, of government, of manufactures, of commerce, of Language, Literature, Science, Art, this same evolution of the simple into the complex through successive differentiations holds throughout. From the earliest traceable cosmical changes to the latest results of civilization, we shall find that the transformation of the homogeneous into the heterogeneous is that in which Progress essentially consists.[15]

In arguing that the "transformation of the homogeneous into the heterogeneous . . . is consequent on the production of many effects by one cause—many changes by one force" (10), Spencer unwittingly exposed his unexamined belief in a unifying and hegemonic moral order in the universe, an assumption that was set outside the bounds of investigation when he argued in *First Principles* (1862) that the analysis of "first" causes lay beyond the scope of science. Thus "law" stands in the place of God in his discourse.

Spencer's analysis of evolution had a profound impact on his early support for feminism, but the conflict between these two ideologies was apparently not immediately clear to him. In 1851, when he met George Eliot, he endorsed at least three principles important to Victorian feminists at mid-century: he recognized the need for the reform of marriage and divorce laws, he supported greater civil rights for women in the public sphere, and he endorsed the rights of women to better education and vocational opportunities. In a section of his *Autobiography,* written when Spencer was 73, he confesses some embarrassment over his "juvenile radicalism," but nonetheless acknowledges his early feminist analysis of marriage by citing a letter written to Edward Lott in 1845. Spencer begins by arguing that women should serve as "the representation of the ideal" to the men they have married, and from this he argues that an "equality of rights" should exist between men and women within marriage and condemns the traditions which converted marriage into "slavery" for women. He writes:

> The present relationship existing between husband and wife, where one claims command over the actions of the other, is nothing more than a *remnant of the old leaven of slavery.* It is necessarily destructive of refined love; for *how can a man continue to regard as his type of the ideal a being whom he has, by denying an equality of privilege with himself, degraded to something below himself?* . . . I feel sure that a man of generous feeling has too much sympathy with the dignity of his wife to think of dictating to her, and that no woman of truly noble mind will submit to be dictated to. (*Autobiography* 1:267–68)

In his concluding point about marriage we can see even more clearly the influence of Shelley, who was at that time his favorite poet, as Spencer comes close to endorsing the philosophy of free love that made the poet so notorious:

> The last important condition I hold to be the forgetting, to as great an extent as possible, the existence of a legal bond, and the continual dependence upon the natural bond of affection. I do not conceive the most perfect happiness attainable while the legal bond continues; for as we can never rid ourselves of the consciousness of it, it must always influence our conduct. But the next best thing to destroying it is to banish it from our minds, and let the husband and wife strive to act towards each other as they would were there no such tie. (*Autobiography* 1:268)

Spencer never again quite so explicitly expressed his hopes that the "legal" bond of marriage would someday die away.

The position Spencer takes here on marriage reflects not only Shelley's influence but also echoes the view of marriage taken by Owenite socialists and feminists of the 1830s and 1840s. According to Barbara Taylor, the following analysis of marriage, written by James Smith in 1833, summarizes the socialist-feminist position on marriage in the dec-

ades after Shelley's death and represents its characteristic rhetoric and
Utopian idealism:

> At present woman is dependent; then she would become equal to man in
> political and personal privileges. Now, the marriage tie binds together for life
> two parties, who are frequently destructive of each other's happiness; then
> each would be free to make such change of circumstances as was necessary for
> their comfort; love would become a perpetual courtship, and not a domestic
> prison. . . . This is the marriage of nature. She is the only priest or rather
> priestess. Hitherto the world has been ruled by priests, let a priestess be substi-
> tuted in their stead. Hitherto has God been worshipped as a Man; let us now
> worship the female God, the goddess Nature—the bride—the Lamb's wife;
> thus fulfilling the words of scripture: Behold I create a new thing in the earth,
> a woman shall compass a man.[16]

Spencer's family had its roots in the evangelical and radical traditions
that Smith draws from here (Peel 73), but Spencer was not at all willing
to "worship the female God," as Smith proposes. While he also turned to
"Nature" in order to repudiate the power and doctrines of orthodox
Christianity, Spencer soon constructed an analysis of the "marriage of
nature" that would prevent the kind of male subjection to the female
that Smith envisioned.

Spencer's critique of the Victorian woman's subordinate place in marriage is articulated in the first edition of his *Social Statics*, but not in the
subsequent substantial revision, completed in 1894, where Spencer
erased nearly the entire chapter on "women's rights."[17] In the first edition, written in 1850, Spencer echoed Owenite feminists by arguing that
the subordination of woman to man in marriage is a vestige of a more
brutal age and inconsistent with civilized society:

> Of all the causes which conspire to produce the disappointment of those glow-
> ing hopes with which married life is usually entered upon, none is so potent as
> the supremacy of sex—this degradation of what should be a free and equal
> relationship—into one of ruler and subject—the supplanting of the sway of
> affection by the sway of authority. (*Social Statics* 166)

Like J. S. Mill several years later, Spencer argued in 1850, reiterating his
comments to Lott, that the subordination of women to men in marriage
perverts the institution that should express the "free bonds of affection."
"Command is a blight to the affections," he writes. "Whatsoever of refine-
ment—whatsoever of beauty—whatsoever of poetry there is in the passion that unites the sexes, withers up and dies in the cold atmosphere of
command" (*Social Statics* 165).

In *Social Statics*, Spencer also reveals his support for women's political
and social emancipation by arguing that a truly equitable society should

grant full civil rights to women as well as men. He explains: "Equity knows no difference of sex. . . . The moral sense by virtue of which the masculine mind responds to that law, exists in the feminine mind as well. Hence the several rights deducible from that law must appertain equally to both sexes" (*Social Statics* 155). Looking forward to the triumph of the "fast spreading recognition of popular rights accompanied by a silent, growing perception of the rights of women," Spencer, with characteristic optimism, imagines a new society where women would be free to define for themselves the proper sphere of their activities:

> We are told, however, that "woman's mission" is a domestic one—that her character and position do not admit of her taking a part in the decision of public questions—that politics are beyond her sphere. . . . Who now will tell us what woman's sphere really is? As the usages of mankind vary so much, let us hear how it is to be shown that the sphere we assign to her is the true one— that the limits we have set to female activity are just the proper limits. Let us hear why on this point of social polity we are exactly right, whilst we are wrong on so many others. (*Social Statics* 169)

Spencer's unquestioned and unshakeable belief in individualism allowed him, in 1850, to approve of removing the legal restrictions which confined women to the domestic realm and to approve of their entry into the public sphere. In taking this position, Spencer also implicitly indicates his support for better education for women and for the improved access to it which would allow them to pursue whatever vocation they chose.

As late as 1854, in "The Art of Education," Spencer repeated the criticisms of girls' education voiced by Victorian feminists at mid-century. He describes, for example, the paltry curriculum offered to young women, noting that "when we have named reading, writing, spelling, grammar, arithemetic, and sewing, we have named about all the things a girl is taught with a view to their direct uses in life."[18] In arguing that better education would make better "parents," Spencer reiterated the arguments of many feminists, including Mary Wollstonecraft. Moreover, by emphasizing the importance of the physical sciences and mathematics in elementary education and by defining vocational training as second only to these subjects, Spencer seemed to authorize an educational program that could remove some of the greatest obstacles to women's entry into the trades, the professions, and to higher education (Bauer and Ritt 113–18). However, by 1858, in "The Moral Discipline of Children," Spencer made it clear that he did not intend that girls should have an education equal to that of boys,[19] and his arguments are explicitly countered in Eliot's *The Mill on the Floss.*

Moreover, as Spencer began to recognize that the physical laws of evolution did not necessarily correspond to the divinely ordained "moral laws" that protected male privilege, he began his dramatic repudiation of his support for marriage reforms, women's emancipation, and better education. By 1856, after his brief nervous collapse in 1853 and his self-diagnosed eighteen-month "nervous breakdown" of 1855–1856, Spencer's retreat from these feminist principles became obvious. Having successfully extricated himself from his alliance with Eliot, Spencer came to see marriage as offering a dangerous "fatality." He includes in his *Autobiography* a letter to his friends, the Potters, written in January 1856, in answer to their advice that he try marriage as a "cure" for his considerable physical complaints and for his mental "exhaustion." He writes:

> I am perfectly willing to try your remedy for rationalism. Indeed, marriage has been prescribed as a means of setting my brain right in quite another sense: the companionship of a wife being considered the best distraction—in the French not the English meaning of the word. But the advice is difficult to follow. I labour under the double difficulty that my choice is very limited and that I am not easy to please. Moral and intellectual beauties do not by themselves suffice to attract me; and owing to the stupidity of our educational system it is rare to find them united to a good physique. Moreover there is the pecuniary difficulty. Literature, and especially philosophical literature, pays badly. If I married, I should soon have to kill myself to get a living. (*Autobiography* 1:478)

In three of his essays of this period, "Personal Beauty" (1854), "The Moral Discipline of Children" (1858), and "Physical Training" (1859), we can see how Spencer used his interpretation of "evolutionary law" to rationalize his claim that a "good physique" was more important than a woman's "moral and intellectual beauties" in the process of sexual selection.

As early as 1854, we can observe—with the advantage of hindsight—how evolutionary theory prompted Spencer to redefine the meaning of gender by reassessing women's place in nature. As he began to recognize some of the fallacies in his own arguments that "moral laws" sanctioned by the Creator controlled the Design of the Universe and began to identify physical laws instead, his belief that women were inherently equal to men apparently collapsed.

Though Spencer does not discuss women per se in his essay on "Personal Beauty," published in April 1854, he does formulate theories that lay the groundwork for his later arguments about their natural inferiority. Spencer's object in this essay is to demonstrate that "beauty of character and beauty of aspect" are related, and he substantiated his analysis by citing numerous examples of biogenetic analogies which compared human babies to animals and ugly people to "inferior races," in order to show that superior physical beauty was an expression of superior mental development. He wrote, for example,

> If the recession of the forehead, protuberance of the jaws, and largeness of the cheekbones, three leading elements of ugliness, are demonstrably indicative of mental inferiority—if such facial defects . . . are habitually associated with these, and disappear along with them as intelligence increases, both in the race and in the individual, is it not a fair inference that all such faulty traits of feature signify deficiencies of mind.[20]

Spencer defended this reasoning by invoking Lamarckian use-inheritance, asserting that there is an "organic relationship between that protuberance of jaws which we consider ugly, and a certain inferiority of nature"; he argued that as the brain evolved, heavy jaws became less necessary, since the hands were used to save the jaws and implements were designed to save the hands ("Personal" 153). Spencer concluded by asserting that the pure and mixed races of the human community are subject to the same rules of heredity that pertain to pure and mixed breeds of sheep. Though genetic accidents do sometimes produce anomalies, he argued that while "plainness may coexist with nobility of nature," generally "mental and facial perfection are fundamentally connected, and will, when the present causes of incongruity have worked themselves out, be ever found united" ("Personal" 162). When we consider how this theory of beauty applied to women, we can see one of the few missing links that explains how Spencer arrived at and justified the radical reversal in his views about women that began to appear in print after 1854.

The clearest evidence of the dramatic change in Spencer's thought appeared in 1858 when he began to speculate about the "supreme end" of all education. In his *Autobiography*, Spencer identifies the two essays on education that he wrote in 1858 as revealing the ways that the developmental hypothesis revolutionized his analysis of society. Spencer wrote "The Moral Discipline of Children" immediately after he composed a "clear outline" for his *Synthetic Philosophy*, the undertaking to which he devoted the rest of his life. Commenting on the background for this essay, Spencer remarks that "consciously or unconsciously the theory of evolution furnished guidance" (*Autobiography* 2:23), thus indicating how central the "doctrine of evolution" was in justifying his view of women's inferior physical, moral, and intellectual capacities.

Spencer spells out the implications of his ideas about the "inherited constitution" in the subsequent essay, "Physical Training," also written in 1858 but not published until 1859 (*Autobiography* 2:18). In this essay, he repeats the arguments and logic from "Personal Beauty" and assumes woman's mental inferiority from her smaller physical size and her earlier sexual maturity, asserting that "a girl develops in body and mind rapidly, and ceases to grow comparatively early. A boy's bodily and mental development is slower and his growth greater" ("Physical Training" 391).

An education that cultivates a woman's mind at the expense of her body, Spencer observes pragmatically, ignores the place of woman in the natural order, where only the fittest will survive:

> The truth is that, out of the many elements uniting in various proportions to produce in a man's breast that complex emotion which we call love, the strongest are those produced by the physical attractions; the weakest are those produced by intellectual attractions; and even those are dependent much less upon acquired knowledge than on natural faculty—quickness, wit, insight. If any think the assertion a derogatory one, and inveigh against the masculine character for being thus swayed; we reply that they know little what they say when they thus call into question the Divine ordinations. . . . It needs but remember that one of Nature's ends, or rather her supreme end, is the welfare of posterity. . . . it needs but to remember that, as far as posterity is concerned, a cultivated intelligence based upon a bad physique is of little worth, seeing that its descendants will die out in a generation or two. ("Physical Training" 395)

Thus, he argued that there was a sexual division of labor that followed from sexual function and insisted that woman's most important contribution to the evolution of the race was a healthy "physique," which her education should cultivate, while man's contribution was a fully developed brain which his schooling, likewise, should foster. In Spencer's analysis of human sexuality, then, we can see his unexamined belief that humans are compelled by the same evolutionary forces which operate "among all lower forms of life, uncontrolled by commands, traditions, or creeds" and his consequent conviction that there is "no other prompter to right physical action than obedience to sensations" (*Autobiography* 2:20). Spencer was unable to see how "commands, traditions, or creeds" shaped his own assessment of the compelling power of "physical sensations" in human sexual selection.

Moreover, by recommending this new educational program, Spencer consciously advocated a system that would amplify the intellectual disparities between men and women, since he believed—along with other Lamarckian evolutionary thinkers of his time—that acquired intellectual and moral characteristics were inherited along with physical ones. In the leap of logic that collapsed "one of Nature's ends" into her "supreme end" ("Physical Training" 395), Spencer assumed that all women were destined by nature to become mothers, and ignored, or defined as un-

natural, the needs and requirements of all women who could not or
would not marry and those who, married or not, declined to bear children. This is the starting point for Eliot's debate with Spencer in *Adam
Bede.*

In 1851 when she met Herbert Spencer, Eliot also supported feminist
reforms in marriage and divorce laws, endorsed women's social emancipation, and recommended better education for women, though she assumed a more ambivalent position in the 1860s on female suffrage.
Eliot's attitude toward marriage reforms during the 1840s and 1850s
reflects perhaps the most obvious ground of agreement between her
and Spencer, as well as the socialist feminists who influenced them both.
In an enigmatic letter to Charles Bray, Eliot indicates her disapproval of
the restrictive divorce laws that bound Rochester to Bertha Mason: "I
have read *Jane Eyre*, mon ami, and shall be glad to know what you admire
in it. All self-sacrifice is good—but one would like it to be in a somewhat
nobler cause than that of a diabolical law which chains a man soul and
body to a putrifying carcass" (*GEL* 1:268). The echoes of Owenite criticisms of marriage evident in this letter, and references to other socialist
concerns in several letters from this period, indicate that Eliot was aware
of this strand of feminist thought, though she was not particularly impressed with Robert Owen when she met him in 1843 at the Brays (*GEL*
1:161).

By 1856, when the parliamentary debates on the reform of divorce
laws were most heated (Poovey 70), Eliot signed Barbara Smith Bodichon's petition supporting the legal rights of married women over their
own property and earnings. Eliot wrote to Sara Hennell that she saw this
measure as a "counteractive to wife-beating and other evils" and successfully urged her friend to sign as well. In a subsequent letter, Eliot writes,
"I'm glad you have taken up the cause, for I do think that with proper
provisions and safeguards, the proposed law would help raise the position and character of women. It is one round of a long ladder stretching
beyond our lives" (*GEL* 2:225). In taking this long-range view of the
changes offered by legislation, however, Eliot reveals the conservatizing
influence that Spencer's evolutionary theory exerted on her feminism in
the interval between 1848 and 1856.

Eliot's objections to the restrictive laws defining women's rights in
marriage and divorce were not purely theoretical, of course, as is suggested by her willingness to establish unconventional liaisons with John
Chapman and Herbert Spencer and, more dramatically, by her revolutionary decision in 1854 to live openly with George Henry Lewes without
the benefit of marriage. Eliot's relation to Lewes did not simply express
a rejection of marriage or a principled commitment to the doctrine of
"free love," as some feminists then and now have assumed, because after

suffering a great deal of pain and anguish in her relationship with both Chapman and Spencer, Eliot would have married Lewes, had this been legally possible.

Nonetheless, in choosing to live with Lewes, Eliot deliberately defied the most cherished conventions of Victorian culture, though she realized that she risked ostracism even from her closest female friends. She refused, for example, to discuss her plans beforehand with either Sara Hennell or Cara Bray. Mrs. Gaskell's gentle regret that she was not married though living with Lewes (*GEL* 3:197), and Mrs. Linton's more acrimonious criticism, reveal only a small measure of the repressive force of Victorian "ladyism" that Eliot resisted. Furthermore, her beloved brother Isaac's repudiation of her when he learned of her decision to live with Lewes and the disapproving silence he kept for twenty-four years until Lewes's death all suggest the radical nature of Eliot's act.

These painful readjustments in her personal life, however, may have made Eliot less willing to make an issue of her unmarried state (*GEL* 3:396). She regarded Lewes as her husband, intended, as Charles Bray delicately explained, to "fulfill all the conditions that belong naturally to the marriage state" (*GEL* 8:131), and adopted Lewes's name. In 1855, shortly after she began living with Lewes, Eliot wrote to Bray:

> Assuredly, if there be one subject on which I feel no levity, it is that of marriage, and the state of the sexes—if there is any one action or relation of my life which is and always has been profoundly serious, it is my relation to Mr. Lewes. . . . Light and easily broken ties are what I neither desire theoretically nor could live for practically. Women who are satisfied with such ties do not act as I have done—they obtain what they desire and still are invited to dinner. (*GEL* 2:213)

Eliot's unwillingness to endorse a more unconstrained philosophy of "free love" and her refusal to take a stand on principle about her unmarried state, should not obscure the fact that her view of marriage was consistent with that of many Owenite feminists before 1850.

Despite the circumstances that pushed Eliot into an act more radical than she perhaps would have otherwise chosen, she, like Lewes, refused to see marriage in the entirely legalistic terms posed by the parliamentary debates of the 1850s. Eliot shared with Lewes a belief that marriage could be conducted on more egalitarian terms and that loveless marriages were destructive. She supported Lewes in his desire to maintain contact with his wife, Agnes, who was living at the time with Thorton Hunt. Similarly, she joined with Lewes in caring for his sons by Agnes, especially after 1860 when they came to live with Eliot and Lewes. Eliot also provided substantial sums toward their education and, eventually, their patrimony (Haight, *George Eliot* 293–94, 332–34, 361–65).

By the 1860s, then, Eliot's attitudes about marriage were understandably complicated, not the least because she was ostracized by women in polite society because Lewes could not marry her. Legally, Lewes had "condoned" Agnes's adultery since he had not sued for divorce after the birth of her first child by Hunt and was subsequently prevented from obtaining a divorce on those grounds. It is important to note, however, that after 1857, the parliamentary debates took a more "moderate course," and the passage of the Matrimonial Causes Act preempted more radical feminist proposals for marriage reform (Poovey 73). By the 1860s, many Victorian feminists began to regard marriage as offering important protections for middle-class women, especially as the plight of the "redundant" woman, the prostitute, and the illegitimate child gained more attention and as the challenges of evolutionary theory began to be heard. Eliot's analysis of marriage and motherhood—and the conflicts between women's work in the public and private sphere—become more important in her later novels, as she worked to reconcile a feminist assessment of women's potential with her increasingly more sophisticated understanding of the social implications of evolutionary theory.

Eliot's support for women's emancipation in the 1850s is perhaps most explicit in her review essay, "Margaret Fuller and Mary Wollstonecraft" (1855), where she demonstrates her agreement with Fuller that "women need, especially at this juncture, a much greater range of occupation than they have to rouse their latent powers" (*Essays* 204). Eliot's understanding of the special vocational problems faced by the unmarried Victorian woman is also frequently displayed in her letters and in her novels, where she presents with heartfelt sympathy the crisis experienced by her heroine when a marriage partner fails to appear and she must ask herself the question posed with such simple eloquence by Dorothea Brooke: "What can I do?"

Eliot, who had herself experienced the uncomfortable confinement of an unmarried daughter's life, was especially close to Barbara Smith Bodichon and Emily Davies in the 1850s; she joined with them in objecting to the enforced leisure of the middle-class woman and in championing the cause both of the "redundant" woman and of her less fortunate sister who worked for very little pay in the sweat shops, mines, and mills of a newly industrialized England. Bodichon and Davies were instrumental in publicizing the economic reality faced by the "redundant" single woman, and both feminists argued that it was the father's responsibility to educate his daughters so that they could support themselves and maintain an independent life if they did not marry, or if the financial need otherwise arose—a position for which Eliot shows her sympathy in the essay on Fuller and Wollstonecraft and, of course, in her novels.

Eliot helped Bodichon write her pamphlet *Women and Work,* and also revealed her sympathy for working women in a letter to Charles Bray in 1857. Commenting on his apparently disapproving description of "female labor in factories," Eliot asked, "How is it that the results have been so different at Lowell [Mass.]?" She goes on to explain that though she has chosen the "part of the Epicurean gods" in her position on the Woman Question, she all the more "highly venerates" those feminist activists who are "struggling in the thick of the contest." She closes by remarking, " '*La carrière ouverte aux talents,*' whether the talents be feminine or masculine, I am quite confident is the right maxim" (*GEL* 2:396). It seems precisely in order to counter this middle-class snobbery about women working in the factories that Eliot gives to Dinah Morris, one of her most morally exalted characters, the occupation not only of preacher but of millworker.

Eliot was also deeply appreciative of the work undertaken by Bessie Parkes in the *English Woman's Journal,* though she declined to write an article for the publication, excusing herself from all occasional journalistic work when her career as a novelist began (*GEL* 2:428). In the same extraordinary letter to Barbara Bodichon describing her response to Darwin in 1859, Eliot praised the work that Parkes was accomplishing, though she complained, characteristically, about the reviewer of novels and about the writing style of the publication: "The *English Woman's Journal* must be doing good substantially—stimulating woman to useful work, and rousing people generally to some consideration of woman's needs. A few mistakes, and a rather feeble presentation of useful matter, will not neutralize the good that lies in a great aim and an honest effort; and I heartily wish all connected with the journal 'God Speed.' " (*GEL* 3:225–26). Eliot's compassion for the condition of the unmarried woman is particularly clear in her early novels: she presents with great sympathy Hetty's recognition of her destitution, Maggie's patient devotion to her poorly paid work at plain sewing, and Priscilla Lammeter's defensiveness about her single state.

Eliot's treatment of Maggie's vocational crisis, like her treatment of similar crises faced by Esther Lyon, Mary Garth, and Gwendolen Harleth, can be better understood in the context of the writing of Victorian feminists like Bodichon and Parkes, who argued that teaching and governessing were already desperately overcrowded professions even for middle-class ladies and that training in these fields was not an adequate way to insure a single woman's financial independence. Teaching was, furthermore, a vocation for which many intellectual women were temperamentally ill-suited, as Maggie Tulliver asserts.

Finally, of all the reforms urged by Victorian feminists in the 1850s, Eliot's support for women's education is the strongest and least equivo-

cal.[21] Her support for women's educational reforms prompted her to
attend a series of lectures at Bedford College for Ladies during these
years and moved her to contribute, albeit modestly, to Emily Davies's
campaign for the establishment of Girton College and to other feminist
efforts to open the professions to women in the 1850s and 1860s
(Haight, *George Eliot* 460; David 178). In uniting with Bodichon and Davies on this issue, Eliot aligned herself with the more radical group of
feminist educational reformers who argued that women should be
granted access to the same university curriculum studied by men and
should be allowed to sit for examinations for the same degrees.

In her essay on Fuller and Wollstonecraft, Eliot argued that inadequate education was one of the major obstacles to women's emancipation, and she defended feminist educational reforms by appealing to
male self-interest, in terms that anticipated and countered Spencer's
concerns about "overly educated" women:

> Men pay a heavy price for their reluctance to encourage self-help and inde-
> pendent resources in women. The precious meridian years of many a man of
> genius have to be spent in the toil of routine, that an "establishment" may be
> kept up for a woman who can understand none of his secret yearnings, who is
> fit for nothing but to sit in her drawing-room like a doll-Madonna in her
> shrine. Anything is more endurable than to change our established formulae
> about women or to run the risk of looking up to our wives instead of down on
> them. (*Essays* 205)

In publicly expressing her appreciation for Wollstonecraft in this essay,
Eliot revealed the radical resistance that shaped her feminism. In taking
Wollstonecraft seriously, Eliot distinguished herself from moderate feminists who, even a century after her death, regarded her as anathema
because of her association with "freethinking, free living, and free loving" and "unwomanly habits of all sorts" (Taylor 15). Perhaps some of
Eliot's own "Epicurean" aloofness from the political activism undertaken
by her friends may be explained, in part, by her consciousness that her
own similar association with "freethinking, free living, and free loving"
might jeopardize the cause. Undoubtedly, however, her acceptance of
Spencer's arguments about the value of specialization in the social division of labor also played a part.

Yet, in her reference to "Nature" in "Margaret Fuller and Mary Wollstonecraft," Eliot makes an attack on Spencer's incipient antifeminism
that indicates the grounds of her debate with him over the application of
his evolutionary theories to women. She praises Margaret Fuller for
pointing out the "folly of absolute definition of woman's nature and
absolute demarcations of woman's mission." She cites, with particular

approval, Fuller's comment that " 'Nature . . . seems to delight in varying the arrangements, as if to show that she will be fettered by no rule' " (*Essays* 203). One hears many echoes of Fuller's words in Eliot's works, especially in her first novel, *Adam Bede* (1859).

It is against the background of Spencer's thought in the 1850s that we can best understand Eliot's most controversial and frequently misunderstood essay, "Woman in France: Madame de Sablé." Eliot wrote this essay in 1854, immediately after she left England with George Henry Lewes, and it is her first public statement addressing feminist issues in the context of evolutionary thought. She recognized that in writing it she ran the risk of alienating the few feminist friends who would not otherwise be scandalized by her choice to live openly with Lewes. Immediately before the essay appeared, she wrote to Bessie Parkes, "If I happen to write anything you don't like about women, you must tolerate me, since in all things I am obliged to say with old Luther, 'This is my belief—I cannot speak otherwise—so help me God! Amen' " (*GEL* 2:174). In retrospect, we can see Eliot struggling in this essay to reconcile her own feminist views with the most difficult aspects of Spencer's developing antifeminist arguments.

In "Woman in France," Eliot chooses for her subject a woman who seems to epitomize the ideal of the perfectly developed woman as Spencer defined her in 1854, for Madame de Sablé was, Eliot reminds us, preeminently and exquisitely beautiful. Eliot goes on to emphasize this woman's physical frailty and, indeed, to generalize in a way most disconcerting to modern feminists, about woman's inferior physical capacities, echoing Spencer's analysis of comparative anatomy and his Lamarckian belief in inherited racial characteristics. In order to explain why women writers were more influential in the French tradition than in the English, Eliot asks:

> What were the causes of this earlier development and more abundant manifestation of womanly intellect in France? The primary one, perhaps, lies in the physiological characteristics of the Gallic race: the small brain and vivacious temperament which permit the fragile system of woman to sustain the superlative activity requisite for intellectual creativeness; while, on the other hand, the larger brain and slower temperament of the English and Germans are, in the womanly organization, generally dreamy and passive. (*Essays* 55)

At this point in 1854, Eliot could find no grounds to argue against Spencer's assertion of woman's weaker physical constitution, but she clearly did not share his conclusion that sex differences necessarily made women intellectually and morally inferior to men. Moreover, as this essay and her subsequent novels demonstrate, she firmly resisted his conclusion that women should be kept ignorant in order to gratify male tastes and thus succeed through sexual selection in taking their proper place as mothers of the race.

What is striking about "Woman in France" is that Eliot employs her description of the beautiful *précieuse* in order to demonstrate the enduring contribution she made to the development of French letters, not because of her beauty but because of her intellectual—and womanly— genius. Eliot ends the essay by arguing eloquently that with better education, both formal and informal, English women could become as accomplished as French women:

> Women become superior in France by being admitted to a common fund of ideas, to common objects of interest with men; and this must ever be the essential condition of true womanly culture and true social well-being. . . . Let the whole field of reality be laid open to women as well as men, and then that which is peculiar in her mental modification, instead of being as it is now, a source of discord and repulsion between the sexes, will be found a necessary complement to the truth and beauty of life. (*Essays* 80–81)

Rejecting the evolutionary logic that led Spencer to argue, by the end of the decade, that female education should be adjusted entirely to the "supreme end" of Nature, by which he meant the demands of motherhood, Eliot maintained throughout her career her belief that women could only achieve a liberation from their "natural" physical subjection by developing their intellectual and moral capacities to the fullest extent through a complete liberal education. The fervor of this passage from "Woman in France" suggests the depth of Eliot's commitment to the reforms in education for women proposed by Victorian feminists and indicates how central the "maternal emotions" were in this defense.

Though Eliot had, by 1854, already recognized several features of Spencer's evolutionary analysis that threatened those feminist concerns she felt most deeply about, she nonetheless found in her acceptance of evolutionary theory a self-justifying and feminist compensation that was particularly liberating to her as a woman writer. As George Levine explains, "Only the establishment of an authority alternate to religious tradition made it possible to extend the rule of science to the human" realm through disinterested observation (*Darwin* 15). Spencer's essay, "The Genesis of Science," which Eliot especially admired, provided her with a useful argument that allowed her to challenge the most fundamental basis of the authority that Spencer claimed as a scientist and to establish on an equal basis her own authority as a poet and realist. In this essay, Spencer exposed the subjectivity of the "natural philosophers" who developed what he called a "new form of the old realism" by reiterating the Hegelian doctrine that "to philosophize on Nature is to re-think the great thought of Creation."[22] To natural philosophers versed in the English empiricist tradition, Spencer observed, the fallacy of this "old realism" is obvious:

> Here we see the experience of quantitative relations which men have gathered from surrounding bodies and generalized (experiences which had been scarcely at all generalized in the beginning of the historic period)—we find these generalized experiences, these intellectual abstractions, elevated into concrete actualities, projected back into Nature, and considered as the internal framework of things—the skeleton by which matter is sustained. (*Essays: Scientific* 2:10–11).

By demonstrating the solipsism of these natural philosophers, and by dissolving the separation between science and fiction through his argument that perception depended on the changing fictions about the "generalized experiences" of an historical period, Spencer unwittingly called his own theories into question.

In exposing the subjectivity of both the natural philosopher and the poet, Spencer reasserted the essential unity of all knowledge. He writes:

> The sciences are branches of one trunk, and they were at first cultivated simultaneously. This harmony becomes the more marked on finding, as we have done, not only that the sciences have a common root, but that science in general has a common root with language, classification, reasoning, art; that throughout civilization these have advanced together, acting and reacting upon each other just as the separate sciences have done; and the development of intelligence in all its divisions and subdivisions has conformed to this same law which we have shown that the sciences conform to. (*Essays: Scientific* 2:71–72)

In the English literary tradition, the poets who were particularly susceptible to Spencer's criticism were those whom the Victorians saw as epic interpreters of Nature, poets who, like Milton, were great antagonists of feminist women writers.[23]

By identifying the interdependence of science and art and by describing the importance of "naming" and classification, Spencer provided a sophisticated philosophical argument that Eliot appropriated in arguing that women writers possessed a superior authority in naming the experiences that were, in Eliot's words, otherwise "unknown to men." In Eliot's hands, then, Spencer's theories could give a new dignity to angry feminist protests like those voiced by Charlotte Brontë's heroine in *Shirley*. Shirley resists the patriarch's exclusive right to read and interpret God's Book as it is manifest in the natural world, and protests against Milton's powerfully authoritative act of "naming" women in *Paradise Lost*, but her only weapon is rage:

Milton's Eve! Milton's Eve! I repeat. No, by the pure Mother of God, she is not!
. . . Milton was great; but was he good? His brain was right; how was his heart?
. . . He saw Satan, and Sin his daughter, and Death their horrible offspring. . . .
Milton tried to see the first woman; but . . . he saw her not.[24]

While Eliot followed Brontë in radically revising the model Milton offered of genesis and maternity in *Paradise Lost*, she no longer needed to
rely on the Divine Authority invoked by Owenite feminists, and by
Brontë herself, in order to challenge and revise the traditional androcentric vision of motherhood, which Spencer was reinscribing into the
fabric of his evolutionary theory. Though Eliot followed Brontë in her
resistance to female stereotypes and to the plots they imposed on
women's fiction, as *Adam Bede* and subsequent novels show, Eliot was
neither as psychologically nor as artistically enthralled by "Milton's
bogey." Because of her wide reading and cultural sophistication, and
especially because of her understanding of evolution and the philosophy
of science, she was able to appropriate an even more sweeping privilege
than her sister writers in challenging the authority of the phallocentric
scientific and literary traditions that defined the interpretation of gender differences and social relations in her own time. In depicting
women's experiences, Eliot was not only to "rename" but also to rupture
and refashion the limits of the realistic novel as she received it, and thus
she succeeded in accommodating more adequately the experiences of
mothers and daughters. To return to her comments in "Woman in
France," Eliot in her great masterworks successfully adjusted the weft
and woof of the English realistic novel so that it reflected not just one
"generalized" and androcentric myth about women, mothers, and the
maternal sentiments, but rather displayed the various and "distinctive
forms and combinations" in the lives of the women who were her chosen
subjects.

3 _____

Beauty, Sexuality, and Evolutionary Process: *Adam Bede* and "Personal Beauty"

SOME of the reasons for Eliot's appreciation of Spencer's essay "The Genesis of Science" may be deduced from her review of Robert William Mackay's *Progress of the Intellect,* where she cites approvingly the following passage from Mackay: "A remnant of the mythical lurks in the very sanctuary of science. Forms or theories ever fall short of nature, though they are ever tending to reach a position above nature, and may often be found really to include more than the maker of them at the time knew" (*Essays* 45). Mackay's words here describe part of the "mystery" that "lies under the process" of evolution that so fascinated Eliot (*GEL* 3:227), a mystery Eliot found to reside as much in the observer of nature as in the exterior world itself.

In *Adam Bede,* written in 1858 and published the following year, Eliot repeatedly calls attention to the perspective the narrator takes on nature and on the myths humanity has constructed in order to explain the origin of human life, the proper relation between men and women, and their place in the natural and supernatural world.[1] In this novel, Eliot's narrator depicts both Christian and classical myths of origin from the "outside," as it were, from a third perspective created and informed by Eliot's reading of German higher criticism and evolutionary theory.[2]

By making it possible to speak of "bodies" and "life processes," rather than "sin" and "salvation," evolutionary theorists created a language that allowed Victorians to question what Michel Foucault calls "the truth about sex" (64). In helping to shift the authority which defined the truth about sex and gender from Biblical scripture to science, Herbert Spencer participated in a second great philosophical revolution of the nineteenth century whereby sex became "something fundamental, useful or dangerous, precious or formidable" (Foucault 56). In March of 1858, Spencer formulated his evolutionary analysis of sexual selection and motherhood, which he published in the essay "Physical Training" in the following year; the relation between sexual instinct and love appears in this work as a "muddled zone" (Foucault 54), one that Eliot tries to clarify in *Adam Bede.*

In "Physical Training," Spencer remystified desire by insisting that sexual instincts primarily defined the dynamics of attraction between the

sexes; the promptings of reason or sensibility or class, or even of friendship, affection, and love, became increasingly irrelevant in his effort to
analyze gender roles and human reproduction in terms consistent with
evolutionary science. In *Adam Bede*, Eliot insists on the fundamental differences between blind instinct and love, and so challenges Spencer's
developing re-definition of human sexuality by demonstrating how simply and easily blind instinct leads to the destruction of Hetty Sorrel and
Arthur Donnithorne. While Spencer's evolutionary theory apparently
moved him to surround sexuality with all the old taboos of silence, it
prompted Eliot to criticize those customs designed to "protect" female
"innocence" and to reconceptualize female love and desire, the subject of so much literature in the female tradition, in light of Victorian
science.

In offering her story of a new English Adam, his fall, and eventual
union with a new Eve, Eliot demonstrates the regressive force of traditional beliefs about Mother Nature, motherhood, love, and female sexuality that Spencer uncritically reinscribed in his evolutionary analysis of
human reproduction and sexual selection. Both Arthur and Adam initially see Hetty Sorrel in Miltonic terms that valorize the androcentric
values of the Christian myth of Genesis; both see her as Eve and assume
that her beauty is a sign of her virtue. In the end, Eliot demonstrates that
both are tragically mistaken.[3] She traces their error to its source in the
teleology that organizes their conceptual world and describes how both
young men are taught to interpret their society, and the women in it, in
light of prevailing cultural myths about the origins of life, love, and
human responsibility. Arthur, though he is offered the double perspective of the Greek and Christian traditions, chooses to see his life as enacting Milton's "fortunate fall." Adam is offered a narrower interpretation
of the Christian myth of origin, and gradually learns to see beyond it.
Thus, in the contrast between Adam Bede and Arthur Donnithorne,
Eliot shows the self-gratifying appeal of the traditional Christian myth of
origin. Arthur's view of Hetty reflects his complacent belief that he lives
in a providentially ordered world, where class is fixed and where his social and moral preeminence is assured. Adam, in contrast, sees his world
in more Darwinian terms, as demanding the fellowship of workers of
both sexes.

Adam Bede counters the analysis Spencer articulates most dramatically
in "Physical Training" by disclosing the more egalitarian and feminist
implications of evolutionary theory (Beer, *Darwin's Plots* 114–15). Eliot
presents Dinah as an alternate Eve; her characterization reveals most
clearly Eliot's feminist resistance to Milton's powerful representation of
women as created by God to serve exclusively as "helpmates" for men
and her skepticism about Spencer's uncritical adoption of this same as-

sumption in his interpretation of gender differences. Disputing Spencer's functional view of women, Eliot asserted her special authority as a woman writer when she describes the failure of maternal instinct in Hetty's character and the triumph of erotic love in Dinah's. By locating woman's greatest gift not in her reproductive potential but rather in her capacity for erotic and maternal love, Eliot shows that Dinah must surrender her sexual innocence. However, Eliot presents this transformation not as the Miltonic fall into sin, but rather as a fall from innocence to knowledge. As Gillian Beer explains, one of the effects of evolutionary thought is that it "offers a new creation myth which challenges the idea of the fall and makes the tree of life and the tree of knowledge one" (*Darwin's Plots* 115). Thus, the marriage Dinah celebrates with Adam avoids the sexual subordination that Milton represents as necessary in order to protect women from their greater temptation to sin. In this way, Eliot registers her feminist resistance not only to Milton's mythology but also to Spencer's emerging analysis of sexual selection and the role of love and instinct in human reproduction.

Eliot's evolutionary perspective in *Adam Bede* is reflected, first of all, in the narrator's descriptions of the natural realm as far more mysterious and less hierarchically ordered than the worlds represented in Greek and Christian myths of origin. Eliot begins by challenging the metaphor of Mother Nature, which was so evocative and powerful in the hands of Milton and the Romantics as to prove irresistible to Darwin in *The Origin of Species* (Beer, *Darwin's Plots* 70). Eliot opposes this sentimental view of maternal Nature by insisting that Nature displays little solicitude for the "individual lot." In *Adam Bede*, Nature performs the same role assigned to Dame Nature in Eliot's letter to the Hennells (*GEL* 1:272–73); it remains "unmindful, unconscious" of the suffering of Adam and Hetty. The narrator asserts:

> There are so many of us, and our lots are so different: what wonder that Nature's mood is often in harsh contrast with the great crisis of our lives? We are children of a large family, and must learn, as such children do, not to expect that our little hurts will be made much of—to be content with little nurture and caressing and help each other the more. (338, ch. 27)[4]

In *Adam Bede* Eliot takes a more Malthusian view of Nature's fertility than does Darwin. In depicting the mothers in this novel, she calls attention to the mysterious genetic laws and social forces that define and restrict the maternal relationships of Rachel Poyser and Lisbeth Bede. Moreover, in presenting Hetty, Dinah, and Arthur as orphans, she reminds her readers that motherhood was often fatal, even in a world of plenty like Hayslope. Finally, by demonstrating the tragic consequences of Hetty's psychological incapacity for motherhood, Eliot makes infant mortality a visceral reality rather than the bland statistic it is in Spencer's "Theory of Population" (1852). For Eliot, and indeed for most feminists since, the capacity for motherhood and for love itself depends upon far more than woman's biological fecundity, and it is in Eliot's disclosure of the differences between physical potential and emotional capacity that we can see the clearest expression of her initial feminist defense of those values she saw as defining what it is to be truly human and female.[5]

Eliot offers an alternate metaphor that personifies Nature as a "great tragic dramatist" which "knits us together by bone and muscle, and divides us by the subtler web of our brains; blends yearning and repulsion; and ties us by our heart strings to the beings that jar us at every movement" (83–84, ch. 4). Reading the language of nature, then, depends on the "subtler web of our brains," on the skill, knowledge, and disciplined self-awareness of the reader, and on a necessary humility before the often inscrutable spectacle of Nature. As the narrator explains, "Nature has her language, and she is not unveracious; but we don't know all the intricacies of her syntax just yet, and in a hasty reading we may happen to extract the very opposite of her real meaning" (198–99, ch. 15). Though Eliot thus replaces the traditional metaphor of Mother Nature with a second traditional metaphor comparing Nature with "God's Book," one that Darwin also employs (Beer, *Darwin's Plots* 44), she selects a metaphor that emphasizes interaction between reader and text. Thus, she focuses attention on the competence of the readers and their self-consciousness about the ways that Nature serves as the ground upon which to "project" the "generalized knowledge" of the period, as Spencer explains in "The Genesis of Science."

Eliot's comments about Nature's inscrutability appear most frequently in the context of her descriptions of Hetty Sorrel and Dinah Morris, and it is here that we can see the special relevance of the new evolutionary analysis of women that Spencer began to formulate between 1852 and 1858. In constructing the theory of sexual selection described in "Physical Training," Spencer ignored the complexity of Nature's "syntax" and assumed that the most beautiful women were those most naturally suited to become the best mothers of the race. Hetty is the perfect Eve, according to Spencer's evolutionary criteria; she possesses great beauty though she conspicuously lacks, for example, the genius of Madame de Sablé. Thus, her story exposes the widening gap between Spencer's evolutionary perspective on sex and gender roles and Eliot's. In presenting her own re-vision of the genesis story, Eliot insists on the radical intellectual, moral, and emotional deficiencies that beauty may hide in both women and men. "Human feeling," she counters in *Adam Bede*, "does not wait for beauty—it flows with resistless force and brings beauty with it" (224, ch. 17).

The narrator invokes and challenges the ideas expressed in Spencer's earlier essay, "Personal Beauty," by describing Hetty's beauty as "impersonal" and not as a sign of a providential design whereby feminine beauty is the perfect complement to masculine intellect. Because Spencer discussed only masculine beauty in this essay, he avoided confronting the inconsistencies in his assumptions about female beauty that find expression in "Physical Training." By describing Hetty's "impersonal" beauty, Eliot questions Spencer's unexamined assumption that perfect beauty reflects intellectual perfection in men but moral virtue in women. Hetty's beauty, indeed, disguises the private and various secrets of her limited inner life. The narrator reminds the reader that "there are faces which nature charges with meaning and pathos not belonging to the single human soul that flutters beneath them, but speaking the joys and sorrows of foregone generations" (330, ch. 26). By the same token, when feminine beauty exists apart from moral virtue, we should recognize it as a mark of humanness, and so the narrator urges us to consider Hetty's condition with sympathy. We may be inclined to see Hetty as one of those "lovely things without souls," because "it is too painful to think that she is a woman, with a woman's destiny before her—a woman spinning in young ignorance a light web of folly and vain hopes which may one day close round her and press upon her, a rancorous poisoned garment, changing all at once her fluttering, trivial butterfly sensations into a life of deep human anguish" (295, ch. 22). In the evolutionary world that Eliot's narrator depicts, nature and women present themselves ambiguously; an accurate assessment of either demands that all the traditional associations linking women and nature be reexamined.

Similarly, the narrator repeatedly warns the reader about the difficulties of reading women's outward appearance as a sign of Nature's "intentions," or of deducing the "nature" of all women from the relatively few examples one encounters in one's own life. Dinah Morris is first seen through the eyes of a travelling stranger who visits Hayslope and, after noting Dinah's fragile beauty, he concludes "surely nature never meant her to be a preacher" (67, ch. 2). The reader, however, is advised to avoid this same mistake when the narrator comments disparagingly on the stranger's habit of mind: "Perhaps he was one of those who think that nature has theatrical properties, and, with a considerate view of facilitating art and psychology, 'makes up' her characters, so that there may be no mistake about them." (67, ch. 2). So corrected, Eliot's readers are urged to see women, and nature, as equally enigmatic and mysteriously complex.

Eliot not only requests the reader to avoid interpreting nature's intentions too hastily; she also comments ironically about this habit of mind in her male characters. The narrator displays withering irony in his descriptions of the fantasies Hetty evokes in both Arthur and Adam when they imagine "what a prize the man gets who wins a sweet bride like Hetty!" (198, ch. 15). Envisioning the "the dear, young, round, soft, flexible thing" in her bridal lace and orange blossoms, they assume Hetty's pliant accommodation to the needs of her future husband and family and conclude: "If anything ever goes wrong, it must be her husband's fault there: he can make her what he likes—that is plain" (158, ch. 15). Commenting on such extravagant flights of male fantasy, Eliot's narrator ironically comments:

> Every man under such circumstances is conscious of being a great physiognomist. Nature, he knows, has a language of her own, which she uses with strict veracity, and he considers himself an adept in the language. Nature has written out his bride's character for him in those exquisite lines of cheek and lip and chin, in those eyelids delicate as petals, in those long lashes curled like the stamen of a flower, in the dark liquid depths of those wonderful eyes. How she will dote on her children! She is almost a child herself, and the little pink round things will hang about her like florets round the central flower; and the husband will look on, smiling benignly, able, whenever he chooses, to withdraw into the sanctuary of his wisdom, towards which his sweet wife will look reverently, and never lift the curtain. It is a marriage such as they made in the golden age, when the men were all wise and majestic, and the women all lovely and loving. (198, ch. 15)

By describing how Arthur and Adam habitually imagine Hetty as a child or a flower, Eliot indicates that both men see her as closer to nature than themselves and assume her capacities and skills for motherhood are therefore innate. By exposing the fatuousness of these fantasies about Hetty, Eliot challenges Spencer's similar view of women. Moreover, by tracing the genesis of this fantasy to myths about a classical "golden age," Eliot exposes Spencer's specious logic in "Personal Beauty," where he argues that that classical sculptures of the Greek gods prove his own "half-instinctive convictions" that the physical "aspects that please are the outward correlatives of inward perfections" (*Essays: Moral* 156).

This passage about Hetty's beauty, however, also reveals Eliot's narrative difficulties, because part of her strategy in creating her narrator's male persona depends upon her appropriation of the "reifying language" of men about women (Goode 28). Too strenuous a protest against traditional "readings" of Nature's definition of a "bride's character" in "those exquisite lines of cheek and lip" would jeopardize the credibility of Eliot's male narrator. Thus, the narrator's sympathy for Hetty in particular seems to vacillate, especially when she is seen against the background of the natural world or when her beauty is compared to that of "kittens" and "downy ducks."[6]

Eliot thus uses Reverend Irwine to voice the skepticism that might otherwise undermine the narrator's male authority. It would violate Eliot's sense of historical realism to allow Irwine to view the world, as the narrator does, through the triple lens provided by Greek, Christian, and evolutionary myths of origin, but of all the characters in this novel, he most resembles the narrator in his cautious reading of nature, female beauty, and gender roles.[7] Early in the novel, Irwine tries, for example, to correct his mother's belief that she can tell what "men are like by their outsides" (108–9, ch. 5), by pointing out that "Nature is clever enough to cheat even you, mother" (108, ch. 5).

The insight that Irwine's "pagan" philosophy gives him is most evident when Arthur seeks him out to confess his susceptibility to Hetty's beauty and to solicit his advice. This episode parallels one later between Adam and Bartle Massey, and in both scenes Eliot shows how Christian and classical myths of origin operate in the psychic machinery of these two young men. Arthur and Adam come to their mentors when they recognize their subjection to Hetty's "absolute loveliness" and feel the original Adam's confusion before the first Eve, when "All higher knowlege in her presence falls/ Degraded" (*Paradise Lost* 8:551–52).[8] In the dialogues that follow, Eliot shows how patriarchal creation myths which define the first woman as "made for man" continue to shape the male psychology of love and desire.

Irwine's conversation with Arthur also reveals the advantages of the formal education given to aristocratic men, for he offers Arthur the superior insight derived from his understanding of both the classical and Christian traditions, advantages which Eliot was herself denied because of her sex. Eliot's description of Arthur's response to Hetty's beauty reflects, of course, her own restricted and vicarious access to this aspect of male experience, a realm which corresponds to the "wild zone" of female experience (Showalter, "Feminist" 200). Arthur's subjection to Hetty's beauty is thus described in highly literary terms; he invokes common Romantic metaphors of sickness and enchantment when he complains, "A man may be very firm in other matters, and yet be under a sort of witchery from a woman" (216, ch. 16). More often, though, it is Milton's version of the Christian genesis myth that, in Arthur's psychology, turns the "small unnoticeable wheel which has a great deal to do with the motion of the large obvious ones" (281, ch. 16). Arthur responds to Hetty's beauty first of all when he sees her surrounded by "each rural sight, each rural sound" (*Paradise Lost* 9:450–51) at Hall Farm. Her work in the dairy calls to mind Eve in her paradisal bower preparing "dulcet creams," and her unruly ringlets, rose-petal cheeks, and blushes all reinforce the parallels between her and Milton's first woman.[9] Irwine tries unsuccessfully to correct Arthur's Miltonic as-

sumptions about women, class, and nature. His knowledge of classical
literature enlarges his sense of the possible and allows him to recognize the fictional appeal of a "golden age" when beauty and virtue were
one. His knowledge of the Greek creation myth about Pandora prompts
him to imagine correctly that Hetty's beauty could also hide her foolishness. Thus, in reminding Arthur of the "alternate doses which a
man may administer to himself by keeping unpleasant consequences
before his mind" (217, ch. 16), Irwine tries to warn his protégé about
the dangers of an imprudent marriage by tactfully alluding to Aeschylus' *Prometheus Bound* (217, ch. 16).[10] Though Irwine isn't himself aware
of all the parallels between Hetty and Io that are illuminated by this
allusion, the reader knows that Hetty is haunted by similarly flattering
visions of a marriage with a social superior. Thus, Io's tragedy foreshadows Hetty's, for she too is maddened by fear and transformed into
the semblance of an animal, condemned to wander in a foreign landscape under the censorious observation of a watchful rural Argus (640–
80).[11]

Arthur, however, completely misunderstands the import of Irwine's
allusions to *Prometheus Bound,* and he remarks, instead, on Hetty's power
to change his "mood." Irwine responds by describing his more determin-
istic view of human nature, a perspective that is the product of Irwine's
more philosophical and "pagan" view of free will: "Ah, but the moods lie
in his nature, my boy, just as much as his reflections did, and more. A
man can never do anything at variance with his own nature. He carries
within him the germ of his most exceptional action" (127, ch. 16). When
Arthur rejects Irwine's warning not to tempt Hetty or feed her vanity by
telling her she is a "great beauty," his infatuation appears as the deliberate indulgence of his own wayward fancy. Arthur is unwilling to surrender his belief that the world is providentially organized to satisfy his own
desires.

Miltonic metaphors retain their appeal for Arthur throughout his affair with Hetty, and Eliot's use of these allusions shows how evolutionary
theory authorized her resistance to the gender and class hierarchies that
Milton's genesis story embodies. The argument which Arthur constructs
to ameliorate his guilt for Hetty's seduction parodies Milton's defense of
the "fortunate fall":

> But Hetty might have had the trouble in some other way if not in this. And
> perhaps hereafter he might be able to do a great deal of good for her, and
> make up to her all the tears she would shed about him. She would owe the
> advantage of his care for her in future years to the sorrow she had incurred
> now. So good comes out of evil. Such is the beautiful arrangement of things!
> (358, ch. 29)

Arthur's complacent faith that "Providence would not treat him harshly" is destroyed when he learns that Hetty has given birth and has been driven to abandon their child.

Eliot's evolutionary re-visioning of the myth of genesis is particularly evident when she describes the meeting between Hetty and Arthur in the wood, a meeting that Adam Bede accidentally observes. In this scene, Arthur amuses himself by imagining that Hetty is a "wood-nymph," but he knows, though Hetty does not, what a pathetically diminished Eve she is. Arthur is aware that the "golden age" has indeed passed away; Hetty, bound by the constraints of gender and class, still lives in her egocentric dream world. In the new world disclosed by evolutionary science, in a world beyond "sin" and "innocence," Arthur's superior knowledge about human nature and sexual desire further amplifies his patriarchal power.[12]

Having herself rejected the arguments whereby "natural theologians justified the ways of God to man" (Levine, *Darwin* 55), Eliot also stages a dialogue between Adam Bede and Bartle Massey that exposes the misogynistic bias of Milton's genesis story and reveals the gender and class hierarchies that structured the "Charities of Father, Son, and Brother" in Milton's poem and in Adam Bede's world (*Paradise Lost* 4:756–57). While Bartle Massey's conversation with Adam about Hetty parallels Irwine's with Arthur about the "charm of Beauty's powerful glance," it exposes the darker side of Milton's version of genesis, but Bartle is no more effective than Irwine in averting the tragedy. When Adam comes to confess his desire to marry Hetty Sorrel, Bartle reminds Adam that he lives in a fallen world:

> "Don't tell me about God having made such creatures to be companions for us! I don't say but He might make Eve to be a companion to Adam in Paradise—there was no cooking to be spoilt there, and no other woman to cackle with and make mischief; though, you see what mischief she did as soon as she'd an opportunity. But it's an impious, unscriptural opinion to say a woman's a blessing to a man now; you might as well say adders and wasps and foxes and wild beasts, are a blessing when they're only the evils that belong to this state of probation, which it's lawful for a man to keep clear of as he can in this life, hoping to get quit of 'em forever in another." (286, ch. 21)

Bartle is correct to identify Adam's excessive sentimentality as rooted in the myth of a domestic paradise that Milton elaborated so beautifully.[13] In the scene preceding this visit, Adam observes Hetty surrounded by the "half-neglected abundance" of the Poyser's garden and sees her as Eve with "Roses blushing round" (*Paradise Lost* 9:425). Hetty's beauty has prompted Adam to imagine her as a woman specially created for his gratification. Yet we see from the contrasts between Adam's conversation with Massey and Arthur's with Irwine, that Adam Bede's apprehension of his beloved as Eve is not the willful expression of fanciful self-indulgence that it is for Arthur Donnithorne but rather a result of his unsophisticated convictions about women and nature, attitudes that remain uncorrected by his rudimentary and class-bound education.

While both Adam and Massey subscribe to the Puritan work ethic that Milton glorified in his presentation of the domestic romance in the concluding books of *Paradise Lost*, Bartle shrewdly notes that Adam shows a mawkish foolishness in viewing Hetty in such idealized terms. With neither Irwine's resources nor his urbanity, Massey tries to correct Adam's vision by reminding him instead of the fatal temptations posed by woman's sexuality. Echoing Milton's Adam after the fall, Massey describes woman as the "fair defect/ Of nature" (*Paradise Lost* 10:891), and insists on her "natural" associations with sin and lawlessness. Because he habitually confuses women with "wild beasts," Massey imagines all the sin on earth as issuing from a feminine source not unlike Milton's monstrous mother, Sin. While Massey's intuition about Hetty's animal nature predicts her future as accurately as Irwine's references to Pandora and Io, his misogynistic interpretation of women's capacities also expose assumptions about woman's "defect" that Spencer similarly rationalized in "Physical Training."

When Bartle elaborates on women's lawlessness, Eliot reveals how he loses the consciousness that he was "using a figure of speech" when he confuses women with animals, thus disclosing a failure of logic that discredits not only his argument but Spencer's as well. Though Bartle asserts woman's innate lawlessness when he declares, "What's the use o' law when a man's once such a fool as to let a woman into his house?" (284, ch. 21), his complaint is not only about women, it is also directed at his dog who has produced a litter of unwanted puppies: "That's the way with these women, they've got no head-pieces to nourish, and so their food runs to fat or to brats" (285, ch. 21). Eliot deflates Massey's misogyny by revealing this humorous crotchet, but her efforts to expose Spencer's similarly unconscious use of metaphors comparing women and animals became a lifelong task.

Massey's conversation also asserts the powerful and continuing appeal of a world defined exclusively by "Spirits Masculine," and by "Charities/ Of Father, Son, and Brother" (*Paradise Lost* 4:756–57). Bartle's conversation exposes the grotesque illogic that prevails in a world where women are seen as "defective" and therefore subject—like animals—to man's ownership and control. In *Adam Bede*, Eliot challenges the logic that requires that women be kept ignorant in order to protect their "innocence" by dramatizing the tragic consequences that result from Hetty's ignorance about her sexuality. By dramatizing the severe punishment that she alone suffers for the sexual lawlessness issuing from her "innocence," Eliot tries to pose an alternate world unstructured by such traditional misogynistic assumptions about women.[14]

For Eliot, evolutionary theory not only redefined the nature of sin and law, as her resistance to the Miltonic formulas in these two dialogues makes clear, it also transformed redemption from a Divine to a "social act" (Levine, *Darwin* 225). Adam Bede suffers a fall comparable to that of Milton's Adam when he surrenders his belief that Hetty was the "prettiest thing God had made" (468, ch. 41) after he learns of Arthur's involvement with her. When he hears about her pregnancy, he not only denounces Arthur, he criticizes the gender and class foundations of patriarchal law itself, saying: "If there's been any crime, it's at his door, not at *hers*. *He* taught her to deceive—*he* deceived me first. Let 'em put *him* on trial—let him stand in court beside her, and I'll tell 'em how he got hold of her heart and 'ticed her t'evil, and then lied to me" (455, ch. 39). Though he later qualifies his view of Hetty as victim and accepts her share of the guilt in exposing the child she bore by Arthur, Adam shows that he has seen the fault in the patriarchal system of justice when he cries: "Is he to go free, while they lay all the punishment on her . . . so weak and so young?" (455, ch. 39). Realizing that his paternalistic protectiveness could not save Hetty, Adam recognizes that she alone must suffer the consequences of her ignorant choices. In protesting that Arthur will go unpunished for his part in the crime, Adam sees some of the inequalities women faced under the laws of church and state in nineteenth-century England.

Eliot gives us only a brief glimpse into Arthur's mortification and self-imposed punishment. If in this she seems to betray an ambivalent allegiance to the patriarchy, we may see her silence, perhaps, as a defense against the same anger that surfaces in her treatment of Hetty, an anger that is most clearly articulated when Adam rages against Massey's suggestion that Hetty's fall might have been a fortunate one:

> "Good will come out of it! . . . That doesn't alter th'evil: *her* ruin can't be undone. I hate that talk o' people, as if there was a way o' making amends for everything. They'd more need be brought to see as the wrong they do can never be altered. When a man's spoiled his fellow-creatur's life, he's no right to comfort himself with thinking good may come out of it it: somebody else's good doesn't alter her shame and misery" (504, ch. 42).

Eliot imagines a world where Milton's God and Milton's justice no longer prevail, and she questions the ethics of love and marriage that Milton envisioned. Adam experiences a "baptism of suffering" because he was mistaken about Hetty and the maudlin paradise he could enter by marrying her, but he is able, as a result, to discover with Dinah a "paradise within" that is "happier far."[15]

There are no scenes in *Adam Bede* where Dinah or Hetty receive the kind of guidance that Irwine offers to Arthur or that Massey gives to Adam; what Eliot represents, instead, is Dinah's and Hetty's exclusion from the discourse of sexuality, knowledge, and power. These young women are left to rely upon their own resources, and the results are tragic. In *Adam Bede*, then, Eliot invokes Milton not only to describe male experiences of love and desire but also to critique the traditional Christian interpretation of female sexuality in a fallen world. In the famous chapter entitled "The Two Bed-Chambers," and in her treatment of Hetty's and Dinah's sexuality more generally, Eliot demonstrates how the biological risks of motherhood are amplified immeasurably by the social and religious customs designed to protect a young woman's "innocence," traditions which actually promote a terrible ignorance. In her depiction of the "alienation" that separates both Hetty and Dinah from an understanding of the female body and its potential, we can see some of the most important signs of Eliot's feminist resistance to both Milton's and Spencer's reading of Genesis.

Conservative Victorians typically defined the ignorance which shrouded a young woman's understanding of her own sexuality as a "remnant of the innocence of Paradise" that had been "mercifully" bestowed upon women.[16] Spencer reembedded this traditional belief in his theory of education by identifying unconscious sexual instinct as the fundamental dynamic of attraction between the sexes. In *Adam Bede*, Eliot registers her serious disagreements with Spencer's basic assumptions about the compelling force of male sexual instinct in the reproductive process. By claiming to reveal the new evolutionary "truth" about sex, Spencer created a theory of education that threatened to amplify the subordination of women to men both outside marriage and inside it. In her 1856 essay "Silly Novels by Lady Novelists," Eliot rejected the "superstition" that a woman's "amazing ignorance both of science and of life" was an adequate basis for moral choice (*Essays* 310). In *Adam Bede* she displays the relation between sexuality and power by contrasting Hetty's and Dinah's ignorance about their sexuality. While Hetty is trapped by her desires, Dinah achieves her fullest human potential by consciously choosing a marriage that honors her autonomy as well as her love.

In the chapter "The Two Bed-Chambers," Eliot invites her readers to see Dinah and Hetty in evolutionary terms.[17] She writes:

> It is our habit to say that while the lower nature can never understand the higher, the higher nature commands a complete view of the lower. But I think that the higher nature has to learn this comprehension, as we learn the art of

vision, by a good deal of hard experience, often with bruises and gashes incurred in taking things up by the wrong end, and fancying our space wider than it is. (206, ch. 15)

Eliot uses the terms "higher" and "lower" here to suggest Dinah's and Hetty's relative positions on an evolutionary scale that discriminates the less complex from the more complex nature, or, to use Herbert Spencer's terms, the homogeneous from the heterogeneous organism.

However, Eliot refused to imagine that scientific law offered a realm that was entirely free of contamination by the same hierarchies of gender and class that structured Milton's epic, and in her comparison of these two women, she reveals one of the avenues that Spencer had used to smuggle misogynistic assumptions into his evolutionary theory. By insisting on the beauty of both women, Eliot highlights some of the reasons for her skepticism over Spencer's conviction that outward appearance is an adequate index of inward perfection. Dinah's "higher" nature is not simply the product of biological heredity but originates, Eliot asserts, from a mysterious and unpredictable blending of her biological gifts and her unique psychological response to the suffering she observed during her childhood in Stoniton. Though Dinah's eyes disclose a family resemblance to Rachel Poyser, which is reinforced by the implicit allusion to the Biblical Dinah, the daughter of Rachel's sister (Genesis 34), Eliot emphasizes the sharp contrast between Mrs. Poyser's "keenness" and Dinah's seraphic "gentleness" (118, ch. 6). In fact, Mrs. Poyser remarks on how unlike her biological mother Dinah really is: "I could fancy you was your aunt Judith, only her hair was a deal darker than yours, and she was stouter and broader i' the shoulders. . . . Oh! your mother little thought as she'd have a daughter cut out after the very pattern o' Judith, and leave her an orphan, too, for Judith to take care on. . . ." (121, ch. 6). Moreover, Mrs. Poyser recognizes the impact of Dinah's early experiences and environment when she tries unsuccessfully to persuade the girl to "come and live i' this country, where there's some shelter and victual for man and beast" (121, ch. 6). Pointing out how Dinah differs from both mother and aunt, Rachel argues, "And then you might get married to some decent man, and there'd be plenty ready to have you, if you'd only leave off preaching as is ten times worse than your aunt Judith ever did" (122, ch. 6). Dinah's early environment thus has been more powerful than nature in allowing her to realize the full potential of her "higher nature."

In demonstrating how Dinah successfully resists her aunt's nurturing, Eliot also shows what Adrienne Rich has identified as some of the advantages of a motherless daughter.[18] Dinah sees her obligations to her aunt as "voluntary"; they are not enforced by the blood bond that converts a "call of duty" into a moral imperative. Because she is an orphan, Dinah is free to elect the vocation that allows her to express her talents and disposition best.

Dinah defends her choice of vocation in a conversation with Reverend Irwine and this dialogue expresses Eliot's sympathy for the feminist reforms which would allow talented women to enter the vocation of their choice.[19] Dinah explains that among the Wesleyans at that time, a woman's sex did not disqualify her from becoming a preacher, and she protests against those who would exclude her from the work she loves. Citing the example of Mrs. Fletcher, the first woman to preach in the Society, Dinah continues: "Mr. Wesley approved of her undertaking the work. She had a great gift, and there are many others now living who are precious fellow-helpers in the work of the ministry. I understand that there's been voices raised against it in the Society of late, but I cannot but think their counsel will come to naught" (134, ch. 8). Irwine accepts Dinah's feminist argument that "it isn't for men to make channels for God's Spirit, as they make channels for the watercourses, and say, 'Flow here, but flow not there' " (134, ch. 8). Seeing her choice as an appropriate one, Irwine notes he "might as well lecture the trees for growing in their own shape" as criticize Dinah for her preaching (136, ch. 8). In Dinah, Eliot thus represents all the female energy and intelligence wasted by narrow definitions of gender roles that recognize woman's only "natural" vocation in marriage and motherhood.

Though Dinah can temporarily claim God's word as legitimizing her choice of a vocation, as did many other feminists, especially before the publication of Darwin's *Origin of Species,* Eliot herself realized how these appeals to Christian scripture as authorizing female emancipation were undermined by the theory of evolution. Moreover, Eliot uses Dinah to show the limitations of feminist appropriations of phallocentric Christian rhetoric and ideology. As her conversation with Reverend Irwine makes clear, Dinah has learned to separate entirely the desires of the flesh from those of the spirit. When Irwine questions her delicately about her awareness of her sexual self, by asking if she feels embarrassment for being "a young woman upon whom men's eyes are fixed," Dinah responds, "I've no room for such feelings and I don't believe that people ever take notice of that" (136, ch. 8). Dinah's asceticism reflects the traditional Christian distinction that Milton articulates when Raphael explains the differences between "heavn'ly Love," which exalts man's spirit, and "carnal pleasure," which debases him to the level of the beasts (*Paradise Lost* 8: 589–94). Beautiful women like Dinah have difficulty escaping these categories, as Seth's gentle romantic attention to her proves.

Dinah ultimately discovers that the separations between "heavn'ly Love" and "carnal pleasure" are painfully confining when she begins to feel a sexual attraction to Adam. Living out the conflict that her faith once allowed her to dismiss, Dinah experiences her passionate feelings for Adam in Miltonic terms, as a "great temptation." Thus, she refuses to sit at Mrs. Poyser's harvest table, because she feels she must "wrestle" against her sexual impulses until she can determine if her "soul had lost its freedom and was becoming enslaved by earthly affection" (533, ch. 52). In the episode, Eliot shows how the ideology which freed Dinah to find a vocation allowing the fullest expression of her nature becomes an obstacle to her participation in the process of creation.

While Eliot's analysis of Dinah Morris suggests the preeminence of nurture over nature, her treatment of Hetty suggests the reverse, and it is in this way also that she registers the impact of evolution on the more optimistic feminist analysis of woman's physical and moral potential. Surrounded by the comfort and plenitude of the Hall Farm and nurtured by the motherly Mrs. Poyser, Hetty remains a plant with "hardly any roots" (199, ch. 15). Nurture does not triumph over nature in the simple organization of Hetty's person and personality. Mrs. Poyser observes that her niece's "heart is as hard as a pibble" (201, ch. 15). The causes of Hetty's selfishness are as mysterious as the origins of Dinah's altruism, though in the passage about Hetty's "roots" Eliot seems to be implying that the unfortunate marriage of Hetty's mother and her early death had damaging effects upon her child, a problem Eliot explores further in her later novels.

Even though nature resists nurture in Hetty's case, biology alone cannot make Hetty a good mother. Martin Poyser quiets his wife's concerns about Hetty's "hardness" by optimistically asserting that biology has predetermined Hetty's destiny. In a parody of Spencer's theories about women, Martin Poyser says, "Them young gells are like unripe grain: they'll make good meal by and by, but they're squashy as yet. Thee't see, Hetty'll be all right when she's got a good husband and children of her own" (201, ch. 15). Eliot insists, by describing Hetty's very different fate, that without the the moral capacity for love or the imaginative capacity for sympathy, women like Hetty, whether or not they are beautiful, cannot perform adequately as wives or mothers.

In Mrs. Poyser's later remarks at the harvest home celebration, Eliot challenges the logic of analogies that equate women with less developed forms of life ("Them young gells are like unripe grain"). Bartle Massey, on this occasion, repeats Mr. Poyser's argument by recommending a peculiarly misogynistic kind of sexual selection:

"You don't value your peas for their roots or your carrots for their flowers. Now that's the way you should choose women; their cleverness'll never come to much—never come to much; but they make excellent simpletons, ripe and strong-favored." (569, ch. 53)

Mrs. Poyser deflates Massey's comically rigid antifeminism by observing sharply:

"I know what men like—a poor soft, as 'ud simper at 'em like the pictur' o' the sun, whether they did right, or wrong, an' say thank you for a kick an' pretend she didna know which end she stood uppermost, till her husband told her. That's what a man wants in a wife mostly; he wants to make sure o' one fool as 'ull tell him he's wise." (569, ch. 53)

Bartle, nonetheless, has the last word in response to her sally, and, for all her penetrating criticism of such biological analogies, Mrs. Poyser is not able to save Hetty from her tragic mistake, as her absence at this second harvest feast makes clear.

All of Mrs. Poyser's astuteness about men's taste in women and her awareness of the false logic of the analogies that link women with nature remains unspoken in her exchanges with her foster daughters. By sheltering both young women in her household from such wisdom, Mrs. Poyser acts in concert with the men in her society. She is, in fact, complicit in teaching Hetty the habits of a pleasure-loving animal, not only because she is "fascinated in spite of herself" by Hetty's beauty (128, ch. 7), but also because she does nothing to enlighten her niece about the meaning of sexuality, knowledge, and power. Acknowledging her husband's greater responsibility for his sister's child, Mrs. Poyser concedes to his wishes and declines to act as a disciplinarian or to interfere with her niece's prospects for marriage: she lets nature take its course.

Despite her shrewdness about birth and breeding, Mrs. Poyser does not notice that Hetty is responsive to some kinds of love; she does not observe her growing infatuation with Arthur and fails to note the consequences when Hetty becomes pregnant. Mrs. Poyser's blindness to the changes in her niece's body neatly reflects patriarchal attitudes about female sexuality; she assumes that Hetty's pleasure-loving nature will be sufficiently disciplined by her "dread of shame," if not by affection for her family. When Hetty is forced to surrender her own "blind trust in some unshapen chance" (411, ch. 35) and recognize that her pregnancy will inexorably lead to the birth of a child, bringing shame upon her family, it is her aunt's censure that she shrinks from most.

Hetty is mistaken in assuming that Mrs. Poyser would be her most severe judge. It is her uncle and grandfather, instead, who feel family dishonor so keenly that they have no room in their hearts for compassion toward Hetty. Their harshness, rather than Mrs. Poyser's more generous sympathy, is reflected in English law, especially after 1834 when the bastardy clause was enacted to prevent women like Hetty from making any financial claims on the father of a child born out of wedlock (Taylor 200).

Eliot was keenly aware of the dangers posed for feminism when the authority defining the truth about sexuality shifted from Biblical scripture to science, especially when the "remnant of the mythical" continued to lurk in the "very sanctuary of science," and when, as in Spencer's case, the role of the "mythical" was disavowed (Eliot, *Essays* 45). In *Adam Bede*, Eliot calls particular attention to the discrepancy between the "language of the soul" and the man-made images, language, and mythology by which her heroines are seen. The element of the "mythical" remains so compelling that it obliterates, for many readers,[20] the submerged "language of the soul" by which Eliot herself tries to honor and express the "difference of view" that is hers as a woman writer and feminist,[21] a difference especially evident when she describes female sexuality and those "maternal emotions" that are "unknown to men" (*Essays* 53). Thus, many critics have argued that Eliot simply reveals her conservative antifeminism in forcing Dinah to abandon her revolutionary career as a preacher and submit to a conventional marriage and motherhood. This reading ignores the second voice in the double-voiced discourse of Eliot's novel.

The "Two Bed-Chambers" chapter also marks one of the places in her text where Eliot represents the female "wild zone" and asserts her special authority as a female writer. Eliot's treatment of Hetty's narcissistic sexuality in this episode has often been read as an expression of her neurotic envy of the female beauty she did not personally possess.[22] In describing the rituals Hetty performs as a "devout worshipper" in the religion of Narcissus, Eliot reveals that it is not simply Hetty's place in the evolutionary scale that holds her in thrall (194, ch. 15); it is her ignorance, fostered by a rudimentary education which, in contrast to Adam's, has given her so few outlets for her ambition. Hetty, like Milton's Eve, responds narcissistically when she sees her image in the glass as a "companion she might complain to" (329, ch. 31). Because she is excluded from Raphael's instruction about love and womanly beauty and from Michael's moral lessons drawn from history, Hetty is not led away from her self-involvement to recognize that "beauty is excelled by manly grace and wisdom" (*Paradise Lost* 4:490–91). Neither is she directed by the voice of God to see herself as the mother of the human race. Instead, she remains lost in contemplation over her own face in the mirror, pining with "vain desire" over a marriage she will never celebrate.[23] Thus, Hetty remains confined by her "narrow bit of imagination," which limits her apprehension of the future and allows her to see only ego-flattering and "ill-defined pictures" woven out of her childish fantasies. The "alternate dose" that Irwine recommended for Arthur, by which he could anticipate the "unpleasant consequences" of his seduction, is clearly out of Hetty's ken.

Hetty's imprisonment by her fantasies is contrasted in this scene with Dinah's expansive and mystic visions, but like Hetty, Dinah's imagination is also confined. Dinah's habits of prayerful self-forgetfulness, so evident in her private devotions, suggest her alienation from, rather than her imprisonment by, her body. Correctly observing the "absence of any warm, self-devoting love in Hetty's nature," Dinah sees her cousin as caught in a "thorny thicket of sin and sorrow" (203, ch. 15) and tries to enlarge Hetty's mind by suggesting the "solemn daily duties of the wife and mother" (203, ch. 15) that lie before her. Dinah's only direction, however, comes from the small, worn Bible, with its alienating language about love, the Bible that she opens at random.

Dinah, unlike Irwine, has not had any experience, vicarious or otherwise, that would allow her to envision or describe Hetty's real future or to intuit correctly her cousin's confused understanding of her own sexuality. Dinah, in fact, has no shared experience, no common language, no words to describe the truth about sex as she understands it; she has only the patriarchal Christian rhetoric that she habitually uses. Dinah's "tender warnings" are not ineffectual because she is too moralistic; they simply cannot take a more specific form than "trouble comes to us all in this life" (205, ch. 15). She, like Hetty, has been prevented from penetrating the mysteries of female sexuality because of her sex and class. In this world where even Mrs. Poyser simply exhorts Hetty to attend to her duties but fails to speak in particular about the dangers of self-absorption and erotic passion or to describe the possible consequences of pregnancy and the shame and guilt of unwed motherhood, it is unthinkable that Dinah could say anything more than she does. Dinah is herself unaware of her own sexuality—as her conversation with Irwine has revealed—and she could not speak to Hetty about anything that would betray her own innocence or insult her cousin's modesty. This wordlessness reflects woman's experience in the "wild zone."[24]

Eliot sends Hetty literally into the wild zone when she is ready to give birth, and in depicting the effects of childbirth on Hetty Eliot challenges traditional assumptions about the force of maternal instinct that Spencer uncritically reinscribes in "Physical Training." Mary Poovey cites the following description by Peter Gaskell as typical of Victorian attitudes toward maternal instinct:

Love of helpless infancy—attention to its wants, its sufferings, and its unintelligible happiness, seem to form the very well-spring of woman's heart. . . . A woman, if removed from all intercourse, all knowledge of her sex and its attributes, from the very hour of her birth, would, should she herself become a mother in the wilderness, lavish as much tenderness upon her babe, cherish it as fondly . . . sacrifice her personal comfort, with as much ardour, as much devotedness, as the most refined, fastidious, and intellectual mother, placed in the very centre of civilized society. (7)

Eliot imagines a very different scene of childbirth in the wilderness.

Hetty does not recognize her imprisonment in her body until, realizing she cannot escape the shame and guilt that will inevitably result when her pregnancy is known, she flees from Hayslope. Eliot shows first how Hetty is driven "to and fro between two equal terrors" and discovers her own passion to survive. Unable to find the resolution to kill herself, Hetty realizes she must endure being seen by those who will regard her as a monster.[25] She awakens to an understanding of the meaning of her sexuality: "Life, now, by the morning light, with the impression of that man's hard wondering look at her, was as full of dread as death:—it was worse; it was a dread to which she felt chained, from which she shrank and shrank as she did from the black pool and yet could find no refuge from it" (435, ch. 37). In this moment, Hetty recognizes, as far as she is able, what it means to be a sexually mature woman, unhoused, and without money or protection. Her terror is amplified by the harsh words of the shepherd who awakens her with his alarming, "Anybody 'ud think you was a wild woman" (434, ch. 37), and Hetty knows she cannot escape his description. When her money is gone, she knows she will really "look like a wild woman"; that is, she will be a woman in the state of nature.

Animal instinct does triumph after Hetty's child is born, as Eliot shows, when Hetty, reduced to an animal-like self-sufficiency, abandons her child because it is born out of season. In Hetty's confession about the birth of her child, Eliot underscores the instinct of self-preservation which counteracts Hetty's "maternal" instincts, and thus calls into question the idealized assumptions underlying notions, like Spencer's, about the mother's "natural" altruism. Hetty confesses to Dinah:

> "And then the little baby was born, when I didn't expect it and the thought of it came into my mind that I might get rid of it and go home again. . . . I don't know how I felt about the baby. I seemed to hate it—it was like a heavy weight hanging around my neck; and yet its crying went through me, and I daredn't look at its little hands and face" (498, ch. 45)

Hetty's description of the child hanging around her neck here recalls the earlier fantasy image of the domestic paradise that Arthur and Adam imagined, where the child-mother appeared as a central blossom surrounded by pendant flower-children. By this repetition, Eliot indicates her commitment to tell the truth about the daughter's sexual initiation, pregnancy, and childbirth rather than subscribe to these male fantasies. Hetty's honest description of her resistance to maternity discloses the tragically mistaken assumptions about the compelling power of maternal instinct that find expression in the Miltonic myth and in the developmental theory Spencer had begun to formulate to replace the Mosaic account of human origins in Genesis.

Eliot reveals the power of the taboos surrounding the description and avowal of female sexuality by presenting through Hetty's long-delayed confession, rather than by direct dramatization, her experience of birth and her confused abandonment of her child. In having Hetty confess to Dinah, Eliot uses one of the "main rituals" that prevailed before the nineteenth century and traditionally defined the truth about sex (Foucault 58). In Hetty's confession, Eliot dramatizes the power of phallocentric language and discourse to define the perspective women take on their own sexuality. Moreover, by depicting Hetty's trial, Eliot calls attention to the process by which the patriarchal word becomes law and envisions an alternative, but submerged, moral system which honors the charities of mother, daughter, and sister.

Once Hetty's crime is known, many see her as a monster, but Eliot keeps Hetty's "impersonal" beauty before us in order to assert that Hetty is still the same young woman with the "same, rounded, pouting, childish prettiness, but with all love departed from it—the sadder for its beauty, like that wondrous Medusa face with the passionate, passionless lips" (430, ch. 37). When she appears in court, terrified into silent defiance by the magistrate and by her dread of the death that will be her punishment, the narrator again calls attention to the way the predispositions of the observers at the trial determine how they see Hetty. Many of the strangers who see her "thought she looked as if some demon had cast a blighting glance upon her and withered up the woman's soul in her" leaving only "a hard, despairing obstinacy" (477, ch. 43).

After his "baptism of suffering," Adam, by contrast, looks at Hetty with a "mother's yearning" which, Eliot asserts, is the "essence of real human love" (477, ch. 43). Defining this love as an expression of learned behavior rather than biology, Eliot insists that when Adam looks at "this pale, hard-looking culprit," he is able to "feel the presence of a cherished child" in the girl "who had smiled at him in the garden under the apple-tree boughs" (477, ch. 43). After he hears Hetty's confession, Adam is able to acknowledge both Hetty's beauty and her "hardness"; she appears to him as one who "had come back to him from the dead to tell him of her misery" (505, ch. 46). In this exchange, Eliot underscores the difficulties of seeing beyond the images projected by desire, yet Adam's sympathy eventually allows him to join in the charities of mother, daughter, and sister.

Dinah also experiences a "fall into knowledge" as a result of sharing Hetty's experience of literal imprisonment; she too seems to understand more of what it means to be a sexually mature woman as a result of listening to Hetty's confession about her "confinement," that euphemism so expressive of the Victorian woman's feeling that she was imprisoned by her biology and her childbearing. Dinah learns the "art of vision" in prison with Hetty; she begins to see the distance between Hetty's experience in the body and her own out of it. Paradoxically, their communion is a leveling one, for Dinah comes to recognize all to which she had earlier been blind when she misinterpreted her cousin's confusion and fear of discovery as a sign of the religious awakening that her randomly-chosen reading of the Bible had led her to expect. As she listens to the agony Hetty experienced because of her pregnancy and the subsequent exposure of her child, Dinah begins to comprehend the power of female sexuality, allowing her to supplement her understanding of "heavn'ly Love" by joining imaginatively in Hetty's passion.

When Dinah tries to bring Hetty to an awareness of God's love and mercy, she realizes not only the limits of Hetty's narrow imagination, but also the constraints of the phallocentric Christian rhetoric she herself uses. When Dinah invokes Christ's presence, saying, "There is someone else in this cell besides me," Hetty assumes she speaks literally, and can only ask in a frightened whisper who that "someone" is. Lacking Dinah's gifted imagination, Hetty cannot conceive of the possibility of redemption except in the form of a legal pardon which would convey a very palpable salvation. Seeing at last the narrowness of Hetty's consciousness, Dinah realizes that natures like her cousin's demand no more comfort than that which can be immediately felt, so she constructs analogies for Hetty: "You believe in my love and pity for you, Hetty; but if you had not let me come near you . . . I couldn't have made you feel my love; I couldn't have told you what I felt for you. Don't shut God's love out in that way by clinging to sin" (495, ch. 45).

In promising to be a "sister to the last," and in thus offering Hetty the charities of mother, daughter, and sister, Dinah helps Hetty see the promise of earthly forgiveness in her own mild eyes. In showing that it is Dinah, rather than the supernatural Christ she invokes, who removes the "stony" from Hetty's heart, Eliot offers a feminist revision of Milton's heavenly universe, which celebrated the power of the patriarchal Word. When Dinah comes to Hetty full of "sad, yearning love" and opens her arms in a maternal embrace, she offers Hetty the only sign of forgiveness her cousin can understand.

In this third excursion into the wild zone Dinah recognizes her own imprisonment as well as Hetty's, and Eliot here uses one of Feuerbach's

most radical transformations of the patriarchal images that were fundamental to Milton's epic vision:

> If then the worship of the Son of God is no idolatry, the worship of the Mother
> of God is no idolatry. If herein we perceive the love of God to us, that he gave
> his only Begotten Son, i.e., that which was dearest to him, for our own salva-
> tion,—we can perceive this love still better when we find in God the beating of
> a mother's heart. The father consoles himself for the loss of his Son; he has a
> stoical principle within him. The mother, on the contrary, is inconsolable; she
> is the sorrowing element, that which cannot be indemnified—the true in
> love.[26]

Dinah's love for Hetty indicates the power of feminist spirituality to dislo-
cate the teleology of the Miltonic version of genesis by asserting the
power of the divine maternal principle that balances the "charities of
father, son, and brother" exalted by Milton. Dinah allows Hetty to feel
the power of the maternal when they hold each other, standing cheek to
cheek, for in this episode Dinah acts not as judge but as the sorrowing,
loving, accepting Titanic mother unrepresented by Milton's Eve or his
Virgin Mary.

Eliot suggests that Dinah has achieved a new sense of her own power
and agency by being initiated into the female mysteries and listening to
Hetty's confession, for this ritual is one, as Foucault says, that recognizes
the power of the listener (59–63). Eliot indicates Dinah's spiritual revolution indirectly when she describes Dinah and Hetty together for the
last time:

> She was clinging close to Dinah; her cheek was against Dinah's. It seemed as
> if her last faint strength and hope lay in that contact; and the pitying love that
> shone out from Dinah's face looked like a visible pledge of the Invisible Mercy.
> (505, ch. 46)

By emphasizing this female image of Divine Mercy, Eliot suggests
Dinah's increased stature and moral authority.

In recounting Hetty's confession later, Dinah speaks in a new way
about God and the power of love. She acknowledges her own instrumen-
tality in bringing Hetty to acknowledge her sin, saying, "she is contrite—
she confessed all to me. The pride of her heart has given way, and she
leans on me for help" (505, ch. 46). By avoiding the Christian idiom we
might expect and saying she "leans on *me*" (italics mine), rather than on
the Lord, for help, Dinah indicates a change in her awareness of the
limits of her religious idiom, an awareness, if followed to its logical conclusion, which would require that she surrender her role as public
preacher so that she could individually assess each of her listeners' capacities.

Eliot does not fully describe the impact of Hetty's confession on Dinah's evangelical faith. Her reluctance to portray explicitly how Dinah recognizes the limited power of the Word and eventually surrenders her role as preacher may in part reflect Eliot's own reticence in speaking of the process by which she herself surrendered her own faith in orthodox Christianity and adopted the Feuerbachian religion of humanity, the religion that finds expression in the narrator's imagery in these climactic episodes of the novel (Knoepflmacher, *Religious* 52–59). Certainly it would violate her commitment to historical realism to give Dinah a consciousness that was so intellectually and historically out of her reach.

Eliot shows clearly, however, that Dinah is changed profoundly by Hetty's confession, as is evident by her willingness to stay with the Poysers after Hetty's deportation. In showing how her heroine comes to understand and avow her own passion, Eliot dramatizes how Dinah comes to a new understanding of love itself, one which transcends the duality of "heavenly" and "sinful."

This submerged narrative about Dinah's "fall" and her experience in the wild zone of female identity is most evident when she returns to the Bede cottage several months after Hetty's trial. In this episode, Dinah achieves a deeper understanding of what it was in Adam's "dark penetrating glance" that once made her feel, for the first time, a "painful self-consciousness" (162, ch. 11). Dinah has reached that dangerous transition period before the sexually awakened daughter becomes a wife, but she has no mother to help her escape the saintly role that has begun to oppress her. While she is visiting Lisbeth, Dinah takes up the duster and begins to clean Adam's study, a scene many critics have read as signaling Eliot's secret antifeminist desire to transform her heroine into a "model bourgeois wife shaping her destiny through her prosperous husband's work."[27] If we attend to the differences between the marriage of Milton's Adam and that of Adam Bede in Eliot's novel, however, we can read a more feminist message in Eliot's treatment of Dinah's love and marriage. Dinah takes up the role of domestic angel in this episode because she does not know how else to show Adam that she loves him. Why Dinah, who is so eloquent about God's love, feels so constrained in her expression of her earthly desires may not be very clear, especially to modern readers. But Dinah's experience parallels that of many Victorian heroines, including Brontë's powerful heroine Shirley, who sickens and nearly dies because she cannot assert her desire. So Dinah acts out her suitability for wifehood even though she feels "inward conflict" when she is regarded "as a convenient household slave" (533, ch. 50). It should be noted that when Dinah plays this sentimental charade of the angel in the house, acting out her embarrassment and desire, Adam joins her in finishing the housework, a gesture which suggests Eliot's rejection of the conventional Victorian definition of men's and women's separate spheres.

Surprisingly it is Lisbeth Bede who helps release Dinah from her mute desire, and in these exchanges Eliot depicts the effects of the same profound sympathy, those charities of mother, daughter, and sister, that Dinah offers to Hetty. Lisbeth recognizes Dinah as a sister by noting that she too was a "working woman" (154, ch. 10), and later she acts the part of mother by translating Dinah's ambiguous gestures into an iconography that Adam understands. Looking at a Bible picture of the "angel seated on the great stone that had been rolled away from the sepulchre," Lisbeth says, "That's her—that's Dinah" (543, ch. 51), which prompts Adam to think of Hetty and his "dead joy" and to consider establishing a more mature attachment to Dinah.

By representing Dinah's behavior in the Bede cottage, Eliot indicates the difficulties women face, whether they are preachers or writers, when the language they use and the cultural iconography by which they are seen does not correspond to the "language" of their souls. When even Lisbeth, the least capable character in the novel, sees Dinah's physicality and desire, surely it is misreading to see Dinah only in terms of these images of angel and madonna. It is through Lisbeth's agency, then, that Dinah is able to voice the feelings which express the "superior language of the soul," that language that transcends patriarchal formulas defining female sexuality and womanhood in terms of sin and salvation. Dinah speaks forthrightly enough once Adam has broken the silence, when she tells him, "My heart is strongly drawn to you" (551, ch. 52).

Dinah finds a wonderful new "strength and sweetness" in the more mature passionate love she shares with Adam, but their love is consummated only after they have healed the separations that divide "heaven'ly Love" from its passionate earthly expression, separations which are central to the Christian genesis myth and the definition of female sexuality it prescribes. By releasing her female hero from feeling guilt over naming Adam and accepting him as the object of her desire, Eliot allows Dinah to recover some of the identity and power of the prehistoric mother, that Titanic presence that Brontë's hero Shirley struggles to see. When Dinah renounces her "divided life," she transcends the simple Miltonic polarities defining woman as a supernatural deity or a tragically flawed genetrix, as Mary or Eve. Prompted by the "ultimate guiding voice from within" and not to the conventional voices that have urged her to give up her career as preacher, Dinah refuses any longer to live a divided life.

Dinah's decision to leave Snowfield and surrender her ministry there need not be read, then, as an acknowledgement that she has sinned in desiring to "work apart." Eliot's Adam, in contrast to Milton's, has seen the futility of such attempts to shield women from "danger and dishonour" (*Paradise Lost* 9:267). Seeing that marriage, could, in his words, "interfere" with Dinah's sense of her moral duties, Adam offers Dinah a marriage that recognizes her autonomy, saying, "I'd never think of putting myself between you and God, and saying you oughtn't to do this, and you oughtn't to do that. You'd follow your conscience as much as you do now" (552, ch. 42). Dinah's marriage is thus premised on a relation that revolutionizes the hierarchical relation that Milton celebrates in the formula, "He for God only, she for God in him" (*Paradise Lost* 4:299). Moreover, theirs is also a marriage that avoids Spencer's reinscription of this traditional formula, in which male intellect compensates for female incapacity, for passionate feeling and moral understanding allow both Dinah and Adam to discover their own completeness.

One of the implications of evolutionary theory that most fascinated Eliot, as is attested by her enthusiasm over "The Genesis of Science" and her appreciation for Mackay's *Progress of the Intellect*, was her awareness that cultural myths, like the literary works that codified them or the science that reflected them, change through time. She created an historical frame for Dinah's and Adam's story to suggest the dynamic quality of their social medium. If Eliot betrays any nostalgia in her depiction of the harvest festivals that give *Adam Bede* its distinctive formal qualities, it is an expression, I would argue, of her appreciation for the more egalitarian domestic life of the Poysers, and not the festivals themselves; in fact, her letters reveal that when Eliot was herself in danger of playing Mrs. Poyser's role she found these celebrations "nauseating" (*GEL* 1:31).

History, Eliot insists, will prohibit both Hetty and Dinah from finding the organic harmony which united work and family life for Rachel and Martin Poyser. Because Mrs. Poyser was able to integrate the productive labor of the dairy and farmhouse with her domestic responsibilities as wife and mother, because she shared in her husband's work, she "finds herself able to give her husband advice on most things" (234, ch. 18). Because he respects her "superior power of putting two and two together," Martin Poyser frequently submits to his wife's judgment (234, ch. 18), though unfortunately he asserts his superior authority in assessing Hetty's potential for the roles of wife and mother. While some of this equality is ultimately reproduced in Dinah's marriage to Adam, the balance of the Poysers' working life is not.

Mrs. Poyser herself calls attention to the forces which are changing life at Hall Farm when she asserts her "little bit of irregular justice" in her conversation with Squire Donnithorne. Her astute observations about "them as is born t'own the land, and them as is born to sweat on 't" (392, ch. 32) suggest the growing exploitation of the nineteenth-century tenant farmer by his aristocratic landlord and express an alternative and less patriarchal standard of justice. Hetty's relation to Arthur discloses a second and more private dimension of class exploitation, one which became increasingly more obvious to Victorians as the century went on.

In setting the novel in 1799,[28] so that Dinah's career is conveniently cut short by the Methodist Conference's decision to prohibit women like her from preaching in public, Eliot indicates how religious defenses of women's emancipation will come increasingly under attack in the coming century. But Dinah's submission to the "brethren" seems to disguise a much more profound rebellion against the fundamental assumptions of the Christian genesis myth and literalist readings of the Bible more generally. Eliot's epilogue is not prescriptive but descriptive; it simply reflects the inexorable advance of those social forces that pushed the Victorian woman into her position as angel or monster, madonna or witch.

By giving Dinah a profession outside the sphere of woman's traditional "mission," and by allowing her to successfully defend her choice to Irwine, Eliot gives Dinah the epic stature of a feminist hero, making her Adam's equal rather than his subordinate. By inviting us to see the parallels between the opening scenes of Adam at work and Dinah preaching on the Green, Eliot indicates that Dinah has a sense of vocation and an acute awareness of her responsiblity, just as Adam does. Though Dinah perhaps does not have Adam's keenness of intelligence, she possesses a compensating imaginative capacity that allows her to envision the suffering hidden in Adam's world. Furthermore, she is gifted with historical foresight—not unlike that of Milton's Adam—because she has lived beyond the hills that shelter Hayslope; she has witnessed the suffering caused by the industrialism that has already transformed Snowfield and will encroach—in time—upon Hayslope also.

If the sun slants more obliquely on the Bede cottage than it did when the novel first began, it is because Hayslope exists in the twilight of its days. Eliot's treatment of the marriage in Hayslope is not a sentimental or nostalgic refusal to face the realities of the nineteenth century, because Dinah, like her Victorian counterpart, feels compelled to choose between two vocations. Unlike Mrs. Poyser, she must choose either to work apart from Adam or to work inside the home, and this choice demonstrates the problem faced by women in middle-class marriages in the coming century, which increasingly enforced the separation between the public and the domestic sphere. When Hayslope proves to be such a paradise lost, Adam's and Dinah's marriage—celebrating the mutual discovery of a "fullness of strength" through love—becomes the only ameliorating sacrament for the future.

4

Feminism and the Problem of Authority:
The Mill on the Floss and "Physical Training"

IN THE FALL of 1858, Herbert Spencer helped precipitate a crisis of naming that forced George Eliot to reconsider the nature and sources of her authority as a woman writer. Shortly before she completed *Adam Bede*, she revealed to Spencer that she had assumed the pseudonym of George Eliot. Spencer was one of the the first people she told about the secret of her authorship, and though Eliot indicated to him that she wished to preserve her anonymity, Spencer broke confidence with her shortly afterwards by refusing to contradict John Chapman when he guessed that George Eliot was, in fact, Marian Evans Lewes (Spencer, *Autobiography* 2:38). To Eliot's great chagrin, Chapman gossiped about her authorship, "carelessly" causing "serious injury," as she later complained, to her literary and personal reputation (*GEL* 2:494).

Eliot had hoped that by maintaining her anonymity she could ensure that *Adam Bede* would be "judged on its own merits, and not prejudged as the work of a woman, or of a particular woman" (*GEL* 3:106). While Eliot revealed her identity to several other friends, she succeeded in keeping her authorship a secret from most of her reviewers, and *Adam Bede* was widely acclaimed. Persistent rumors, however, attributed *Scenes of Clerical Life* and *Adam Bede* to Joseph Liggins of Nuneaton and to several other male imposters, allegations Eliot could not effectively deny as long as she preserved her anonymity. By July 1859, Eliot's incognito had worn so thin that William Hepworth Dixon, in a notice in the *Athenaeum*, could sneer: "It is time to end this pother about the authorship of 'Adam Bede.' The writer is in no sense a 'great unknown'; the tale, if bright in parts, and such as a clever woman with an observant eye and unschooled moral nature might have written, has no great quality of any kind" (Haight, *George Eliot* 290). Eliot knew, then, shortly after she began writing *The Mill on the Floss*, that she could not hope to shield herself from similarly malicious attacks on her personal morality and on her authority as a woman writer by continuing to use her male pseudonym. She was thus forced to recognize that the authority she claimed as a woman writer remained a serious liability which would determine the critical reception of *The Mill on the Floss* and subsequent novels.[1]

The role Spencer played in unmasking her undoubtedly helped widen the serious rift that developed between them during 1858 and 1859, when she began writing *The Mill on the Floss* and he completed the last three of his essays on education, republished in 1860 in the collection *Education: Intellectual, Moral and Physical*. By March of 1859, George Henry Lewes identified the following motives for Spencer's "coolness" toward them:

> He used to be one of our friends on whom we most relied; but his jealousy, too patent and too unequivocal, of our success, acting on his own bitterness at nonsuccess, has of late cooled him visibly. He always tells us the disagreeable things he hears or reads of us and never the agreeable things. His jealousy of me has been growing these last two years, and it is more excusable than his jealousy of [Marian Evans Lewes]. (Haight, *George Eliot* 292)

Eight months after its publication, Spencer redeemed himself somewhat by finally reading and praising *Adam Bede*. He wrote to Eliot that her novel measured up to his "ideal of a work of art" because it possessed "all the requisite qualities in due balance; which is more than I can say of any fiction I ever read" (*GEL* 8:247). He concluded this backhanded compliment by saying: "I feel greatly better for having read it; and can scarcely imagine anyone reading it without having their sympathies widened and their better resolves strengthened. Not only in the interests of literature but in the interests of progress I hope that we shall have many more such books from you" (*GEL* 8:247). Nonetheless, *The Mill on the Floss*, published in 1860, reveals that there were many serious intellectual as well as personal reasons for the disagreements that divided George Eliot and Herbert Spencer during 1858 and 1859, and several of these issues were never resolved.

In 1859, when Eliot began her research for *The Mill on the Floss*, she planned it as a companion piece to *Adam Bede*. Her analysis of the "provincial life" of St. Ogg's (*GEL* 3:41) shows her continuing skepticism about Spencer's glib readings of Nature's syntax. Yet, in this novel, Eliot is more preoccupied with examining the origins of gender identity and with representing the inhibiting force of Victorian gender roles, a concern prompted, perhaps, by her recognition that she could no longer prevent critics from judging her own work by Victorian double standards defining men's and women's writing and morality. Moreover, Eliot's fascination with tracing the origins of gender difference was given new impetus by her reading of Darwin's *On the Origin of Species* in December of 1859, when she was writing the second volume of her novel, and *The Mill on the Floss* demonstrates her fundamental agreement with many of the premises of the evolutionary theories developed by both Spencer and Darwin in these years.[2]

Like Spencer and in contrast to Darwin, Eliot was interested in exploring the perspective that evolutionary theory offered on the development
of individual human life. Eliot's use of biogenetic analogies comparing
Tom and Maggie with young animals in *The Mill on the Floss* indicates that
she shared Spencer's belief that human life was "subject to the same
organic laws as inferior creatures" ("Physical Training" 364).[3] However,
as this novel also shows, Eliot disagreed with many of Spencer's conclusions about the "superior powers" that place all human beings at a
"proud distance from the chimpanzee,"[4] and gender is shown to be a
fundamental factor in the development of these superior powers in the
lives of Tom and Maggie. In contrast to Spencer, Eliot demystifies gender difference in this novel; for while he treats gender as a biological
given in his essays on education, Eliot asks her readers to observe how
Nature "under these average boyish physiognomies . . . conceals some of
her most rigid inflexible purposes, some of her most unmodifiable characters," and how "the dark-eyed rebellious girl may after all turn out to
be a passive being" (85, bk. 1, ch. 5). Though Eliot believed that a
woman's sex defined "the deepest and subtlest sort of education life
gives" (*GEL* 4:468), *The Mill on the Floss* shows finally that she, in contrast
to Spencer, saw sex differences not only as determined by biological
function but also as constructed by profoundly misogynistic cultural traditions and ideologies.

Spencer's essays on education challenged some of the most cherished
Victorian ideas about parents and children, and *The Mill on the Floss*
reveals some points of agreement that Eliot shared with him in her analysis of the "physical" and "moral" education that boys and girls receive
both at home and at school. In "What Knowledge is of Most Worth,"[5]
Spencer proposed revolutionary changes for formal education by recommending a pedagogy based on developmental psychology, by de-
emphasizing the study of classical languages and literatures, and by
proposing, instead, a more vocationally based curriculum. These particular reforms threatened several feminist educational goals that were
close to Eliot's heart. By locating gender as a central problem, which
Spencer ignored in his critique of contemporary educational practices
and by raising "far-reaching questions about the functioning both of
sexual ideology and language" (Jacobus 213), Eliot in *The Mill on the
Floss* challenged many of Spencer's conclusions. By dramatizing the
"tragedy" that lies "under the process" of social evolution (*GEL* 3:227),
Eliot exposed the basic assumption that underlay Spencer's argument
in "What Knowledge is of Most Worth": his belief that "progress" could
be equated with industrialization. In describing the impact of the industrialism that had appeared only as a shadowy force in Adam Bede's
life, Eliot represents the destruction it brought to the world of the Dod-

sons and Tullivers and details its consequences for both Maggie and Tom.

Mr. Tulliver's first words in the novel announce the importance of the theme of education in *The Mill on the Floss*, "It's about my boy Tom. . . . You see I want to put him to a new school at Midsummer" (64–65, bk. 1, ch. 2).[6] His subsequent remarks about both Tom and Maggie suggest the problems in the family that have been created by what he calls the "crossing o' the breeds." Jeremy Tulliver has chosen his wife, as he notes in this first episode, according to Spencerian criteria, because she was a "good looking woman" but not "o'er 'cute" (68, bk. 1, ch. 3); yet, nature unaccountably has frustrated his paternal desires, since his wife has produced only "stupid lads and 'cute wenches" (69, bk. 1, ch. 3). Jeremy Tulliver evaluates Maggie's intelligence in a similarly Spencerian fashion for, as he says, "an o'er 'cute woman is no better nor a long-tailed sheep—she'll fetch none the bigger price for that" (60, bk. 1, ch. 2).[7] Tulliver's comments expose Spencer's similar failure to explain why men—but not women—were able to develop fully the intelligence they inherited.[8]

In "The Moral Discipline of Children," Spencer argues that the "difficulties of moral education are necessarily of dual origin—necessarily result from the combined faults of the parents and children" (387). In this way, Spencer indicates his rejection of the idealization of motherhood that finds expression, for example, in Darwin's personification of Mother Nature in *The Origin of Species*. By emphasizing the vanity, inconsistency, and ignorance of Victorian mothers and the detrimental effects they have on their children's moral and physical education, Spencer echoes the concerns of many contemporary feminist educational reformers. By dramatizing Mrs. Tulliver's failure as the first teacher of her children, Eliot presents a similarly unsentimental view of Victorian motherhood.[9]

Though Eliot implicitly criticizes Mrs. Tulliver in some regards, however, she allows her to avoid the two most common failings that Spencer identified in the mothers he describes in "Physical Training." Bessie Tulliver does not feed her children less in order to discipline their "animalism" (365–69), nor does she forbid them necessary physical exercise but rather allows them a surprising amount of freedom in their outdoor play, except, of course, when the children are wearing their best clothes. Her flexibility in both matters is unexpected in light of her sisters' "saving habits": Mrs. Glegg's obsessions concerning mildewed gowns and money; Mrs. Pullet's concerning food, filth, and funerals; and Mrs. Deane's concerning locks, medicine, and tidy daughters. Eliot's most basic criticism of Mrs. Tulliver concerns her intellectual and moral failings as the mother of a domineering son and an unconventional daughter. Mrs. Tulliver assumes that Tom's preeminence over his sister and other women is natural, and her passive maternal affection for him prevents her from adequately disciplining his egotism. Eliot thus shows how rigid and conventional definitions of gender produce "demoralizing" effects (6, bk. 1, ch. 2) in both sons and daughters.

Spencer argues that fathers should involve themselves in their children's education in order to correct the excesses and failures he finds in the moral and physical training provided by mothers ("Physical Training" 362–63). Eliot, by contrast, demonstrates the inadequacy of this solution by showing that fathers are equally fallible. Mr. Tulliver is willing to give Tom a "good eddication: an eddication as'll be bread to him" (58, bk. 1, ch. 1), but he takes no notice of Tom's particular talents and imagines his son's future entirely in egocentric terms. Shrewdly anticipating the generational conflict between father and son, Mr. Tulliver decides not to train his son for his own profession but instead prepares Tom for "a business, as he may make a nest for himself and not want to push me out o' mine" (58, bk. 1, ch. 3). Because Tom's education is designed according to his father's needs rather than his own, it does not help him develop his best skills.

In his essays on education written between 1858 and 1860, Spencer also disputes Victorian conventions by rejecting the Wordsworthian view of the child as inherently good. Children in Spencer's analysis do not come "trailing clouds of glory"; they are naturally domineering rather than naturally innocent. In "What Knowledge is of Most Worth," for example, Spencer locates the "struggle for survival," that famous phrase he coined, in the bosom of the family itself.[10] Children, he explains, develop according to the same natural laws that operate in both the animal kingdom and in the laissez-faire world of human commerce:

> To get above some and be reverenced by them, to propitiate those who are above us, is the universal struggle in which the chief energies of life are expended. By the accumulation of wealth, by style of living, by beauty of dress, by display of knowledge or intellect, each tries to subjugate others and so aids in weaving that ramified network of restraints by which society is kept in order. (3)

Tom shows a similar domineering disposition "in very tender years" when he "scolded the sheep with an inarticulate burr, intended to strike terror into their astonished minds," but he remains this "Rhadamanthine personage" because, unlike Maggie, he possesses a "wonderful, instinctive discernment of what would turn to his own advantage or disadvantage" (121, bk. 1, ch. 7). Yet Eliot shows that though Tom is, by nature, "much more wilful and inflexible than Maggie," he remains so because of the prevailing conventions defining gender. His mother indulgently accepts his forcefulness because she sees it as a sign of his inherent masculinity.

Moreover, in her treatment of Tom's moral development, Eliot questions Spencer's conclusions about the social value of "that desire for mastery over inferior animals, wild and domestic, including cockchafers, neighbors' dogs, and small sisters, which in all ages has been an attribute of so much promise of our race" (153, bk. 1, ch. 9), as her satirical yoking of dogs and small sisters suggests. In comparing Tom's potential for "mastery" with Maggie's divided nature, which finds expression in her spontaneous rebelliousness and subsequent loving contrition, Eliot discriminates between the egotism that is natural and that which is fostered by a patriarchal society and used to justify the unsympathetic and authoritarian domination of the self-conscious male adult. In contrast to Spencer, Eliot refused to regard as "natural" the egotism that allowed the older brother to domineer over the small sister. Moreover, as she goes on to note in this passage, nature also does not authorize the "British man" to rationalize his subjugation of the "foreign brute," a presumption increasingly more evident in Spencer's thought after 1860. The most powerful discipline for this egotism can be found for Eliot in those "loves and sanctities of our life" that have "deep immovable roots in memory" (222, bk. 2, ch. 1). The puzzle she analyzes in Tom is why he is able to violate these sanctities so readily.

Part of the answer can be found in Tom's relation to his father and uncle during his premature apprenticeship at Guest and Company. Tom's formal education, like his education in the home, has opened no new moral horizons for him and his feelings for the men of his father's generation continue to reflect his earliest attitudes about authority. Tom grudgingly agrees with his uncle that his "Latin" and "rigmarole" are useless in the business world of St. Ogg's. Moreover, Eliot asserts, Tom's behavior is typical of most young men raised in patriarchal society:

> Not that Tom was in awe of his uncle's mental superiority.... A boy's sheepishness is by no means a sign of overmastering reverence: and while you are making encouraging advances to him under the idea that he is overwhelmed by a sense of your age and wisdom, ten to one he is thinking you extremely queer. The only consolation I can suggest to you is that the Greek boys probably thought the same of Aristotle. It is only when you have mastered a restive horse, or thrashed a drayman, or have got a gun in your hand, that these shy juniors feel you to be a truly admirable and enviable character. (152–53, bk. 1, ch. 9)

Though Tom assumes his place in the working world of St. Ogg's as he grows older and feels a "common cause with his father which springs from family pride," he continues to equate masculinity with mastery and to judge his father with severity because the world has been "too many" for him. Tom's resolute dutifulness is compounded of little piety, reverence, or sympathy, and he passes "much silent criticism on the rashness and imprudence of his father" (406, bk. 5, ch. 2) as he finds his place in the business world of St. Ogg's, a world Eliot characterizes as ruthless and destructive.

By comparing Tom's and Maggie's educations, Eliot exposes and questions Spencer's assumptions about the biological fixity of gender differences and their implications for human morality. In "The Moral Discipline of Children" (1858), Spencer argues that the object of all education should be to produce a child capable of "self-mastery." He writes:

> Bear constantly in mind the truth that the aim of your discipline should be to produce a self-governing being; not to produce a being to be governed by others. Were your children fated to pass their lives as slaves, you could not too much accustom them to slavery during their childhood, but as they are by and by free men, with no one to control their daily conduct, you cannot too much accustom them to self-control while they are still under your eye. (411)

Spencer's assumption, reflected in his rhetoric, especially in his use of the term "slavery" and in his shift from "children" to "men," reveals a contradiction in his thinking about women's education that Eliot dramatized in *The Mill on the Floss* by showing that while self-government may be expected of boys, submission is expected and cultivated in girls.[11]

In her early years, Maggie reveals the same irrepressible impulse to "get above some and be reverenced by them" that Tom displays; her first act in the novel is to attempt to impress Mr. Riley with her cleverness (66, bk. 1, ch. 3). Similarly, Maggie's most famous childhood transgressions repeat two examples Spencer cites of childish misbehavior in "The Moral Discipline of Children." Spencer mentions a boy who carelessly and habitually soils his clothes with mud and recommends that he suffer the "natural" punishment for this act by being excluded from family fetes (397). Eliot pokes fun at Spencer by showing that children like Tom and Maggie usually regard the attendance at such events as a punishment in itself. Moreover, when Maggie, impelled by her natural and overmastering desire for dominance, similarly misbehaves, she damages not only herself but poor "little pink and white Lucy" when she pushes her cousin into the "cow-trodden mud" (164, bk. 1, ch. 10).

In "The Moral Discipline of Children," Spencer goes on to describe a boy who cuts his brother's hair and recommends that the father punish the culprit by temporarily withholding affection (401). Again, while Maggie performs a similar childish prank, Eliot indicates that she is prompted to cut her own hair *because* she already suffers the disapproval Spencer describes as the most appropriate punishment for misbehavior. Because her mother regards her as a "small mistake of nature" (61, bk. 1, ch. 2), Maggie's life cannot be reformed by the disciplinary system

Spencer recommends, since she suffers perpetually from the withholding of her mother's approbation. Moreover, Eliot shows that gender itself is part of this disciplinary system, for Mrs. Tulliver enforces Victorian notions of femininity, hoping, in time, to transform her daughter into a miniature version of the asexual Victorian lady, with artificially curled hair, a lace tucker, and an unpocketed, uncomfortable dress. Limited by her feeble mind and tradition-bound imagination, Mrs. Tulliver regards Lucy Deane not as the highly artificial doll she is but as the normal type of femininity. Though Maggie is clearly the more natural child, her mother, far from trusting Maggie's "nature," sees her daughter as a "wild thing," one of the more "comical" tricks of Providence in a world where Lucy should have been her child (60, bk. 1, ch. 2). Under such treatment Maggie learns to see herself as one of the "things out o' nature" (82, bk. 1, ch. 4), destined, like lop-eared rabbits, not to thrive because she is so unlike the pattern of normal femininity in her world. Maggie is starved for the parental love that Spencer assumes is part of the (male) child's natural heritage, and her subsequent development is determined by her "hunger" for love and by the frustration of all her other natural appetites that are denied or ignored by her family.

In describing Maggie's childhood, Eliot asserts that the heart's needs, though they are not scientifically estimable, are no less powerful than the desire for preeminence that Spencer identified as the only force motivating and controlling human behavior. When Maggie retreats to the attic vowing to "stay up there and starve herself" (89, bk. 1, ch. 5) because Tom has quarrelled with her over the rabbits she forgot to feed, Eliot describes her heart's hunger as "a wonderful subduing force" and compares it to the "peremptory" force of "that other hunger by which nature forces us to submit to the yoke and change the face of the world" (91, bk. 1, ch. 5).

Having exposed the most common faults of Victorian parents in "The Moral Discipline of Children," Spencer optimistically recommends that they can provide the correct guidance for their children by assuming the role of "ministers and interpreters of Nature" (392). Spencer argued that the family should be reorganized according to a kind of laissez-faire system of child discipline whereby parents "see that their children habitually experience the true consequences of their conduct—the natural reactions: neither warding them off, nor intensifying them, nor putting artificial consequences in place of them" (392). Eliot, by contrast, dramatizes how Bessie and Jeremy Tulliver fail as "interpreters of Nature" for their children, because their ignorance and egotism render them both incapable of recognizing their children's capacities or of conveying Nature's laws to them.

The "moral" education of girls, of course, posed particular problems that Spencer entirely ignored in these essays. The introduction to nature that Maggie receives from her parents demonstrates how patriarchal society intervenes to distort the mother's and daughter's understanding of their own sexuality and experience in the "wild zone" (Showalter, "Feminist" 200; Homans, "Eliot" 230–41). Mrs. Tulliver constantly worries that her daughter will drown if Maggie ever gives in to the promptings of her own passionate nature. These metaphors reveal Mrs. Tulliver's unconscious concern with Maggie's sexuality, for throughout the novel river images are associated with Maggie's overflowing desires. Thus Eliot alludes to the role mothers have traditionally played in the "moral education" of girls by damming this flow and channeling it into the proper subliminal passages in the young woman's psyche.

Even at age nine, though, Maggie precociously sees the contradictions that define a woman's relation to her sexuality and to the natural world. Not yet having learned to censor her own intuitions about women's experience in the "wild zone," Maggie recognizes the paradox that underlies the orthodox Christian view of woman's inherently sinful nature when she interprets the witch's dunking trial in Defoe's *History of the Devil:* "If she's drowned—and killed, you know,—she's innocent, and not a witch but only a poor silly woman. But what good would it do her then, you know, when she was drowned?" (66, bk. 1, ch. 3).[12] By revealing Maggie's pleasure in imagining a world beyond such contradictions, Eliot suggests one of the origins of Maggie's divided life. Her mother's silence and prohibitions concerning her displays of passion inadvertently teach Maggie to seek her freedom apart from the natural world— where nature provides its great correction and control—and to find it instead in the private, undisciplined world of imagination and romance, where female egotism flourishes unreproved.

Maggie makes several journeys into the literal landscape of the wild zone; her flight to join the gypsies marks her first attempt to visit that region where daughters confront the meaning of their own sexuality. But in all her physical excursions into that zone, Maggie's experience is defined by the men she confronts there. *The Mill on the Floss* differs markedly from *Adam Bede* in this respect, for the "metaphysical" space identified as part of the wild zone in this novel is much narrower.[13] Maggie's first doubts about her plan to join her "unknown kindred" arise when she, like Hetty, meets "formidable" strangers along the road, who inspire her with fear and cause her to imagine an encounter with Defoe's "diabolical blacksmith" (171, bk. 1, ch. 11). Maggie's experiences with the gypsies disabuse her of her dreams about becoming their "queen," and she begins to worry that after robbing her they meant to "kill her as soon as it was dark and cut her body up for gradual cooking" afterwards. Thus, Maggie realizes both her physical and sexual vulnerability through her flight to join the gypsies, but she is prevented from bringing to consciousness these intimations about her own sexuality, disguised as they are in her childish fantasies of darkness and dismemberment.

When Maggie returns to the family, her father acts to preserve her innocence by imposing upon the family a patriarchal silence about women's sexuality. Though he forbids any discussion about Maggie's transgression in order to protect her from her mother's and brother's criticism, he also prevents her from learning anything more about the desires that prompted her to try to run away from home. Thus, Eliot shows that Jeremy Tulliver, like his wife, lacks the capacity to act as one of the "ministers and interpreters of nature" ("Moral Discipline" 392), because he too fails to help Maggie understand the sexual impulses that, for an evolutionary thinker like Eliot, unite humanity with the rest of the biological world. Maggie learns instead the essential shame that prevents her from recognizing the compelling power of her response to Stephen Guest and begins to practice the habit of silent passivity that ultimately causes her paralysis of will when she glides with him down the river.

In this and subsequent episodes, Eliot also emphasizes the father's superior authority over both wife and children, which allows him to impose his own "reading" of nature upon them. Though Tulliver recognizes that his sister, Gerty Moss, has the obligation to prepare her four daughters to "fend for themselves" by obtaining training that will make them financially independent (140, bk. 1, ch. 8), he assesses Maggie's capacities in Spencerian fashion and prepares her only for wifehood and middle-class leisure. Were it not for her Aunt Pullet's generosity, Maggie would even have been denied the woefully inadequate education in the provincial ladies' finishing school that allows her to become a governess or a teacher in a "third-rate schoolroom," work Maggie dislikes but accepts because of economic necessity (494, bk. 6, ch. 3).

Eliot's treatment of the formal education that Tom and Maggie receive and her dramatization of their later effort to "make their way" in the world reveal her belief in the mitigating force of nurture over nature, and her analysis of the very different resources cultivated in men and women by an education not designed to teach self-mastery to both sexes but rather to encourage domination in men and submission in women. In *The Mill on the Floss*, Eliot omits any depiction of Maggie's formal education, and this may, at first, seem at odds with her support for the feminist educational reforms expressed in her essay "Margaret Fuller and Mary Wollstonecraft," as well as in her letters where she protests, for example, against the "domestic misery" that results from the "presumption that women must be kept ignorant and superstitious" (*GEL* 4:568).

Yet, Eliot's depiction of Maggie's intellectual frustrations at King's Lorton and her representation of her futile efforts to earn money for the family by plain sewing, indicate her awareness, and understated endorsement, of those feminist reforms designed to expand women's educational opportunities so as to allow them to achieve economic self-sufficiency.

By directly describing Tom's formal education rather than Maggie's in *The Mill on the Floss*, Eliot takes up a subject for which she was uniquely qualified, and she exposes the less obvious antifeminist implications of Spencer's theories of education. Many of the principles articulated in Spencer's essays on education could be used to support feminist reforms in women's education since he included informal as well as formal training and suggested a greater emphasis on its vocational function. However, the different educations that Tom and Maggie receive show how Spencer's underlying assumptions about women's "supreme function" subverted the apparently emancipationist reforms he recommended in educational practices and curriculum. Spencer's argument in these essays leads directly to the conclusions articulated in "Physical Training" that women are inherently "less developed" than men by "nature," and should, for the sake of the race, remain less educated than the men they wish to attract.

Eliot's depiction of Tom's schooling at King's Lorton does reveal some ground of agreement between Spencer and herself in her criticism of Victorian education.[14] In "What Knowledge is of Most Worth," Spencer writes that children should be educated, first of all, in the skills that would allow for their direct self-preservation, by learning mathematics, geometry, physics, chemistry, and biology; second, for their indirect self-preservation, by studying the skills necessary in the vocation or trade appropriate to their particular talents; third, for parenting, by mastering the knowledge and skills necessary for nurturing and educating children; fourth, for the maintenance of proper social and political relations, by learning what Spencer called "descriptive sociology," including the aspects of history and geography that Spencer defined as relevant to this study; and, finally, for leisure, by studying the beauties of Nature, literature, and the fine arts (10–34).

Eliot clearly agreed with Spencer—and with George Henry Lewes— that the conventional classical education given to middle- and upper-class young Englishmen at the time was too narrow and too authoritarian. In describing Tom's experience as a student, Eliot shows that he fails, in part, because of his teacher's unexamined elitism, his authoritarian pedagogy, and his inflexible belief that the only "natural method" of instilling the Eton Grammar into the mind of a recalcitrant student is by rote. Eliot turns evolutionary theory against Mr. Stelling by comparing his "unerring instinct" for teaching to that of an "amiable beaver" who performs his function with instinctive unconsciousness (207, bk. 2, ch. 1). Nonetheless, Tom's failure to master "masculine" subjects teaches him at least one salutary moral lesson, for by feeling "more like a girl than he had ever been in his life" (210, bk. 2, ch. 1) and by fleetingly sharing what Eliot calls a girl's "susceptibility," Tom experiences emotions that, Eliot asserts, should provide a more adequate understanding of "true manliness." By describing Tom's intellectual failures in these terms, Eliot assserts an alternate interpretation of gender differences, one which would define masculinity as rooted in a "protecting pity for the weak" (213, bk. 2, ch. 1) rather than in the masterful domination that Tom—and Spencer—regard as the "natural" expression of male identity.

Thus, Eliot particularizes Tom's formal education at King's Lorton in order to dramatize how gender roles are reproduced and "maximized" by his education, thereby revealing how it fosters Tom's censorious domination of Maggie later in his life. Through Mr. Stelling, Tom receives an indoctrination in male supremacy that he hardly needs. It begins with the lesson about the gender of nouns and is reinforced by readings like the one about the "astronomer who hated women generally," which causes Maggie such "puzzling speculation" (220, bk. 2, ch. 1).[15] Mr. Stelling provides Tom with a most emphatic lesson about feminine inferiority, a lesson which, though it lacks the evolutionary theory that rationalizes woman's lesser physical and intellectual capacities as a function of "natural law," otherwise echoes Spencer's conclusions about female capacities.

Eliot, however, took issue with Spencer's estimation of the value of studying literature, fine art, and classical languages, an estimation which, coincidentally, defined Spencer's scientific writing as central to the curriculum while marginalizing the artistic accomplishments of many women, including Eliot herself. By 1861, Eliot noted that a "great gulf was fixed" between herself and Spencer concerning the study of "art and the classics" (*GEL* 3:469). The King's Lorton episodes show that Tom is capable of understanding Greek and Latin literature when Maggie and Philip are available to reinterpret the texts in terms he understands.

Moreover, in representing Maggie's visits to King's Lorton, Eliot challenges the pervasive misogyny that operated to exclude women from such "masculine" studies, a misogyny that Spencer uncritically reinscribed in the final pages of "Physical Training." Eliot makes it clear in describing Maggie's first visit to her brother that she has the intellectual aptitude for Latin and geometry, but when she asks Mr. Stelling if she could do Euclid, he echoes Spencer in replying that girls "can pick up a little of everything I daresay. . . . They've a great deal of superficial cleverness, but they couldn't go far into anything. They're quick and shallow" (220–21, bk. 2, ch. 1). Though Mr. Stelling appreciates Maggie's dark eyes and seems to enjoy her cleverness, he is unable to see beyond his prejudices in assessing her larger capacities and judges her in Spencerian terms based on her physiology alone, seeing her as "mentally less developed" than a man. Eliot is affectionately humorous in commenting that Maggie was "oppressed by this dreadful destiny"—by the peculiar "brand of inferiority" (221, bk. 2, ch. 1) that applies to quickness in women—but she also demonstrates the natural force of Maggie's intelligence and so proves that Stelling's assessment of her is inaccurate. Nonetheless, this episode shows how social expectations limit the free development of a daughter's capacities by revealing the persistence of the traditional prejudices that Stelling and Spencer shared.

By portraying Maggie's subsequent frustration when she attempts to study Tom's schoolbooks after her own superficial boarding school education has been abruptly terminated, Eliot similarly focuses on one of the most influential aspects of Spencer's argument in "Physical Training," one that posed the greatest threat to feminist efforts to open higher education to women. In this essay, Spencer began the hazy speculations about how gender differences were affected by the "fixed energy" model of the human body that he described in "The Development Hypothesis" (1852) and subsequent essays (Russett 118). Young women, he argued, should educate themselves at home rather than attend college in those "wasted years" between finishing school and marriage, because, as he later explained more fully in *The Principles of Biology*, girls did not have the same physical energy available to pursue advanced study because of their reproductive function. While he protests against the excessive demands that higher education puts on the brains of students of both sexes, holding that too much study diverted the energy necessary to sustain physical vitality, he cites only examples of young women to illustrate this point in "Physical Training." He writes, "At the present time we have daily under our eyes a young lady whose system was damaged for life by the college-course through which she passed" (385). He concludes by describing the "pale, angular, flat-chested bluestockings" that inhabit London drawing rooms and criticizes the "anxious" mothers who have supervised their daughters' rigorously intellectual education and have inadvertently fostered the "physical degeneracy" that will doom them to a life of celibacy (394).

Eliot's endorsement of feminist efforts to open higher education to women was grounded, in part, in her belief that women needed access to the world of ideas not only so that they could become adequate companions to men in marriage and good mothers to their children, but also so that single women could find in the world of ideas a "defense against passionate affliction." She writes:

> We women are always in danger of living too exclusively in the affections; and though our affections are perhaps the best gifts we have, we ought to have our share in the more independent life—some joy in things for their own sake. It is piteous to see the helplessness of some sweet women when their affections are disappointed—because all their teaching has been that they can only delight in study of any kind for the sake of personal love. They have never contemplated an independent delight in ideas as an experience which they could express without being laughed at. (*GEL* 5:107)

Unlike Spencer, then, who defined women's sexuality as their primary allure and motherhood as their "supreme function," Eliot shows her rejection of such simple biological determinism by casting Maggie in the role of what the Victorians called a "redundant woman" and by portraying her sufferings when, because of circumstance and moral scruples, she rejects marriage and maternity.

Though Maggie feels as if she were "the only girl in the civilized world of her day" who had "come out of her school-life with a soul untrained for inevitable struggles," Eliot's narrator suggests that her deprivation is common by noting that she, like so many young women, possessed "no other part of her inherited share in the hard-won treasures of thought, which generations of painful toil has laid up for the race of men than shreds and patches of feeble literature and false history" (381, bk. 4, ch. 3). Because her father's bankruptcy cut short her education, Maggie is "unhappily quite without that knowledge of the irreversible laws within and without her which, governing the habits, becomes morality, and, developing the feelings of submission and dependence, becomes religion" (381, bk 4, ch 3).

Eliot counters Spencer's low estimate of female strength and intelligence by insisting that Maggie's "unconscious appetites" for knowledge are as peremptory as her need for love, and that both are as powerful as the forces within a "living plant-seed," which "will make a way for themselves, often in a shattering, violent manner" (320, ch. 5, bk. 3). No anxious mama can be blamed for Maggie's ambitious desire to enter the "masculine" province of knowledge; and her only access is through her brother's schoolbooks. While Maggie's lonely efforts to nibble at the "thick-rinded fruit of the tree of knowledge" end in a failure to find any sustaining joy in her repeatedly interrupted study of "Latin, geometry, and the forms of syllogisms" (380, bk. 4, ch. 3), her experience is not represented as a sign of her biologically determined ineptitude but rather as a function of the self-doubt learned under the oppressive domestic conditions of English provincial life. Thus Eliot indicates that larger educational and social changes are necessary in order to cultivate the "higher sensibilities" of women like Maggie and to allow them to pursue a life of independent study that would provide a sustaining moral purpose for their lives.

Having no quarrel with traditional gender roles, Spencer assumed the "beneficient" discipline of "inorganic Nature" and argued that Nature's physical discipline is "pure justice" ("Moral Discipline" 397). Eliot, in contrast, provides an alternative view of justice that defines the moral ground for Maggie's resistance to her family's narrow interpretations of law and gender differences. The treatment of Maggie's conflict with Tom in the second volume of the novel and with Stephen Guest in the third dramatizes Eliot's belief that human life is defined by an "inner" as well as an "outer law." In her 1856 essay "The Antigone and Its Moral," Eliot argued that while the law of force may often triumph, "inner" laws ultimately prevail so that the "outer life of man" is "gradually and painfully being brought into harmony with his inward needs" (*Essays* 264). While her acceptance of evolutionary theory prompted her to refine her ideas about "inner law," as as we see in *The Mill on the Floss,* Eliot was not willing to accept Spencer's paradigm of law and "pure justice," which entirely ignored the force of what Eliot called "moral law."

The Mill on the Floss thus illustrates how difficult it is to interpret the meaning and force of the "outward" and "inward" laws that define complex human behavior in historically determined societies. As the shape of Tom's and Maggie's lives reveals, Eliot did not find in the forward rush of time the promise of inexorable "progress" that Spencer celebrated. The best hope for insuring the gradual, uncertain progress of human society lay, for Eliot, in recognizing the conflict between those "outward" laws that Spencer identified by reference to biology and social analysis and the less tangible "inward" laws that move mysteriously in the human heart and mind. Eliot's paradigm for human society, in contrast to Spencer's, is based on the assumption that the flowering of all human potentiality, of all that is "beautiful and good" in the individual and the society, will eventually find expression in the "onward tendency of human things" (363, bk.4, ch. 1). By identifying Maggie with the forces of "inward" moral law, defined by conscience, love, loyalty, and filial piety, Eliot lends her heroine an epic authority in her resistance to the demands of those "outward" laws defined by the patriarchal traditions and biological imperatives that Tom and Stephen invoke.

Though Tom repeats Spencer's analysis of family "law" and "pure justice," Eliot shows that he is driven by an impulse for dominance which is based on the "very negations" of his more complex human potentialities (407, bk. 5, ch. 2). Tom is, by Spencer's definition, fit to survive in the world of St. Ogg's, but Eliot questions Spencer's criteria by revealing how Tom is "imprisoned" because he "judges only by what he could see" (630, bk. 7, ch. 3). Tom succeeds briefly in the business world of St. Ogg's because he possesses a "nature in which family feeling has lost the character of clanship in taking a doubly deep dye of personal pride" (631, bk. 7, ch. 3), but it is precisely Tom's "personal pride"—his individualism and self-righteousness—that causes his destruction by giving him a "character at unity with itself—that performs what it intends, subdues every counteracting impulse, and has no visions beyond the visible" (407, bk. 5, ch. 2).

Tom's commitment to the ethics of force and domination emerges dramatically when he joins with his father in swearing vengeance upon Wakem. In that primal moment of male bonding, he literally spells out the terms of his alliance with his father in the family Bible, and through this richly evocative act, Eliot demonstrates the power of the father to legitimize and sanction patriarchal domination by defining it as "law."

In this scene, Maggie challenges the "morality" of such an interpretation of law by asserting the insight she achieved as a result of the vague religious quest she pursued during these years, a quest she undertook without the aid of "established" religious authorities. Seeing the terrible irony of Tom's inscription of a curse in the pages of the Bible, she protests that this pact between father and son is "wicked" because it violates the moral premises of Christianity requiring love and forgiveness. Though Maggie is silenced in this episode by Tom's peremptory, "Be quiet, Maggie . . . I *shall* write it" (357, bk. 3 ch.8), Eliot valorizes Maggie's resistance by revealing her commitment to the same principles that guided Antigone when she declared, "I cannot share in hatred but in love."[16] Later, on the day of reckoning when her father attacks Wakem, Maggie enacts her superior moral authority when she prevents her father from killing him (461, bk. 5, ch. 7).

Eliot lends a similarly mythic dimension to the final episode of Maggie's adolescence played out in the Red Deeps, where she confronts Tom and again asserts her more comprehensive vision of moral law, an understanding which has been deepened and refined through her conversations with Philip in the landscape of the wild zone. Eliot casts Tom in the role of Creon and Maggie as Antigone in this deeply symbolic episode. In the debate about law and justice that takes place there, Tom defines duty in traditional patriarchal terms and urges Maggie to submit to him in the name of the father by invoking the prevailing religious and social conventions that demand the daughter's subordination to father and brother. Maggie, in opposition, asserts a "wider" moral law which legitimizes her resistance by disclosing the inadequate basis of Tom's "judgment" and authority.

Tom expresses a Spencerian complacency about the superior force of the "outward" over the "inward" law when he locates the essential basis of his right to command in his threats of violence. He warns Philip that he has the right to "take care of" Maggie, by force if necessary, saying: "If you dare to make the least attempt to come near her, or to write to her, or to keep the slightest hold on her mind . . . I'll thrash you—I'll hold you up to public scorn" (448, bk. 5, ch. 5). Maggie protests that Tom, in conceiving of her as a possession to be defended, has distorted the true meaning of love, protection, "manhood," and familial duty. Protesting Tom's self-righteousness as well as his "insulting unmanly allusions" to Philip's "deformity," Maggie concludes: "You have been always sure you yourself are right: it is because you have not a mind large enough to see that there is anything better than your own conduct and your own petty aims" (449, bk. 5, ch. 5). Maggie's exposure in this scene of the aggressive dominance that is fostered by patriarchal privilege demonstrates Eliot's skepticism about the impulses that Spencer redefined as biological law in his interpretation of the "survival of the fittest."

Ultimately, Tom defends himself against Maggie in this scene by resorting to more pragmatic sexist arguments. Eliot emphasizes the sexual politics of their relationship when Maggie protests that Tom lacks sympathy because he is "a man" and has "power and can do something in the world" (450, bk, 5, ch. 5). Tom responds by articulating the same logic that underlies Spencer's analysis of sexual selection: "If you can do nothing, submit to those who can" (450, ch. 5, bk. 5). Thus, Tom bluntly restates the same problem posed by Spencer's theories, and Maggie's difficulties in establishing a legitimate basis for her resistance to such "outward" laws parallels Eliot's own. By her own logic, however, Maggie must obey those moral obligations she sees as based on the higher laws of love and filial duty, and so she submits to "what is unreasonable" from her father, if not from Tom, and agrees to discontinue her conversations with Philip.[17] In the end, then, Tom prevails over his sister, just as Creon prevailed over Antigone, by invoking the power of patriarchal law, but Maggie nonetheless acts in accordance with a "higher law" based on the primacy of love, which, through acts of resistance like hers, eventually brings the outward law into greater harmony with the inward.

Philip's conversations with Maggie in the "wild zone" also reveal some "negations" in Maggie's behavior.[18] While he confirms the healthiness of Maggie's thirst for knowledge, truth, and beauty, he asserts the differences between genuine religious resignation and the "stupefaction" that Maggie practices in the name of religion. Philip protests that Maggie's impulse to "seek safety in negations" cannot form the basis of religion or genuine morality: "No character becomes strong in that way. You will be thrown into the world someday and every rational satisfaction of your nature that you deny will assault you like a savage appetite" (429, bk. 5, ch. 3). By correctly predicting Maggie's future, Philip demonstrates, as well, the logical failure in paradigms like Spencer's which depend upon an interpretation of "outward law" to preserve existing class and gender arrangements and which locate the "pure justice" of nature in laws which require a similar "negation" of human potential in both men and women. In demonstrating the consequences of denial and false submission in Maggie's life and by portraying the more complete understanding of moral law that she achieves after she leaves Stephen behind, Eliot identifies the epic authority she would herself claim in asserting the force of "inward" laws that transcend the "outward law" Spencer defined as supreme.

Nevertheless, in showing that Phillip's own motives are not entirely disinterested when he urges Maggie to meet him against the wishes of her father and brother, Eliot acknowledges the difficulties of imagining moral laws that transcend the limits of gender and sex entirely. Philip approaches an understanding of the "charities of mother, daughter, and sister," because he, like Maggie, has not been "soothed by that mother's love which flows out to us in the greater abundance because our need is greater" (431, bk. 5, ch. 3). Similarly, he has felt the soul's hunger, because he is prevented by his "accidental deformity" from assuming a more traditional male role in society (543, bk. 6, ch. 8). However, though Philip is "half feminine" in his sensibilities, he is not immune to Maggie's sexual appeal. Eliot implicitly criticizes Spencer's basic assumptions about how the biological laws of adaption and Lamarckian use-inheritance apply to moral growth when she explains that Philip is not naturally altruistic:

> Do not think too hardly of Philip. Ugly and deformed people have great need of unusual virtues, because they are likely to be extremely uncomfortable without them: but the theory that unusual virtues spring by a direct consequence out of personal disadvantages, as animals get thicker wool in severe climates, is perhaps a little overstrained. The temptations of beauty are much dwelt upon, but I fancy they only bear the same relation to those of ugliness, as the temptation to excess at a feast, where the delights are varied for eye and ear as well as palate, bears to the temptations that assail the desperation of hunger. (430, bk. 5, ch. 3)

The remarks about beauty in this passage interrogate the assumptions that allowed Spencer to make female beauty the keystone of his misogynistic arguments against higher education for women and his functional definition of women's place in the "struggle to survive." In generalizing about the effects of the hunger of the mind and soul upon both Maggie and Philip, Eliot resists Spencer's dismissal of the invisible force of "moral laws" in his assessment of human society. Eliot concludes this passage with the question, "Does not the Hunger Tower stand as the type of the utmost trial to what is human in us?", in order to assert an alternative vision of human potentiality, glimpsed in the "wild zone" and grounded in the assumption that the appetites of the mind and spirit, like those of the body, exist in women as well as men and must be fed, if humanity is to achieve its fullest development.

In the final volume of the novel Eliot indicates her reservations about Spencer's identification of progress with industrial development by describing Maggie's failure to adapt to the social milieu of St. Ogg's. The new aggressive, individualistic social order promoted by laissez-faire capitalism has reorganized the society that once insured the Dodsons' success; and those values they most venerated—"obedience to parents, faithfulness to kindred, industry, rigid honesty, thrift"—have been marginalized in this new society (364, bk. 4, ch. 1). Stephen Guest and Lucy Deane represent the values of this new rising society, where "light irony" has become the prevailing mode (385, bk, 4, ch. 3) and where Lucy is destined to become the "world's wife." Guest's views are juxtaposed to Philip's and Maggie's larger, more comprehensive understanding of human nature and the transcendent moral values that provide the basis of a more genuine and affirmative culture, deserving of the Keatsian terms that Philip habitually uses. Their cultural ideal, like Eliot's, escapes the flattery and petty misogyny that characterizes the life of polite society in St. Ogg's, rejects the paternalistic appropriation of culture that Stephen enacts, and opposes the rigid conformity and intolerance that Tom Tulliver displays.

The central chapter of Book Four foreshadows the critical perspective Eliot later brings to bear upon Stephen Guest and on the business practices that give his father and Lawyer Wakem their competitive edge in St. Ogg's.[19] In this passage, she emphasizes the "expensive" costs of a national life "based entirely" on the "emphasis of want," by referring to the "arduous national life condensed in unfragrant, deafening factories, cramping itself in mines, sweating at furnaces, grinding, hammering, weaving under more or less oppression of carbonic acid, or else, spread over sheepwalks, and scattered in lonely houses and huts on the clayey chalky cornlands, where the rainy days look dreary" (385, bk. 4, ch. 3). Stephen and Lucy both live on the fringes of the "good society" that is a parasite on this national life; their fathers have profited extensively from a laissez-faire capitalism based on the emphasis of "want." Moreover, this system of "want" has submerged the "charities of mother, daughter, and sister" even more deeply than they were submerged in *Adam Bede*, and while these charities do find expression at the end of the novel, Eliot also portrays the destructive counterforce exerted by "the world's wife," that invention of the industrial middle class.

The Mill on the Floss shows, then, that industrial development has transformed not only public life but domestic arrangements as well, changing in consequence the conventions defining courtship, sexual attraction, and heterosexual love. Mary Poovey cites a passage from the *Saturday Review* written in 1859 which criticizes Bessie Parkes's work. This commentary shows how the rhetoric of laissez-faire capitalism infected the analysis of marriage and the problem of the "redundant woman" in particular:

> Married life is women's profession; and to this life her training—that of dependence—is modelled. Of course by not getting a husband, or losing him, she may find that she is without resources. All that can be said of her is, she has failed in business; and no social reform can prevent such failures. The mischance of the distressed governess and the unprovided widow, is that of every insolvent tradesman. . . . Men do not like, and would not seek, to mate with an independent factor. . . . (154).

Indeed, the meaning of Maggie's life and death depends upon whether we see her final rejection of Stephen as her refusal to accept the biological destiny he urges on her, which locates the essential fulfillment of a woman's life in sexual union and, like Spencer—and Freud—in maternity, or whether we see her choice in her own terms, as an affirmation of painfully achieved personal integrity.[20]

Stephen Guest assumes the role of spokesman for Spencerian values in Book III by enthusiastically advocating industrial capitalism, while Lucy and Maggie try to soften its effects. Stephen shares with his father's subordinate partner a Spencerian appreciation for rapid industrial development; as Mr. Deane reports, "It's this steam, you see, that has made the difference—it drives on every wheel double pace and the wheel of fortune along with 'em, as our Mr. Stephen Guest said" (507, bk. 5, ch. 5).

Stephen is equally complacent about the changes capitalism has fostered in gender relations, and he assumes a utilitarian attitude toward art, music, and literature that is in accord with the view Spencer takes in "What Knowledge is of Most Worth." In his first appearance in the novel, Stephen shows his "half-ardent, half-sarcastic" view of culture when he invites Lucy to sing with him the duet from "The Creation": "Now then, the recitative for the sake of the moral. You will sing the whole duty of women—'And from obedience grows my pride and happiness' " (474, bk. 6, ch. 1). Though Eliot mocks Stephen humorously here by describing his cumbersome and fatuous attempts to use "light irony," she indicates, nonetheless, the power he has acquired because, in contrast to Mr. Glegg whose readings of the first chapters of Genesis could only yield "puzzlement," Stephen, like Spencer, has learned to read Genesis for the sake of its misogynistic "moral."

In her first meeting with Stephen, Maggie challenges his conception of female beauty and demonstrates her cleverness by suggesting an alternate reading of Genesis, contained in the Bridgewater Treatises. When Maggie reveals her defiance of his conventional expectations about female submissiveness and mental incompetence, Stephen's first impulse is to conclude that there must be "an alarming amount of the devil" in her (485, bk 6, ch. 2). In her subsequent conversations with him, Maggie voices Eliot's more specific objections to Spencer's theory of sexual selection. In these conversations, Stephen echoes Spencer in elevating "sexual instinct" to the level of a biological law which supercedes all moral considerations. Though Stephen sees his pursuit of Maggie as a betrayal of his friendship with Philip, as a breach of his tacit engagement with Lucy, and as a violation of his obligation as a gentleman to honor Maggie's repeated requests that he give her up, he rationalizes his persistence because of his Spencerian confidence in the superior power and authority of the "natural laws" which he sees as controlling their affections. Maggie defends herself against Stephen's Spencerian arguments by asserting the binding nature of the same "moral law" that justified her resistance to Tom, but this law requires that she honor those loyalties that are most deeply rooted in her personal past.

Just before Stephen kisses Maggie in the conservatory at Park House, he notices that there must be "some attachment" between Philip and Maggie, and he thus recognizes a "claim which called him to resist the attraction that was constantly threatening to overpower him" (559, bk. 6, ch. 10). He chooses, though, to act instead on a "certain savage resistance" to his friendship with Philip and to his commitments to Lucy. Intoxicated by the "grave mutual gaze" that marks their first mute confession of love, Stephen resorts to the language of gesture when a "mad impulse" prompts him to kiss Maggie's arm. Stephen is moved to this display of passionate desire because of Maggie's beauty, as Spencer's analysis of sexual selection would predict, but she responds by expressing the rage, humiliation, and guilt that makes this "moment's happiness" seem to her to be a "treachery to Lucy, to Philip—to her own better soul" (562, bk. 6, ch. 10). In this way, Eliot exposes the same male egocentricity that informs the psychology of desire represented in *Adam Bede*.

The first time that Maggie and Stephen enter the literal landscape of the "wild zone" together is when Stephen, impelled by "love, rage, and confused despair" (380, bk. 4, ch. 3), visits Maggie at her aunt's home at

Basset. In this excursion into the wild zone, Stephen claims a scientific authority by arguing that their love is "natural" and that Maggie should submit to the "laws of attraction" (512, bk. 6, ch. 6) as he interprets them, thus alluding obliquely to Spencer's theory of sexual selection. Stephen insists that his tacit engagement to Lucy cannot be fulfilled because "it is unnatural"; he tells Maggie, "We can only pretend to give ourselves to anyone else" (570, bk. 6, ch. 11). Thus, Stephen demonstrates the powerful appeal of an analysis of human love and passion based on natural "scientific" laws like those Spencer defined in "Physical Training." Maggie's response exposes Stephen's—and Spencer's—narrow-mindedness in elevating sexual feelings over all the other affections and emotions: "Love is natural," she argues, "but surely pity and faithfulness and memory are natural too. And they would live in me still, and punish me if I didn't obey them" (571, bk. 6, ch. ll). Maggie does not here or later justify her resistance to Stephen by simply invoking the abstract principles of duty, religion, or social convention; instead, she asserts the compelling power of the "inward" laws that have shaped her own personality, by claiming that she cannot silence her memories or ignore the affectionate bonds of the past.

The last time Maggie and Stephen enter the wild zone is when they go out rowing on the river, and in this episode Eliot dramatizes her most serious reservations about the moral implications of Spencer's analysis of sexual selection and the way in which it limits woman's full humanity by defining her social role exclusively in terms of her reproductive function. Eliot acknowledges the "natural joy" to be found in an erotic surrender to physicality in the wild zone by describing Maggie's rapt absorption in the natural beauty of the world around her as she allows Stephen to "bear her along" on the "backward flowing tide."[21] When Maggie protests, however, that in taking advantage of her thoughtlessness, Stephen has acted to "deprive" her of choice, Eliot reveals her similar objection to Spencer's analysis of sexual selection which, by definition, deprives all women of "choice" by making the male sexual instinct aroused by woman's "impersonal" beauty preeminent and by denying women a similar instinct or agency in selecting a mate. This is, perhaps, why Eliot puts such emphasis on Maggie's passionate nature, an emphasis which, when the secret of her authorship was disclosed, prompted one outraged critic, writing in 1860, to protest that Eliot "enthrones physical law so far above both affections and conscience in point of strength, that she represents Maggie as drifting helplessly into a vortex of passion and rescued at last only by the last spasmodic effort of a nearly overpowered will."[22]

Maggie's behavior in this scene also shows, I would argue, Eliot's subtle effort to counter Spencer's assertion that "nature" alone defines sexual selection; Maggie surrenders to Stephen not only because of the sexual imperatives she feels but also because of her social conditioning as a woman. Maggie has repeatedly been taught to "submerge" the needs of her own personality and attend to those of "another." The physical forces, the gliding of the boat, her fatigue, and her own awareness of the compromising complications of their situation amplify her sensual response and help "to bring her into more complete subjection to that strong mysterious charm which made a last parting with Stephen seem the death of all joy" (592, bk. 6, ch. 13). Thus, alone with Stephen in the natural world, Maggie reexperiences the physical and emotional vulnerability she felt in her flight to join the gypsies and surrenders, once again, to the familiar and "unspeakable charm in being told what to do" (592, bk. 6, ch. 13).

In depicting Maggie's final renunciation of Stephen, however, Eliot asserts her own definition of human potential by revealing her heroine's commitment to a view of erotic love that does not pit the promptings of the mind and the spirit against the desires of the body, as Spencer's paradigm required. Maggie's decision to leave Stephen is not an expression of her aversion to sex, but rather her rejection of the divided state in which passion is not willingly embraced as an expression of one's best self but is felt instead as submission, humiliation, and betrayal. Eliot writes that the "sins" Maggie recoils from are her "breach of faith and cruel selfishness," and not sex itself. Affirming once again the importance of conscious choice, which, for Eliot, distinguishes sexual attraction from love, Maggie reasserts her ability to choose (600, bk. 1, ch. 14) and tells Stephen she must leave him in the morning: "There was at least this fruit from all her years of striving after the highest and best—that her soul, though betrayed, beguiled, ensnared, could never deliberately consent to a choice of the lower. And a choice of what? O God—not a choice of joy—but of conscious cruelty and hardness, for could she ever cease to see before her Lucy and Philip with their murdered trust and hopes?" (597, bk. 6, ch. 14).

In this final scene, Stephen's counterarguments about the compelling force of sexual instinct are so commonplace in modern thought that they are often accepted uncritically.[23] Eliot's sympathies, however, are clearly with Maggie in this scene, for the narrator asserts that Maggie acts on particular inward commands of the "mind and heart," which are dictated by the "divine voice within." This "divine voice" authorizes Maggie's resistance to the demands of a passion that, Stephen insists, are determined by natural "outward law." For Maggie, as for Eliot, honoring the private, particular, inward law that grows from being "true to to all the motives that sanctify our lives" (604, bk. 6, ch. 14) is the superior obligation, just as love which encompasses all motives and not simply the sexual impulse is the more developed expression of affection.

In Maggie's last conversation with Stephen, Eliot reveals her heroine's belief in a love that includes passion, but to be true to this faith Maggie must reject both Stephen and Philip. Thus, she repudiates Stephen's final Spencerian argument that the "natural law surmounts every other—we can't help what it clashes with' " (610, bk. 6, ch. 14), and asks instead, "if the past is not to bind us, where can duty lie?" (602, bk. 6, ch. 14). When Stephen challenges her definition of the "past,"[24] and reminds her that the "world" will believe that she is "his" and that a "duty" must spring out of these conventional expectations, Maggie reminds him of their relationships with Philip and Lucy, saying, "I cannot marry you—I cannot take a good for myself that has been wrung out of their misery" (605, bk. 6, ch. 14). Maggie's answer to each of Stephen's arguments thus insists on the primacy of the inward over the outward law, just as the "natural piety" she describes is individual, private, and personal, and defies the generalized language that Stephen uses, and that Spencer himself employed in formulating the "laws" of sexual selection.

It is an expression of Eliot's tragic realism that in devoting herself to the commands of inward rather than outward law, Maggie becomes a martyr for moral progress. Maggie's sufferings upon her return to St. Ogg's do not imply that Eliot regards renunciation and suffering as preferable to self-fulfillment,[25] but it does reveal her belief that without morally courageous revolutionaries like Maggie, who suffer because of their devotion to an inward law, there would be no progressive social change. It is through individual resistance to the outward law rather than submission to it that, as Eliot explains in her essay on Antigone, the outward law is brought into greater harmony with the inward (*Essays* 264).

The Mill on the Floss is, finally, an elegy for a lost society and a depiction of the tragedy that lies "under the process of evolution" (*GEL* 3:227). The new society of St. Ogg's has little room for the Dodson matriarchs or for their strong-willed daughter, as is emphasized by Mrs. Tulliver's position as a housekeeper and Maggie's as guest in her cousin's home. Against Tom, Stephen, the "men of maxims," and "the world's wife," all of whom articulate the values of this new industrial society, Eliot sets Maggie, her mother, Mrs. Glegg, and, belatedly, Lucy. This grouping indicates Eliot's ongoing defense of the "charities of mother, daughter, and sister." Certainly one of the most touching moments in the novel occurs when Maggie returns to Dorlcote Mill and her mother, acting on the "simple human pity that will not forsake us," rejects Tom's judgmental repudiation of Maggie and tells her daughter, instead, "My child, I'll go with you. You've got a mother" (614, bk, 7, ch. 1).

Eliot does not idealize this reunion between mother and daughter. Instead, she shows that Mrs. Tulliver is economically dependent upon Tom and must accept money from him in order to help Maggie. Mrs.

Glegg too, when she comes to Maggie's defense, must quarrel with her husband, who is as "hard in his judgment of Maggie" as Mr. Deane himself was (630, bk. 7, ch. 3). Finally, Lucy must steal out of her house to meet her cousin and accept her confession and penitence; she too acknowledges her powerlessness and recognizes Maggie's superior moral stature, saying, "You are better than I am" (643, bk. 7, ch. 4).

Thus, we see that the "charities of mother, daughter, and sister," which promote and underlie the marriage of Dinah and Adam in *Adam Bede*, are more deeply submerged by the flood of time that sweeps through *The Mill on the Floss*. Though Maggie, directed by memory, awakening hope, and strength of will, survives one dangerous trip across the flood to rescue her mother and Tom, brother and sister go down to their death when she submits to Tom's command, "Give me the oars, Maggie" (654, bk. 7, ch. 5). Though the flood seems "too pat," the machinery too fortituous, and the symbolism too facile,[26] this conclusion does reflect a certain honesty about female culture and ambition—both Maggie's and Eliot's—in a world where the moral authorities legitimizing the "charities of mother, daughter, and sister" were being eroded not only by industrialism but also by evolutionary theories which redefined love as biological instinct and so stripped women of their dignity by denying their intellectual and moral capacities.

In a world where natural, moral, and social laws are being reformulated in evolutionary terms, Eliot acknowledges the power of characters, who, like Tom and Spencer, are "at unity with themselves because their vision is so limited." Tom's commitment to judging "by what he had been able to see," reflects his unquestioning belief in "facts observed through years by his own eyes which gave no warning of their imperfections" (630, bk. 7, ch. 3). For the authoritarian male personality who, like Tom, possesses "strength of will, conscious rectitude of purpose, narrowness of imagination and intellect, a great power of self-control, and a disposition to exert control over others—prejudices come as the natural food of tendencies which can get no sustenance out of that complex, fragmentary, doubt-provoking knowledge we call truth" (579, bk. 6, ch. 12). While Eliot concludes this passage by asserting that the "responsibility of tolerance lies with those who have a wider vision" (630, bk. 7, ch. 3), she is forced by this logic to sacrifice Maggie because of her love, tolerance, and understanding of Tom.

In the end, Eliot surrenders to her own wishfulness when she allows Tom, in his extremity, to glimpse the "depths of life, that had lain beyond his vision which he fancied so keen and clear" (654, bk. 7, ch. 5) and to recognize his sister's superior moral authority. Only by invoking the appealing romance of childhood, when brother and sister "roamed the daisied field together," can Eliot find hope for a reconciliation between a brother and sister so fundamentally separated by their experiences in a world deeply divided by gender. Because of her own experiences in a gendered world, Eliot, in contrast to Spencer, could find no solace in the belief that those who adapt successfully are the most "fit to survive."

By describing Maggie's death by drowning, Eliot insists that we recognize, in spite of the false providence of the flood and the glorification of brother-sister love, the destruction of the highest life that St. Ogg's had produced. And by insisting on the tragic death of her heroine, Eliot makes an appeal for the recognition of those fundamentally heroic impulses that reside in all men and women who choose, as Maggie does in this last gesture, to resist outward laws with a full understanding of the meaning and consequences of their acts. "To eyes that have dwelt on the past, there is no thorough repair," Eliot admits in her conclusion, and this epigram, rather than the lines chiseled on the tomb of Tom and Maggie, discloses the reality of her heroine's sacrifice, a reality that cannot be entirely ameliorated by hopes for the future redefined by Maggie's brave resistance to the demands of outward law.

5

The Origins of Morality:
Silas Marner and *First Principles*

OF ALL the full-length works Spencer produced in his long and prolific career, Eliot was perhaps most impressed and surprised by his *First Principles* (1862), which she read in page proof in the fall of 1860, shortly after she began writing *Silas Marner* (Haight, *George Eliot* 341).[1] On December 20, 1860, she explained to Sara Hennell that she felt "supremely gratified" by this work because Spencer "brings his argument to a point which I did not anticipate from him" (*GEL* 3:364).

First Principles begins with Spencer's untypical acknowledgment that the "production of matter out of nothing is the real mystery, which neither this simile nor any other enables us to conceive" (25). He subsequently identifies the Absolute or First Cause of all life as "unknowable" since "the Power which the universe manifests to us is utterly inscrutable," and thus he admits the limits of scientific research by recognizing the "unknown" as a realm beyond the reach of science (46). Nonetheless, Spencer asserts that evolutionary scientists who refrain from speculating about the ultimate causes of life may claim an authority which supersedes that of the Bible or the priest in the analysis of the laws which organize the natural world, for, as Spencer explains, "that which to most will seem an essentially irreligious position is an essentially religious one—nay is the religious one, to which . . . all others are but approximations" (109).

During these years, Eliot articulated one of her major criticism of Darwin's *Origin of Species* by observing that he was unwilling to discuss in this text the "mystery which lies under the process" of biological law (*GEL* 3:227), while Spencer's *First Principles*, by contrast, earned her praise because it acknowledged the limits of scientific inquiry and addressed the problem of the Unknown. Spencer's speculations in this work about the epistemological issues raised by his recognition of the Unknown parallel Eliot's concern with similar issues in *Silas Marner*. When it is read in the context of Spencer's work of this period, Eliot's novel reveals her ongoing interest in the irreducible "mystery" of creation, suggested by Silas's weaving, and the related epistemological issues raised by those invisible weavers who turn Molly Cass's child into a blessing for Silas and produce that "mild" Nemesis that checks Godfrey Cass (*GEL* 3:382).

In the early chapters of *First Principles* which Eliot especially admired, Spencer uncharacteristically acknowledges the difficulties of interpretation caused when metaphorical language is used to describe the invisible or abstract forces of nature. He explains: "As repeatedly shown in various ways, the deepest truths we can reach, are simply statements of the widest uniformities in our experience of the relations of Matter, Motion, and Force; and Matter, Motion, and Force are but *symbols of the Unknown Reality*. That Power of which the nature remains forever inconceivable and to which no limits in Time or Space can be imagined, works in us certain effects" (501; my italics). Repeating the ideas that Eliot found provocative in his essay "The Genesis of Science" (1852), Spencer here recognizes the limits of scientific research, by articulating more fully his skepticism about the efficacy of metaphors in scientific discourse and by noting the problem of human subjectivity in the interpretation of the "symbols of the Unknown Reality."

Silas Marner (1861) dramatizes Eliot's similar analysis of the ways that the perception and interpretation of the Unknown are complicated by human subjectivity. While Spencer confidently outlined those evolutionary *First Principles* that could, within proper limits, accurately represent the hidden biological and psychological realities of human life, Eliot invokes Spencer's evolutionary vocabulary to demonstrate those mysterious processes in Silas's "inward" life that escape definition by Spencer's terms. In analyzing Silas's intellectual and moral development, Eliot demonstrates the difficulties of discriminating the effects of inward movements from those produced and reinforced by the outward laws that operate in traditional patriarchal societies like the urban and rural worlds depicted in this novel. While Eliot focuses on the same basic conflict between "outward" and "inward" laws that she dramatized in *The Mill on the Floss*, she relies more upon the language of associationist psychology to describe Silas Marner's inner world and his apprehension of those "inward" religious and moral laws that transform his life.

Eliot's representation of the origins and development of Silas's religious feelings shows that she shared Spencer's belief, first outlined in *The Principles of Psychology* (1855),[2] that evolutionary science offered an effective means to demystify the study of the human "soul" through the "naturalization of mind" offered by an evolutionary associationist psychology (Russett 109). In *First Principles*, Spencer dismisses the claim that "the feeling that responds to religious ideas resulted, along with all other human faculties, from an act of special creation" and proposes, instead, that these feelings "in common with the rest, arose by a process of evolution" (15). In other words, Spencer argues that in each individual, religious feelings arise from the same mental processes of association and repetition that establish other human impulses. Describing this process as the theory of "correspondences," Spencer writes, "If in the surrounding world there are objects, attributes, or actions that usually occur together, the effects severally produced by them in the organism will become so connected by these repetitions which we call experience, that they also will occur together" (298–99). Spencer's application of evolutionary principles deeply influenced the direction of British associationist psychology in the second half of the nineteenth century and redefined the Victorian perspective on the relationship between mind and body.[3]

Eliot's acceptance of Spencer's theory of correspondences is especially evident in her presentation of the process by which Silas loses all the "treasures" of his past life, of which his gold is simply the last and most durable token. In describing how Silas first acquired his "simple untaught" faith, Eliot identifies the associations that established his religious feelings and sensibilities by locating "the fostering home of his religious emotions" in those familiar objects connected with his worship, the "white-washed walls and the little pews" of the chapel, and in the "occult and familiar phrases of the minister and the couplets of the hymn" (63, ch. 2). When Silas leaves these familiar objects behind, thus disassociating his religious feelings from their original referents in Lantern Yard, the foundation of his faith is destroyed and he is left in a state of "benumbing unbelief" (62, ch. 1). This demystified description of the developmental process which established and then undermined Silas's religious faith shows that Eliot joined with George Henry Lewes in accepting the validity of the theory of mental "correspondences" enunciated by Spencer during this period.

Eliot similarly traces the origins of Silas's hoarding impulse by identifying the process of association that allows Marner's golden guineas gradually to absorb all his attention. In describing how the "little light he possessed" is blocked by Silas's "frustrated belief," Eliot's narrator directs the following question to the reader:

> Do we not wile away moments of inanity or fatigued waiting by repeating some trivial movement or sound, until the repetition has bred a want, which is incipient habit? That will help us to understand how the love of accumulating money grows an absorbing passion in men whose imaginations . . . showed them no purpose beyond it. (67, ch. 2)

Yet, Eliot also reveals her skepticism about the ease with which Spencer deduces the meaning of such inward changes by the interpretation of outward signs when she notes that Silas's obsession takes this particular form because the culture in Raveloe promotes and reinforces the hoarding of gold and silver as typical obsessions (68, ch. 2).

In his analysis of the psychology of belief in *First Principles*, Spencer cites Calvinism as a case in point, and Eliot similarly focuses on the role Calvinism played in shaping Silas's apprehension of the Unknown. Spencer's analysis of Calvinism is, however, far more critical than Eliot's in *Silas Marner*. He condescendingly concludes that most Calvinists, and indeed most religious people in general, have been content to embrace a "lower" creed whereby God is envisioned anthropomorphically, though Spencer does not use this term. Thus, he argues, the believer who resists those "successively less concrete conceptions" of the Godhead "which have been forced upon him" by scientific discoveries remains confined within the narrow limits of his faith because he is psychologically satisfied by finding a "community of nature between himself and the object of his worship" (84–85).

Eliot, in contrast, illustrates the appeal of Calvinism by describing the processes which established Silas's faith while, at the same time, demonstrating Spencer's failure to notice that the conception of God the Father, which he regards as central to Calvinism, is already an abstraction created by a phallocentric culture. Indeed, throughout *Silas Marner*—as in *The Mill on the Floss* and in her later novels as well—Eliot resisted Spencer's more pragmatic and judgmental conclusions about religion and analyzed instead how her characters respond psychologically to the mystery of the Unknown and find in it a source of the outward and inward laws which determine religious feelings and morality. Near the end of *Silas Marner*, Eliot warns against the arrogantly superior attitude Spencer, for example, takes toward religious doctrines and practices established before the rise of evolutionary science. She writes, "the gods of the hearth exist for us still; and let all new faith be tolerant of that fetichism, lest it bruise its own roots" (200, ch. 16). Moreover, Eliot invites her readers to share in this tolerant spirit when she identifies the origins of Silas's primitive religious emotions: "A weaver who finds hard words in his hymn book knows nothing of abstractions; as the little child knows nothing of parental love, but only knows one face and one lap towards which it stretches its arms for refuge and nurture" (ch. 2, p. 63). In passages like this, Eliot expresses her recognition of the various ways human subjectivity functions to determine the prevailing interpretations of the Unknown.

Eliot's most specific critique of Calvinism appears in her comparison of the ways in which Silas and William Dane respond to the religion practiced in Lantern Yard. She uses an evolutionary vocabulary to distinguish Silas's authentic religious intuitions about the Unknown from those superstitions and "false" ideas for which "no man is culpable" (62, ch. 1). In this way, Eliot exposes the self-serving functions of the subjectivity that Spencer recognized but failed to investigate in the first edition of *Principles of Psychology* (1855) and in *First Principles*. William Dane's egotism allows him to find an "unshaken assurance" of his own salvation in his dreams about "the words 'calling and election sure' standing by themselves on a white page in the open Bible" (57–58, ch. 1). Because Silas, by contrast, is "one of those impressible self-doubting natures which, at an inexperienced age, admire imperativeness and lean on contradiction" (57, ch. 1), he is vulnerable to egoists like Dane who invoke religious law in order to exploit others. To hide his betrayal of Silas, and the sexual transgression that prompted it, Dane persuades his brother in the faith to submit to a ritual where chance becomes the sign of Divine justice in the drawing of lots. In this episode, then, Eliot shows how Dane uses religious language to interpret the Unknown but does so in order to "authorize" his own self-interested reading of it, by claiming that the mysterious cause of Silas's trances "looked more like a visitation of Satan than a proof of divine favor" (58, ch. 1). Dane thus prevents the detection of his own guilt by casting suspicion on Silas.[4]

While Eliot uses Spencerian terms in her depiction of the development and destruction of Silas's religious faith, she also emphasizes the role of gender as a structuring principle in his Calvinism, by disclosing the patriarchal bias of the interpretation of the Unknown that prevails in Lantern Yard. While Spencer looked no further than the Divine Father as the image of the believer's sense of his "community" with God, Eliot identifies the illogic of this conclusion by noting that the original biological source of this sense of community should more properly be located in the body of the mother.

In his youth, before he converted to Calvinism, Silas was introduced to some of the mysteries of the natural world by his mother who taught him about "medicinal herbs and their preparation—a little store of wisdom which she had imparted to him as a solemn bequest" (57, ch. 1). After his mother's death and after Silas's acceptance of the strict Calvinism practiced in the "little hidden world" of Lantern Yard, he began to feel "doubts about the lawfulness of applying this knowledge, believing that herbs could have no efficacy without prayer, and that prayer might suffice without herbs" (57, ch. 1). Thus, the interpretation of the Unknown, as it is codified in the religious doctrines that prevail in Lantern Yard, causes Silas to reject his mother's heritage and distrust the "natural piety" that defined her understanding of the Unknown.[5] In learning to regard his "inherited delight" both in his mother's knowledge and in his own wanderings in the natural world as a "temptation," Silas seals off a fundamental "channel for his sense of mystery" and blocks the "proper pathway of inquiry and knowledge" (57, ch. 1). Eliot indicates in this way how the early "growth" of Silas's religious feelings is selectively shaped by an interpretation of the Unknown that excludes the maternal principle.

Evolutionary theory provided an "integrated vocabulary" which, as Sally Shuttleworth argues, allowed Eliot to move "easily between different levels of analysis, combining intricate psychological analysis with wider social and moral conclusions" (89). The language of evolutionary psychology thus permits Eliot to shift the register of her maternal metaphors frequently in *Silas Marner*, in order to identify several related dimensions of the "wild zone": in Silas's personal history and responses, in his religious faith as it develops in Lantern Yard, and in his moral sensibilities as they find expression in his life in Raveloe.

In moving from the urban to the rural world of Raveloe, Silas enters a region that provides easier access to the natural world and to the "wild zone" that Calvinism has taught him to distrust, but in suggesting the inner developments that allow Silas to recognize and recover the repressed maternal in himself, Eliot shows that he experiences a psychological regression, a process that evolutionary theorists at the time described as "psychic atavism" (Russett 66). In thus depicting the disorientation and alienation that nearly transform Silas into the semblance of a spider in a web, Eliot underlines the primitive nature of his response to the Unknown, which is most clearly revealed after his relocation in Raveloe. His flight from Lantern Yard is prompted by an archaic impulse "not unlike the feeling of primitive men, when they fled thus, in fear or in sullenness, from the face of an unpropitious deity" (64, ch. 2). In describing Silas's failure to adjust to the new, unfamiliar rural landscape of Raveloe, Eliot appropriates the language Spencer used to describe the Unknown in *First Principles*. By using the terms "symbol" and "Power" (*First* 501) rather than a more specific religious idiom, Eliot suggests Silas's reversion to a more primitive religious sensibility: "It seemed to him that the Power he had vainly trusted in among the streets and at the prayer-meetings, was very far away from this land in which he had taken refuge, where men lived in careless abundance, knowing and needing nothing of that trust, which, for him, had been turned to bitterness" (64, ch. 2). In moving beyond the reach of the patriarchal religious laws of his former Calvinistic creed, Silas returns to the primordial mother, to that place where "mother earth shows another lap, and human life has other forms" than those on which his soul has been "nourished" (62, ch. 2).

The evolutionary terminology Spencer developed in outlining his associationist psychology also allowed Eliot to compare Silas's inward and outward journeys, for in coming to Raveloe, Silas experiences a social as well as a psychological regression. Raveloe is socially less developed, in Spencerian terms, than the city that surrounds Lantern Yard. It remains a region virtually untouched by the historical forces that created the great industrial centers like that unnamed city where Silas lived and worked.[6] Yet Raveloe is not an ideal Wordsworthian community; it is not a world where "natural piety" is universally practiced or where more humane—or more maternal—values prevail. Eliot's critics rarely note the grimness in her presentation of rural life in Raveloe, yet Eliot's perspective on this community is informed by her scientific understanding of evolution, medicine, and demography, and by her personal and vicarious experiences as a Victorian woman, an intellectual, a religious skeptic, a feminist sympathizer, and a potential mother.[7] Her representation of life in Raveloe thus disputes Wordsworth's pastoralism, on the one hand, and Spencer's sexism, on the other.

Eliot challenges Wordsworthian sentimentalizing about the association between mothers and Mother Nature in traditional rural communities like Raveloe by showing us instead the misogyny that characterizes the primitive religious and moral life of Silas's neighbors. Raveloe is a darker world, where witches and demons are regarded with religious awe and where women wear charms to protect them from bearing an idiot child. Eliot invokes Spencer's analysis of the Unknown when she comments on the psychological basis of the primitive superstitions that define this community's apprehension of the supernatural: "The rude mind with difficulty associates the ideas of power and benignity. A shadowy conception of power that by much persuasion can be induced to refrain from inflicting harm, is the shape most easily taken by the sense of the Invisible in the minds of men who have always been pressed close by primitive wants" (53, ch. 1).

Moreover, Eliot identifies the basis of the misogyny in Raveloe, and at the same time exposes Spencer's exclusion of the mother from his analysis of Calvinism, by demonstrating the primal associations that surround the mother as the source of life. Silas is himself regarded with suspicion because his "origins" are unknown, because no one knew his father or his mother. Moreover, Silas is deeply distrusted because he performs traditionally feminine work; as one of the "wandering men," he carries with him an aura of "vagueness and mystery," since his skills as a weaver are "wholly hidden," like a woman's reproductive powers and partake of the "nature of conjuring" to the untutored imagination (52, ch. 1).

Eliot shows that these fears find their most familiar and concrete expression in the superstitions about the mother's reproductive capacities when she outlines the associations that allow the villagers to identify Silas's healing art with witchcraft. Silas's relation to Sally Oates demonstrates, with great economy, how primitive misogynistic fears about the Invisible find expression in unexamined beliefs which associate mothers not with Wordsworth's benign Mother Nature but with the powers of darkness. After his successful cure of Sally Oates, the villagers see Silas as possessing magical powers, but when he refuses to pander to their superstitions, they see his healing skills as evidence that he, like the Wise Woman at Tarley, is able to command more diabolical powers.

By showing that Silas's psychological "regression" allows him to reconnect with the maternal in himself and thus achieve a more positive reintegration of his personality, Eliot reiterates her criticism of Spencer's definition of social evolution, which in valuing urban over rural life, privileged male dominance, social stratification, and technological advances. In coming to Raveloe, Silas gains greater access to the "wild zone" and to the maternal in himself. His contact with Sally opens "channels" that allow him to recover his memories about his mother and to reclaim her heritage as a healer. When Sally shows symptoms which remind Silas of the diseases his mother suffered as the "precursors" of her death, he feels a "rush of pity at the mingled sight and remembrance" (66, ch. 2). Yet for Eliot, outward and inward progress are not necessarily coordinated, for "the movement" of his pity which gives Silas "a transient sense of brotherhood" only "heightened the repulsion between him and his neighbors" (67, ch. 2).

Eliot similarly registers her resistance to the Wordsworthian logic that would protect the force and purity of woman's maternal instincts by idealizing the superstitions and illiteracy common in rural communities like Raveloe. In this community mothers are generally categorized as either "lazy" or "notable" (178, ch. 14). While Dolly is represented as the most morally mature woman in this community, she is also associated with death since she is the "first person always thought of in Raveloe when there was illness or death in a family" (134, ch. 10). Similarly, Dolly, whose maternal generosity is often seen as the embodiment of ideal community values in Raveloe, cannot read and does not know the significance of the letters "IHS" pricked on her pastries.[8] Eliot thus demonstrates that while Raveloe contrasts to Lantern Yard as a world less structured by phallocentric law and language, a world where religious beliefs are defined by an oral as well as a written tradition, the maternal remains nonetheless ambiguous and subject to interpretation. And when the maternal Unknown is deciphered in this community, phallocentric language is used to describe it, and the written word is given precedence.

In contrasting Silas's sympathetic response to that dark mother, Molly Cass, with the impassiveness shown by the other members of the Raveloe community, Eliot similarly challenges Wordsworthian sentimentalizing about motherhood itself. None of the villagers share Silas's sensitivity to Molly's suffering; they regard her lonely passing as an event "as trivial as the fall of a summer leaf" (178, ch. 14). Seeing Eppie's mother as a wandering intruder, they witness her death with an unemotional detach-

ment that recalls Spencer's personification of Nature as a "strict disciplinarian" and Eliot's equally uncongenial representation of "Dame Nature" in her birthday letter to the Hennells (*GEL* 1:272–73).

Eliot also corrects Wordsworthian pastoralism by showing how the hierarchies of class and gender operate in this seemingly ideal rural community to suppress the knowledge not only about Molly's death but also
about her secret marriage to Godfrey Cass. When Silas comes to Red
House bearing Eppie and the news of her mother's death, Mr. Cracken-
thorpe silences him, lest his disclosure "shock the ladies" (172, ch. 13);
thus, the rector unknowingly acts to protect Godfrey, just as earlier he
shielded Dunstan from suspicion in the theft of Silas's gold. Mr. Kimble
too, because he does not know of Godfrey's secret alliance with this
"fallen woman," maintains his efficient professional distance and scolds
his nephew for coming out into the cold to see this "vagrant." Without
any curiosity about this woman who, he observes, wears a wedding ring,
Mr. Kimble simply notes impersonally, "They must fetch her away to the
workhouse tomorrow" (175, ch. 13). Thus, Eliot's ironic evocation of
parallels to the Christmas story in the ladies' question, "What child is
this?", underscores the indifference that prevails when the blessed child
is a girl whose parents are unknown but presumed to be from the working classes. Godfrey's private marriage thus exposes the complicity between the religious and civil authorities of this community that allows
him to maintain his secret.[9]

In describing the domestic life at Red House, Eliot represents a more
sophisticated version of the misogyny that characterizes the religious
and moral life of the less fortunate members of Silas's community, but in
the Squire's family, too, Eliot identifies a pervasive distrust of mothers
and maternity. In this respect, too, Eliot resists presenting Raveloe as a
"wild zone" where the maternal values can be apprehended in their un-
alloyed form. One of the causes of Godfrey's moral irregularities, Eliot
suggests, is that he has been raised in a household "without that presence of the wife and mother which is the fountain of wholesome love
and fear in parlour and kitchen" (72, ch. 3). Godfrey's irascible father is
untouched by that Victorian hypocrisy that prompted the husband to
profess a reverence for his wife and the mother of his children—especially after her death. Instead, he criticizes his son for being a "shilly-
shally fellow" like his "poor mother." He continues, "She never had a will
of her own; a woman has no call for one, if she's got a proper man for her
husband. But *your* wife had need have one, for you hardly know your
own mind enough to make both your legs walk one way" (125, ch. 9).

The Squire, like Mr. Tulliver, seems unable to acknowledge or discipline the traits in both his sons that mirror his own: his irresolution and
his profligacy (73, ch. 3). Though Squire Cass married the mindless wife

that Spencer idealized in "Physical Training," she fails to survive her children's infancy. Though the Squire identifies himself as his wife's intellectual and moral superior, he patently fails to convey to his son the necessary moral lessons which will lead him to a harmonious and happy marriage.

Eliot uses an evolutionary vocabulary, then, not only to characterize the superstitions that separate men from women, and the customs that divide class from class in Raveloe, she also uses it to expose an underlying similarity in the patriarchal laws that bind father, son, and brother and form the social compact of civil laws prevailing in both the rural world of Raveloe and the seemingly more "developed" community of Lantern Yard. Mr. Macey's ritualistic retelling of the story of the Lammeters' irregular marriage defines the laws of marriage and paternity as central to this covenant. Telling how distressed he was when the minister put the marriage vow "by the role of contrary" to the bride and groom, Mr. Macey describes his anxious concern lest the marriage vows of the Lammeters be annulled by the accidental confusion of the words actually spoken. Then he asks, "Is't the meanin' or the words as makes folks fast i' wedlock? For the parson meant right, and the bride and bridegroom meant right. But then, when I come to think on it, meanin' goes but a little way i' most things" (101, ch. 6). When the minister resolves this problem by insisting that "it's the regester does it—that's the glue," he acknowledges the power the patriarchal word gains by inscription. Thus, civil law functions to recognize the otherwise unknown biological father, just as religious law in Lantern Yard recognizes the Unknown by reference to a metaphysical Father.

However, Eliot shows that in both Raveloe and Lantern Yard the bonds between father and son, and between brother and brother, are strained by secret or illicit sexual alliances with women, a perspective Spencer ignores in *The Principles of Psychology* (1855) by focusing exclusively on the male psychology of desire that leads to married love. Godfrey becomes alienated from his brother when he acts on his sexual passion and initiates his secret liaison with Molly Cass, just as Silas became alienated from William Dane upon his engagement to Sarah, though Godfrey and Dunstan seem not to have ever shared that deep affection that Silas felt for his brother in the faith. The mutual disaffection between Godfrey and Dunstan allows "brotherly love" to become the basis for blackmail, as Dunstan satirically reminds Godfrey when he threatens to expose the secret of his brother's marriage unless he forgives a debt Dunstan owes (74, ch. 3).[10] By comparing the psychological and social changes that follow Godfrey's sexual initiation with those of Silas's regression, Eliot challenges Spencer's progressivism and exposes the male bias of the associationist psychology outlined in *The Principles of Psychology* (1855) and reiterated in *First Principles* (1862).

In *First Principles,* Spencer came close to questioning his own assumption that the general direction of psychological and social change was necessarily progressive, but he posited instead a "theory of rhythm" to account for the rise and fall of individual members of particular "races" or of species as a whole:

> Life as it exists in all the members of such species, is an extremely complex kind of movement, more or less distinct from the kinds of movement which constitutes life in other species. In each individual of each species, this extremely complex kind of movement rises to its climax, declines, and ceases to exist in death, and every successive generation thus exhibits a wave of that peculiar activity characterizing the species as a whole. (325)

Though Spencer, in this passage, momentarily admits the difficulty of finding a clear and orderly progression in the "complex movement" of inward and outward change, he clung to the notion that some progressive order defines the direction of individual and social "growth." By the end of *First Principles,* he optimistically asserts that

> there is a gradual harmony between man's mental nature and the conditions of his existence. After finding that from it are deducible the various characteristics of evolution, we finally draw from it a warrant for the belief, that evolution can end only in the establishment of the greatest perfection and the most complete happiness. (486)

Eliot, in contrast to Spencer, takes a more Darwinian view of change by stressing the role of chance in the mental life of both Godfrey and Silas. Moreover, by portraying Silas's psychological regression and, later, the regeneration, also promoted by chance, that begins when Eppie wanders onto his hearth, Eliot registers her skepticism about Spencer's assumption that individual development and social change are both defined by a clearly progressive improvement.

Moreover, in bringing to light the psychological and social roots of Godfrey's and Silas's contrasting attitudes toward marriage, family, and paternity, Eliot extends her criticism of Spencer's analysis of erotic and parental love. In *The Principles of Psychology* (1855), Spencer reinscribed the patriarchal traditions defining wives and children as property and asserted the scientific validity of these traditions by asserting their physiological basis. Eliot uses the terms Spencer employed in *The Principles of Psychology* when she describes Godfrey's "patient worship" (81, ch. 3) of Nancy Lammeter. In describing Godfrey's fantasy of a future domestic "paradise" with Nancy, however, Eliot uses the same rhetoric she developed to expose the fatuous and self-involved daydreams of Adam Bede and Arthur Donnithorne, language that anticipates Lydgate's "spots of commonness." Godfrey imagines Nancy as a domestic idol who would make it "easy, when she was always near, to shake off those habits that were no pleasure, but only a feverish way of annulling vacancy" (80–81, ch. 3).

Having shed the male persona of *Adam Bede*, however, Eliot is freer in this text to criticize the psychology of male sexuality. She analyzes Godfrey's feelings for Nancy in the terms Spencer elaborated in *The Principles of Psychology* (1855). In this text, he anatomizes the psychology of romantic love by describing the "highly complex impressions produced by personal beauty," "affection," the "love of approbation," the gratification of "self-esteem," and finally the "pleasure of possession" whereby lovers claim each other as a "species of property" (601–2). By showing how Godfrey fails to keep "fast-hold on the strong silken rope by which Nancy would have drawn him safe to the green banks where it was easy to step firmly" and lets "himself be dragged back into the mud and slime" when he becomes "enslaved" by his secret marriage to Molly Cass, Eliot reiterates her criticism of Spencer's views on female beauty and sexual instinct that found expression in *Adam Bede* and *The Mill on the Floss*. Godfrey's private indulgence of his sexual instincts precipitates his fall and places the green paradise he dreamed of out of his reach, as Eliot neatly suggests by the metaphor of the slippery banks. While his feeling for Nancy conforms to Spencer's definition of love in that it expresses both his "love of approbation" and his "self-esteem," Godfrey's sexual instincts override all his other emotions, exposing his worship of Nancy as hypocritical and fundamentally egocentric and rendering his subsequent marriage to her barren.[11]

In *The Principles of Psychology* (1855), Spencer reiterated the equation between fatherhood and ownership which he first expressed in *Social Statics*, by characterizing children as a "species of property."[12] In Silas's first meeting with Godfrey, Eliot reveals how easily Godfrey evades the responsibilities of fatherhood by keeping secret his relation to Molly and Eppie. In describing Godfrey's "strange mixture of feelings," when he recognizes Eppie as his daughter and experiences a "conflict of regret and joy" because "that little heart had no response for the half-jealous yearning in his own," Eliot dramatizes the father's psychological alienation from the birth process and the child's subsequent vulnerability because it can assert no claim on the blood father.

When Godfrey renounces the child, who is to become Silas's best treasure, he gives the old weaver half a guinea, a sign that he estimates the meaning of paternity in economic terms. In this and subsequent meetings between Eppie's natural and adoptive fathers, Eliot dramatizes the basis of her resistance to Spencer's similar impulse to define fatherhood in economic terms. When he leaves Eppie behind, Godfrey rationalizes his abandonment as follows: "As for the child, he would see that it was cared for: he would never forsake it; he would do everything but own it. Perhaps it would be just as happy in life without being owned by its father, seeing that nobody could tell how things would turn out and that—is there any other reason wanted?—well, then, that the father would be much happier without owning the child" (177, ch. 13). By his defiance of the biological laws that make Eppie a part of himself, and by this desecration of the ancient values represented by the hearth which Silas venerates, Godfrey invites his own Nemesis. In this way, Eliot exposes the premises supporting Godfrey's mistaken belief that marriage to Nancy would offer a way back to a domestic paradise where he would find shelter from the inexorable realities of biological law.

Lest we ignore the hollowness of Godfrey's "deliverance" and marriage to Nancy Lammeter, Eliot repeats her emphasis on the "father's duty," when she describes Godfrey's fantasy of himself playing happily with his children on the hearth, with Nancy smiling on. The narrator concludes, ironically, "And that other child, not on the hearth—he would not forget it; he would see that it was well provided for. That was a father's duty" (192, ch. 15). The rest of the story, of course, dramatizes his sixteen years of neglect. Thus, Godfrey's notion of fatherhood exposes the values which perpetuate the emotional impoverishment that he suffered in the patriarchal family at Red House, an impoverishment that Eppie avoids because she is adopted into a household governed by more maternal values.

Eliot shows that before he adopts Eppie, Silas similarly confuses children and money, for he associates the half-finished work in his loom with the promise of "unborn children." In her descriptions of Silas's nights of "revelry," when he "bathes his hands" in the heaps of coins he has saved, Eliot employs associationist psychology to lay bare the process whereby Godfrey and Silas confuse the products of productive and reproductive labor. Invoking her own cultural context as well, by brilliantly parodying the cozy scenes of the overpopulated hearth that appear in so many Victorian novels, Eliot describes Silas as he relaxes after a long day of monotonous labor, like the typical Dickensian paterfamilias beside his bright fireside; but in Eliot's novel, gold magically replaces the children.[13] By emphasizing the metaphors of getting and spending, then, in Silas's response to the profiles on the golden guineas that have spilled out of the "dark leathern mouths" of those heavy skin bags that he keeps hidden in his house and in his fond anticipation "of the guineas that were coming slowly through the coming years" (70, ch. 2), Eliot identifies the male psychology that allows children, and their mothers, to be imagined as possessions.[14]

Silas's unwillingness to "exchange those coins, which had become his familiars, for other coins with unknown faces" (68, ch. 2) nonetheless foreshadows the subsequent triumph of affection over materialism, and altruism over self-absorption, which is enacted when Eppie's natural and adoptive fathers meet. When Silas first discovers that a real child has mysteriously replaced the gold on his hearth, he reacts with a wonder and pity that stirs his deepest memories about his mother and sister in the time before he became a member of the brotherhood at Lantern Yard. When he then sees Eppie, he ponders, "Could this be his little sister come back to him in a dream?" (167, ch. 12), and feels the "old quiverings of tenderness" in "fibres that had never been moved in Raveloe," tremors which revive "old impressions of awe at the presentment of some Power presiding over his life" (168, ch. 12).

Once he has awakened to Eppie's material reality, Silas retraces the inward movement of his own "psychic atavism" by following Eppie's trail backward to the "human body, with the head sunk low in the furze, and half-covered with the shaken snow," showing the subconscious power that the maternal Mystery still exerts as a power shaping his life (Shuttleworth 90–91). In depicting the fatal cost by which this child is brought into Silas's world, Eliot exposes the false logic that allows children to be objectified, a logic that Spencer reinscribes in his economic analysis of the father's relation to his child.[15]

Eppie's advent not only causes Silas to reexperience this "influx of memories" about his lost mother and sister, which prompts him to give Eppie his sister's name, it also heals his separation from the natural world that once gave him such delight. So Silas "began to look for the once familiar herbs again; and as the leaves, with their unchanged outline and markings, lay on his palm, there was a sense of crowding remembrances" (185, ch. 14). By sharing Eppie's joy and by responding instinctively to her "endless claims and ever growing desires", Silas is thus led out of the "cold narrow prison" of the self, gradually to acquire "full consciousness" (185, ch. 14). Silas does not return to the Calvinistic values of his youth, but instead, as he rediscovers his lost joy in the "lap" of his Immortal Mother Earth, he reidentifies himself with the more deeply buried values of the maternal. Thus, Eliot anticipates Freud in demonstrating the psychological validity of the metaphor whereby mothers are associated with the "known" and with "nature's Lap," while fathers are linked to the "unknown" abstractions of paternal love (63, ch. 2).

Eppie embodies the metaphor Eliot used earlier to describe Silas's response to Raveloe's rural landscape, for she literally becomes the "little child" who "knows nothing about paternal love but only one face and one lap towards which it stretches its arms for refuge and nurture" (63, ch. 2). Tracing the pattern of Eppie's psychological development, Eliot repeats her insistence on the psychological primacy of the mother which is dramatized when Eppie's cries for "Mammy" lead Silas literally back to her dead mother and prompt him to assume both the mother's and the father's part in adopting and caring for Eppie. As a young woman growing into maturity in a family that allows her an easier access to the "wild zone," Eppie hardly ever imagines her biological or metaphysical father. The idea of the father remained an "unknown" mystery to her, Eliot explains, and "for a long while it did not even occur to her that she must have had a father" (206, ch. 16). Though Eppie recognizes for the first time that her mother must have had a husband when Silas shows her the wedding ring, still "she thought hardly at all about the father of whom it was a symbol" (206, ch. 16). The questions that "most often pressed on Eppie's mind" remain those about "who her mother was and how she came to die in that forlornness" (206, ch. 16).

This emphasis on the mother's role in the psychological growth of both Silas and Eppie and the literalization of the maternal metaphors in the foregoing episodes point out a curious paradox in *Silas Marner*, for, on the one hand, Eliot insists on the psychological primacy of the mother, while, on the other, she demonstrates how Eppie thrives in being raised apart from her biological mother and father. Moreover, despite Eliot's emphasis on the power and value of the mother in teaching the child and bestowing on it a sense of religious awe, she shows the growth of maternal tenderness in the most unlikely person of old Master Marner, while presenting Eppie's biological mother as a woman who is almost entirely devoid of maternal altruism.

Eliot presents the story of Molly's marriage and motherhood enigmatically; it is inexplicably shadowed by darkness.[16] Eliot withholds from us exactly what has prompted Molly to rebel against the "degradation" of her lot on this particular New Year's Eve and tells us nothing about how her "barmaid's paradise of pink ribbons and gentleman's jokes" is destroyed or how the child who becomes Silas's salvation is conceived and born. Though Eliot insists on Molly's unrooted alienation from work, family, community, and nature—which mirrors Silas's similar condition before Eppie's advent—Molly remains unredeemed. In comparing Molly and Silas, then, Eliot exposes Spencer's confusion of the biological and moral dimensions of motherhood; for by showing that Molly is an inadequate mother while Silas is a good one, Eliot reveals the gap between sex and gender roles.

Molly Cass has only the most fleeting sense of maternal responsibility, in contrast to Silas's tender, possessive affection. This contrast expresses Eliot's ongoing feminist efforts to demystify "maternal instinct" by not-

ing, as in *Adam Bede*, the differences between the capacity for reproduction and the psychological disposition for maternity. But in this
novel, she questions a functional analysis of motherhood itself by dramatizing Silas's surprising development of maternal capacities. Eppie's
mother is deprived of the comfort that Hetty Sorrel finds in her contact
with Dinah Morris, for Molly Cass recognizes "but one comforter," Eliot
writes melodramatically, "the demon Opium" which lies "in her bosom"
(164, ch. 12). In her extremity, a physical compulsion prompts Molly to
ignore the "mother's love" which "pleaded for painful consciousness
rather than oblivion—pleaded to be left in aching weariness, rather than
to have the encircling arms benumbed so that they could not feel
the dear burden" (164, ch. 12). Alone and in pain, Molly is unvisited
by those "white-winged delicate messengers," which save other "fallen
women" like Hetty or Mrs. Gaskell's Ruth, and she takes the opium,
choosing oblivion and finding an "easy pillow" against the furze bush
and a fatal "bed of snow" outside Silas's cottage. Maternal "tenderness"
(164, ch. 12) or "mother's love"—and Eliot is careful to use these terms
rather than "instinct"—remains, in this presentation, a force less strong
than this mother's basic egoistic desire for release from pain.

By sending Molly Cass and her daughter back to the "wild zone," Eliot
returns to the theme she explored in *Adam Bede*: that maternal altruism
is a moral capacity which must be cultivated; that it is not biologically
inherent in all mothers, as Spencer and most of Eliot's contemporaries
assumed. While the daughter's story in *Silas Marner* preempts the more
obscure mystery in the mother's heart—that mystery which lies hidden
"under" the laws and myths of individual and collective development—
Eliot later brings her understanding of evolutionary theory to bear on
the mystery of maternal love in *Romola*, the novel that she was working on
when the inspiration for *Silas Marner* cut across her plans.

In *Silas Marner*, Eliot focuses attention on the male psychology of love
and attachment by contrasting Silas's regeneration through the recovery
of the maternal in himself with the repression of parental feelings that
prevents Godfrey's similar redemption and integration. Though he feels
some guilt in denying his tie to both Molly Cass and his daughter,
Godfrey does not confess the secret of his past marriage and his relation
to Eppie until after he witnesses a clear showing of the power of Nemesis
in his life. When the waters at the Stone-pits recede, they expose Dunstan's skeleton and Silas's gold, and suggest, by their juxtaposition, the
killing power of the obsession with money that destroys brotherly love.
Godfrey is not himself immune from this obsession, for when he arrives
at Silas's cottage sixteen years after he renounced his daughter, he approaches the disclosure of his paternity awkwardly, though not coinci-

dentally, by talking about the recovery of Silas's gold and hinting that it might not be sufficient to meet his needs in old age.

In the exchange between Godfrey and Silas, which enunciates two differing views of fatherhood, Eliot demonstrates how Godfrey's assumptions based on the "natural" law of biological paternity are defeated by Silas's appeals to a "moral" law that transcends it. Godfrey's rhetoric shows that he still views Eppie as a possession that could be exchanged for money. He begins with an economic argument that seems to him to be the most obvious and persuasive one to convince Silas to surrender Eppie: he asks if Silas wouldn't "like to see her taken care of by those who can leave her well off and make a lady of her" and promises him "every reward" as a compensation (228–29, ch. 19). Godfrey's embarrassed assertion of his "preeminent" and "natural claim" on Eppie shows that his first impulse is to use the economic metaphors which associate fatherhood with possession, metaphors Spencer unself-consciously employs in his analysis of erotic and parental love in *The Principles of Psychology*.

When Godfrey fails to claim Eppie by this "natural" right of the father, he resorts to an assertion of his patriarchal authority as chief lawgiver in Raveloe. Reminding Silas of his daughter's permanent minority under the law, Godfrey again addresses himself to Silas: "You ought to remember your own life's uncertain, and she's at an age now when her lot may soon be fixed in a way different from what it would be in her father's home; she may marry some low working man, and then, whatever I might do, I couldn't make her well off" (232, ch. 19). Godfrey's very bluntness discloses the stark reality of the social compact between fathers and daughters in Eppie's world—and in Eliot's own—where married women were still denied the right to claim their own wages or to own property.[17] In resorting to such economic and legal arguments, Godfrey reveals an understanding of kinship that attends to the letter rather than the spirit of the law, a perspective that is evident in Spencer's brief discussion of marriage and fatherhood in *The Principles of Psychology*.

Eliot counters this traditional view of fatherhood by asserting an alternative interpretation, and investing not only Silas but Eppie with some of the epic authority she gave to Maggie Tulliver in *The Mill on the Floss*. Though Silas appeals to a superior Divine Authority in resisting Godfrey's offers, he ultimately refuses to speak for Eppie. Silas identifies a moral authority that supersedes natural and civil law in Eppie's case: "God gave her to me because you turned your back upon her, and he looks upon her as mine; you've no right to her! When a man turns a blessing from his door, it falls to them as take it in" (231, ch. 19). In spite of his desperate desire to "keep her," though, Silas submits himself finally to Eppie's will, saying, "Eppie, my child speak. I won't stand in your way" (229, ch. 19), and later reminds Godfrey that he will not bargain with him for the child he loves (232, ch. 19). In this way, Silas shows that he has freed himself from the delusion that originally prompted him to confuse the foundling on his hearth with his lost gold; Godfrey, in contrast, remains imprisoned by similar economic metaphors until he is forced to see beyond them when his daughter repudiates his claims.

Eliot is quite explicit about Eppie's refusal to surrender herself to the traditional compact which allows the father to transform the daughter into a "treasure" to be exchanged in marriage.[18] Eppie feels her heart swell in sympathy at Silas's sudden understanding of Godfrey's intention to separate him from the child he has loved with "perfect love" (205, ch. 16), but her choice to stand loyally by him is not a blind act of filial obedience but rather an expression of her capacity to "judge" and speak for herself. When Godfrey describes all the fine things he would give her in exchange if she would come to live at Red House, Eppie sees his offer as a bribe and feels a "repulsion toward the offered lot and the newly revealed father" (232, ch. 19). She says, "It'd be poor work for me to put on things, and ride in a gig, and sit in a place at church, as 'ud make them as I'm fond of think me unfitting company for 'em" (234, ch. 19).

In emphasizing those capacities for language and love that separate humans from other animals, Eliot thus registers her disagreement with Spencer, who focused primarily on mankind's economic and productive capacities. Silas counters Godfrey's appeal, by saying: "Your coming now and saying 'I'm her father' doesn't alter the feeling inside us. It's me she's been calling her father ever since she could say the word" (232, ch. 19). Eppie's feelings likewise "vibrate" to "every word" Silas speaks, and so she rejects Godfrey's offer and acts instead on her profound sympathy for the man who has "loved her from the first," and has played the part of both mother and father in her life. Thus, Eppie transcends the word of law as it is patriarchally defined and asserts instead her own right to the power of naming, when she says, "I can't feel as I've got any father but one" (234, ch. 19). Her words, and later her appropriation of her right to name her own desire to marry Aaron Winthrop, make Godfrey realize, finally, that "there's debts we can't pay like money debts" (236, ch. 20).

In thus challenging the very basis of the religious and civil laws that codify the "Unknown" in both Lantern Yard and Raveloe, Eliot indicates one final dimension of her criticism of Spencer's assumption that inward psychological processes move in harmony with outward social progress. In the final chapter of the first part of *First Principles*, Spencer misquotes a famous passage from *The Winter's Tale* in order to suggest that "Unknown" mystery that lies outside the reach of evolutionary science; but he ends instead by asserting the authority of the trained scientist who confines his study to the proper parameters of scientific investigation:

> While he is a descendant of that past, he is a parent of the future; and his thoughts are children born to him, which he may not carelessly let die. Like every other man he may properly consider himself as one of the myriad agencies through whom works the Unknown Cause, and when the Unknown Cause produces in him a certain belief, he is thereby authorized to profess and act out that belief. For to render in their highest sense the words of the poet:
>
> > . . . Nature is made better by no mean,
> > But nature makes that mean: over that art
> > Which you say adds to nature, is an art
> > That nature makes. (123)[19]

For Eliot, Spencer's effort here to claim a scientific authority for his brainchildren disclosed his characteristic—and usually unself-conscious—habit of reinscribing traditional patriarchal prejudices into his evolutionary theory, in the name of science.

Eliot also alludes to *The Winter's Tale* in *Silas Marner*, but her references emphasize her faith in the superior force of a "moral" law which honors both feeling and reason, a law which is limited by an individual's physical capacity and social environment but which provides, nonetheless, the only authentic apprehension of adequate knowledge, informed moral choice, and responsible action. Commenting on Godfrey's temporizing when his father orders him to marry Nancy, Eliot writes, "Favorable chance is the god of all men who follow their own devices instead of obeying a law they believe in" (126, ch. 9). Unlike Silas, who submits humbly to the mysterious movement of the "Unseen Power" he venerates, Godfrey willfully ignores the moral law against "prevarication and deceit" that he "believes in," a belief that is revealed by his reluctance to enter into his secret marriage with Molly in the first place and by his acknowledgment, as he stands outside in the snow on the night Molly dies, that he ought to "own" his wife and child. Unlike Silas, who only later is able to recognize the mysterious process that has brought him the child in place of his gold, Godfrey deliberately resists the moral law he, in fact, recognizes, which decrees that the "seed brings forth a crop after its kind" (127, ch. 9).

Eliot's effort in *Silas Marner* to define a superior moral law which works in concert with the biological, psychological, and social laws identified by Spencer causes some formal inconsistencies in her novel. From Silas' point of view, the novel is a comedy, but from either the mother's or the daughter's perspective, the novel remains stubbornly tragic, and, in this way, it anticipates all of Eliot's later novels.[20] Eppie and Nancy Lammeter

Cass suffer innocently as a consequence of Godfrey's and Molly's secret sin, and it is this suffering that women experience because of their biological and social roles that Eliot later identifies—in dramatic contrast to Spencer—as the source of the moral "art which does mend nature" (*GEL* 4:364). By examining Eliot's use of allusions to *The Winter's Tale*, we can see the tragedy that Eliot finds hidden "under" evolutionary law.

Allusions to *The Winter's Tale* cluster around Eppie's sudden decision to plant a garden, described after the sixteen-year interval in the narrative. Eliot uses the same *typos* of the garden that Shakespeare employs in *The Winter's Tale* (4.4) to reveal the heroine's innocent apprehension of her own sexual power.[21] Eppie, like Perdita, signals her desire to move into the wild zone, where love and sexual delight are experienced outside the patriarchy's controlling structures, when she uses the symbolic language of flowers to express her sexuality. But unlike Perdita, Eppie awakens, at the same time, to the threat of mortality that hangs over female sexuality, a threat amplified in the evolutionary struggle to survive, when she indicates her wish to honor the mother who died in bringing her to Silas's hearth by transplanting to her garden the furze bush that sheltered Molly on the last night of her life.

For both Perdita and Eppie, talking about the garden allows them to broach the subject of marriage with their beloveds, but while Perdita's conversation reveals her unwillingness to mix her aristocratic blood with that of the commoners who have nurtured her, Eppie's words show just the opposite.[22] Indeed, Eliot uses this dialogue about the new flowers to be planted in the garden to emphasize the sexual and material profligacy of the patriarchal family at Red House, for Aaron, who is a gardener there, says to Eppie, "I can bring you slips of anything; I'm forced to cut no end of 'em . . . and throw 'em away mostly" (198, ch. 16).

In honoring her promise to marry Aaron even after she learns of her biological parentage and social status in Raveloe, as defined by the law of the father, Eppie dramatizes Eliot's rejection of the similarly patriarchal values that underlie Shakespeare's pastoral. While Perdita, apparently without a word, leaves behind the shepherd who has raised her to maturity, acting out Shakespeare's belief in the superior power of nature over nurture, Eppie acts out Eliot's opposite conviction of the preeminence of nurture over nature. Because Eppie has become aware of her legal father's profligacy, she dislikes him, and her refusal to join his family becomes part of his "punishment."

Both Eppie and Nancy Lammeter Cass are, nonetheless, forced to give up "something," as Nancy says, and the relationship between Eppie and her prospective stepmother reveals how Eliot uses allusions to *The Winter's Tale* to emphasize another aspect of the hidden tragedy of mothers and daughters. While Shakespeare endows Hermione with all the powers of "great creating Nature" and in the end allows her magically to reunite the lost mother and daughter with the father, Eliot refuses to employ any similar art to transform the painful realities of Godfrey's and Molly's story. Eppie loses her mother forever, just as Nancy loses both her infant child and the stepdaughter whose love, she feels, would have been a "treasure to her" (233, ch. 19).

Not knowing that Eppie is Godfrey's child, Nancy has resisted his wish to adopt her after their own infant dies. Nancy believes that adoption expresses a willful desire to "try to choose your lot in spite of Providence," when children have been denied for "some high purpose." While Eliot notes that Nancy's belief is based on her inadequate understanding of the Unknown, she insists that her "difficult resistance" to her husband's wishes reveals her honest "clinging to the right"; for Nancy, in contrast to her husband, acts on the basis of a "moral" law that she "believes in." Her imperfect understanding of moral law, like Maggie Tulliver's, is a consequence of her experiences as a motherless daughter in a society that restricts her access to full knowledge:

> It might seem singular that Nancy—with her religious theory pieced together out of narrow social traditions, fragments of church doctrine imperfectly understood, and girlish reasoning on her small experience—should have arrived by herself at a way of thinking so nearly akin to that of many devout people whose beliefs are held in the shape of a system quite remote from her knowledge: singular, if we did not know that human beliefs, like all other natural growths, elude the barriers of system. (224, ch. 17)

Though Godfrey once worshiped her as an idol during their courtship, Nancy cannot perform Hermione's redemptive metamorphosis that finally unites father with lost mother and daughter in Shakespeare's pastoral. In *Silas Marner*, biological realism overturns pastoral fantasy.

In providing a happy ending, despite this darkness, for Silas, Eppie, Aaron, and Dolly, if not for the two mothers who are lost to Eppie, Eliot assumes Athena's part, but in reversing the Apollonian judgment in the *Oresteia* which defined the child by law as the offspring of the father alone and banished the Eumenides from the Earth, she also indicates her rejection of the traditional hierarchical and patriarchal values that found a new expression in the evolutionary laws Spencer outlined in *First Principles*. So Eppie succeeds in finding a family by following her natural leadings, first to Silas's warm hearth, then to Dolly, and finally to Aaron, and this is why the Nemesis seems so "mild" in this novel (*GEL* 3:382).

In *Silas Marner*, Eliot counters logic like Spencer's which associates fatherhood with ownership by noting that though the father is excluded from the primary psychological bond that unites the mother and child, he can—and should—share the joy of nurturing the child; for only so can he overcome his fundamental alienation from the birth process and help sustain the "fountain of wholesome love and fear" that exists in a household where the hearth is honored and where human potentiality—in both men and women—is nourished to the fullest. Silas, then, seems justly rewarded for his very special reverence for those veiled goddesses who preside over the hearth. In refusing to change the "old brick hearth" where he found the child he loved, Silas acts out Eliot's belief that "the gods of the hearth exist for us still: and let all new faith be tolerant of that fetichism, lest it bruise its own roots" (200, ch. 16). The problems Eliot seems to resolve so traditionally in the marriage that marks the end of *Silas Marner* are more than the formal ones suggested by the childless family at Red House and by the absence of Dolly's husband in the final scene. In her subsequent novels, Eliot goes on to depict the tragedies of mothers and daughters more fully. Never again will she simplify her realistic vision or soften the power of Nemesis in quite the same way.

6

Feminism, History, and Cultural Determinism: *Romola* and *The Principles of Biology* I

WHILE Eliot joined Spencer, as *Silas Marner* shows, in looking forward to a time when "the growing belief" in the "Universality of Law" would prevail (Spencer, *First* 112), she was not nearly so optimistic as he about the ease with which "cultured minds" could recognize and interpret the operation of scientific laws. By the time she began to write *Romola* in January of 1862, Darwin's authority in defining the "natural laws" governing all biological life was widely recognized. While her private insight into Herbert Spencer's personality and psychology gave her particular advantages in discerning and resisting the most sexist implications of his evolutionary analysis of human potential, she could not claim the same authority, either as a woman writer or as a particular woman, in her effort to counter Darwin's reiteration in *The Origin of Species* (1859) of many of Spencer's most sexist premises.

In November of 1862, Spencer turned his attention to elaborating the evolutionary laws of biology in his two volume *Principles of Biology* (1864–1867).[1] In this work, Spencer does not often address himself to the problem of sexual differentiation in human beings, but in his efforts to extend his analysis of plant and animal reproduction to include human sexuality, we can see how the "muddled zone" widens in his thinking about sex and gender (Foucault 54). Before Spencer began this work, his ideas about womanly beauty and female inferiority were confined to a realm of discourse separate from his "synthetic principles," since they appeared in his essays primarily about education and in a few comments about love in *The Principles of Psychology* (1855), which was written, of course, before he fully realized the implications of evolutionary theory for his analysis of gender. Similarly, though in *First Principles* Spencer frequently refers to the "antagonism" between reproduction and individuation, he had not as yet identified any mechanism to explain why women remained especially disadvantaged by evolution or why inheritance did not distribute these disabilities to men and women equally.

Both volumes of Spencer's *Principles of Biology* bear the signs of his anxiety of influence in relation to Darwin, on the one hand, and Eliot, on the other. In the final chapters of the first volume of *Principles of Biology*, first published in numbers beginning in January 1863 and reissued in volume form in October of 1864, Spencer acknowledged Darwin's contributions to evolutionary theory and attempted to define the most significant differences between their theories. He writes:

> This survival of the fittest, which I have here sought to express in mechanical terms, is that which Mr. Darwin has called 'natural selection, or the preservation of favoured races in the struggle for life.' That there is going on a process of this kind throughout the organic world, Mr. Darwin's work has shown to the satisfaction of nearly all naturalists. . . . Doubtless many who have looked at Nature with philosophic eyes, have observed that death of the worst and multiplication of the best, must result in the maintenance of a constitution in harmony with surrounding circumstances. That the average vigour of any race would be diminished, did the diseased and feeble habitually survive and propagate; and that the destruction of such, through failure to fulfill some of the conditions of life, leaves behind those which are able to fulfill the conditions of life, are almost self-evident truths. (*Biology* 1:449)

In this passage, Spencer distinguishes his position from Darwin's by identifying three areas of disagreement, seeing his analysis, in contrast to Darwin's, as characterized by a greater emphasis on the inheritability of acquired traits, on the adjustment of inward to outward "relations," and on the "moving equilibrium" that assured progressive development in both the individual and in human society (1:457). Eliot had disputed these arguments in *The Mill on the Floss* and *Silas Marner*, but the success of his essays on education seemed to relieve Spencer of many of his earlier inhibitions. Morever, because Darwin, in the *Origin of Species*, reiterated Spencer's analysis of the physiological division of labor, the dominance of the male in natural selection, and the importance of sexual selection in human evolution, Spencer felt that the scientific credibility of these hypotheses had been confirmed. Thus, in *The Principles of Biology*, Spencer amplified many of the ideas about women's inferiority that had appeared in his essays on education and claimed a far greater authority for them in the new arguments he constructed about the natural—by which he meant biological—hierarchies of gender and race.

Nonetheless, the biological evidence he marshalled in *The Principles of Biology* in some ways proved recalcitrant. In his discussion of sexual reproduction in the first volume of this work, Spencer was forced to revise his earlier theory that sexual differentiation in human beings was guaranteed from conception because sperm contained "co-ordinating matter" while ova contained "matter to be co-ordinated" ("Theory of Population" 490). By July 1863, he acknowledged that "the union of sperm-cell and germ-cell" simply permitted "mixing the slightly different physiological units of slightly different individuals" (*Biology* 1:234). In order to rationalize his assumption that the female was less developed than the male, Spencer was now forced to rely, instead, upon his newly formulated theories about heredity, the physiological division of labor, and the "moving equilibrium" that he saw as characterizing evolutionary development.

In *The Principles of Biology*, then, Spencer located a biologically permanent basis for sex differences in his theories about the sexual "division of labor" which allowed him to assert, henceforth, that women were physically and intellectually inferior to men. In arguing that there was a biological "division of labor" in human reproduction, Spencer unself-consciously relied upon analogies that reinscribed existing social relations. In this way, he smuggled sexism and racism into his evolutionary analysis of biology in general and of human development and social evolution in particular. Describing the evolutionary "advance from vital activity in its lowest forms to vital activity in its highest forms," he writes:

> And probably the general reader cannot in any other way obtain so clear a conception of functional development in organisms as he can by tracing out functional development in societies; noting how first there comes a distinction between the governing class and the governed; how, while in the governing class there slowly grow up such differences of duty as the civil, military, and ecclesiastical, there arise in the governed class fundamentally industrial differences like those between the agriculturists and artizans; and how there is a continual multiplication of such specialized occupations, and specialized shares of each occupation. (*Biology* 1:160)

Spencer subsequently elaborated on his earlier ideas about homogeneity and heterogeneity by extending this metaphor in order to illustrate "the increasing physiological co-operation that accompanies increasing physiological division of labour" (*Biology* 1:163).[2]

The social functions Spencer identified as the basis for this division of labor in society and in the human body show the unacknowledged impact of Comte's *Positivist Philosophy*[3] on his thinking:

> Just as we see in an advanced community the magisterial, the clerical, the medical, the legal, the manufacturing, and the commercial activities have grown distinct, they have yet their agencies mingled together in every locality; so in a developed organism, we see that while the general functions of circulation, secretion, absorption, excretion, contraction, excitation, &c., have become differentiated, yet through the ramifications of the systems apportioned to them, they are closely combined with each other in every organ. (*Biology* 1:164)

By asserting that form followed function—that is, that "inward relations" were forced to conform to "outward relations"—Spencer would later come to the conclusion, in *The Study of Sociology* (1873) and *The Principles of Sociology* (1873–1896), that woman's biological function thus ensured her "lower development."

In *The Principles of Biology*, Spencer laid the foundation for his argument about woman's biological inferiority by positing that a "moving equilibrium" characterized the development of various species, a principle which superseded his earlier "theory of rhythm" which he relied upon to describe individual development in *First Principles*. In *The Principles of Biology*, Spencer organized his survey of plants and animals in such a way as to demonstrate the logic summarized in his claim that "since evolution describes the passage from a structureless to a structured state . . . it follows that function is from beginning to end the determining cause of structure" (*Biology* 1:167). Spencer then applied this premise about structure to explain the natural "equilibrium" of organisms and the fixed capacity for energy within them. In this way, he was able to explain how the sexual differences between men and women illustrated the "antagonism" between individuation and reproduction, whereby women in each generation sacrificed more to reproduction than men did. Repeating verbatim in *The Principles of Biology* several passages from "Physical Training," Spencer argued that when women achieved reproductive maturity, their intellectual development was biologically arrested, and because the amount of energy in each organism was fixed, females were thus prevented from achieving the same physical and intellectual capacities as males (*Biology* 2:479). Moreover, females could not escape this disadvantage since it was a biological consequence of their reproductive function. These principles formed the cornerstone of Spencer's definition of women's role in what he called "super-organic" evolution, that is, the development of human society and its institutions which became the focus of his attention for the rest of his career.

Like Spencer, Eliot also suffered extreme anxiety of influence during these years, and, of all her novels, *Romola*, posed the greatest creative and metaphysical difficulties for her. *Romola*, which was first published serially in *Cornhill Magazine* beginning in July 1862, differs from all of Eliot's other novels because it represents the life of one woman in a time far beyond the reach of living memory. It is shaped by her effort to lend history an authority "coextensive with that of science," in order to counter Spencer's increasing biological determinism and to valorize the role of the maternal principle in what she called the "moral evolution" of human society.[4]

The basis of Eliot's resistance to Spencer's developing biological analysis of human sexuality and gender differences that finds expression in *The Principles of Biology* is suggested by a letter she wrote to John Morley in 1867. While we have already seen how Eliot's allusion in *Silas Manner* to *"an art which does mend nature"* repeats Spencer's allusion to *The Win-*

ter's Tale in his discussion of the "unknowable" in *First Principles*, it is useful to consider it now in the larger context of Eliot's debate with Spencer between 1862 and 1867, when he was writing the numbers for *The Principles of Biology*. In this letter Eliot explains:

> I would certainly not oppose any plan which held out any reasonable promise of tending to establish as far as possible an equivalence of advantages for two sexes, as to education and the possibilities of free development. I fear you have misunderstood something I said the other evening about nature. I meant to urge the "intention of Nature" argument, which is to me a pitiable fallacy, I mean that as a fact of mere zoological evolution, woman seems to have the worse share in existence. But for that very reason, I would the more contend that in the moral evolution we have "*an art which does mend nature.*" It is the function of love in the largest sense to mitigate the harshness of all fatalities, and in the thorough recognition of that worse share, I think there is a basis for a sublimer recognition in women and a more regenerating tenderness in man. (*GEL* 4:364)

In her comments about the "pitiable fallacy" of the "'intention of Nature'" argument, Eliot registers her skepticism about Spencer's developing analysis of human potentiality as determined by biological function alone. *Romola* thus demonstrates Eliot's efforts to counter Spencer's biological functionalism by discriminating more precisely between the forces of what she called "zoological" and "moral" evolution. *Romola* also reveals her desire to construct an intellectually responsible definition of the "moral evolution" of human society, one which recognized how historical forces and cultural ideologies had directed the interpretation of gender differences in the past and had consequently determined prevailing ideas about gender that found expression in the social arrangements of Eliot's own time.

While she was involved in the painstaking research for and writing of *Romola*, Eliot admitted that she felt particularly impatient with Spencer. She writes to Sara Hennell: "I, as usual, had been too ready to find fault with the excellent champion of heterogeneity. I get a little impatient sometimes with his contentment in abstractions, and allow myself to look at the seamy side of an old friend's mind more than is right or kind" (*GEL* 4:66). Eliot's criticism of Spencer's "contentment in abstractions" highlights a profound difference between them as to the place of history in evolutionary theories about human progress, a difference which is subsequently inscribed in Eliot's design and approach to history in *Romola* as a whole.[5]

During these years, Spencer disputed the authority of history in social analysis, an attitude he defends perhaps most succinctly in his *Autobiography*, in which he describes a visit to Pompeii in 1868. Comparing the validity of history to that of sociology, Spencer writes: "Nothing I saw in Italy impressed me so much as this dead town. I take but little interest in what are called histories, but am interested only in sociology, which stands related to these so-called histories much as a vast building stands related to the heaps of stone and brick around it" (2:215). Interested in houses rather than homes, Spencer argued that the "primitive types of habitations" at Pompeii formed a sort of missing link in the evolution of what he calls that "abstraction 'society' " that made these architectural correspondences appear to him to be "a good example of super-organic evolution" (2:216). Though Spencer claimed that his historical research for *The Principles of Sociology* in the 1870s gave him a greater readiness to recognize the "relative goodness of forms which have passed away," his comments about history and historians continue to reveal a thinly disguised contempt and a jealous insistence on the superiority of sociological analysis.

In 1860, when Eliot wandered through this same "silent city of the past" in Pompeii, she marveled over the "sight of utensils and eatables and ornaments and half-washed linens" (*GEL* 3:293). Though she, like Spencer, found much evidence of historical continuity in these and "hundreds of other traces so startlingly like our own" (*GEL* 3:293), her tour of Pompeii, in contrast to his, inspired her with awe and prompted her to wonder over these traces of the past that had been so remarkably preserved. The "Proem" of *Romola* and the novel as a whole, which displays Eliot's detailed historical research on the Italian Renaissance, thus indicates why she turned to history as a basis for resisting Spencer's evolutionary analysis of human development.

In *Romola*, then, Eliot attempted to locate a "wild zone" in the history of Western culture that would allow her to illustrate the force of the "maternal principle" by representing her heroine's life and acts of heroism. By selecting Florence in the late fifteenth-century as her setting, Eliot describes a period in Renaissance history when the "maternal emotions" were a more visible and powerful force defining both private and public life. Similarly, by focusing on the period of political crisis when the Medicis were temporarily overthrown by Savonarola, she represents historical events that raise profound questions about Spencer's theory of the dominance of "outward" over "inward" forces. *Romola* thus reveals the power of moral resistance completely ignored by Spencer in his theory of the "moving equilibrium" that characterizes human development. By exploring how and why men and women, living in this city devoted to the "Unseen Madonna," responded to Savonarola's moral appeals, Eliot identifies several components of the resistance that Savonarola authorized by reference to sacred "maternal" emotions, as they manifested themselves in this crisis in the government of the Catholic church and in the nation state.

Ironically, though, in researching and writing *Romola*, Eliot was at the same time forced to recognize women's invisibility in the written historical record. Eliot's decision to represent the life of a young woman in Florence in 1492 created almost insurmountable obstacles in her effort to delineate her heroine with the historically accurate particularity demanded by her realistic aesthetics. Eliot articulates the difficulties she faced in reconstructing a woman's life history in one letter to her illustrator, Frederic Leighton. After asking him to notice if the women in Ghirlandajo's frescoes wear that "plain piece of opaque drapery over the head that haunts my memory," she comments on the absence of historical records about women:

> We have in Varchi a sufficiently fit and clear description of the ordinary male costume of dignified Florentines in my period; but, for the corresponding feminine costume the best authority I have seen is the very incomplete one of a certain Genevra's trousseau in the Ricori of the Rinuccini family of rather an earlier period. . . . Approximate truth is the only truth available, but at least one must strive for that and not wander off into arbitrary falsehood. (*GEL* 4:43)

The frustration Eliot experienced in trying to recapture the "approximate truth" about the lives of women otherwise lost to history informs *Romola* in fundamental ways, but her awareness of these gaps in the historical record hampered her efforts to define a historical determinism which could effectively counter the biological functionalism that became increasingly more prominent in Spencer's *Principles of Biology* and subsequent works.

In imagining Romola's contributions to human development, Eliot drew on the work of Harriet Martineau and August Comte, who influenced many Victorian feminists' analyses of women's social and moral role in private and public life.[6] However, in locating the "likeness in human building . . . broader and deeper than all possible change" in women's domestic and religious lives (*Romola*, "Proem" 44), Eliot risked seeming to endorse the essentialist analysis of gender put forward by Spencer and other conservatives.

Romola is, in many respects, Eliot's most feminist hero, and in describing her efforts to resolve the conflicting demands of love and duty, submission and rebellion, that she confronted in the family and the church, Eliot reveals her ongoing support for the educational and legal reforms proposed by many Victorian feminists. Mrs. Peter Taylor, Bessie Parkes, Emily Faithfull, and other Victorian feminists echoed Comte in stressing woman's essential moral role in family life.[7] Though they promoted the rights of unmarried women by arguing that "redundant" women needed an alternative outlet for their energies outside the family, they were anxious to avoid alienating or discrediting the vast majority of Victorian women who chose to marry and raise a family rather than pursue a professional career. J. A. and Olive Banks describe how Victorian and modern feminists differ in their view of domestic life: "Time and time again, these early feminists stressed that they did not want to remove women from the sphere of the home. This was the view of Emily Faithfull and of Bessie Parkes, who argued that the 'married household is the first constituent element in national life' and that the immense majority of women are and ought to be, employed in the 'noble duties which go to make up the Christian household'" (48–49). Because prominent English intellectual feminists, especially if they were also socialists or Catholics, often reiterated Comte's analysis of woman's moral role in the family and the church, Eliot's similar efforts to recognize women's moral contributions to the development of Western culture cannot be seen as evidence of her "anti-feminist" sympathies.[8] In fact, Eliot differed not only from Spencer—who is notorious for his refusal to acknowledge his debts to Comte—but also from George Henry Lewes (*GEL* 4:333) in her appreciation for Comte's *Système de politique positive ou Traité de sociologie instituant la religion de l'humanité (1851–1854)*, and, by 1866, she had convinced Lewes to reconsider his negative view of it (Haight, *George Eliot* 390).

Nonetheless, Comte's and Spencer's analysis converged in arguments which normalized male dominance in both the private and public realm. For Comte, the only way women could maintain their moral disinterestedness was by voluntarily renouncing participation in the public sphere. Since women could, in Comte's view, "never do more than modify the harshness with which men exercise their authority," they should "renounce" the "political power which some visionaries have claimed for [them] without their consent" (Comte, *General* 224–25). Thus, Comte's analysis of male authority in both the family and the church became an important point of contention between Positivists and feminists in the 1860s, and these tensions are clearly evident in Eliot's treatment of Romola's relation to Bardo, Tito, and Savonarola.[9]

Romola is, first of all, a character explicitly designed to counter Spencer's and other anti-feminists' arguments that women will be "unsexed" by a rigorous classical education (*GEL* 4:467). As her letter to John Morley in 1867 indicates, Eliot remained steadfast in her support of women's right to higher education, which would allow them to enjoy all the "possibilities of free development" (*GEL* 4:364). In taking this position, Eliot sided with the more radical group of educational reformers who felt that women who were intellectually, emotionally, and physically fit for careers in medicine and law should not be excluded simply because of their sex from the classical education required for entry into these professions. Eliot underlined her heroine's role as a champion of women's higher education in 1867 when she sent £50 to Emily Davies for the development of Girton College and signed her contribution "from the Author of *Romola*" (Haight, *George Eliot* 397). Yet, Eliot acknowledges the impact that Spencer's educational theories had made on feminist defenses of women's education by insisting that Romola's splendid classical education has not diminished her "lovable womanliness."

Bardo's education of Romola also suggests one reason why historical analysis proved so threatening to Spencer: that is, it presented a record of the long-standing traditions of misogyny whereby gender roles were constructed and imposed. Eliot saw classical literature as providing an important source of definitions of the maternal principle. The passage that Romola reads from Politian's account of the myth of Teiresias, for example, emphasizes the sanctity and redemptive power of the mother. However, just as Romola is describing how Pallas is moved by her beloved Chariclo to mitigate Teiresias's punishment by endowing him "with prophecy and length of days . . . so that an oracle spoke from his tomb" (94, ch. 5), Bardo interrupts her. By thus describing the censorship practiced by patriarchal authorities, Eliot demonstrates how maternal values have traditionally been suppressed and denigrated.

In reminding Romola that she inherits the intellectual and moral deficiencies of her mother because of her sex, Bardo articulates essentially the same argument about how heredity enforces female inferiority that Spencer began to outline in *The Principles of Biology*. Bardo chastens Romola, saying, "It is true, I have been careful to keep thee aloof from the debasing influence of thy own sex, with their sparrow-like frivolity and enslaving superstition," but, he continues, "I cannot boast that thou art entirely lifted out of that lower category to which Nature assigned thee, nor even that in erudition thou art on a par with the more learned women of this age" (100–1, ch. 5). Bardo echoes Spencer's assessment in "Physical Training" (1859) of women's physical and intellectual potential when he declares that the "zeal and unconquerable patience demanded from those who would tread the unbeaten paths of knowledge are still less reconcilable with the wandering vagrant propensity of the feminine mind than with the feeble powers of the feminine body" (97, ch. 5). In Bardo's view, and in Spencer's, woman's nature always triumphs over nurture.

Eliot shows, though, that it is her father's tutorship, and not biological mechanics, that prevents the "large claims" of Romola's nature from being fully developed; Romola's best energies remain divided between her loving submission to her father and her proud resistance to his misogyny. Romola's education shows the psychological violence women experience in patriarchal societies where the maternal emotions are devalued or repressed. In the world of Florence, filial duty operates to inhibit Romola's resistance, for she is taught to honor her father and silently to accept his disparagement of her mother and herself.[10] Eliot invokes the classical past in this episode in order to disclose some of the "things which have not changed" in the lives of intellectually gifted young women. Thus, while Romola devotes herself to becoming as "learned as Cassandra Fidele," she remains divided against herself; like Maggie Tulliver, she learns to see herself as having a "man's nobility of soul" trapped in a woman's feeble body.

In contrasting Romola's bookish "innocence" about her womanhood with Tessa's loving spontaneity and more integrated femininity, Eliot acknowledges what Romola has sacrificed in order to live more fully in the sophisticated patriarchal culture of Florentine society. Tessa, by contrast, inhabits the literal landscape of the wild zone, a world less structured by phallocentric culture. Tessa's security in her female identity is perhaps best displayed when she and Tito walk outside the walls of Florence, and Eliot identifies something "sweeter than a smile" in her "childish calm." Eliot draws iconographic parallels between Tessa and the Virgin Mary, as she describes her sitting contentedly under the plane tree cradling Tito's head in her lap—like one of Leonardo da Vinci's Madonnas—sitting at the still point of the universe, beyond the city's gates. Throughout the novel, Eliot contrasts Tessa's earthy sense of her own womanhood with Romola's intellectual alienation and cultivated "innocence" about female sexuality and maternal love.

However, Tessa also represents the "zoological" attributes that Spencer recognized as woman's only contribution to human evolution in all times and societies; and the contrast between her and Romola defines more precisely what Eliot imagined as woman's moral contributions to the development of human culture by focusing on her role in the family and the church. *Romola* demonstrates the problems Eliot faced, then, in locating the maternal in the wild zone of Renaissance history when larger economic, political, and cultural forces were transforming the family and the church into increasingly more patriarchal institutions, even in this city devoted to the worship of the Madonna. Tessa possesses a more integrated and more joyful sense of her own nature and sexual identity, because she, in contrast to Romola, recognizes the "natural authority" of the mother and has worshiped at the feet of the Madonna.[11] While Eliot portrays Tessa's childlike faith in the power of the "potent Virgin" in the Church of the Annunciation as an expression of her undivided female consciousness, she nonetheless shows that Tessa has not developed beyond what Comte identified as the earliest fetichistic stage of religious life, when natural forces, including women's fertility, were worshiped as an expression of the divine (*Positivist* 548).

When Tessa enters the urban world of Florence, a world divided by "belief and unbelief," "Epicurean levity and fetichistic dread" (48, "Proem"), her spontaneous sexuality and religious sensibility become a liability, for in this city, power derives from the kind of knowledge that transforms female sexuality into a commodity and male desire into an instrument of domination. Far from sentimentalizing the education Tessa has been given by her mother, Eliot, in contrast to Comte, repeatedly portrays Tessa as a victim of her mother's superstitions and her own naiveté. In dramatizing Tessa's early meetings with Tito, Eliot emphasizes the ways that Tessa is victimized. Tessa is moved by Tito's angelic beauty and associates him with the archangel Michael, but when Tito sees his power over her, he exploits it, literally blocking Tessa's view of the Divine Mother and leading her out of the church.

Tito subsequently deceives Tessa into mistaking a sham ceremony for the marriage rites that, according to Comte, recognized in their original form the sacred place of the maternal in the family. Tito's deception shows how his power over Tessa is enhanced by those patriarchal privileges that allow him to withhold fundamental information from her and to sustain her delusion that they are legally married. Tito decides that it would "spoil Tessa" if he were to reveal his deception or make her "the least particle wiser or more suspicious" (206, ch. 14). Thus, in exercising the same power to control women's access to knowledge that Bardo exerted in his tutorship of Romola, Tito shows how the institution of the family operates in Florentine society to promote male domination and enforce female submission by restricting women's knowledge about sexuality and power.[12]

In comparing Tessa's fertile union with Tito and Romola's childless marriage, Eliot critiques Comte's—and Spencer's—notion of a natural gender-defined division of labor in society, for she shows that the family cannot be seen as a "moral institution" exempt from the legal, social, and economic forces that otherwise shape human culture. By juxtaposing the two young women, Eliot demonstrates that sophisticated Florentines no longer respect those natural powers of female sexuality and fertility that Tessa so innocently worships; the figure of the Madonna has been transformed into a sterile icon. Moreover, Tessa's role as Tito's "second wife" exposes the underside of Florentine life, and by representing it, Eliot reveals the feminist sympathies that would later find expression when she and other middle-class women sided with the prostitutes during the campaign to repeal the Contagious Diseases Acts in the 1870s.[13]

In Tessa's relationship with Tito, Eliot portrays the compelling power of erotic love and the fundamental blood bonds uniting parents and children, even in relations unsanctified by the civil and religious laws that codified marriage in Renaissance Florence. Tessa's artlessness is never completely corrupted by the sophisticated culture that surrounds her, and when she, out of the naturalness of her affection, bears Tito's two children, they help him keep "open the fountains of kindness" in his heart. Eliot stresses Tito's "fondness" for Tessa and his children: "When he thought of leaving Florence, he never thought of leaving Tessa and the little ones behind. He was very fond of these round-cheeked, wide-eyed human things that clung about him and knew no evil of him. And wherever affection can spring, it is like the green leaf and the blossom—pure, and breathing purity, whatever soil it may grow in" (503–4, ch. 50). Thus, Eliot shows how erotic love, even outside marriage as legally defined, can exert a moral influence that mitigates some of the "fatalities" of both Tessa's and Tito's life.

Eliot, however, does not exaggerate the power of Tessa's love or her motherhood, for she shows that Tito, despite his good intentions, later abandons Tessa when he flees from Florence, leaving her helpless and destitute in a world she does not understand. Eliot thus suggests why "zoological" definitions of women's potential are inadequate to describe their full participation in human culture. Tessa's powerlessness is demonstrated in the two episodes in which she leaves the enclosed world that Tito has prescribed for her and confronts the institutions of the family and the church in their more legalistic and patriarchal urban forms. Tessa is first drawn outside her home by Baldasarre. Not knowing that Tito was raised by this man and has now forsaken him, Tessa simply observes his need for love and offers him shelter and food. To cheer him, she brings her child to him and naively calls attention to the parallels between herself and the Madonna saying, "This is my baby. . . . It is like the little Gesù, and I should think that Santa Madonna would be kinder to me now, is it not true?" (367, ch. 33).

Tessa's comments disclose the unconscious egotism which her sheltered life has fostered, but her altruistic gestures to include Baldasarre in her extended family have precisely the opposite effect. As he holds her child, Baldasarre mutters, "Poor thing," with "something strangely threatening in his apparent pity" because "it did not seem . . . as if this guileless, loving little woman could reconcile him to the world at all, but rather that she was with him against the world, that she was a creature who would need to be avenged" (367–68). Baldasarre's response indicates that even though he has lost his mastery of Greek, he still exercises his prerogative to use patriarchal language to define woman's place in society. Florence appears to be deeply antipathetic to the values of spontaneous love and familial affection that Tessa instinctively embraces, and her dishonor becomes a further cause for Baldasarre's revenge on Tito.

When Tessa leaves home a second time, she is able to break through her innocently egocentric identification with the Madonna for, by confronting Romola, she recognizes that she is in the presence of a love greater and stronger than her own. Just before this meeting, Tessa looks at an image of the Holy Mother and Child and feels an expansive power in her belief that the Divine Mother loves her "more and more since she had had her babies" (510, ch. 50). Yet Romola appears as the living and breathing embodiment of a more comprehensive definition of maternal love when she intervenes to prevent Tessa from being harassed by some of Savonarola's zealots who demand that she surrender her jewels for the bonfire of vanities. In this meeting between Tessa and Romola, then, Eliot contrasts the "natural authority" of the mother, which has allowed Tessa to worship the divine feminine as a projection of her ideal self, with Romola's moral authority, which provides a corrective for Tessa's innocent egotism. An alliance between Tessa and Romola, combining the biological and moral forces of the maternal, suggests the power of resistance that could be liberated by female solidarity. Recognizing this threat, Tito exerts his authority to try to correct Tessa's impressions about Romola, but he fails, for "in the dream-like combination of small experiences which made up Tessa's thoughts, Romola remained confusedly associated with the pictures of churches, and when she reappeared, the grateful remembrance of her protection was slightly tinctured with religious awe" (546, ch. 56).

Thus, in her depiction of Tessa's illegitimate marriage with Tito, Eliot shows how the domestic seclusion of women operated historically to enhance male dominance and female submission, and by comparing this marriage with Romola's legitimate one, she shows how civil and religious marriage laws operated to enforce this subordination. Eliot's analysis of the effects of marriage laws on Romola suggests some of "the things which have not changed" in women's lives, for in Romola's time, as in Eliot's own, the patriarchal laws which structured the family were used to prevent women's full development, to exclude them from education, and to restrict their participation in public life. *Romola* demonstrates, however, that the forces of resistance cannot be perpetually contained without transforming the institution of the family itself. By revealing the conflicts between civil and moral definitions of marriage that are played out in Romola's relationship with Tito, Eliot shows how inward moral law eventually triumphs over outward civil law.

"Marriage," Eliot notes in *Romola*, "must be either a relation of sympathy or of conquest," and in her depiction of Romola's relation to Tito, she reveals the unrealized potential for "sympathy" in this union while she shows, at the same time, how marriage laws operate to make it instead into a relation of conquest. Tito begins his engagement to Romola with a promising moral susceptibility to that "loving awe in the presence of noble womanhood, which is something like the worship paid of old to a great nature-goddess, who was not all-knowing, but whose life and power were something deeper and more primordial than knowledge" (145, ch. 9). His motives for seeking Romola's hand in marriage are subtly transformed, however, by his desire for material gain and by his lust for political power. In the urban world of Florence, Tito begins to see Romola as a "prize" he "wished to have" (170, ch. 12), and marriage itself becomes an attractive avenue to power in the city's government.

By the time Tito and Romola are married, then, he has begun to resent and resist her "primordial power," as he recognizes that she possesses a "nature which could judge him" (371, ch. 34). In her presentation of Romola's private life with Tito, Eliot anatomizes the operation of that "passion or inclination" that is, according to J. S. Mill, "permanently incompatible" with woman's "moral power" in marriage, that impulse which renders women powerless in the patriarchal family that Comte—and Spencer—would normalize. Mill explains: "For everyone who desires power, desires it most over those who are nearest to him, with whom his life is passed, with whom he has most concerns in common, and in whom any independence of his authority is oftenest likely to interfere with his individual preferences."[14] By invoking this example from Florentine history, Eliot suggests how the civil laws governing marriage have enhanced the authority of the husband at the wife's expense, even when she possesses Romola's "large intelligence" and penetrating moral vision.

The episode which most dramatically displays Eliot's belief that marriage cannot be isolated as a moral institution, exempt from the changes that shape other political and social institutions in the culture, occurs when Tito refuses to honor Romola's promise to preserve her father's library as a legacy for the people of Florence. In acting on that "sense of power over a wife which makes a husband risk betrayals that a lover never ventures on" (345, ch. 31), Tito asserts his legal prerogatives as husband. In describing how marriage laws buttress Tito's power and prevent Romola from taking any legal action to preserve her father's bequest, Eliot repeatedly characterizes his exploitation as typical of "husbands," thus highlighting the patriarchal nature of the marriage laws in Renaissance Italy, laws which remained essentially intact, as Victorian feminists argued, in nineteenth-century England.[15]

In this episode, Eliot's sympathetic treatment of Romola as a victim of Tito's domination expresses her continuing support for reforms in marriage property laws, for she joined with Victorian feminists in arguing that married as well as single women should be legally protected from the "exercise of unrighteous power" (*GEL* 4:366). Tito uses physical force to compel Romola to submit to his decision to convert Bardo's library into capital, by literally locking her in their house; and later he asserts his legal right to act on her behalf without her consent, saying, "The very care of a husband for his wife's interest compels him to that separate action sometimes" (355, ch. 32). In this way, Eliot deflates the idealism of Comte's theory of domestic relations by dramatizing the male domination that has characterized marriage as a social institution.

Eliot similarly counters Spencer's appropriation of Comte's categories in his paradigm for the physiological division of labor by insisting that Romola's desire to "subdue her nature to her husband's" is not an expression of instinctive feminine submissiveness but rather a product of her particular history and response to the misogyny she faced in her family and culture. Romola's impulse to submit to Tito is carefully qualified as the reaction of an insecure and "loving woman"; it is not the response of all women who become wives. In representing Romola's efforts to divorce herself from Tito, however, Eliot acknowledges the threats that the emancipation of women posed for the Victorian family and for her own conception of those "moral laws" that she wished to preserve in the family.

In this way, she returns to the problem of defining the moral limits of principled resistance to both outward and inward law, a problem she first broached in *The Mill on the Floss*. *Romola* shows that Eliot was not willing to endorse all acts of resistance—by women or by men—undertaken on the authority of inward law alone. Four years after she completed *Romola*, for example, in a famous letter to Barbara Bodichon, Eliot explained that she hoped that many well-educated women could be induced to accept voluntarily the roles of wife and mother and undertake the "great amount of social unproductive labor which needs to be done by women" (*GEL* 4:425). Though she agreed with Bodichon and other feminists that women should not be prevented from devoting themselves to the "highest work" they were able to perform, she offers the following qualification:

> No good can come to women, more than to any class of male mortals, while each aims at doing the highest kind of work, which ought to be held in sanctity as what only the few can do well. I believe—and I want it to be well shown—that a more thorough education will tend to do away with the odious vulgarity of our notions about functions and employment, and to propagate the true gospel that the deepest disgrace is to insist on doing work for which we are unfit—to do work of any sort badly. (*GEL* 4:425)

Clearly, Eliot would prefer to see women become good wives and mothers rather than inadequate lawyers, or—more to the point—second-rate novelists, but in an age when woman's "highest calling" was defined as motherhood, her remarks about the "odious vulgarity of our notions about functions and employment" also reiterate her persistent skepticism about Spencer's appeals to biological functionalism in defining gender roles.

Eliot uses the examples of both Romola and Savonarola, then, to challenge Spencer's developing conception of that "moving equilibrium" he imagined as serenely directing the course of human history. In this novel Eliot exposes Spencer's silence about the moral force of erotic and religious love in determining human potentiality, and she dramatizes instead the power of "resistance" authorized by moral law that finds expression in the struggle between the outward and inward forces that she saw as shaping human history and woman's place in it. Both Romola and Savonarola serve to refine Eliot's notion of inward law and to suggest the moral limits for resistance authorized by reference to the maternal principle. Romola's first effort to break her marriage bonds with Tito indicates that she cannot responsibly repudiate outward—that is, external—law until she has learned to see beyond the limits of her individualist's view of "love," which is, at this point in the novel, the only "law of her affections" and the only religion of her life (391, ch. 36).

Romola first decides to separate from Tito when she discovers his perfidy in selling her father's library. Though she is, by her own lights, morally justified in acting to dissolve her marriage bond, since "it no longer represented the inward bond of love" (391, ch. 36), Eliot insists that she cannot so easily repudiate the "inexorable external identity" that has been created by the public laws and ceremonies that formalized her marriage to him.

This acknowledgment of the "external" force of marriage laws has been read by many of Eliot's readers as an endorsement of women's traditional subordination to male authority in marriage. By preventing Romola from acting on the principle of what Victorians called "free love," however, Eliot clears the way for a more convincing defense of Romola's right to participate in the larger public sphere. It is her acceptance of wider civic duties which ultimately frees her to act responsibly, on the basis of a "higher law," when Romola successfully separates from Tito later in the novel. Eliot noted in her copy of Comte's *Catechism,* "How can there be duties without corresponding claims?" and in Romola's case, she demonstrates how, by assuming her larger duties to both the church and state, Romola is eventually justified in separating from Tito.[16]

In describing how Savonarola stops Romola in her first effort to escape from Florence, Eliot also reveals how the church reinforced male dominance in both the private and the public sphere. Eliot's treatment of Catholicism in this novel thus reveals her sympathy with those Victorian feminists who argued that maternal values had been suppressed in the codification of church doctrine as they had in the civil and religious laws legalizing marriage. In 1860, a noted Victorian feminist activist, Francis Power Cobbe, identified the patriarchal quality of Christian law and doctrine:

> We come nearer to God through the affections, wherein lie woman's great power, than through the intellect wherein man excels. . . . We have had enough of *man's* thoughts of God—of God first as the King, the "Man of War," the Demiurge, the Mover of all things, and then, at last, since Christian times, of God as the Father of the World. . . . But the woman's thought of God as the "Parent of Good, Almighty," who unites in one the father's care and the mother's tenderness, *that* we have never yet heard. . . . And we want her Moral intuition also. We want her sense of the law of love to complete man's sense of the law of justice. (Bauer and Ritt 87–88)

Eliot's thorough knowledge of Feuerbach and Strauss, and her familiarity with the evolutionary theories of Spencer and Comte, allowed her to bring an intellectual rigor to these feminist critiques of religion. In representing how the Catholic Church responded to the challenges mobilized by Savonarola, Eliot eventually exposes the patriarchal basis of the authority that Savonarola claims for himself as priest.

Romola is initially attracted to Savonarola even before her first flight from the city because his definition of Christian love emphasizes its maternal qualities. When she hears him preaching in the Duomo at that moment when he experiences the "rapture and glory of martyrdom, without its agony," she is arrested by the maternal metaphors that characterize his address:

> "Listen, O people, over whom my heart yearns, as the heart of a mother over the children she has travailed for! God is my witness that but for your sakes I would willingly live as a turtle in the depths of the forest, singing low to my Beloved, who is mine and I am his." (293, ch. 24)

In describing his listeners as a family united in love and saved by the merciful intervention of the Virgin Mother, Savonarola defines "love" as the moral element that mystically transforms the church into a family in Christ.

Moreover, Savonarola, in contrast to Romola's brother Dino, has chosen the active reformer's rather than the contemplative's path to sainthood, and so he coordinates the forces of resistance to restore Florence's more democratic traditions of popular government.[17] It is not the theology he preaches but rather the heroic scope of Savonarola's aspiration that prompts Romola to submit to his direction and return to Florence. She is moved by Savonarola's lofty desire to promote the "universal regeneration" of his world, and her enthusiasm is "continually stirred to fresh vigor" because of her "strong affinity for his passionate sympathy and the splendor of his aims" (463, ch. 44). The scope of Savonarola's reforming spirit reaches far beyond the cloister:

> His burning indignation against the abuses and oppression that made the daily story of the Church and of States had kindled a ready fire in her too. His special care for liberty and purity of government in Florence, with his constant reference of this immediate object to the wider end of a universal regeneration, had created in her a new consciousness of the great drama of human existence in which her life was a part; and through her daily helpful contact with the less fortunate of her fellow-citizens this new consciousness became something stronger than a vague sentiment; it grew into a more and more definite motive of self-denying practice. (464, ch. 44)

Savonarola defines his moral responsibilities in social and political as well as religious terms, and so helps Romola find a means to "keep alive the flame of unselfish emotions by which a life of sadness might be a life of active love" (464, ch. 44). Romola submits to his teaching, then, even though she regards the "superstitions" of his faith with contempt (463, ch. 44).

Romola is persuaded by Savonarola's heroic example, if not by his theology, to return to her husband and to undertake the work of caring for the needy and nursing the sick in Florence. But Savonarola's instruction, like her father's, also creates internal conflicts which divide Romola's best energies. Savonarola urges Romola to play the part of Tito's "good angel" in their failing marriage, and echoes Comte in arguing that marriage is a sacrament that requires absolute obedience and cannot be dissolved (Comte, *General* 254). Though Romola tries valiantly to act the part of Tito's angel wife—she tells him, "If we are united, I am that part of you that will save you from crime" (482, ch. 46)—she is powerless, Eliot shows, to prevent her husband's treachery.

In fact, the very qualities that define Romola as morally superior to Tito enable her husband to "master" her even more thoroughly. Far from preventing his crimes, Romola's quietism allows him to spin even more quickly the web of political intrigue that jeopardizes the lives of the two other men Romola loves most in Florence: Bernardo del Nero and Savonarola himself. When she learns of Tito's involvement in a plot to assassinate Savonarola, Romola is prompted to try a more active means to dissuade Tito. Meeting him in the street, she pleads with him to sever his political alliances, but Tito resists, by grasping her wrists and whispering bitterly, "I am master of you. You shall not set yourself in opposition to me" (483, ch. 46). Disparaging her intellect, Tito insists that she does not have the capacity to understand the details of politics, that she is a "fair creature" who "lives in the clouds" (484, ch. 46).

By showing how Tito eventually converts the "angelic qualities" he originally admired into a reason to dismiss Romola's moral vision, Eliot ironically underscores the ineffectuality of the self-sacrifice Savonarola urged upon Romola in her marriage. Thus, she extends the problem of authority that Mill identified in Comte's ideology of the family and traces its implications in the larger public realm by showing how the altruist, armed with moral power alone, must submit to the egoist, who exercises the physical or political force that Spencer imagined as man's "natural" attribute.

Romola finds herself in a similar dilemma when she plays her role as the "visible Madonna" of Florence. By lending moral authority to Romola's acts of public service, Savonarola licenses her escape from the narrow confines of the domestic world of husband and family, and in this way, Eliot indicates how women like Romola have traditionally used religion to legitimize their entry into the larger public world. In valorizing Romola's nursing as an expression of "womanly sympathy" (463, ch. 44), Eliot goes further than Florence Nightingale was prepared to go in admitting nursing as appropriate work for a married woman.[18] Yet Romola does not choose this work naturally, for she must struggle against the bias of her education in order to transform herself into the semblance of the Madonna. Of Romola, Eliot writes: "She had no innate taste for tending the sick and clothing the ragged, like some women to whom the details of such work are welcome in themselves, simply as an occupation. Her early training had kept her aloof from such womanly labours; and if she had not brought to them the inspiration of her deepest feelings, they would have been irksome to her" (463, ch. 44). Romola assumes the role of the Madonna, then, because her culture offers it as the only admissible one which will allow her to move freely about the city and still be regarded with respect.

In playing the part of the Madonna, Romola begins to recover a sense of the dignity and power of the maternal principle in her own life, but she ultimately recognizes that this role, like that of Tito's "angel wife," simply disguises the reality of her actual powerlessness in Florentine society. The men who control religious and political life in this city regard the figure of the Madonna in a thoroughly egoistic light; "Florentines are convinced," Eliot writes, "that they had a Madonna who would do what they pleased," a saying that Romola recalls as she watches a procession accompanying the ancient icon of the sorrowing Mother that is brought into the city during the famine (445, ch. 42). Viewing this figure, Romola sees that the freedom and power she had felt in playing the

part of the "visible Madonna" in Florence is illusory. Romola's acknowledgement of the limits of all women's power in Florence reflects
Eliot's concessions to Spencer's analysis of the "survival of the fittest"
and its impact on her estimation of the power of the "moral" forces
that find expression in domestic and religious life. When Romola is
threatened by a crowd of rough, irreligious men, she tells them, "You
have the power to take this bread if you will. It was saved for sick women
and children. You are strong men; but if you do not choose to suffer
because you are strong, you have the power to take everything from the
weak" (449, ch. 42). In this confrontation, Romola recognizes that she
cannot exercise her moral authority as madonna without supporting the
institutions of the state and the church. Though Florentines ostensibly
worship various "visible Madonnas" as figures of maternal solicitude and
supernatural goodness, civil and religious laws operate to subvert the
earthly expression of these values in the material world. Women are confined, as a consequence, to two very narrow roles, that of angel wife or
holy virgin.

In the series of revelations which allow Romola to escape the control
of both her husband and priest, Eliot indicates her resistance to Spencer's theory of a "moving equilibrium" directing social development, on
the one hand, and to Comte's authoritarian analysis of moral law, on the
other.[19] Though Eliot shared the Positivist conception of moral laws transcending those presently regulating the church, she was unwilling to in-
vest authority, as Comte did, in the more paternalistic, hierarchical, and
ritualistic elements of the Catholic Church or any other. Eliot was far
more willing to confront in her life—and entertain in her fiction—the
possibility of an ideal society divested of institutionalized patriarchal
authority in both the family and the church. She explains to Barbara
Bodichon:

> But I have faith in the working-out of higher possibilities than the Catholic or
> any other church has presented, and those who have strength to wait and
> endure, are bound to accept no formula which their whole souls—their intel-
> lect as well as their emotions—do not embrace with entire reverence. The
> "highest calling and election" is to do *without opium* and live through all our
> pain with conscious clear-eyed endurance. (*GEL* 3:366)

It is the problem of authority, then, in both the private and public
spheres, that prompted Eliot's most serious reservations about Comte's
definition of the family and the church as moral institutions.

Though Romola initially submits to Savonarola's spiritual guidance,
she experiences no real conversion, and she eventually comes to recognize, instead, the patriarchal and authoritarian forces that undermine

Savonarola's moral vision. Once Romola discovers that Tito has ignored even the most basic, biologically defined duties to the man who raised him and to the two children he has fathered by Tessa, she again decides to separate herself from him, but she does so by recalling Savonarola's defiance of Church law in the name of a higher moral duty. Recognizing that "the problem before her was essentially the same as that which had lain before Savonarola—the problem where the sacredness of obedience ended, and where the sacredness of rebellion began" (553, ch. 56)—Romola claims her freedom from the "external law" which binds her to Tito, declaring, "I too am a human being. I have a soul that abhors your actions. Our union is a pretence—as if a perpetual lie could be a sacred marriage" (567, ch. 58). In choosing this course, Romola asserts the preeminence of an internal and individual "moral" law over "external" laws, though she has come to recognize, too, the larger responsibilities which come with acting on the "soul's own warrant"—responsibilities to which she had been blind before she met Savonarola.

Before she leaves Florence, Romola is also forced to question the nature of the Divine Authority which Savonarola claims, and this consequently frees her to move beyond his interpretation of moral law. Romola becomes aware of the limits of his vision shortly after she learns that her uncle has been charged with treason against the State. Realizing that Savonarola would compromise his own authority if he tried to contradict the prophecies of the "spirit-seeing" women that prompt her uncle's arrest, Romola observes that Savonarola "was fettered inwardly by the consciousness that such revelations were not, in their basis, distinctly separable from his own visions; he was fettered outwardly by the foreseen consequences of raising a cry against himself even among members of his own party, as one who would suppress all Divine inspiration of which he himself was not the vehicle" (526, ch. 52). Romola's understanding of the basis and limits of Savonarola's moral authority is accompanied by a recognition that all actions—morally or otherwise defined—are compromised by the social and cultural institutions which constrain and interpret them.

In this way, Romola experiences that moment when the "soul must have no guide but the voice within it" (576, ch. 59), and so moves beyond patriarachal interpretations of the Word.[20] When Savonarola refuses to grant her uncle a trial, Romola detects the personal and political considerations that prevent him from acting justly and consistently, and she denounces him indignantly:

> "Do you, then, know so well what will further the coming of God's kingdom, father, that you will dare to despise the plea of mercy—of justice—of faithfulness to your own teaching. . . . Take care, father, lest your enemies have some

reason when they say, that in your visions of what will further God's kingdom you see only what will strengthen your own party." (578, ch. 59)

Thus, Romola rejects Savonarola's authority to interpret the Divine and to demand obedience to moral laws; she claims her own right to define God's kingdom as "something wider" than Savonarola will allow (578, ch. 59).

Having already recognized in her marriage this discrepancy between outward and inward law, Romola is moved by the "full force of sympathy" for her uncle to see the same discrepancy on a larger public scale. Understanding that her uncle is caught in the collision of "two kinds of faithfulness," Romola sees the inadequacies of a system of law which depends upon inflexible "formulae by which actions and parties are judged" (583, ch. 60). Eliot emphasizes the patriarchal nature of these laws when Romola observes that the prevailing notion of justice is untempered by mercy and reflects "that hard systematic judgment of men which measures them in assents and denials quite superficial to the manhood within them" (526–27, ch. 55).

This second great crisis in Romola's moral life prompts her again to leave Florence, and in this flight she moves beyond the reach of Savonarola's moral appeals. Thus, Romola rises to an apprehension of the problem of duty that anticipates the existential position of Eliot and Spencer when she asks herself: "What force was there to create for her that supremely hallowed motive men call duty, but which can have no constraining existence save through some form of believing love?" (586, ch. 61).[21] Romola's loss of faith in Savonarola moves her, in despair, to question the power of "invisible Goodness" to provide any object for her sense of duty, and her disillusionment nearly kills her.

In the end, then, Eliot sends Romola out into the literal landscape of the wild zone, back to the natural world, back to a place where she can "stand for the first time in her life . . . alone in the presence of the earth and sky; with no human presence interposing and making a law for her" (p. 430, ch. 40). Having experienced the moral discipline of family and church, Romola arrives at the existential position where she recognizes no external authorities, and she recovers a sense of her own authority through a regressive movement backward into a world of pregnant silence and primordial beauty, a regression similar to Silas Marner's. Surrounded by the images of serene natural beauty—the crescent-shaped beach, the sapphire sea, the green, ripened corn; all recalling the symbols of a prehistoric mother goddess who predates Florence's icon of the Virgin Mother—Romola discovers a sense of her own power by recognizing the "natural authority" of her maternal impulses and by claiming her right to define a moral code that more fully honors them.

In representing Romola's experience in the wild zone, Eliot tried to resolve a fundamental issue that was raised by her reading of Spencer and Comte: if Mother Nature replaces a supernatural Divine Authority as the source and symbol of moral law, then, as Eliot noted in the margin of her copy of Comte's *Catechism,* "What shall women worship?"[22] While Spencer was content to see women as permanent victims of their "zoological" development and Comte erred in the opposite direction by regarding them as symbols—but not agents—of moral law, as otherworldly angels or madonnas, Eliot was satisfied with neither solution. Romola takes a position in the wild zone, then, that expresses Eliot's own evolutionary perspective on physical and moral law.

From this serene vantage point Romola reassesses her obligations to the patriarchal family, church, and state:

> The memory of her life with Tito, of the conditions which made their real union impossible, while their external union imposed a set of false duties on her which were essentially the concealment and sanctioning of what her mind revolted from, told her that flight had been her only resource. All minds, except such as are delivered by dulness of sensibility, must be subject to this recurring conflict where the many-twisted conditions of life have forbidden the fulfillment of a bond. (651, ch. 69)

Having come to peace with herself, Romola understands the ideal power of the maternal in a world beyond the reach of Florentine culture. In this realm she is able to see how the "special ties of marriage, the State, and religious discipleship" have complicated the "simpler relations of the human being to his fellow-men" (650, ch. 69). Romola's ruminations there offer some tentative answers to Eliot's question, "What shall women worship"? A woman is not simply to worship the parents to whom she is bound by blood, or the husband she has chosen and promised to cherish in love, or the children she has suffered to bear and nourish, but all those whom the heart recognizes in spontaneous sympathy: the sick, the weak, the helpless, the forlorn. For as Romola concludes, "If everything else is doubtful, this suffering that I can help is certain; if the glory of the cross is an illusion, the sorrow is only the truer. While the strength is in my arm I will stretch it out to the fainting; while the light visits my eyes they will seek the forsaken" (650, ch. 69). And in this epitome of Romola's final sense of her moral duty, Eliot registers her rejection of Spencer's notion that women's only contribution to human evolution is "zoological," as well his implicit assumptions that a "natural division" of labor confined women to the domestic realm and that a self-adjusting "equilibrium" characterized the development of all human societies.

In this primitive, almost prehistoric world then, outside the boundaries of "civilized" Florence, Romola reconstructs a woman-centered culture and exercises her own power as moral leader in it. The community she visits is a remnant of an earlier social order, as is evident when the priest and villagers recognize her as the "Mother with the glory about her tending the sick" (646, ch. 68). But Romola is no longer willing to cooperate with those patriarchal interpretions of the Word that so limited her role as the "visible Madonna" in Florence. There are no miracles in the many legends that are "afterwards told in that valley about the blessed Lady who came over the sea" (649, ch. 68); she leaves behind, instead, "legends by which all who heard might know that in times gone by a woman had done beautiful loving deeds there, rescuing those who were ready to perish" (649, ch. 68).[23] Similarly, Romola refrains from enacting the miracle of the virgin birth, for though she cares for the little Hebrew child orphaned by the plague, she does not bring him with her when she leaves this "wild zone."

Instead, upon her return to Florence, Romola creates a family that provides a wider scope for moral resistance in the urban world. Defying the prevailing patriarchal model, Romola gathers Monna Brigida and Tessa with her two children into a family that transcends the more restrictive patriarchal model formalized by the laws of marriage and legitimacy; for Romola accepts the responsibility of caring for Tessa's children as warmly as if they were her own. In this way, Eliot indicates her resistance to Spencer's theory that individuation and reproduction are at odds with one another, and that men embody one force while women embody the other. Instead, she presents in Romola an example of how the impulses of individuation and reproduction do battle within women as well as men, and that, though the need for individuation may defeat the impulse to reproduce, as it does in Romola, this resolution does not signal the denial of the maternal qualities of that woman.

Finally, Romola creates a family that transcends the law of the father and recognizes a basis for moral resistance beyond it. The deaths of Tito and Baldasarre show the power of dominance and hate that no earthly wife or mother alone could counteract or redeem. The absence of fathers in Romola's created family suggests that it will escape the old pattern of patricide, in which the adopted son rejects the father and is ultimately killed by him in revenge. Moreover, within this household, Romola generates and interprets a new history, teaching Lillo and Nello to recognize the more inclusive ties that unite them to family and community. Thus, she escapes from the Madonna's role as a symbol of "immanence" and claims the right to effect change, achieving and articulating a vision of moral law and social duty which honors not only the memory of Savonarola's acts of heroic resistance but also the sacredness of the maternal in herself.

7

Women's Suffrage and Women's Suffering:
Felix Holt and *The Principles of Biology* II

THE 1860s witnessed the greatest display of feminist political activity that Spencer and Eliot were to see in the course of their lives. The campaign for women's suffrage, in particular, reached its climax in 1866, when J. S. Mill presented the Ladies' Petition to the House of Commons. Barbara Bodichon, one of Eliot's closest friends, was a major figure in the campaign for women's vote and one of the founders of London's first suffrage society (Bauer and Ritt 214). The political debates of 1865–1866, precipitated by the Representation of the People Bill and by the campaign for women's suffrage, prompted both Spencer and Eliot to confront the darker side of social change and to reconsider woman's actual and ideal place in society.[1] While Spencer's *Principles of Biology* (1864–1867) and Eliot's *Felix Holt* (1866)[2] reveal the conservatizing force that evolutionary theory exerted on their analyses of political change, their reactions to women's suffrage show a sharp difference of opinion. The theory of social development that Spencer formulated in the 1860s justified female subordination by appropriating biological mechanisms in order to naturalize the existing social hierarchies of gender, class, and race. Eliot, by contrast, in reconsidering woman's relation to civil and moral law was impelled to emphasize the value of intellectual disinterestedness in the assessment of public questions.

Spencer's work in *The Principles of Biology* (1864–1867) was negatively informed by the feminist politics of the 1860s, though he would certainly not have acknowledged it, for this work shows how his theory of the physiological division of labor facilitated his increasingly more sexist and racist analysis of human reproduction. In the second volume of *The Principles of Biology*, he extended his theory about the fixed quantity of energy to explain male dominance and so established a defense of sexual and racial subordination in what Foucault calls its "modern biologizing statist form" (149). Arguing that women expended more energy in reproduction than men, Spencer concluded that when women achieved reproductive maturity, the development of their intellect was biologically— and permanently—arrested, causing all women to exhibit a "lower" mental development than men: "Among the higher vertebrata the substance lost by one sex in the shape of sperm cells is small compared with that lost by the other sex in the shape of albumen stored up in the eggs, or blood supplied to the foetus, or milk given to the young" (*Biology* 2:416). Though Spencer goes on to acknowledge that women may avoid the largest and most prolonged "indirect tax" on their energy by sharing "the fostering of the young" with men, he constructed an explanation of their lesser development that included all women in their childbearing years, whether they actually bear children or not.[3]

Spencer supported his analysis of women's biologically determined inferiority by arguing that variations in the birthrates of different races proved that there was a universal "antagonism" between "individuation and reproduction," a theory which, coincidentally, demonstrated that the Anglo-Saxon race was the most developed. In other words, the birth-rates of each race became, for Spencer, a reliable index of its place in a universal racial hierarchy. "Human races differ considerably in their size and notably in their degree of cerebral development," Spencer observed, and though he conceded that some of these differences might be attributed to variations in climate, they were primarily caused by the evolutionary mechanisms that ensure the "survival of the fittest" (*Biology* 2:480, 472–73). Contrasting the birth rates of "less developed" African peasants who have "six to seven" or even a "dozen or twenty" children to the "more developed" Hottentots who have "two or three," and comparing the more prolific Irish with the less prolific Anglo-Saxons (2:481–83), Spencer argued, with amazing circularity, that these statistics demonstrated that "genesis decreases" as "individuation increases" (2:477). The "below average" fertility rates of both Hottentots and Anglo-Saxons thus came to signify their relative physical and mental superiority (2:480), since Spencer regarded these lower rates as the manifestation of greater individuation.

Spencer subsequently extended his arguments naturalizing gender and racial hierarchies to include class structure. Citing French and Austrian studies showing that working-class women reach puberty one year later than middle-class women, Spencer concluded that working-class women were therefore less developed than their middle-class counterparts. Though this study posed an unacknowledged challenge to his theory of individuation—since it might have been interpreted to mean that working-class women achieved greater individuation than their bourgeois sisters—Spencer explained this discrepancy by referring to his theory about the conservation of energy. He argued, instead, that this later onset of the menarche was caused by the greater "muscular expenditure" required of working-class women. Assuming that mental labor was more taxing than physical labor, Spencer concluded by warning middle-class women of too great an expenditure of "mental labor," since "absolute or relative infertility was generally produced in women by mental labor carried to excess" (2:486). Conferring scientific authority on the ideas he initially outlined in "Physical Training" (1859), Spencer reasoned:

> Though the regimen of upper-class girls is not what it should be, yet, considering that their feeding is better than that of girls belonging to the poorer classes, while, in most other respects, their physical treatment is not worse, the deficiency of reproductive power among them may be reasonably attributed to the overtaxing of their brains—an overtaxing which produces a serious reaction of the physique. This diminution of reproductive power is not shown only by the greater frequency of absolute sterility nor is it shown only in the earlier cessation of childbearing; but it is also shown in the very frequent inability of such women to suckle their infants. In its fullest sense the reproductive power means the power to bear a well developed infant and to supply the natural food for the natural period. Most of the flat-chested girls who survive their high-pressure education, are incompetent to do this. (2:486)

What is extraordinary about this passage is that Spencer apparently failed to consider that educated Englishwomen in the 1850s and 1860s, in part because of feminist activities, had a better understanding of and access to methods of birth control and some were beginning to assert their power to control their rate of reproduction, thereby artificially depressing the rate of fertility for their class and race. Similarly, Spencer ignored the impact of customs that delayed middle-class marriages and thus further depressed the birth rates of this group. In this recurrence of the anxiety Spencer expressed in "Physical Training" about overly intellectual, flat-chested women, we can see how evolutionary science produced what Foucault calls the "hysterization" of women, that peculiar blindness to the distinction between women and mothers (104). This biological functionalism allowed Spencer to define all women as mothers of the race in the remaining years of his career—the years of his greatest prominence, during which he wrote *The Study of Sociology*, *The Principles of Sociology*, and *The Principles of Ethics*.

Spencer's more frequent references to "savages" or "the less developed races," so important in this crucial passage of *The Principles of Biology*, also characterize his revised version of *The Principles of Psychology*. Spencer reconceptualized and rewrote this work between 1868 and 1872, publishing it first in numbers and later reissuing it in two volumes in 1870 and 1872.[4] His references to race reflect Spencer's reception of the work of several influential cultural anthropologists of the 1860s, as well as his own research for a digest of the cultures of "lesser races" in his *Descriptive Sociology* (1874–1881). In 1861, Spencer met J. F. McLennan, author of *Primitive Marriage* (1865), and in 1864, he began meeting monthly with a group called the "X Club," which included Thomas Huxley, John Tyndall, Sir Edward Frankland, George Busk, T. Archer Hirst, and Sir John Lubbock, author of *Pre-Historic Times* (1865) and *The Origin of Civilization and the Primitive Condition of Man* (1870).[5] In these years, Spencer familiarized himself with the work of McLennan and Lubbock, which extended the arguments of Sir Henry Maine and Lewis Henry Morgan to counter the feminist challenges of the 1860s. Thus, Spencer's texts helped to construct a "solid, historical evolutionary justification" for women's subordination within the family and the state by "presenting 'civilized marriage' as the end point of cultural evolution."[6] In this decade, feminist activists and Eliot herself raised "severe questions about the nature of the 'natural family' " and women's subordinate position in marriage, as Elizabeth Fee has argued. Interrogating "the elemental source" of male authority in the family, Victorian feminists asked: "If the power of father-husbands were proved not to be a natural, God-given, timeless fact of life, then might not the basis of sexual, imperial, and, to some extent, even political authority be undermined?" (Fee 87–88).

Spencer's effort to defend and justify the traditional structure of the patriarchal family was also directed toward refuting Johann Bachofen's *Das Mütterrecht*, published in English in 1861.[7] Bachofen provoked consternation among English social theorists because he used the *Oresteia* and other classical Greek texts to argue that in the prehistoric stage of social development, women were victims of male aggression, but that women had themselves initiated the second, matriarchal stage by establishing the institution of marriage and enforcing it through the authority of the mother. Later, this matriarchal order was overthrown by a patriarchal order, a social revolution which is dramatized in the *Oresteia* where, as Bachofen writes:

> Triumphant paternity partakes of heavenly light while childbearing is bound up with the earth that bears all things; the establishment of paternal right is universally represented as an act of the Uranian solar hero, while the defense of the motherright is the first duty of the Cthonian mother goddess. (109–10)

McLennan, Lubbock, and Spencer attempted to refute Bachofen's theory by contending that men rather than women were responsible for the revolutionary changes which transformed the family into its most advanced, monogamous, patriarchal configuration and that modern marriage developed in conjunction with systems for the transmission of private property. By 1877, in his expanded version of the first volume of *The Principles of Sociology*,[8] Spencer would argue, for example, that not only reproduction rates but also patriarchal, monogamous marriage customs could be used as an index to determine the evolutionary superiority of the Anglo-Saxon race.

In contrast to Spencer, Eliot maintained her support throughout the 1860s and 1870s for feminist reforms in the marriage and divorce laws, for women's emancipation, and for improved education. Because of her increasing prestige and authority as a woman writer, Eliot was frequently approached during the suffrage campaign by feminists who hoped to enlist her support and who urged her to express her sympathies through overt political action. At the height of feminist activism in 1867, Eliot summarized her position on women's issues in a letter to Mrs. Peter Taylor: "I do sympathize with you most emphatically in the desire to see women socially elevated—educated equally with men, and secured as far as possible along with every other breathing creature from suffering the exercise of unrighteous power" (*GEL* 4:366). Nonetheless, as this letter reveals, Eliot would not endorse women's suffrage.

Eliot indicates here that she was unwilling to sign the petition in support of women's suffrage because of her reservations about the effectiveness of legislative reforms and her desire to maintain a nonpartisan position on the suffrage question. She writes that though she was "inclined to hope for much good from the serious presentation of women's claims before Parliament," she felt that a "broader ground of sympathy than agreement as to . . . a particular issue" would be secured only when the public arrived at a fuller understanding of woman's actual and ideal place in society. Eliot was, as this letter reveals, far more skeptical about the process of political reform than Mrs. Taylor or other leading suffragists, and this caution prompted her refusal to sign the petition for women's vote. In a letter to Sara Hennell from the same period, Eliot wrote that she regarded the campaign for women's suffrage as an "extremely doubtful good," and objected to "the proportionate toil and interruption such labors cause to women whose habits and duties differ so much" from politically active suffragists like Mrs. Taylor (*GEL* 4:390).

Nonetheless, Eliot's position on women's suffrage should be understood as part of her unwillingness to extend the vote to the disenfranchised members of either sex: she felt that electors, without proper education, could not achieve that "disinterestedness" that would allow them to transcend their own narrow personal interests in assessing the larger national good (Gallagher 229). Because she, like Spencer, hoped to see institutionalized government reduced to the "smallest amount possible," Eliot distrusted the machinery of government and believed that permanent social change was best initiated and directed by moral appeals rather than political negotiations. In 1865, for example, when she learned that J. S. Mill was running for a seat in Parliament, she expressed dismay, commenting that "thinkers can do more outside than inside the House" (*GEL* 4:196).

Felix Holt demonstrates how the conservative force of evolutionary psychology cast doubt on the possibility of achieving rapid social reform through political legislation, particularly in areas which required changes in feelings as fundamental as any could be—those which bind men to women and to their families. The question of women's suffrage forced Eliot to reevaluate her definition of the maternal principle and to reassess the resistance that was justified by reference to moral laws. In this novel, then, Eliot reconsiders how public opinion promotes political change and social reform. There is an apocalyptic note in *Felix Holt* that distinguishes it from Eliot's earlier works, suggesting her fear of the changes that an expanded franchise could bring. Eliot's allusions to the *Oresteia* in this text suggest her concern that Victorian England was on the verge of a social revolution perhaps as profound as the one Bachofen had described.

Nonetheless, *Felix Holt* and subsequent novels show Eliot's desire to see beyond the existing social hierarchies of gender, class, and nationality, and in this respect her response to evolutionary theory differs dramatically from Spencer's. *Felix Holt* also reveals Eliot's effort to envision a society that transcends the subordination enforced by "unrighteous power" and explores one viable means to that end. When it is read in the context of theories developed in *The Principles of Biology*, *Felix Holt* challenges Spencer's increasing emphasis on the irrefutable authority of biological science, on reproduction as a process that naturalizes gender and class hierarchies, and on women's subordination to male authority in the family and the nation-state. Recognizing that social theorists like Spencer used analyses of women's nature to set "structural limits" to the debates about women's social, legal, and economic rights, Eliot attempts in this novel to bring those limits to light.[9] While in *Romola* Eliot attempted to locate a "wild zone" in the distant past, in order to examine how maternal principles found expression in ancient moral laws, in *Felix Holt* she focuses instead on a period of recent history already mapped by another important feminist intellectual, Harriet Martineau (David 63). By this route, Eliot returns to the questions which lie at the heart of *Silas Marner* by reexamining the sources of moral sensibility in the family and by interrogating to what extent men, as well women, can recognize and act on "maternal" principles that find expression in moral law.

In *Felix Holt*, then, Eliot uses allusions to the *Oresteia* to invoke the current debate, aroused by Bachofen, about the nature and function of marriage, and these allusions highlight the conflict between two definitions of the family, one based on the prehistoric motherright and the other based on the prerogatives of the father and enforced by patriarchal marriage laws. Eliot invites us, in the introduction to *Felix Holt*, to see Mrs. Transome's tragedy in the monumental terms of ancient Greek drama, to find "some tragic mark of kinship" binding her life to "the far-stretching life that went before, and to the life that is to come after, such as has raised the pity and terror of men ever since they began to discern between will and destiny" (83).[10] Arabella Transome's proud and imperious stoicism in the "monotonously narrowing life" of the "poorer gentry" (104, ch. 1) evokes comparisons with the valiant-hearted queens and goddesses of Greek tragedy (102, ch. 1). Yet, while she imitates Clytemnestra's defiance by taking the lawyer Jermyn as her secret lover, subverting the rule of her all-but-absent husband, Mrs. Transome wins only a slightly widened scope for her energies. Though she plays the part of the chief bailiff on her estate, Mrs. Transome reigns like a Clytemnestra fallen out of her proper place in time; her kingdom has shrunk to the size of a drawing room, and her grandest public demonstration of her power is to "insist that a tenant should stand bare-headed below her as she sat on horseback" (106, ch. 1).

In disclosing the motives that prompt Mrs. Transome to adopt Clytemnestra's ancient defiance of the patriarchal laws of marriage and paternity, Eliot reiterates her support for better women's education—that cause about which she would say, in 1867, she had "no doubt" (*GEL* 4:399). Like the heroic women in Eliot's earlier novels, Mrs. Transome has been inadequately educated; her "larger self" has been starved because she has learned nothing of those transcendent moral laws epitomized, for example, by Aeschylus's premise that "our days are heritors of days gone by" (582, ch. 48). Similarly, while Mrs. Transome's education was designed to make her more attractive to the men who once courted her, it has become obsolete since, "what once passed for signs of her accomplishment or cleverness have become as insubstantial and valueless as an old fashioned stucco ornament, of which the substance was never worth anything, while the form is no longer to the taste of any living mortal" (106, ch. 1). Because of her uncorrected belief that "what is true and, in general, good for mankind is stupid and drug-like" (105, ch. 1), Mrs. Transome enters into her illicit relationship with Jermyn.

While Eliot reiterates her protest against the inadequacies of women's education voiced in *The Mill on the Floss* and *Romola*, she reveals more pointedly in this novel how the values shaping Mrs. Transome's education have also narrowed her vision and reinforced the prejudices of her class, imprisoning her even more securely in her misery. Mrs. Transome has found that "many sinful things were highly agreeable to her," but she acts, like Godfrey Cass, in defiance of moral laws whose validity she herself acknowledges. Despite her affected Byronism, Arabella Transome "believed all the while that truth and safety lay in due attendance on prayers and sermons, in the admirable doctrines and rituals of the Church of England" and "in such a view of this world and the next as

would preserve the existing arrangements of English society quite unshaken, keeping down the obtrusiveness of the vulgar and the discontent
of the poor" (105, ch. 1). Eliot expresses her distaste for the Tory politics
practiced at Transome Court, by noting that Mrs. Transome acted, like
Dunstan Cass, on her faith in "luck and lotteries," in hoping that "her
first, rickety, ugly, imbecile child should die and leave room for her dar-
ling, of whom she could be proud" (98, ch. 1). This faith in luck is typical, Eliot claims, both here and later in *Daniel Deronda,* of many of the
men and women "who have the softest beds and the most delicate eating,
who have a very large share of the earth and sky" (98, ch. 1).

Moreover, in one of the most famous passages in the novel, Eliot uses
a glancing reference to the *Oresteia* to dramatize how the primordial
power that women once claimed as mothers has been eroded over time.
In the distant world of Greek tragedy, a world more deeply grounded in
the "maternal" values, Clytemnestra had the power to ensnare and kill
Agamemnon; Mrs. Transome, by contrast, is herself bound by the "fatal
threads" linking her with her secret lover:

> The finest threads, such as no eye sees, if bound cunningly about the sensitive
> flesh, so that the movement to break them would bring torture, may make a
> worse bondage than any fetters. Mrs. Transome felt the fatal threads about her
> and the bitterness of this helpless bondage mingled itself with the new elegan-
> cies . . . which Harold had ordered to be brought about with magical quick-
> ness. (198–99, ch. 8)

This echo from the story of Agamemnon's murder serves to accent Mrs.
Transome's suffering in a world where the entangling threads pull only
one way.[11]

Furthermore, we never see Mrs. Transome at a moment parallel to
that of Clytemnestra's triumph in *Agamemnon*; we see her instead just as
Nemesis is about to seize her—when her son has assumed the patriarch's
privileges, and she is obsessed by fear and dread. By inviting comparisons with this later portion of the *Oresteia,* Eliot dramatizes how female
adultery and illegitimacy challenge Spencer's theories of "natural" gender hierarchy. In describing Mrs. Transome's relation to her illegitimate
son, Eliot disputes Spencer's functional analysis of motherhood and the
sweeping biological conclusions he draws from differential birth rates in
The Principles of Biology; that is, she exposes the false logic in his unwar-
ranted assumption that maternity is necessarily constrained within the
legal limits of patriarchal marriage. Similarly, in uncovering the secret
profligacy of both the men and the women of Transome Court, Eliot
reveals the destructive egotism that is sheltered by legalistic definitions
of paternity. Jermyn's manipulation of Arabella's shame concerning Ha-

rold's illegitimate birth exemplifies the morally corrosive effects of legal and economic systems which reproduce sexual double standards that brand female adultery as reprehensible while overlooking male adultery.

Eliot's portrayal of the "woeful progeny" at Transome Court invites us to consider Mrs. Transome's marriage and maternity in evolutionary as well as classical terms, by showing how economic and social pressures have prompted Arabella to contract a loveless marriage to a man whose frame never "expressed much vigor, either bodily or mentally" (88, ch. 1). Mr. Transome is, in turn, the progenitor of a "rickety, ugly imbecile child" who, as he grows into manhood, exhibits the cumulative results of generations of vice. Though he is "tenacious of a despicable squandering life," the only career that Durfey Transome seemed likely to enter is one in which "vice might kill him" (98, ch. 1), and in fact, at the point at which Eliot's narrative begins, Durfey is indeed dead. Mr. Transome likewise is, as Harold says, a "wreck" of a man, "terribly shrunk and shaken," who crawls about his books and beetles," as if to seek the company of similarly simple and decayed specimens (91, ch. 1). By thus representing the dark secrets of this vice-ridden class, where degenerate fathers engender still more unhealthy and vicious sons, Eliot anticipates the feminist outrage of the late 1860s that found expression in the struggle to revoke the Contagious Diseases Acts.[12]

Mrs. Transome succumbs to Jermyn's seductive "homage," however, for a good Spencerian reason—she desires a healthy son—and after she gives birth to Harold, she clings "to the belief that somehow the possession of this son was the best thing she lived for," because "to believe otherwise would have made her memory too ghastly a companion" (98, ch. 1). Thus, Eliot challenges Spencer's "hysterization" of women by demonstrating the moral questions that a biological analysis of human reproduction fails to take into account. Mrs. Transome's "larger self" is frustrated not only by the lovelessness of her marriage but also by the non-reciprocal qualities of motherlove: "After sharing the common dream that when a beautiful man-child was born to her, her cup of happiness would be full, she had travelled through long years apart from that child to find herself at last in the presence of a son of whom she was afraid, who was utterly unmanageable by her, and to whose sentiments in any given case she possessed no key" (198, ch. 8). In presenting the conflict between mother and child in such unsentimental terms, Eliot amplifies one of her earliest arguments, evident in *Adam Bede*, which exposed how Spencer conflated the biological and moral functions of mothers:

> The mother's love is at first an absorbing delight, blunting all other sensibilities; it is an expansion of the animal existence; it enlarges the imagined range for self to move in; but in after years it can only continue to be a joy on the

same terms as other long-lived love—that is by much suppression of self, and power of living in the experience of another. Mrs. Transome had darkly felt the pressure of that unchangeable fact. (98, ch. 1)

By noting once more that maternal love is not a function of a woman's "animal existence" but rather a product of her moral nature, Eliot indicates that Mrs. Transome's culpability lies not in her refusal to conform to the biological imperative that Spencer described, requiring women's complete sacrifice to the "supreme" end of motherhood, but rather in her resistance to those moral laws which dictate that "our days are heritors of days gone by."

Recording the "blanks" in Mrs. Transome's life as Harold's mother, Eliot also challenges the new scientific authority that Spencer's *Principles of Biology* lent to the conservative program for women's education first outlined in "Physical Training" (1859). The "blanks" Mrs. Transome experiences occur not only in the lives of childless women but in mothers' lives as well, as Eliot's narrator observes: "It is a fact perhaps kept a little too much in the background that mothers have a self larger than their maternity, and that when their sons have become taller than themselves, and are gone from them to college or into the world, there are wide spaces of time which are not filled with praying for their boys, reading old letters, and envying yet blessing those who are attending to their shirt buttons" (198, ch. 8). Mrs. Transome's adultery, however, also calls into question the nature of the "maternal principle" that was so central to Eliot's ideas about "moral law" in *Romola*.

In her delineation of Mrs. Transome's relationship with her natural son, Eliot likewise shows why human reproduction cannot be assessed in the simple biological terms that Spencer developed in *The Principles of Biology*, but must be seen, instead, as determined by the larger social and moral forces of a changing patriarchal culture. In *Felix Holt*, she contextualizes Mrs. Transome's adultery in order to show how the maternal principle is defeated, to demonstrate why a son learns to like "many things better than his mother's caresses" and why he comes to possess a "much keener consciousness of his independent existence in relation to her" (98, ch. 1). Treby Magna, Eliot makes plain, is being transformed by an industrial capitalism that encourages sons to repress their compensating sense of duty and devotion to their families and renders mother-love—and altruism more generally—powerless in the contest with the more assertive egotism of this rising generation. Eliot's desire to preserve the "sacredness" of the bond between mother and child is thus easily confused with a conservatism which would maintain the family in its traditional patriarchal form.

In selecting the 1830s as the period for this novel, Eliot chose a decade that witnessed not only great political upheaval but also the apogee of the Victorian cult of the mother (Trudgill 256). From the moment of Harold's return, though, Mrs. Transome is shrewdly aware that her son practices a false chivalry towards her, emblematic of the hypocrisy underlying Victorian attitudes about motherhood in this period. In their first meeting, Harold tries to assign her to the part of "grandmama on satin cushions" (95, ch. 1) in order to guarantee more freedom for himself in making changes and improvements at Transome Court. Harold's sense of filial duty is thus evacuated of meaning; it merely masks his impulse to dominate.

By casting Harold as a Victorian Oedipus, determined to inaugurate a new "reign" which would allow him to exercise complete control over all the things that "don't properly belong to a woman" (95, ch. 1), Eliot unveils the male dominance so effectively disguised by the sentimental glorification of motherhood in the 1830s and suggests, by implication, what was likewise obscured by Spencer's reconstruction of motherhood in the 1860s. Mrs. Transome sees through Harold's pretense and is humiliated by the emptiness of his grand gestures; she realizes that Harold "had no wish opposed to filial kindness, but his busy thoughts were imperiously determined by habits which had no reference to any woman's feelings; and even if he had conceived what his mother's feeling was, his mind, after that momentary arrest, would have darted forward in his usual course" (93, ch. 1). In this patriarchal household, filial duty becomes a disguise for domineering paternalism.

Harold's impulse to domination has been reinforced by his career as a banker and businessman in Smyrna. Though he has traveled nearly to the geographical omphalos of the maternal wild zone, Harold's sojourn in the East has brought him no closer to an understanding of the ancient authority of the mother. In fact, Harold has defied the ancient moral law which, according to Bachofen, originally defined and enforced marriage; for Harold buys a Greek woman slave for his consort and later asserts his patriarchal right to claim the son of this union as his property. Though Harry's mother is dead and conveniently out of the way by the time Harold returns to Transome Court, he is not inclined to contract a more legitimate marriage, for he finds that "Western women were not to his taste; they showed a transition from the feebly animal to the thinking being, which was simply troublesome" (497, ch. 40). Harold expects that the "possession on any terms of a healthy grandchild" will mollify his mother, but he is mistaken. By suggesting Harold's small part in the "white slave trade,"[13] Eliot indicates how, in Harold's mind at least, the property ethic transforms marriage into a kind of prostitution and fatherhood into a business proposition. The juxtaposition of Harold's illegitimate sexual union and his mother's secret liaison suggests once again the double standard, reinforced by patriarchal marriage laws, which overlooks the sexual transgressions of the male while punishing those of the female with great severity.

By keeping Harold ignorant of his true paternity throughout most of the novel, Eliot also unmasks the murderous competition between him and his father that is fostered by the emerging industrial society in Treby Magna. Jermyn, one of the community's most successful "practical" capitalists, recognizes no duties of kinship that bind him to Harold, because he sees his relationship to his natural son in entirely legalistic terms. Since no patriarchal law formalizes his connection with Harold, Jermyn feels free to defend himself and his legitimate family at all costs. Even though he acknowledges the biological heritage his son has acquired from him in his "deuced faculty for business," Jermyn disavows any of the obligations of paternity and plots revenge by pledging that he will make Harold "feel something if he makes signs of setting the dogs on me" (286, ch. 17). Declaring that "the people named Transome owe me a good deal more than I owe them" (286, ch. 17), Jermyn reveals himself to be utterly without what Auguste Comte called "filiation."[14]

It is this patriarchal and legalistic view of his obligations to Harold and to his mother that reduces Jermyn, in Eliot's view, to the level of a hunted "animal." As Harold's desire to restore his family's fortune grows keener and he considers prosecuting Jermyn for legal malfeasance in handling the Transomes' affairs, Jermyn resembles more and more a "doomed animal, with every issue earthed up except where its enemy stands" (579, ch. 47). This animal metaphor demonstrates how the principles of egotism and self-interest, encouraged by ambitious materialism, have reduced Jermyn to "mere lawlessness," and it is against his legalistic but immoral assessment of his personal and parental obligations that Mrs. Transome stands in proud resistance.

Mrs. Transome's memories of her adulterous affair contrast sharply with Jermyn's, and Eliot uses this contrast to reiterate her ongoing feminist critique of the sexual double standards of Victorian England. No episode in the novel dramatizes more clearly the differing views Mrs. Transome and Jermyn entertain of their shared past than her conversation with him about the duties that they both owe to Harold. Quotations from Sophocles' *Electra* and *Ajax* preface this confrontation, providing a definition of manhood which emphasizes the moral obligation to "cherish memory." Judged by this standard, Jermyn proves himself to be "for ever an ignoble man" (510, ch. 42). In this scene, Jermyn asks Mrs. Transome to recognize her "debt" to him by sacrificing the thing most precious to her—her son's respectful attention, cool and superficial though it is. While Eliot recognizes that Jermyn is justified in requesting that Harold be told the secret of his paternity, she points out as well the "selfish insensibility" which makes Jermyn's moral appeal a sacrilege.

Moreover, Eliot shows that the materialism of Jermyn's "pushing middle-class culture" has not only turned his personal selfishness into a habit but also has converted his "tenderness" into "calculation," as each memory of his love affair is rationalized into "a claim." Fearing his son's threats to seek redress through law, Jermyn argues that prevailing "law" can't "represent justice in this case" (515, ch. 42); instead, he urges Mrs. Transome to tell Harold the "whole truth" about his paternity in order to forestall any possible legal action. By showing how Jermyn is led by this logic to break the "deep silence about the past," Eliot represents one of those "terrible" ironies of the human lot whereby "a deep truth" comes to be uttered "by lips that have no right to it" (517, ch. 42).

In describing Mrs. Transome's impulse to "remember" her love affair, while Jermyn "more and more forgot" it (201, ch. 9), Eliot returns to the same historical wild zone that she invoked in *Romola* by alluding to Dante's famous lovers. Locating a "heroism even in the circles of hell for fellow sinners who cling to each other in the fiery whirlwind and never recriminate" (520, ch. 42), Eliot affirms the redeeming potential in erotic love, even when it is illicit, that she described in Tessa's love for Tito.[15] Yet, as *Felix Holt* indicates, egotism can also masquerade as love, and, lacking the passionate loyalty that redeems erotic love, Jermyn has simply evinced his "selfishness in the form of homage" (515, ch. 42). Seeing the use to which he would put their "tender relations . . . when they have ceased to be tender" (512, ch. 42), Mrs. Transome bitterly reminds Jermyn of the love he once professed, pointing out how his calculus of "sacrifices" belies it: "You reckon up your sacrifices for me: you have kept good account of them, and it is needful; they are some of them what no one else could guess or find out. But you made your sacrifices when they seemed pleasant to you; when you told me they were your happiness; when you told me it was I who stooped, and I who bestowed favours" (518, ch. 42). Seeing Jermyn's dishonorable betrayal as a predictable consequence of male privilege, Mrs. Transome denounces him in a moment of passionate anger: "I would not lose the misery of being a woman, now I see what can be the baseness of a man. One must be a man—first of all to tell a woman that her love has made her your debtor, and then ask her to pay you by breaking the last poor threads between her and her son" (519, ch. 42). Eliot acknowledges the mutual guilt that underlies Mrs. Transome's recriminations, but she focuses on exposing why Jermyn is innured to them. His lifestory dramatizes how his insensitivity has been cultivated by his participation in a legal and social system that defines kinship in patriarchal terms, overvalues wealth and power, and assesses love by determining if it is a "good bargain."

Mrs. Transome's adultery, however, also gives Eliot the opportunity to explore the dark side of female sexuality and to consider the evolutionary implications of resisting systems which would contain or control it. In this endeavor, Eliot's feminism collides with her evolutionism. Eliot's own life, of course, suggested a radical alternative to marriage, in her illegal but scrupulously moral relationship with George Henry Lewes, but she was reluctant to endorse either Mrs. Transome's secret adultery or to recommend her own choice of a more public resistance to restrictive patriarchal marriage laws. Mrs. Transome, through her adulterous liaison, moves beyond the limits of moral resistance that Eliot charted in *Romola.* Her example allowed Eliot to reconsider the place of female sexuality in the wild zone and to reassess the moral valence she attached to "maternal" emotions and to moral "resistance." By demonstrating how class prejudices and economic motives corrupt the basis of Mrs. Transome's sexual unions both with her husband and with her lover and by disclosing how the secret of Harold's birth could destroy family feeling entirely, Eliot reveals how she came to regard marriage as the most effective institution for preserving the values of love, honor, sympathy, and altruism against the forces of patriarchal law and industrial capitalism that undermined them. The more successful marriage of Esther Lyon and Felix Holt suggests that this social institution functions, ideally, to protect the most morally elevated values associated with erotic and parental love.[16]

Eliot's reading of social and cultural evolution prevented her from imagining a possible return to the matriarchal order that Clytemnestra defended in the *Oresteia,* a kind of nostalgia exploited by Ruskin's sentimental pronouncement that women could become queens once more, though they could only reign over the hearth and not the world.[17] Because Eliot understood the process of social evolution, she realized that such easy retrogressions were impossible. But the same process suggested an alternative to her: that is, that marriage itself was not exempt from evolutionary change and could serve to coordinate a whole range of moral and social reforms. Esther sees through the Ruskinian illusions about women's domestic power that allowed her to reign as "Queen Esther" in Reverend Lyon's house when she discovers the secrets of her birth and inheritance. She explicitly rejects the bargain that Ruskin offered to middle-class Victorian women—an offer of specious power in the domestic realm that leaves traditional hierarchies of gender and class untouched—when she repudiates a life of "silken ease" with Harold Transome and chooses instead a marriage of downward mobility with Felix Holt.

Mrs. Transome's relation with Jermyn also illustrates why Eliot continued to resist Spencer's assumption that industrial capitalism would naturally allow the greatest fulfillment of human potential, an assumption which provided the foundation for his hypotheses concerning the "biological division of labor." Eliot was unwilling to measure progressive change—in the individual, in a social institution like marriage, or in society at large—according to Spencer's standards of progress. In her letters from these years, she comments on the "hideous" consequences of industrialism, noting, for example, after a trip to Holbeck and Wakefield, that "it is difficult to keep up one's faith in a millennium within sight of this modern civilization which consists in 'development of industries.' Egypt and her big calm gods seems quite as good" (*GEL* 4:162).

Because of her reservations about industrial progress, Eliot is often seen as more politically conservative than Herbert Spencer and other evolutionary theorists.[18] Sally Shuttleworth, for example, argues that Eliot's appreciation for the organic unity of rural English life, her objections to the changes prompted by industrialism, and her reverence for the past form the basis of her political conservativism. Shuttleworth explains that "though class distinctions are disguised in the form of cultural distinctions, the organic model to which Felix adheres is clearly the nostalgic static one rather than the Spencerian model which would encompass industrial and social change" (125). Shuttleworth concludes that Eliot, like Felix, accepted a static rather than a dynamic model of social change and so opposed democratizing reforms, while Spencer, as an apologist for industrial development, was more open to wider participation in the political process.

In fact, the remarks Spencer makes in letters from this period about social change engineered by legislation reveal a political standpoint much closer to Eliot's than is usually recognized. In 1866, Spencer cast his only vote in a parliamentary election. In his *Autobiography*, he comments that some property he had inherited gave him the qualification to vote in that year, though shortly afterwards when he sold the property he was again disenfranchised. Explaining why he did not ever cast another ballot, even after regaining the qualification to vote in London, he observes:

> In most cases my dissent from the beliefs tacitly held by both political parties on the question of the functions of the State, which I regard as the question of most importance, has been such that I have had little motive to support one candidate rather than another. In fact as of late years, Liberals have vied with Conservatives in extending legislative regulations in all directions, there has been nothing to choose between them, and therefore, to me, no temptation to vote. (*Autobiography* 2:125)

When we remember that a self-supporting intellectual like Spencer did not meet the economic requirements for suffrage until he was in his mid-forties, we can understand one possible reason for Eliot's reservations about extending the franchise. Eliot, who could not vote, of course, because of her sex, takes a perspective not unlike Spencer's in her evaluation of the legislative activity of her time. "No system, religious or political," she writes in *Felix Holt*, "has laid it down as a principle that all men are alike virtuous, or even that all the people rated for £50 are an honour to their species" (472, ch. 37).

Eliot's treatment of the process of political reform in *Felix Holt*, reveals, then, that she agreed with Spencer, and other Radicals of the 1840s, about the ideal relation between government and "public opinion" (Peel 69–76). While Spencer's attitudes about women and feminism underwent many vicissitudes in the course of his career, he maintained a firm belief that the legislative machinery of government should be reduced to a minimum. In 1864 he writes:

> The form of society towards which we are progressing, I hold to be one in which government will be reduced to the smallest amount possible and freedom increased to the greatest degree possible, in which human nature will have become so moulded by social discipline into fitness with the social stance that it will need little external restraint, but will be self-restrained. (*Essays: Scientific* 2:131)

Spencer, like other Radicals of the 1840s, assumed this position because, as J.D.Y. Peel explains, he hoped that "the state would become functionless" as " 'public opinion,' based on 'moral principle and general information,' would and should necessarily take over many, if not most, of the former functions of politics; and the mass of the population would acquire the franchise when they really needed it no longer" (72).

The contrast in Eliot's novel between Harold Transome and Felix Holt sets forth the consequences of this "Radical" skepticism about reforms initiated and enforced by political processes. By questioning the efficacy of labels like "Radical" or "Liberal" to adequately define a political position, Eliot indicates her faith in a moral disinterestedness that transcends such labels. *Felix Holt* shows that political labels are, in fact, a thoroughly unreliable index of morality, and in Eliot's analysis of the political struggle in North Loamshire, she stresses the confusion that results from the absence of any real consistency in the use or meaning of these terms:

> The Tories were far from being all oppressors; disposed to grind down the working classes into serfdom, and it was undeniable that the inspector at the tape manufactory, who spoke with much eloquence on the extension of

the suffrage, was a more tyrannical personage than the openhanded Mr. Wace, whose chief political tenet was that it was all nonsense giving men votes when they had no stake in the country. (128, ch. 3)

The ambiguity of the term "Radical" is precisely the point of the comparison between Felix and Harold (130, ch. 3), and by demonstrating the inadequacy of such labels as signifiers of political positions, Eliot invites the reader to consider political affiliation in the context of a larger moral code which embraces private as well as public life.

Moreover, Eliot's feminism intensified her skepticism about taking political terms at face value. Since neither Liberals nor Conservatives took a consistent position on women's issues, she felt justified in her use of private morality as a test of public ethics. Eliot clearly endorses Esther's assessment of "what is severely true" about Harold's Radicalism when her heroine observes that "he had a way of virtually measuring the value of everything by the contribution it made to his own pleasure" (529, ch. 43). Just as the "unsympathetic" nature that is revealed in Harold's relationship with his mother and with others belies "any thorough understanding or deep respect for what was in the mind of the person he obliged or indulged," so his "political views" are an extension of this attitude. "The utmost enjoyment of his own advantages was the solvent that blended pride in his family and position, with the adhesion to changes that were to obliterate tradition and melt down enchased gold heirlooms into plating for the egg-spoons of 'the people' " (529, ch. 43).[19] While this passage, like Eliot's treatment of the election riots, suggests her fear of sudden democratizing change, the ironically underscored reference to "the people," reveals, most of all, her profound distrust of any political rhetoric which allowed powerful and wealthy men like Harold Transome to cloak their self-aggrandizement beneath their professed but utterly unsympathetic concern for the poor. Where political demagoguery allowed such promises of "egg spoons for 'the people' " to take the place of real attention to the sufferings of the oppressed, references to private morality became, for Eliot, a more reliable way to assess public policy.

While *Felix Holt* thus reveals Eliot's skepticism about social reforms instituted by political means, it acknowledges, nonetheless, the need for reform through its extensive use of evolutionary metaphors to characterize the members of the Tory Establishment at Treby Magna. Eliot identifies as superannuated not only the patriarch at Transome Court, who fathers a still less capable "imbecile" son, but all the members of the older generation of this elite group. Sir Maximus, for example, is compared to one of those "antediluvian animals whom the system of things condemned to carry such a huge bulk that they really could not inspect their bodily appurtenance, and had no conception of their own tails" (182, ch. 7). Though he "snarled in a subdued way when he looked over the accounts," Sir Maximus is willing to "endure some personal inconvenience in order to keep up the institutions of the country, to maintain his hereditary establishment and do his duty in that station of life—the station of the long-tailed saurian—to which it had pleased Providence to call him" (183, ch. 7). In comparing the healthiest and most moral representative of the Tory aristocracy to a dinosaur, Eliot intimates that this particular "hereditary establishment" is doomed to a fairly speedy extinction.[20] She is no less critical of the Anglican clergy who help maintain the ascendancy of these Tory aristocrats and lead the attack on the workers. Likewise, she condemns Christian and the "parasite" servant class who pander to their employers while attempting to profit from an inside knowledge of family secrets.

Moreover, by selecting Felix Holt as the hero of this novel Eliot indicates her recognition that more active resistance to a corrupt political system is sometimes both morally justifiable and socially necessary. In *Felix Holt*, she extends the analysis she developed in *Romola* concerning the problem of outward and inward law and of active and passive resistance to the existing social order. Eliot's exploration of Holt's moral position as a Radical shows her continuing interest in the problem of determining where the "sacredness of obedience ended, and where the sacredness of rebellion began" (*Romola* 553, ch. 56). In 1865, Eliot described her "real reverence" for Mazzini in the following terms:

> Now, though I believe there are cases in which conspiracy may be a sacred, necessary struggle against organized wrong, there are also cases in which it is hopeless, and can produce nothing but misery; or needless, because it is not the best means attainable of reaching the desired end; or unjustifiable because it resorts to acts which are more unsociable in their character than the very wrong they are directed to extinguish. (*GEL* 4:200)

Eliot thus indicates her recognition, on the one hand, of the power exercised by the political and social Establishment in preventing necessary reform, and her reluctance, on the other, to condone violence and destruction.

In dramatizing the causes and consequences of "organized wrong" during the election riots, however, Eliot also shows how easily existing political processes are manipulated, and, in this instance, how the rising generation participates in this corruption. Thus, she indicts both Harold Transome, who has paid the operatives to provide the election "treating," and Jermyn, who makes the arrangements. By showing how the disenfranchised fail to influence the political process, Eliot demonstrates that she, like Spencer, would prefer a more gradual method of social reform. By dramatizing Felix's inability to control the rioters and by describing the entangling circumstances which lead to his arrest and trial, Eliot indicates that active resistance is, in this case, both "needless" and "unjustifiable." Thus she registers her preference for a less violent means of resistance that promotes consensus and cooperation.

As her comments on women's suffrage indicate, Eliot saw participation in a corrupt political system as itself dangerously corrupting for both men and women, and Felix Holt expresses this view earlier in the novel when he tries to explain the moral advantages of disenfranchisement. He tells the workers at the Sugar Loaf that they should refrain from agitating for the extension of the suffrage until a future time when the existing political system is actually reformed and when participation in it would be less morally compromising:

> And while public opinion is what it is—while men have no better beliefs about public duty—while corruption is not felt to be a damning disgrace—while men are not ashamed in parliament and out of it to make public questions which concern the welfare of millions a mere screen for their own petty private ends—I say, no fresh scheme of voting will much mend our condition. (401, ch. 30)

Though Holt's speech betrays his condescending attitude toward the working men he addresses in this scene, his outlook nonetheless reflects Eliot's own willingness to confront the social problems that Spencer evaded through his unquestioning acceptance of the positive social value of laissez-faire industrialism and the political and social hierarchies his evolutionary theory allowed him to justify.[21]

This episode also reveals that Eliot was less optimistic than Spencer in her estimation of the power of public opinion to encourage positive change, especially when she considered the outraged opposition to women's emancipation. Nonetheless, since Eliot also doubted the efficacy of social change engineered by legislation, she rejected women's suffrage as the best political solution to women's subordination. Barbara Bodichon could argue cheerfully about the instantly transforming effects of women's suffrage: "When women have votes, they will read with closer attention than heretofore the daily histories of our times, and will converse with each other and with their fathers and brothers about social and political questions. They will become interested in a wider circle of ideas, and where they now think and feel somewhat vaguely, they will form definite and decided opinions."[22] But Eliot's evolutionary understanding of human psychology and social development prevented her from accepting such an optimistic prediction about the immediate intellectual and moral benefits of the vote for disenfranchised women or men.

Though Eliot shared Spencer's skepticism about the political process as the best means for achieving permanent social reforms, she grew increasingly more sensitive to the ways that industrialism inhibited positive social change by controlling the ambiguous force of public opinion. During these years, Eliot expressed her "indignation at the comparative indulgence which the worst corruption of our society meets with," while social activists "are persecuted for simply pointing out the unfairness with which crime is estimated" (*GEL* 4:374). In her selection of Felix Holt as the hero of her novel, then, we can see how Eliot's attitude toward the status quo differs from Spencer's. Because he put his faith in the authority of science—in biology, psychology, and, finally, sociology—to promote what he regarded as positive social change, Spencer was able to preserve covertly the hierarchies of sex, class, and race, as *The Principles of Biology* demonstrates and as the development of his thought in later works confirms.

In 1868, in the revision of *The Principles of Psychology*, Spencer admitted that "feelings are in all cases the material out of which, in the superior tracts of consciousness, intellect is evolved by structural combination" (1:192), but he apparently did not recognize how his evolutionary reading of human psychology undercut his earlier dependence upon public opinion as an adequate agent of social change. Having separated psychology from social analysis, Spencer apparently did not concern himself with the contradictions that arose. Eliot, by contrast, had long insisted that feelings often direct reason. As the political debate about women's emancipation made Spencer's continued reliance on the reforming power of "public opinion" appear more and more untenable, Eliot was forced to reassess the relation between "public opinion" and those other agencies charged with initiating positive social reform.

In *Felix Holt*, then, Eliot acknowledges the problems evolutionary psychology posed for Victorian theories of social reform through her representation of the two social institutions that were most frequently identified as the source and agent of "public opinion": the church and the family. Her study of the role of the Catholic church in *Romola* gave Eliot a new perspective on both the Anglican and the Dissenting Protestant traditions in Victorian England. In a letter written in 1865, for example, Eliot described the Anglican church as the "least morally dignified of all forms of Christianity" (*GEL* 4:214), and her depiction of the Anglican clergymen in *Felix Holt* reflects this view. Personal and political alliances bind Mr. Lingon, Parson Jack, and Augustus Debarry to the dying social order, and their impulses to preserve their dominant position in the social hierarchy inevitably compromise their moral vision. Lingon and Parson Jack oppose Harold's Radical candidacy because of a self-interestedness that is frankly expressed in deliberate policy.

Likewise, the "old-fashioned aristocratic" Rector Augustus Debarry displays an even more egocentric vision of his moral obligations, and, as Eliot shows, he is able to command resources that literally allow him to silence dissent. Already convinced that "the political sermons of the Industrial preacher" were, in their way, "as pernicious sources of intoxication as the beerhouses," Debarry urges his brother, Sir Maximus, to "take care lest" the Dissenters "should get land to build more chapels" (127, ch. 3). Debarry answers Reverend Lyon's "clerical challenge" for a public debate by protesting against "these busy prating men" who would "make the ignorant multitude the judges of the largest questions, both political and religious, till we shall soon have no institution left that is not on a level with the comprehension of a huckster and a drayman" (330, ch. 23). In concluding his tirade, Debarry justifies his position by expressing his concern that sudden democratizing change could jeopardize priceless intellectual and cultural traditions: "There can be nothing more retrograde to losing all the results of civilization—all the lessons of Providence—letting the windlass run down after men have been turning it painfully for generations" (330, ch. 23). While his concerns partly echo Eliot's own,[23] his characterization reveals, nonetheless, Eliot's objections to his narrow-mindedness and to the defensive stance he takes which prevents him from recognizing the moral authority of alternative traditions of dissent.

While Debarry imagines his work as that of preservation and retrieval and assigns himself the role of the only guardian of truth, his class prejudices prevent him from seeing Rufus Lyon as an equally competent and more disinterested seeker after truth. Lyon, in contrast to Debarry, regards himself as obligated to pursue an ongoing "good and necessary" search for truth and defines himself as a member of a company of visionary prophets, who look not only to the past but to the future for their inspiration. In the contrast between Lyon and Debarry, then, Eliot neatly separates the forward-looking quality that she admired in both Spencerian and Positivist thought from its conservative social policy.

Eliot highlights Reverend Lyon's otherworldliness and dramatizes his resistance to the materialism and fundamentalism of his flock in order to display his intellectual disinterestedness, a quality that Eliot particularly admired in J. S. Mill's *Political Economy*.[24] Shortly before *Felix Holt* was published, Eliot commented in a letter: "I was brought up in the Church of England, and never belonged to any other religious body. I care that this should be known, not at all on personal grounds, but because as I have been, and perhaps shall be, depicting Dissenters with much sympathy, I would not have it supposed that the sympathy springs from any partiality of association" (*GEL* 4:213). Lyon indicates his commitment to this same disinterested position by locating the ultimate authority to compel obedience neither in the letter of the law nor in any other exist-ing mechanism of the church or state, but rather in a superior moral law that will unite "all men" in the future (242, ch. 13).

In this spirit, he accepts Felix not as a religious disciple but as a fellow searcher after things "honest and true," unexpectedly overlooking the younger man's iconoclasm and "license in language." Lyon carefully de-fines the conditions under which moral law may prompt resistance to civil law, noting that Felix's "bold" Radicalism could be easily misinter-preted as anarchism. Reiterating Romola's lesson, Lyon urges Felix not to forget that "the right to rebellion is the right to seek a higher rule, and not to wander in mere lawlessness." "True liberty" he concludes, "can be nought but the transfer of obedience from the will of one or of a few to that will which is the norm for all men" (242, ch. 13). At his trial, Felix displays his acceptance of Lyon's view of moral and civil responsibility. He defends his right to resist the law when "it is a pretext for wrong, which it should be the very object of law to hinder" and refers to a higher law which authorizes his resistance: "I hold it blasphemy to say that a man ought not to fight against authority; there is no great religion and no great freedom that has not done it in the beginning" (565, ch. 46).

But Lyon is less successful in conveying his moral vision to his parish-ioners; in the episode of the sabotaged religious debate, for example, he cannot overcome the intellectual obtuseness of his audience. Moreover, the way in which the Dissenters close ranks against Felix when he is brought to trial shows that Dissent alone does not guarantee moral disin-terestedness, that a similar collective selfishness can compromise this alternative "moral" institution, just as it does the Establishment. Lyon's congregation is unable to find any "edification in what had befallen Felix" because his action did not define him as the "champion distinctly of Dissent and Liberalism" (465, ch. 37). In this way, Eliot reveals a nar-rowness in this tradition of Dissent which assesses morality in terms of self interest. In representing Mr. Lyon's failure to alter the view that his congregation takes of Felix, Eliot demonstrates the stubborn ignorance which was, for her, one of the most pressing reasons she resisted extend-ing the suffrage to disenfranchised men or women.

Having thus demonstrated how both the Anglican and Dissenting tra-ditions are compromised as instruments of moral reform, Eliot seems to have fairly successfully painted herself into a corner. Nonetheless, the moral stance assumed by Reverend Lyon, Felix Holt, and, ultimately, Esther indicates the compromise Eliot finally reached in her effort to reconcile her recognition of the necessity to resist an entrenched Estab-lishment when it blocks essential political and social reform with her preference for gradual social change promoted by disinterested analysis. In *Felix Holt* Eliot returns, then, to the "wild zone," to reassess the mother's role in the family and to recommend an individualist solution by suggesting one way that those who recognize the transcendent moral laws defining human evolution may separate themselves from the decadent power elite so as to hasten its decline. Thus, Eliot seeks to identify the powers at work in family life that may help bring about the "transfer of obedience" from the "will of one or of a few men to that will which is the norm for all men" (242, ch. 13).

Eliot's treatment of the family and her representation of Felix and Esther's marriage as an act of resistance can perhaps be better understood in the context of Spencer's comments on "moral law" in the expanded edition of *The Principles of Psychology* (1870–1872).[25] In a rare moment in this text, Spencer uses the term "moral evolution," but he applies it only in his discussion of the social evolution of marriage customs, showing how, for him, "moral" issues cluster around the problems posed by women and the control of their sexuality:

> Along with but a partially established relation between the sexes, along with a parental relation which, on the man's side at least, is vague or not persistent, and along with a relatively small power of representation, the lowest types show us a moral nature in which fellow-feeling, relatively feeble where it is shown, is not shown at all in its higher ranges. During the progress from these types up to the highest types yet evolved, sympathy and sociality under its three forms, have been acting and reacting, each as cause and consequence— greater sympathy making possible greater sociality, public and domestic, and greater sociality serving further to cultivate sympathy. All along, however, this moral evolution, negatively restrained at each stage by defects of intelligence, has been positively restrained by the predatory activities—partly those necessitated by the destruction of inferior creatures but chiefly those necessitated by the antagonisms of societies. (*Psychology*, 2:576–77)

Eliot, in contrast, defined the domain of "moral law" far more broadly, and in *Felix Holt* she challenges Spencer's assumption, evident in the passage above, that the force of outward law prevails over all inward resistance and so sustains the hierarchies of gender and class that it "naturalizes":

> The stronger will always rule, some say, with an air of confidence which is like a lawyer's flourish, forbidding exceptions or additions. But what is strength? Is it blind willfulness that sees no terror, no many-linked consequences, no bruises and wounds of those whose cord it tightens? Is it the narrowness of a brain that conceives no needs differing from its own, and looks to no results beyond the bargains of to-day; that tugs with emphasis for every small purpose, and thinks it weakness to exercise the sublime power of resolved renunciation? (160, ch. 6)

The concept of "moral law" proposed in this passage valorizes the insight women have gained as a consequence of the submission forced upon them by their biology and by the traditional gender arrangements of the patriarchal family. Because Eliot wished to formulate a "moral law" that would eventually transcend the harsher physical ones, she attempted to identify those qualities in family life that make it a viable agent for progressive social change. She focuses, as a result, on the sympathy, imagination, and love that makes the "renunciation" of egotism an important feature of Felix and Esther's marriage. But her commitment to disinterestedness forces her to acknowledge how the "vices of the oppressed" sometimes compromised "maternal principles" and to admit that men as well as women could gain access to this moral wild zone through the experience of love and parenthood. In comparing Mrs. Holt's, Mrs. Transome's, and Esther's experiences of family life, Eliot depicts the vices as well as the virtues of the "oppressed," tries to imagine a means of social change which would allow women to continue to love the men who exercise power over them, and envisions a way for women to escape from reproducing these vices.

Mrs. Holt refers to the crucial moral role in society that sentimental Victorian reformers frequently assigned to mothers when she says, "If everybody's son was guided by their mothers, the world 'ud be different" (532, ch,. 43). But we see in Mrs. Holt not only the destructive consequences of her aggressive ignorance, a quality Eliot had portrayed earlier in Mrs. Tulliver, but also the dangerous conservatism of a moral vision defined entirely by domestic values. Mrs. Holt misunderstands the nature of the "sacred obligations" that bind the child to the family and the community and so interprets Felix's obligations to her in completely egocentric and materialistic terms. She insists that he owes her grandchildren and a gig, and protests his decision not to marry. In characterizing her, Eliot shows how subtly motherlove is blended with the desire to maintain mastery over the child and dramatizes how easily a moral code that defines women's duties to the state exclusively in domestic terms can be corrupted by such egotism and by the principles of "getting on."

Similarly, Mrs. Transome displays, in her compromising relation to Esther, what was perhaps a more politically threatening consequence of women's subordination in the family. During Esther's visit to Transome Court, she and Mrs. Transome meet privately and explore the "wild zone" in their conversations about the meaning of their identity as women. Arabella is gratified by Esther's "deference" and exclaims, "My dear, you make me wish I had a daughter" (495, ch. 40), but Eliot shows that her affection does not counter her more ingrained pride and egotism. Though she anticipates that by marrying Harold, Esther would suf-

fer domestic unhappiness like her own, Mrs. Transome is willing to sacrifice the girl, because she realizes it would prevent Harold from discover-
ing the secret of his paternity. Though she admits to Denner that Esther
would never "master" Harold, and imagines that he would "make her
fond of him, and afraid of him," she nonetheless advises Esther to accept
his proposal of marriage. Unable to see beyond the alternatives of victimization and passive aggression that have shaped her own life, Mrs.
Transome remains imprisoned not only by her class prejudices but also
by her own sufferings as a woman. She would see her own choices
repeated in Esther's life. Generalizing from her own experience, she
concludes:

> A woman's love is always freezing into fear. She wants everything, she is secure
> in nothing. This girl has a fine spirit—plenty of fire and pride and wit. Men
> like such captives, as they like horses that champ the bit and paw the ground:
> they feel more triumph in their mastery. What is the use of woman's will—if
> she tries, she doesn't get it, and she ceases to be loved. God was cruel when he
> made women. (488, ch. 39)

While Eliot uses evolutionary terms to anatomize this psychology of victimization, they provide her with no means either to ameliorate it or to
prevent it from being reproduced in women's subsequent experience in
the "wild zone" or in their analysis of political and social issues beyond
the domestic sphere. Eliot was, of course, especially sensitive in her analysis of this aspect of female psychology because she had herself suffered
from the censure motivated by it.

Felix Holt's concept of fatherhood, by contrast, is designed to counter
evolutionary definitions of paternity which normalize the separation of
the public and the private spheres and the female subordination that is
reinforced by it. Felix urges the workers at the Sugar Loaf to reconsider
their responsibilities as fathers, for he believes that by laying "hold of
them by their fatherhood" he will touch a "more sympathetic fibre than
. . . any ribbon in the buttonhole" (219, ch. 11). In a world where men
dominate the institutions determining both public and private life, fathers must learn to modify their authority and share the responsibilities
and the discipline of self-renouncing love with mothers, before true egalitarian reform can be accomplished: "I'll take one of their little fellows
and set him in the midst. Till they can show there's something they love
better than swilling themselves with ale, extension of the suffrage can
never mean anything for them but extension of boozing" (219, ch. 11).
While Felix betrays his puritanical asceticism and messianic aloofness in
imitating Christ with the children in this scene, his desire to reform the
prevailing attitudes toward fatherhood nevertheless challenges Spencer's claim that men are less inclined, by nature, to respond to parental

love. Felix's moral arguments gain authenticity when he recognizes his own love for Esther, marries her, and himself fathers a son.

Eliot reveals her endorsement of Felix's program for political change based on the cooperation and renunciation ideally practiced in the family when she later repeats his emphasis on fatherhood in her essay entitled "Address to Working Men, by Felix Holt." Here Felix argues that some "parents' misery has made parents' wickedness," when he notes that "there are numbers of our fellow workmen who . . . never use the imperfect opportunities already offered them for giving their children some schooling, but turn their little ones of tender age into breadwinners, often at cruel tasks, exposed to the horrible infection of childish vice" (*Essays* 427). But, emphasizing the difference between biological paternity and morally responsible fatherhood, Felix concludes by recommending a program for social change based on the ideals of family life: "We who are still blessed with the hearts of fathers and the consciences of men—we who have some knowledge of the curse entailed on broods of creatures in human shape, whose enfeebled bodies and dull perverted minds are mere centres of uneasiness, in whom even appetite is feeble and joy impossible—I say we are bound to use all the means at our command to help in putting a stop to this horror" (*Essays* 427). By consistently invoking "parental duties" rather than "mother's duties" in *Felix Holt* and in this essay, Eliot challenges the "hysterization" of women that allowed Spencer, on the one hand, to argue for women's inferiority and, on the other, to identify their instinctive altruism as preventing them from recognizing justice—a notion which, in *The Principles of Ethics*,[26] became his rationale for excluding them from all participation in public life. In Eliot's view, mothers could not oversee the moral reform of the world alone—especially since, as a group, they had been ill-educated and so lacked the disinterestedness that would allow them to see beyond the domestic walls that confined them.

Similarly, though marriage could, in Eliot's view, serve a socially conservative function by allying women—and men—to a dying or corrupt social hierarchy, it could also be used for more revolutionary ends. In defining Esther's marriage to Felix as a "partnership," then, Eliot indicates her rejection of the traditional hierarchy of gender arrangements and expresses her alternative assumption that the moral evolution that is gradually transforming the family will eventually make the traditional subordination of woman to man obsolete both inside marriage and outside it. Early in the novel, Felix Holt points out the socially regressive impact of the traditional middle-class marriage when he explains why he is unwilling to acquire a "discontented wife and several unhopeful children," and his analysis echoes the views Eliot expressed in "Margaret Fuller and Mary Wollstonecraft." In this early essay, Eliot objected to the "established formulae" which define women as inferior and keep them ignorant: "The precious meridian years of many a man of genius have to be spent in the toil of routine, that an 'establishment' may be kept up for a woman who can understand none of his secret yearnings, who is fit for nothing but to sit in her drawing-room like a doll-Madonna in her shrine" (*Essays* 204–5). Felix's objections to the fetich Esther has made of good taste and fine ladyism reiterates Eliot's criticism of marriage à la mode.

Felix's definition of an ideal marriage both anticipates and rejects Spencer's contention that women's submission to men in marriage is justified by their natural inferiority. Felix argues, instead, "If a woman really believes herself to be a lower kind of being, she should place her-self in subjection: she should be ruled by the thoughts of her father or husband. If not, let her show her power of choosing something better" (210, ch. 10). Eliot demonstrates, though, that women do not have the unlimited power of choice that Felix assumes, for when Esther indicates her desire to choose "something better" by loving him, Felix retreats, seeing her as little more than an "idol," a "useless absorbent of precious things" (*Essays* 205). Felix has difficulty believing in Esther's constancy and prescribes, instead of the love she longs for, a "good strong terrible vision," so that she may never lose her best self (366, ch. 27). In this way, then, Eliot acknowledges the self-righteousness which may separate the reformer from those who need his or her help. Felix, at this point, does not properly understand the mutual "subjection" of genuine love that can offset such egotism, as is evident both in his rejection of Esther's advances and in his bemusement over Lyon's "subjection" to his adopted daughter.

Though Esther is tempted to repeat Mrs. Transome's mistake and enter a marriage of "silken bondage" to Harold Transome, she chooses, instead, to act on the "highest kind of love" in renouncing her heritage at Transome Court. Esther makes her choice before she is assured of Felix's love, and by describing her pain when she fears that his choice "lay aloof from her," Eliot acknowledges the intractability of both men's and women's desire. Yet, while Eliot thus confirms Esther's intuition that she lives in a culture where "it is difficult for a woman ever to try to be anything good when she is not believed in—when it is always supposed that she must be contemptible" (365, ch. 27), she asserts her feminist resistance to the Spencerian theories which would define women's moral as well as her intellectual and physical traits as signs of permanent inferiority.

By rejecting Harold's proposal, Esther acts on what is, for Eliot, a fundamental moral "law": she has found "the love that gave strength to obey the law." In thus renouncing the life of "silken bondage," Esther is moved by "the first religious experience of her life—the first self-questioning, the first voluntary subjection, the first longings to acquire the strength of greater motives and obey the more strenuous rule," and this revolutionary experience has "come to her through Felix Holt" (369, ch. 27). Esther submits, however, to the principle of love and not to male domination, though Eliot does not sentimentalize about the power of love in providing compensation for such a renunciation. The narrator observes:

> There was something which she now felt profoundly to be the best thing that life could give her. But—if it was to be had at all—it was not to be had without paying a heavy price for it, such as we must pay for all that is greatly good. A supreme love, a motive that gives a sublime rhythm to a woman's life, and exalts habit into partnership with the soul's highest needs, is not to be had where and how she wills: to know that high initiation, she must often tread where it is hard to tread, and feel the chill air, and watch through darkness. It is not true that love makes all things easy; it makes us choose what is difficult. (591, ch. 49)

Passages like these suggest Eliot's desire to preserve the self-sacrifice prompted by such experiences of erotic and parental love and to apply a similar standard of altruism to public life. This logic allowed her to argue that disenfranchised women (and men) should refrain, temporarily, from pressing demands for expanded rights, until they realized within themselves the full power of such altruism. While Victorian suffragists contended that the only remedy for women's legal subordination in marriage was to be found in the vote, Eliot saw such legalistic analyses of marriage as obscuring and corrupting its moral basis.[27] She turned instead to redefining marriage as a sublime "partnership" and to celebrating the mutual submission to a self-renouncing love which would eventually produce a social transformation more in harmony with "moral evolution."

The potentially radical consequences of Esther's choice to resist the conventional marriage of convenience and upward mobility is dramatized when she testifies at Felix Holt's trial, inspired by a higher moral law that authorizes her resistance to the status quo.[28] In describing the "sublime ignorance" that prompts Esther to testify on Felix's behalf, Eliot asserts her cautiously qualified belief that women's experience in the wild zone promotes a "sublimer recognition" of the power of love as a force in "moral evolution" (*GEL* 4:364). She emphasizes the virtue of disinterestedness that Esther possesses as an inexperienced woman, an "inspired ignorance" which allows her to recognize moral laws that remain invisible to the men who are more powerful and worldly. Esther

acts on the basis of her experience in the "wild zone" when she speaks at
Felix's trial, and the results of her testimony are socially transforming:

> When a woman feels purely and nobly, that ardor of hers which breaks
> through formulas too rigorously urged on men by daily practical needs, makes
> one of her most precious influences: she is the added impulse that shatters the
> stiffening crust of cautious experience. . . . Some of that ardour which has
> flashed out and illuminated all poetry was burning to-day in the bosom of
> sweet Esther Lyon. In this, at least, her woman's lot was perfect: that the man
> she loved was her hero; that her woman's passion and her reverence for rarest
> goodness rushed together in an undivided current. (571, ch. 46)

This glancing allusion to *Romola* and to the passage from the *Eumenides*
about the reverence for the "right" that makes love and duty "flow in one
stream" (169, ch. 11) reminds us that while Aeschylus's trilogy ends with
the pacification of the Eumenides by Apollo, Eliot's novel concludes by
exposing the limits and failures of patriarchal laws defining justice.

Though Esther allies herself at Felix's trial against the powers of patriarchal law and justice, as Mrs. Transome did earlier, her action is not
qualified by a self-justification akin to Mrs. Transome's. Instead, Esther's
"maidenly fervor" inspires a response in "certain just-spirited men and
good fathers" and prompts Sir Maximus to intervene on Felix's behalf.
"So Esther's deed had its effect beyond the momentary one," Eliot
writes, "but the effect was not visible in the rigid necessities of legal pro-
cedure" (573, ch. 46). By indicating her skepticism about the justice defined by civil law, Eliot shows her preference for a definition of justice
provided by moral rather than legal terms and by "inward" rather than
"outward" laws. Similarly, she shows, lest we read Sir Maximus's effort to
obtain a pardon for Felix Holt as a mark of Eliot's unqualified appreciation of his Tory politics and values, that it was Philip Debarry—who later
renounces many of his class privileges in becoming a Catholic—who had
urged his father to intervene "benevolently" in the "loaded" workings of
the legal system.[29]

The marriage of Esther and Felix that follows the trial, like the trial
itself, demonstrates Eliot's refusal to repeat the triumph of patriarchal
law dramatized in the *Eumenides*, which requires women's submission, a
submission which is reinscribed in Spencer's biological and sociological
principles that assign men to the public, and women to the private
sphere. Until the moral revolution in attitudes about fatherhood has
been accomplished and until education is more universally available, the
best place for Esther and Felix to stand—the position Eliot herself
chose—is outside the patriarchy's dying institutions. Esther's and Felix's
rejection of ruling class ideologies which reinforce patterns of domi-

nance and submission is demonstrated by the unconventional marriage they celebrate. Theirs is to be a mutual partnership. Because of her legacy, Esther brings "money to spare" to this marriage. She tells Felix: "You could do wonders, and be obliged to work, too, only not if sickness came. And then I think of a little income for your mother, enough for her to live as she has been used to live; and a little income for my father to save him from being a dependent when he is no longer able to preach" (602, ch. 51). Though she reveres Felix because she sees him as "greater and nobler" than herself, Esther brings to their marriage a good-humored sense of self-esteem that allows her to deflate Felix's moral seriousness and to correct him when he is mistaken: "You will not attribute stupid thoughts to me before I have uttered them," she tells him (602, ch. 51). With this remark Eliot reminds us of the personal vision that Esther too has achieved in coming to understand not only Felix's and her father's view of moral law but also her mother's and Mrs. Transome's secret histories. Eliot even hints that Esther may continue her work as a teacher in order to fill up those "wide spaces of time" which are not filled by motherhood: she warns Felix, "You think you are to do everything. You don't know how clever I am. I mean to go on teaching a great many things" (601–2, ch. 51).

Though Eliot muffles this last detail, as she does in *Middlemarch,* so we cannot tell whether Esther intends to teach other pupils in addition to Felix himself, she gives Esther an economic advantage in marriage which brings balance to the relationship and signals Eliot's endorsement of egalitarian marriage and the emancipationist values of the more moderate Victorian feminists. Eliot has encumbered her novel with an elaborate machinery in order to bestow on her heroine this heritage which guarantees her moral and financial independence, and she has sacrificed her hero's purely working-class status to bring equality to this relationship of husband and wife. But their son's relation to the existing patriarchy—like their own—is symbolized by the fact that he has a "great deal more science" but "not much more money" (606, Epilogue). Esther's marriage suggests that only by remaining aloof from such patriarchal institutions can she escape from becoming a victim in the murderous struggle for dominance between husbands and wives, fathers and sons. By electing this life of "mutual submission," Esther escapes the destructive resistance practiced by both Mrs. Holt and Mrs. Transome. Thus, the hero and heroine achieve a marriage that reflects Eliot's rejection of the profoundly antifeminist implications of Spencer's biological and political ideas as set forth in *The Principles of Biology* and anticipates the extension of those ideas in *The Study of Sociology* and *The Principles of Sociology.*

8

Theories of Origin and Knowledge:
Middlemarch and *The Study of Sociology*

By 1871, it was clear that Darwin had acquiesced to Spencer's misogynistic analysis of women's capacities in *The Principles of Biology* (1864–1867) and in the revised version of *The Principles of Psychology* (1870–1872). With Darwin's authorization of the biological defense of the inferiority of women, Spencer began in *The Principles of Biology* to generalize more broadly and confidently about women's inferior mental and physical capacities. While he was completing the revisions of *The Principles of Psychology* in 1871, Spencer decided to add an extra volume to his *Synthetic Philosophy* in order to elaborate the "special truths in Psychology which have to be handed on to Sociology as part of its data" (*Autobiography* 2:241). This work was originally published as a series of articles beginning in April 1872, when Eliot was writing Book 5 of *Middlemarch*, and was reissued in book form on November 1, 1873 as *The Study of Sociology*. It was, as Spencer himself says, "pecuniarily considered, unusually successful for a book of its kind" and yielded well over £1300 in royalties (*Autobiography* 2:254).

One of these essays, "Psychology of the Sexes," published in 1872 and later incorporated into *The Study of Sociology*, epitomizes Spencer's new freedom in asserting women's physical and mental inferiority and suggests how these sexist arguments shaped his analysis of gender arrangements and marriage customs in his later works.[1] Spencer began his "Psychology of the Sexes" by repeating the theory articulated in *The Principles of Biology* about the conservation of energy which arrested woman's mental development when she reached sexual maturity. Assuming, as he did rather offhandedly in "Physical Training" in 1859, and more defensively in *The Principles of Biology* in 1867, that woman's smaller size and less complete brain development prohibited "the most recent and most complex faculties" of the mind from maturing as they did in man, Spencer concludes in "Psychology of the Sexes" that woman has

> somewhat less of general power or massiveness, and beyond this there is a perceptible falling short in those two faculties, intellectual and emotional, which are the latest products of evolution—the power of abstract reason and that most abstract of the emotions, the sentiment of justice, the sentiment

which regulates conduct irrespective of personal attachments and the likes or dislikes felt for individuals. (32)

Spencer's expansiveness in asserting woman's intellectual inferiority here may have been encouraged by Darwin, who, in *The Descent of Man* (1871), similarly argued that the male is more "courageous, pugnacious, and energetic than woman" and "had a more inventive genius."[2] Darwin remained more cautious than Spencer in his assessment of fixed sexual difference, noting, for example, that the "male's brain is absolutely larger but whether or not proportionately to his larger body, has not, I believe, been fully ascertained" (*Descent* 2:316–17).

Nonetheless, in *The Descent of Man*, Darwin reiterated Spencer's assumption that sexual and racial differences create a natural hierarchy.[3] He wrote in this volume, for example, that women were closer to the "childhood of humanity," like other "less developed" races, and he concluded that women's intellectual capacity for "intuition" showed that they were mentally less developed than men: "It is generally admitted that with women the power of intuition, of rapid perception, and perhaps of imitation, are more strongly marked than in man; in some, at least, of these faculties are characteristics of the lower races, and therefore a past and lower state of civilization" (*Descent* 2:362). For both Spencer and Darwin, then, the male's more strenuous part in the struggle to survive promoted and maintained his physical and mental superiority, and justified, "as a consequence," as Darwin asserts, "the present inequality between the sexes" (*Descent* 2:329–30). For both Spencer and Darwin, as these works make clear, woman's physical and psychological qualities, and especially her conscious and unconscious adaptation to the demands of motherhood, became the keystone of their analysis of sexual difference, though Spencer was more unequivocal than Darwin in maintaining that the inequality between men and women followed necessarily from permanent biological differences.

Middlemarch, which Eliot began in August 1869 and completed September 1872, is profoundly shaped by her awareness of the contemporary debates about evolutionary theory, sexual selection, and female inferiority. During these years, Spencer frequently visited George Eliot and George Henry Lewes at the Priory; as Spencer explains in his *Autobiography*, "There arose a standing engagement to go and lunch with them whenever I found it convenient. The motive for the arrangement was in part that we might have opportunities for conversations, enjoyed on both sides, which were impracticable during their Sunday-afternoon assemblies" (2:202). *Middlemarch* displays Eliot's increasing sophistication in both anticipating and challenging Spencer's hypotheses about women's capacities and his conclusions about motherhood as the "supreme end" of their lives. By dramatizing the consequences of Lydgate's failure to question his "feeling and judgment about women and furniture" (179, ch. 15) in this novel, Eliot invites her readers to consider similar patterns of thinking in Spencer's *Principles of Biology*, patterns which Darwin uncritically repeated in *The Descent of Man* and *The Expression of Emotions in Men and Animals*.[4] Similarly, while Darwin in *The Descent of Man* (811) reiterated the argument that Spencer presented in the first number of *The Study of Sociology*, published in April 1872, that women were compensated for their physical disadvantages because sexual selection allowed them to exercise their preference in courtship by rejecting unattractive suitors (*Study* 95), Eliot refuted this argument by displaying the poverty of choice and meanness of opportunity that confronted women, even those with the beauty, wealth, and status of Dorothea Brooke.

In dramatizing her challenge to Spencer's biologically based arguments for female inferiority, Eliot applied Darwin's theory of "diversification" to the problem of sexual difference. In *Middlemarch*, Eliot illustrates the difficulty of drawing conclusions about the "inconvenient indefiniteness with which the Supreme Power has fashioned the nature of women" (25–26, Prelude), and suggests, as Gillian Beer argues, that "diversification, not truth to type, is the creative principle" in the evolutionary process.[5] In a letter written in 1874, Eliot voices particular objections to Darwin's and Spencer's interpretation of sexual selection when she criticizes "those widowers who are always expecting women to take compassion on them. . . . This is the fine principle of natural selection, they will say. I admit it, but it is also the selection of conceited gentlemen" (*GEL* 6:81). *Middlemarch* thus demonstrates the depth of Eliot's concern about the license that sexual selection, in both its Spencerian and Darwinian forms, seemed to give to male egotism. Moreover, when we see *Middlemarch* in the broader context of Spencer's evolutionary theory, this novel also displays Eliot's serious reservations about the conclusions Spencer drew from the "data" of biology and psychology for his analysis of marriage, motherhood, altruism, and justice.[6]

One of the most celebrated passages in *Middlemarch* suggests the importance of Spencer's theory of knowledge in Eliot's conception and design of the novel. Eliot alludes both to Spencer himself[7] and to a crucial passage in his newly revised edition of *The Principles of Psychology* (1870–1872) to indicate her profound skepticism about the "data" that, according to Spencer, psychology "handed" on to sociology. Eliot writes:

An eminent philosopher among my friends, who can dignify even your ugly furniture by lifting it into the serene light of science, has shown me this pregnant little fact. Your pier-glass or extensive surface of polished steel made to be rubbed by a housemaid, will be minutely and multitudinously scratched in all directions; but place now against it a lighted candle as a center of illumination, and lo! the scratches will seem to arrange themselves in a fine series of concentric circles round that little sun. It is demonstrable that the scratches are going everywhere impartially, and it is only your candle which produces the flattering illusion of concentric arrangement, its light falling with an exclusive optical selection. (297, ch. 27)

In this beautiful passage, Eliot presents, of course, a memorable metaphor revealing Rosamond's dauntless egotism, but she also repeats a parable that Spencer included in the October 1871 number of *The Principles of Psychology* to illustrate a failure in "class reasoning." Spencer uses this same analogy to demonstrate how "the very act of predication" brings into "prominence those members of the class which fulfill the predication" and leaves "in the background those members of the class which do not fulfill it," just as a candle before a mirror creates the illusion of "arcs of circles having the light at its center" and renders invisible all the other scratches in the mirror (*Psychology* 2:398).

Eliot uses this metaphor, moreover, to disclose parallels between Rosamond's self-involvement and the similar and powerful intellectual egotism that defeats Lydgate's scientific ambitions and distorts Casaubon's quest for the key to all mythologies. By invoking this passage so central to Spencer's theory of knowledge, Eliot raises much larger questions about contemporary scientific methods as well. Lydgate's inability to see Rosamond with the same penetrating imaginative vision that directs him in his search for the "primary tissue" is mirrored by Casaubon's more dim-sighted quest, and their common failures expose similar errors of "class reasoning." Moreover, the research that Lydgate and Casaubon undertake corresponds to central themes in Spencer's more ambitious effort to devise a "synthetic philosophy" which would organize all the physical, mental, and social aspects of human life. Spencer is thus implicated when Eliot observes that the failures of Lydgate and Casaubon show how "all of us, grave or light, get our thoughts entangled in metaphors and act fatally on the strength on them" (111, ch. 10).

Lydgate is trapped not only by his "spots of commonness" (179, ch. 15), then, but also by scientific methods which overemphasize the visible and do not acknowledge the subjective power of the imagination in the observer who intuits the "subtle actions inaccessible by any sort of lens" (194, ch. 16), and who interprets both the seen and the imagined in light of a particular theoretical paradigm.[8] From our more privileged vantage nearly a century and a half later, Lydgate's story presents a cautionary tale not only about the supposedly "natural" basis for sexual selection but also about the revenge that history takes on pioneers of science like Lydgate or—for that matter—like Herbert Spencer himself. Moreover,

Eliot extends this theme by emphasizing the interplay between the "fictions" of science and art in Middlemarch during the 1830s and, by implication, in England during the 1870s.

While her characterization of Lydgate demonstrates Eliot's critique of the unself-conscious use of metaphors in the construction of scientific theories of his day—and her own—so her treatment of Casaubon dramatizes her reservations about the similarly "inductive" use of history in the analysis of the "moral evolution" of human society.[9] Casaubon is equally trapped by fatal "metaphors" and by his ethnocentric view of the development of history, culture, and religion; and his unconscious egocentricity consequently subverts his search for the origins of "belief." Eliot's treatment of Casaubon thus recapitulates her critique in *Romola* and *Felix Holt* of the theories about history that Spencer developed in the 1860s and addresses related issues that would emerge more fully in *The Study of Sociology*, *The Principles of Sociology*, and *Descriptive Sociology*.[10] While Spencer employed more historical material in his sociological analyses of the 1870s, especially in *Descriptive Sociology* (Peel 158), he was very selective in citing historical data and called this edited version of history a "moral science."

In his *Autobiography*, Spencer indirectly acknowledged Eliot's influence on his thought by identifying a force that directs the "moral evolution" of society, but he, in contrast to Eliot, locates it in the unconscious alone. "To make my position fully understood," he writes, "it seems needful to add that corresponding to the fundamental propositions of a developed Moral Science, there have been, and still are, developing in the race certain fundamental moral intuitions; and that, though these moral intuitions are the results of accumulated experiences of utility, gradually organized and inherited, they have come to be quite independent of conscious experience" (2:101). George Eliot remained profoundly critical of Spencer's commitment to deducing human capacities from a functional analysis of biological structure and his effort to define moral behavior as determined primarily by inherited and unconscious impulses. Nowhere is Eliot's skepticism about the dangers posed by a selective reading of "moral history" clearer than in her depiction of Casaubon's myopic historical research.

In her treatment of Casaubon, Eliot also reveals some of the difficulties of interpretation she faced in her own move "away from structure to function and to history" (Beer, *Darwin's Plots* 160), the move she began in *Romola* and *Felix Holt*. By placing Lydgate and Casaubon in the specific intellectual milieu of the 1830s, Eliot creates enough distance between them and her readers so that she may expose the role human subjectivity plays both in the formulation of scientific and philosophical theory and in the reconstruction of history. Eliot's increased interest in history prompted her to analyze, among other things, why there had been so little variation in the social arrangements that defined the gender roles of women—and men—in the past. *Middlemarch* addresses itself, therefore, to the scientific and philosophical theories which have defined women in the past and shows how these theories are particularly compromised by the failures of "class reasoning" that Spencer described and inadvertently exemplified in *The Principles of Psychology* (1870–1872) and subsequent works.

By dramatizing in *Middlemarch* the life that traditionally lies beyond the "bourne of so many narratives" (890, Finale), Eliot locates a more specific failure of "class reasoning" in Spencer's theory of sexual selection: for Spencer focused exclusively on courtship and ignored the domestic discord that could result when marriage partners were "selected" according to his "natural" criteria. Lydgate's determination to take a more "strictly scientific view of woman" (183, ch. 15) after his disastrous affair with Madame Laure becomes doubly ironic when we recognize not only that Lydgate succumbs, in spite of himself, to Rosamond's similarly superficial charms, but also that he marries a woman who, according to the most advanced scientific principles of evolutionary theory in the 1870s, is the perfect mate.

In accord with Spencer's theories of sexual selection, Rosamond displays no "unbecoming knowledge and always was that combination of correct sentiments, music, dancing, and perfect blond loveliness" (301, ch. 27). By noting Rosamond's musical talent and her skill in imitation, Eliot identifies two specific qualities that Spencer and Darwin considered advantageous to females in sexual selection. Rosamond makes herself more attractive in Spencerian terms by playing the piano with the "precision of an echo" and by presenting her beauty to best advantage because of her talent as an "actress of parts that entered into her physique" (144, ch. 12). Eliot insists, though, that both skills expose Rosamond's emptiness as well as the shallowness of these evolutionary criteria which ignore a woman's inner life in assessing her value to society and her usefulness to the race. If Lydgate's "spots of commonness" impel him to mistake Rosamond's beauty for virtue, his prejudices about women reflect, in this context, the persistence of the "hereditary habits" of English gentlemen, which Spencer and Darwin reinscribed in the most advanced Victorian theories of human evolution.

Lydgate is attracted by the impersonal force of beauty in Rosamond and this responsiveness reflects his erotic vitality, but Eliot, unlike Spencer, was unwilling to see the unconscious power of sexual attraction as necessarily promoting the best interests of the individual or the race. When Lydgate and Rosamond act on their mutual physical attraction and marry, they cross a threshold that, according to Spencer, redefines men's and women's relation to the process of natural selection. In *The Principles of Psychology*, he writes: "Up to a certain point, while the individual is young and not yet fertile, its welfare and the welfare of the race go together; but when the reproductive age is reached, the welfare of the individual and the race cease to be the same and may be diametrically opposed" (1:285). In other words, once adults become part of the reproductive process, natural selection no longer operates to the advantage of the individual but rather, as Spencer put it, for the benefit of the "race."

The quality of Lydgate's life after marriage shows that the egotism Spencer privileged in his analysis of sexual selection has the power to destroy the capacity of both women and men to contribute biologically and morally to the progress of the race. In *Middlemarch*, then, Eliot questions Spencer's basic assumption that if men and women would submit to the principles of sexual selection as he defined them, the "welfare of the race" would be assured. The event, of course, which most dramatically reveals how Rosamond's egotism counteracts the benefit she could provide for the race occurs when she persists in going riding in defiance of Lydgate's prescription that she give it up for the sake of their unborn child. Rosamond's subsequent miscarriage reveals a fundamental failure of class reasoning in Spencer's assumptions about women's maternal instincts by showing how they are defeated, in Rosamond's case, when an egotistic desire conflicts with a less palpable obligation.

Moreover, in describing Rosamond's disappointment in her marriage to Lydgate, Eliot similarly demonstrates the "new difficulties" (Beer, *Darwin's Plots* 213) that emerged when Spencer's developmental psychology was applied to his analysis of sexual selection, and especially to his assumptions about female egotism and altruism that find expression in *The Study of Sociology*. Eliot alludes to Spencer's most enduring contribution to psychology when she describes how Rosamond's mental "associations" determine her response both to marriage and to motherhood,[11] but it is Rosamond's stubborn egotism that Eliot accents. Trained to see her life as a race toward marriage and her beauty as a sign that she is destined to be the "best girl in the world," Rosamond looks forward to married life not because it offers her the opportunity to contribute altruistically to the welfare of the race but because it offers her the prospect of "rising in rank" (195, ch. 16). When her ambitions are frustrated by the realities of her married life with Lydgate, Rosamond begins "to associate her husband with feelings of disappointment" (711, ch. 66), and so "the terribly inflexible relation of marriage had lost its charm of encouraging delightful dreams." By thus exposing the "inflexible" psychological laws that move Rosamond toward disillusionment,[12] Eliot challenges Spencer's certainty concerning the instinctive altruism of beautiful women, expressed with such confidence in *The Study of Sociology*.

In *Middlemarch*, then, Eliot expands on the theme she developed earlier in *Adam Bede* about male responsiveness to the ego-gratifications offered by simple womanly beauty, and more specifically identifies the educational and cultural values that support the similar and more universal male egotism portrayed in this novel. "Nature had inspired many arts in finishing Miss Lemon's favorite pupil," she writes in reference to Rosamond, and *Middlemarch* discloses how Lydgate is defeated not only by his own egotism, as well as his wife's, but also by the cultural arrangements that protect male preeminence by educating women to be not only physically but also intellectually and morally disadvantaged.

Lydgate enters into his marriage to Rosamond not only because he appreciates her beauty but also because he is gratified to find that she has been "instructed to the true womanly limit and not one hair's-breadth beyond"; he concludes she will be "docile, therefore, and ready to carry out behests which came from beyond" the limits of her knowledge (387, ch. 36). After their marriage, Lydgate eventually realizes that he is "powerless" to influence Rosamond, because she is incapable of recognizing "his superior knowledge and mental force" and because "affection did not make her compliant" (631, ch. 58). Gradually, he comes to see that his opinion, "instead of being, as he imagined, a shrine to consult on all occasions, was simply set aside on every practical question," for "she believed in her own opinion more than she did in his" (631, ch. 58). Thus, Lydgate achieves his tragic recognition that, in spite of her weaknesses, Rosamond "nevertheless . . . had mastered him" (719, ch. 65). By depicting Lydgate's "mastery" by his wife, Eliot exposes the force of egotism that undermines Lydgate's—and Spencer's—assumptions that altruism will necessarily triumph over egotism and that men will necessarily dominate women in married life.

In chronicling Lydgate's gradual defeat by Rosamond, Eliot also shows how he is misled by his scientific gift for "generalizing," which, she says, gives "men so much of the superiority of mistake over dumb animals" (638, ch. 58).[13] Eliot's wry observation about the ambiguous power of the uniquely human capacity for generalizing applies equally, of course, to Spencer's formulation of biological and psychological laws that reflect his unexamined traditional assumptions about gender arrangements. To underscore the terrible irony of Lydgate's defeat by Rosamond, Eliot reveals how his habit of seeing his wife as a "lesser creature" leads to its logical, and self-defeating, conclusion. During their courtship, Lydgate disingenuously tells Rosamond, "I am sure you could teach me a thousand things—as an exquisite bird could teach a bear if there were a common language" (189, ch. 16), and in the exaggeration of this analogy, Eliot highlights the false logic evident in both Spencer's and Darwin's assumptions that women and men are as unlike as animals of different species. Eventually, the economic crisis in their marriage forces Lydgate to see how these metaphors have sabotaged it: he realizes that Rosamond "no more identified herself with him than if they had been creatures of different species and opposing interests" (643, ch. 58).

Eliot invites us to see this beautiful woman, then, in the context of Spencer's functional analysis of women's capacities, as well as in relation to the older feminists' criticism of the "new" emancipated women of the 1860s and 1870s.[14] Spencer's study of biology apparently prompted him to place less and less faith in the conscious intervention and adaptation of human behavior through education, and to stress more and more the impact of biological functions on the development of "certain fundamental moral intuitions" which enforced the traditional separation of women's and men's spheres. In "Psychology of the Sexes," Spencer repeated the claim he made in "Physical Training" that the women who compete most successfully in the struggle to survive are those who are best adapted to serve the "supreme end" of their existence through motherhood and child-rearing.

Fifteen years after he originally formulated his philosophy of education, Spencer apparently no longer found it necessary to criticize the mother's willfulness, misguided education, and ignorance of the "moral" principles in the education of her children. Instead, he asserted, with no acknowledgment of his inconsistency, that a mother was guided by a more fundamental and invariable maternal instinct which worked unconsciously to promote the survival of her offspring. Spencer admitted in "Psychology of the Sexes" that men also possess a "parental instinct," but he countered Eliot's arguments in *Felix Holt* by claiming that fathers' feelings differ by nature from the emotions experienced by women; for women have acquired through evolution "special aptitudes for dealing with infantine life—an adapted power of intuition and fit adjustment of behavior." He explains:

> Though the parental instinct, which considered in its essential nature, is a love of the helpless, is common to the two [parents], yet it is obviously not identical in the two. That the particular form of it which responds to infantine helplessness is more dominant in women than in men, cannot be questioned. In man the instinct is not so habitually excited by the very helpless but has a more generalized relation to all the relatively weak who are dependent upon him. ("Psychology" 32)

Not only is the female peculiarly adapted to childbearing, but her imagination and her intellect are likewise determined by this function. Woman possesses, Spencer explains, "a vivid imagination of simple and direct consequences" which "shuts out from her mind the imagination of consequences that are complex and indirect." Mothers think "chiefly of present effects on the conduct of children," while fathers "often repress the promptings of their sympathies with a view to ultimate benefits" (36).

When *Middlemarch* is read in the context of Spencer's arguments exalting the power of nature over nurture and asserting women's innate mental and moral inferiority, Eliot's novel clearly reveals her effort to refute Spencer's biological assessment of women's capacities by demonstrating how gender expectations shape women's lives by limiting their intellectual potential and predetermining their choices. Eliot's characterizations of Rosamond Vincy, Mary Garth, Dorothea Brooke, and Celia Brooke all show her continued support for feminist educational reforms and indicate her agreement with the position taken by J. S. Mill in *The Subjection of Women* (1869): that women would become better companions for their husbands when they had access to a fuller and more adequate education (Graver 207–7, 212–3). But in contrasting Rosamond Vincy with Mary Garth, Eliot also registers her dismay over the "New Woman" who seemed to be the beneficiary and product of feminist educational reforms[15] and reiterates her critique of English industrialism by showing the morally corrosive effects of the "plutocracy" it fostered.[16]

As an articled pupil at Miss Lemon's school, Mary studies to follow her mother's profession as a teacher, and escapes being trained to be a "useless doll" like Rosamond. By valorizing Mary for her independence, her integrity, and her commitment to the work ethic, Eliot reveals her continued endorsement of the older feminist program of the 1850s, which championed women's right to a better education by stressing the moral as well as the social value of women's work. Eliot's concern was not unique among older feminists. In 1872, for example, Emily Davies explained how industrial development had undermined feminist reforms in education when she wrote:

> The young unmarried women of the present generation are not called upon to take an active part in household work. It is needless to insist on this, for everyone knows it, and yet there is an undertone of lamentation and reproach as the admission is made. There is nothing for them to do, we confess; and yet sometimes we have a feeling that they ought to be doing it. We sigh, and say—yes domestic employments are gone out of fashion. But why have they gone out of fashion? There are two reasons—the increase in wealth, and the supply of domestic wants by machinery. . . . The fact is patent, . . . unless we came to dismissing the servants . . . a healthy young woman will find no adequate pull on her energies in the domestic employments of a well-to-do household. (Bauer and Ritt 127)

Unlike Davies, Eliot was willing, at least in her fiction, to present positively the alternative of "dismissing the servants," as is hinted in her nostalgic treatment of the Garths' domestic life and in her obvious approval of the "downwardly mobile" marriages of Fred with Mary and Dorothea with Will Ladislaw.

The characterization of Dorothea Brooke also suggests a more specific line of argument against Spencer's assertions in "Psychology of the Sexes" that women's education should be premised on assumptions about their innate mental inferiority. In a letter written a year after she completed *Middlemarch*, Eliot indicates that she regarded Spencer's biological arguments about women's physical disadvantages as a serious threat to the feminist efforts to improve women's education. She writes: "One is anxious that in the beginning of a higher education for women, the immediate nature of which is chiefly the social recognition of its desirableness, the students would be favourable subjects for experiment—girls or young women whose natures are large and rich enough not to be used up in their efforts after knowledge" (*GEL* 5:406). Dorothea's "grand woman's frame," her powerful and "theoretic" mind, and her large ambitions for a life of "intensity and greatness" all show that she possesses the physical and intellectual capacities which will allow her to partake fully in the "common fund of ideas," to share "common objects of interest with men" (Eliot, *Essays* 80).

The pathos of Dorothea's intellectual frustration in her life before and after marriage in itself constitutes a defense of better education for women and counters the biological functionalism underlying Spencer's increasingly restrictive emphasis, in *The Principles of Biology* and *The Study of Sociology*, on women's role as mother. In 1870, Eliot defended female access to higher education by noting that women often needed the resources it offered as a "defense against passionate affliction," and her treatment of Dorothea shows why young women need to have an equal "share of the more independent life" of the mind (*GEL* 5:107). While Dorothea and Celia Brooke received schooling which is less provincial than that of Rosamond Vincy or Mary Garth, all of the women have been excluded from the kind of education that allows Lydgate to find such joy in his vocation and Ladislaw such delight in the great pageant of life and history—the pageant Dorothea glimpses only confusedly in the churches and museums of Rome.[17] Dorothea is led into her marriage with Casaubon because she has been denied access to the discourse of higher learning and so hopes to find a husband "who was a sort of father who could teach you Hebrew if you wished it" (32, ch. 1).

Moreover, by describing the "stifling depression" which descends upon Dorothea after her marriage, as she begins to realize that she has been mistaken in her estimation of the spaciousness of Casaubon's mind, Eliot dramatizes another defense of women's education by asserting a second reason that Dorothea needs an education that would enable her to find an "independent delight in ideas." If Dorothea's interest in Casaubon's *Key to All Mythologies* reveals her passive aggression or her intellectual vampirism,[18] it shows as well a disease in Victorian social arrangements, which provided no other objects for a woman's intellectual energy than the vicarious pleasures of marriage and motherhood. The morbid egotism which prompts Casaubon to try to imprison Dorothea in the labyrinth of his scholarship finds an analogous expression in Spencer's theory of sexual selection which would cement the Victorian definition of men's and women's spheres and make women prisoners of biology by providing an increasingly more rigorous "scientific" defense of traditional gender arrangements.

In focusing on Dorothea's and Casaubon's life after they have crossed the "threshold" that Spencer identified in the newly revised edition of *The Principles of Psychology*, Eliot presents a second analysis of the "inflexible" conditions of married life, one which invites comparison to her portrait of the Lydgates and amplifies the theme of egotism and altruism that emerged in her treatment of this other couple. The way in which the forces of egotism and altruism affect Dorothea's marriage shows that Eliot regarded altruism as an act of will, in contrast to Spencer, who assumed that female altruism in marriage and motherhood was an expression of natural instinct. It is Dorothea, of course, rather than her husband, who plays the altruist's role in their marriage, and in presenting this contrast, Eliot again attacks a favorite Victorian shibboleth about the redeeming power of women's love in marriage. Dorothea's altruism, like Romola's, paralyzes her; she is trapped in moral "subjection" to her husband and feels imprisoned by the "close union" of their marriage. Unlike Lydgate, Dorothea quickly recognizes not only the egotism of her husband but also the hidden egotism in herself which had prompted her to accept Casaubon as a mate, when she discovers the reality of "that center of self" in her husband "whence the lights and shadows must always fall with a certain difference" (243, ch. 20). Yet in comparing Dorothea's subsequent "submission" to the consequences of her choice to marry Casaubon, with Lydgate's similar "sad resignation," Eliot identifies an altruism which transcends sexual differences.

Moreover, when Dorothea resolves to submit herself to the "ideal" yoke of marriage, she is compared to a "man who begins with a movement toward striking and ends with conquering his desire to strike," for, as Eliot notes, the "energy that would animate a crime is not more than is wanted to inspire resolved submission" (464, ch. 42). Thus, Eliot, in contrast to Spencer, asserts that the highest expressions of altruism in women, as in men, are the product of intellectual understanding as well as spontaneous generosity, and result from the recognition of the "supreme" egotism of the self, as well as the voluntary suppression of its demands in deference to the needs of others. Such altruism is not bestowed on either sex by nature, but is achieved, as Dorothea's example suggests, as a consequence of "the reaching forward of the whole consciousness towards the fullest truth, the least partial good" (235, ch. 20).[19]

Eliot's stanch defense of Dorothea's special capacities for sympathy and imagination and her valorization of her acute consciousness of the ties that bind her to her family, her husband, and her community, appear suddenly both more liberal and more feminist when they are compared with Spencer's misogynistic interpretation of the significance of women's physical, mental, and moral differences in *The Study of Sociology*. Eliot's letters show that by 1871, she was more forceful in her rejection of social theories like Spencer's that located woman's contributions to humanity solely in her capacity for reproduction.[20] "Men," she wrote, "are very fond of glorying in that sort of dog-like attachment" that is taken as a sign of women's instinctive loyalty to the men who protect them (*GEL* 5:132), and *Middlemarch* reflects her rejection of such sentimentality about woman's capacity for "animal constancy." Her heroic characterizations of Lydgate, Dorothea, and Will disclose, instead, the goodness that "belongs to the finest natures" of both men and women, and this goodness does not arise from animal instinct or adaptation but rather from a "responsiveness to duty and pity," under the command of human intelligence and will.

Throughout the 1870s, George Eliot and George Henry Lewes collaborated in resisting Spencer's—and Darwin's—easy application of the principles of natural selection to human life; they stressed, instead, the mediating power of human society in shaping and qualifying human behavior.[21] Eliot prepared Lewes's own *Study of Psychology* (1879) for publication after his death in 1878, and the following passage, in particular, shows their alternative perspective on the "human organism" and its place in society, a view that both informs this work and finds expression in Eliot's *Middlemarch*:

> In relation to Nature, man is an animal; in relation to culture, he is social. As the ideal world rises above and transforms the sensible world, so culture transforms nature physically and morally, fashioning the forest and the swamp into the garden and meadow-lands, the selfish savage into the sympathetic citizen. The organism adjusts itself to the external medium; it creates, and is in turn modified by, the social medium, for society is the product of human feelings, and its existence is *pari passu* developed with the feelings which in turn it modifies and enlarges at each stage.[22]

By pointing out how inner forces transform society and how outer forces are internalized, Lewes refutes Spencer's argument that outward forces

simply determine inward life. Eliot, of course, uses these same metaphors of the swamp and forest to characterize her most unconscious
egotists in *Middlemarch*: Rosamond, Casaubon, and Fred Vincy.[23]

One of the most striking features of Lewes's *Study of Psychology*, in this
context, is his analysis of motherhood, and it is in his criticism of the
emphasis laid by Spencer and Darwin on the power of maternal instinct
that Eliot's influence in this work can perhaps be seen most clearly.
Lewes argued that a capacity for conscious altruism distinguishes the
human mother from, to use his example, the baboon. Animals, he insisted, know neither love nor true altruism; their "tenderness vanishes in
the presence of any egotistic impulse." The human mother, by contrast,
is able to experience a far wider range of emotions because of the wondrous human capacity for language:

> In the case of human responses, language allows the human mother to trans-
> form a maternal instinct into a maternal sentiment because it can communi-
> cate the results of the experience of others to those who have not personally
> experienced them, whereas the baboon or any animal only has its personal
> experience. Thus a human mother can appreciate the claims of offspring in
> general, not just her own. She can have an intellectual appreciation of the
> claims of the helpless which is denied the baboon. (71–72)

Lewes concluded by opposing a "motto" that summarizes Spencer's analysis of individualism with one that posits altruism as the highest social
good: "The law of animal action is individualism, its motto is 'each for
himself against all,' the ideal of human action is altruism, its motto is
'each with others, all for each.' "[24] By carefully distinguishing "maternal
instinct" from "maternal sentiment," Lewes echoed Eliot's long-standing
analysis of motherhood and her criticism of Spencer's theory of maternal
instinct. Thus, Lewes acknowledged his debt to the woman he affectionately called "Madonna" by repeating the distinction that Eliot explored
in all of her novels, but especially in *Middlemarch* and *Daniel Deronda*.

In "Psychology of the Sexes," Spencer drew explicit social and political
conclusions from his analysis of woman's special adaptation for motherhood that extinguished what little was left of his youthful liberalism on
the Woman Question. In this essay, published in April 1872, Spencer not
only opposed woman's suffrage, he defined woman as excluded by nature from any responsible participation in public life. Arguing that
woman's especially adapted capacities for love, sympathy, imagination,
and reverence prevent her from fully understanding justice, freedom,
and social obligations, Spencer writes:

> Women err still more than men do in seeking what seems an immediate public
> good without thought of distant public evils. Once more, we have women in

awe of power and authority, swaying their ideas and sentiments about all institutions. This tends toward strengthening of government, political and ecclesiastical. . . . Reverencing power more than men do, women, by implication,
respect freedom less—freedom, that is, not of the nominal kind, but of that
real kind which consists in the ability of each to carry on his own life without
hindrance from others, so long as he does not hinder them. (36–37)

While Darwin remained prudently silent about the social implications of
woman's role in the evolutionary process, Spencer devoted the rest of his
career to exploring the implications of sexual selection. The conclusions
Spencer articulates here are applied and developed in *The Principles of
Sociology*, especially in his analysis of domestic institutions, and in *The
Principles of Ethics*.[25]

In *Middlemarch*, Eliot refers to mother's love at crucial moments in
each of the "three love problems" outlined in this text, and in all of these
episodes we witness Eliot's effort to distinguish between maternal instinct and maternal sentiment and to illustrate her definition of altruism
as an expression of willed action rather than an instinctive reflex. Mary
Garth is an interesting anomaly in *Middlemarch* because she is the only
altruist who succeeds in teaching an egoist to control his selfishness
while she, at the same time, escapes destructive self-sacrifice. Mary's example extends Eliot's analysis of the role of egotism and altruism in
Dorothea's and Lydgate's marriages and illuminates another aspect of
Eliot's disagreement with Spencer about the function and power of the
instincts in the "moral evolution" of the race. Fred seems at least as un-
promising a subject for reform as his sister Rosamond because he is as
conventional as she. His obsession with horses, his compulsive gambling,
and his careless spending are traits that he shares with Eliot's most famous villains, but Mary succeeds in helping him find the strength to
renounce these egocentric habits.

Though Mary is generally seen as her father's daughter, she possess
two qualities that give her authority in her relation to Fred, qualities Eliot
presents as capacities developed by her experience in the "wild zone"
and nurtured by her mother.[26] In contrast to Fred, Mary has been raised
in a family that has "slipped a little downwards" in Middlemarch society
(122, ch. 11), and she learns early in life not to make any unreasonable
claims on others. Eliot shows that Mary's sense of duty is a direct consequence of her mother's teaching whereby the Garth children are led out
of the self by being taught to recognize the "claims of offspring in general," a trait which Lewes defined in his *Study of Psychology* as an essential
ingredient of "maternal sentiment."

Moreover, the authority that both Susan and Mary claim as women—
and the sources of that authority—present a challenge to Spencer's

claim that women cannot comprehend the demands of freedom and justice as well as men.[27] Mary's mother possesses a shrewdness and a skill with words that make her both the teacher and the voice of justice in the family, while her husband plays the traditional feminine role by making understated appeals for mercy and understanding. Mary, who has her mother's sharp tongue, as Caleb Garth observes on more than one occasion, assumes her mother's role as critic and arbiter of justice in her relationship with Fred. However, while Susan Garth shows some of the "awe of power and authority" that Spencer assumed to be part of woman's natural instincts, Mary is far more independent.

When she learns that Fred has defaulted on his loan and has, as a result, jeopardized her family's welfare, Mary forcefully reminds him of his selfishness, though her righteous indignation is qualified by sympathy when he appeals to her for understanding. When Fred protests, "It is not generous to believe the worst of a man. When you have any power over him, I think you might try to use it to make him better" (287, ch. 25), his complaint awakens a "maternal impulse" in Mary. Mary's response reflects Eliot's effort to identify consciousness rather than instinct as the source of women's maternal feelings:

> There is often something maternal even in girlish love, and Mary's hard experience had wrought her nature to an impressibility very different from that hard slight thing which we call girlishness. At Fred's last words, she felt an instantaneous pang, something like what a mother feels at the imagined sobs or cries of her naughty truant child, which may lose itself and get harm. (287, ch. 26).

By thus depicting "maternal" love as a gift conveyed by language and sustained by the imagination and the sensibilities, and by locating these emotions in a childless young woman, Eliot detaches maternal sentiments from the biological facts of maternity. Moreover, she associates the maternal sentiments with the least selfish forms of erotic love instead of identifying both forms of love, as Spencer does, with the involuntary and unconscious compulsions of biological instinct. In contrast to Spencer, then, Eliot defines the "maternal" altruism revealed when Mary's pity for Fred conquers her anger as the source of a more complex and contextualized definition of justice. Mary's sense of both justice and compassion is produced by her family experience and her "impressibility" rather than by biology alone, and this definition of the sources of her moral sensibility resembles the paradigm of female morality that Carol Gilligan has described.[28]

Finally, it is mutual love which allows Mary to lead Fred far enough out of his egocentricity so that she will consent to marry him. Fred differs from Rosamond in that he feels a genuine love for the woman he wishes to marry, a love which is determined not by Mary's physical appearance alone but also by their mutual childhood memories, gratitude, and affection. By describing how Fred and Mary's love was established when Fred "espoused her with the umbrella ring" (561, ch. 52), Eliot invokes the "wild zone" of childhood when both were innocent of the economic and social motives that shape, and often deform, the sexual attraction of adults. In making the basis of their love only a little less incestuous than the love of Maggie Tulliver for her brother, Eliot reveals one of the ways, perhaps, that she overcompensated in her effort to rescue erotic love from an evolutionary analysis which emphasized the instinctual and unconscious power of sexual attraction.

Mary's power over Fred suggests a reversal of traditional sex roles that has often been regarded as one of the features dividing the Garths' "comic" subplot from the more "heroic" stories of Lydgate and Dorothea. But it is seldom noted that Eliot presents a consistent and more woman-centered definition of justice in all three plots which unites the novel by grounding it in the "wild zone." Eliot represents the effects of the same "maternal sentiments" of love, sympathy, compassion, and justice when she describes Dorothea's two life-changing visits to Rosamond's home. Eliot's frequent use of metaphors associating erotic love and maternity has been read as a sign of her fear of uncontrolled female eroticism or as a token of the incestuous taboos which prevented her from endorsing less conscious control of sexual desire.[29] But when these metaphors are seen in the context of evolutionary thought, they show Eliot's resistance to Spencer's assertion in "Psychology of the Sexes," for example, that men were, by nature, better equipped to maintain a moral as well as intellectual and physical preeminence in the family and in society. In invoking "maternal" love, Eliot refers to a relationship that is founded on "temporary" inequality since, as Carol Gilligan has explained, the mother's power is ideally used to foster the development that removes the "initial disparity" between the adult and the child, while traditional power relations between husband and wife, as Spencer describes them, uphold more "permanent inequalities." [30]

In describing the crisis Rosamond creates when she throws herself upon Ladislaw in the "dreary sadness of her heart" (387, ch. 78), Eliot demonstrates how erotic love gives an "awful" meaning to responsibility both inside and outside marriage (855, ch. 81). Certainly Dorothea's first visit to Rosamond dramatizes the damage that can result when an egotist acts on uncontrolled erotic desires. Because Rosamond is so insulated by her flattering fantasies, only the "bewildering novelty of pain" that results from Ladislaw's angry rejection can convince her of the "terrible existence" of the world outside the self (836, ch. 78). After witnessing Rosamond's ill-timed profession of love, Dorothea misinterprets Ladislaw's passionate response as a sign that he is sexually involved with Rosamond and concludes that he has betrayed the worshipful love he once professed for her. In her deepest despair, Dorothea imagines her unavowed love for Ladislaw as a child divided in the name of justice. Eliot writes that Dorothea saw "two images that tore her heart in two, as if it had been the heart of a mother who seems to see her child divided by the sword, and presses one bleeding half to her breast while her gaze goes forth in agony towards the half which is carried away by the lying woman that has never known the mother's pang" (844, ch. 80). By this allusion to Solomon's justice, Eliot demonstrates the heartrending injustice of the altruist's contest with the egotist, the true mother's defeat by the "lying woman who never knew the mother's pang" (844, ch. 80).[31] By using these maternal metaphors invoking the "wild zone," Eliot suggests an alternative standard of justice and mercy that honors ancient maternal principles.[32]

Up to this point in the novel, Eliot has defined Dorothea's love for Ladislaw in altruistic, quasi-religious terms; her "believing conception" of Will expresses one of the "great powers of her womanhood" and is a "sort of baptism and consecration" to her (829, ch. 77). When Dorothea discovers Ladislaw alone with Rosamond, though, her entire faith in "goodness" is shaken. Eliot uses this episode, then, to explore the boundaries between maternal and erotic love and to acknowledge fundamental differences between the love experienced by the mother who, because of the physical and emotional conditions of maternity, exercises power over her young child, and the woman who, in her sexual relation to a man, is vulnerable to all the uncertainties fostered by traditional gender arrangements. Such insecurities result in the painful rivalry between women that Eliot exposes in Dorothea's jealousy of Rosamond.

However, after Dorothea survives her long night of doubt about Ladislaw's personal "goodness," and about the omnipotence of the "divine power" which "widens the skirts of light, making the struggle with the darkness narrower" (427, ch. 39), she, like Romola, awakens to see the world in more Darwinian terms, and her sense of justice is subtly transformed. In transcending her irremediable grief over the loss of Ladislaw and the destruction of her faith in goodness, Dorothea refuses to find solace in Spencerian individualism. She feels, instead, her participation in the "involuntary, palpitating life" of the natural and social world that surrounds her. Voluntarily moving out of the "narrow cell" of the self, Dorothea asks, "What should I do?" (846, ch. 81). By opening herself to these maternal sentiments, she moves beyond the undeniable self-involvement of passionate love to a state of altruistic disinterestedness. Eliot remarks upon the boundary that Dorothea crosses in coming a second time to talk to Rosamond:

She had enveloped both Will and Rosamond in her burning scorn, and it seemed to her as if Rosamond were burned out of her sight for ever. But that base prompting which makes a woman more cruel to a rival than to a faithless lover, could have no strength of recurrence in Dorothea when the dominant spirit of justice within her had once overcome the tumult and had once shown her the truer measure of things. (846, ch. 80)

Just as Dorothea's avowal of her passion for Ladislaw marks Eliot's effort to redefine the highest form of erotic love as that which is consciously chosen, in contrast to Spencer's emphasis on the force of the unconscious in sexual selection, so Dorothea and Rosamond's embrace represents another standard of justice, one which reconciles rigid oppositions like Spencer's which contrast male justice with female sympathy.

Similarly, while Rosamond demonstrates the advantages that the egotist enjoys in contests with the altruist, she is moved by a more compelling standard of justice when Dorothea offers her a wordless and redemptive sympathy that frees her, though only temporarily, from the narrow cell of self. Rosamond has remained impervious to Lydgate's appeals to her love and reason, and she is stunned by the "shattering" violence of Ladislaw's rejection and anger. It is the "reflex" of Dorothea's unexpected generosity, however, that prompts Rosamond first to listen wonderingly to her avowal of Lydgate's innocence in the death of Raffles and then to sob out her willingness to forgive her husband. When Rosamond "is taken hold of by an emotion stronger than her own," she delivers her "soul under impulses which she had not known before" and, after she kisses Dorothea, she acts with spontaneous generosity by telling Dorothea that "no other woman existed" for Will (856, ch. 81). This moment when Rosamond kisses Dorothea, when "the two women clasped each other as if they had been in a shipwreck" (856, ch. 81), dramatizes once more the transforming power of the charities of mother, daughter, and sister.

In *Middlemarch*, however, Dorothea is given the power to act on this alternate standard of justice in her relationship to Lydgate and Ladislaw as well, in both these friendships, Dorothea acts in defiance of "prejudices about rank and status" (473, ch. 43). Dorothea's rejection of the "cautious weighing of consequences" and her commitment to the "efforts of justice and mercy which would conquer by their emotional force" (789, ch. 72) suggest the broad ground of Eliot's resistance to Spencer's scientific arguments reinscribing the traditional hierarchies that allow men to dominate women, reason to subjugate feeling, and justice to counteract mercy. Rejecting the self-justifying arguments of her uncle and brother-in-law, Dorothea—and Eliot—call into question the concept of justice that rests on masculine reason alone and advocate an alternate concept, marked by a fuller awareness of the problems created by social inequality and the personal egotism fostered by it. Dorothea's justice and sympathy move her beyond mere "rational" analysis when she provides the legacy that restores Lydgate's faith in goodness.

Many readers find *Middlemarch,* finally, to be characterized by a conservatism that shows itself in Dorothea Casaubon's and Mary Garth's marriages, in the subsequent birth of sons to each woman, and in the property settlements which conclude the novel. Sally Shuttleworth, for example, argues that "significantly, it is in marriage to the vital Will that [Dorothea] produces the desired heir. . . . Though Will has twice been the victim of irresponsible inheritance, Dorothea, in marrying him, returns him to his rightful role of property owner" (161). Dorothea's marriage to Will demonstrates, she maintains, Eliot's commitment to an "organicism" which restrains her feminism and compels her to deny Dorothea any outlet for her heroic ambitions except in marriage and to define her life as "absorbed" finally in the life of her husband. Such an ending, Shuttleworth explains, shows how the "question of property is linked to both the continuity and solidarity of the social organism; just inheritance insures the perpetuation of social order, while just administration establishes organizing harmony among the different social strata. Unlike Mr. Brooke or Featherstone, Dorothea, on accession to her estate demonstrates responsible administration: she appoints Mr. Farebrother, releases Lydgate from his debt to Bulstrode, and engineers the reappointment of Caleb Garth" (161). In this way, Shuttleworth concludes, Eliot reveals her conservative desire to preserve the traditional hierarchies of gender and class in a world otherwise destabilized by evolutionary change.

Yet, if we compare Eliot's treatment of marriage in *Middlemarch* to Spencer's analysis of this "domestic institution" in his long-delayed addendum to *The Principles of Sociology,* published in 1877, we can see how Eliot's organicism differs from Spencer's and how she anticipates the arguments that Spencer subsequently used to shelter not only gender roles but also the institution of patriarchal marriage from the evolutionary process of historical change and modification. Spencer began his work on the first volume of his *Principles of Sociology*[33] in 1872, but he unaccountably resisted including a discussion of marriage, that social institution which was, for Victorians, the preeminent "moral institution," though his work in *The Study of Sociology* certainly shows that he was giving much thought to it. In his *Autobiography,* Spencer explains this curious omission by noting that he began to define *The Principles of Sociology* from the "political" side and so did not at first realize "that domestic institutions had to be dealt with" (2:289).

Moreover, Spencer was inclined to analyze marriage only in legal terms, as his treatment of marriage in this work ultimately reveals. Elizabeth Fee explains the extraordinary logic that allowed Spencer, finally, to transcend the problem he perceived but could not solve in his analysis of male egotism and female altruism:

> With Spencer, the anthropological invigoration of a moribund patriarchalism reached its peak. . . . The anthropologists had jettisoned a key provision of [Maine's] old theory that had appeared increasingly untenable in the light of investigations of alien cultures. No longer did they posit that patriarchal monogamy was the natural, eternal human family. Quite the reverse: in the beginning there was a natural and despicable licentiousness, and if not female power, certainly female independence from male control. But they argued that the course of history and evolution flowed away from such an unnatural nature in the direction of patriarchal monogamy. Indeed, patriarchalism was not inextricably linked with the progress of civilization. Victorian culture and its attendant social relations represented the capstone of all evolution. Male superiority then, was sanctioned not by nature, but by civilization. (100–1)

While Spencer quibbled with Sir Henry Maine's conclusions, he accepted Maine's basic emphasis on marriage law as the key to comparative sociological analysis and conceded to his claim that patriarchal marriage was the highest form of marriage. Spencer explains his position in his *Autobiography*:

> It was not that I accepted in full the views of Sir Henry Maine; for my studies of primitive societies had familiarized me with the truths that the patriarchal form of family is not the earliest, and that the relations of parents to one another and to children have sundry more archaic forms. But I became conscious that these more archaic forms, as well as the more developed form supposed by him to be universal, influence deeply the type of social organization assumed. Further, reflection made it clear that intrinsically as well as extrinsically, the traits of its family-life form an important group in the traits presented by each society; and that a great omission had been made in ignoring them. (2:289)

Thus, in the earliest version of *The Principles of Sociology* (1876), Spencer argued that patriarchal marriage customs could be used as an index to the "average power of altruistic sentiments" in a given society. Primitive men who were cruel to their wives or treated them "as mere belongings" proved that their society was less developed than the English, because "whatever occasional displays of altruism there may be, the ordinary flow of altruistic feeling is small" compared to that in English society (1876, 1:78).

Despite these remarks about the moral inferiority of primitive men who regard their wives as "possessions," Spencer, like his friends Sir John Lubbock and John McLennan associated the development of monogamous patriarchal marriage with the rise of a system of private property and with the social and political progress that, by his circular reasoning, accompanied it. In the expanded version of *The Principles of Sociology*, first published in 1877, Spencer wrote, "While the notion of private ownership did not exist, there did not exist the notion of private ownership of women" (1:663). The customs of patriarchal monogamous marriage developed, he argued, when fathers began to see their daughters as property to be "given" in marriage to other men, and when they acquired enough property that they desired a method to ensure the orderly transmission of it to their male heirs.

Eliot did not accept Spencer's self-congratulating conclusions about the altruism expressed in the patriarchal marriage laws of modern England, as *Felix Holt* and *Middlemarch* reveal. Eliot's summary of Sir Henry Maine's *Ancient Law* suggests that she reached very different conclusions from Spencer's in her analysis of marriage law and its role in the transmission of property for, as she noted in the margin of this book, "The modern position of women [is] chiefly determined by barbarian elements."[34] *Middlemarch* displays, in fact, the destructive consequences of this traditional association between the patriarchal laws of inheritance and those of marriage and asserts the moral superiority of marriages defined in alternate terms.

In *Middlemarch*, then, Eliot dramatizes how the "dead hand" of the law stifles and nearly kills Dorothea in her marriage to Casaubon.[35] Even as a young girl, Dorothea achieved an "independent clearness," as Eliot notes, in her understanding of the contrast between the legal and the moral laws of inheritance and marriage. While her elders impressed her by describing the "historical, political reasons why eldest sons had superior rights and why land should be entailed," Dorothea nonetheless recognized that inheritance also presented a moral "question of ties" and responsibilities. Such defenses of the status quo ignored the moral obligation to fulfill those "claims founded on our own deeds, such as marriage and parentage" (407, ch. 37) which pertained to men and women, and to sons and daughters, alike. Dorothea's unorthodox view of inheritance, of course, is what causes the first serious breach between Casaubon and herself, when she presumes to correct the property settlement Casaubon formulated before their marriage.

In presenting Dorothea's analysis of the "unjust" law of entail which allowed Casaubon to acquire the property that should have gone to Ladislaw, Eliot contrasts the young woman's disinterested generosity with her husband's wounded jealousy and suspicion. Dorothea's appeal to

Casaubon to change his will so as to restore Ladislaw's "rightful income" and property dramatizes even more strikingly than in *Felix Holt* the contrast between legal and moral rights of inheritance. While this episode demonstrates Dorothea's unselfish definition of her moral obligations, it discloses, at the same time, her minority before the law. Having no power to correct this injustice which was done on her behalf, she must appeal to her husband to correct the terms of their marriage settlement: "You are so good, so just—you have done everything you thought to be right. But it seems to me clear that more than that is right; and I must speak about it since I am the person who would get what is called benefit by that 'more' not being done" (409–10, ch. 37). Stung not only by the threat to his legal prerogatives within marriage but also, unknown to Dorothea, by his sense that her concern for Ladislaw seems to confirm his worst suspicions that his cousin has designs on his wife, Casaubon refuses her request. Casaubon echoes Spencer's ideas about justice when he replies that Dorothea is "not qualified to discriminate" the justice of her marriage settlement and declares, resentfully, that he will accept no "revision, still less dictation within that range of affairs which I have deliberated upon as distinctly mine" (410, ch. 37).

Eliot draws a similar contrast between the legal and moral definition of marriage laws in Dorothea's second midnight debate with her husband, and here she also dramatizes how male egotism is flattered not only by the legal preeminence the husband is given over his wife but also by his role as lawmaker and judge in questions of inheritance. In this scene, Eliot demonstrates how the husband's legal right to his wife's possessions encourages him to regard her person and her talents as "a peculiar possession for himself" (517, ch. 48). Casaubon makes a terrible mockery of the marriage vows exchanged in love when he demands that Dorothea commit herself blindly to carrying out his wishes. In response, Dorothea points out the distinction between the moral obligations compelled by love and affection and those defined by patriarchal prerogatives which require female subordination in marriage: "It is not right . . . to make a promise when I am ignorant what it will bind me to. Whatever affection prompted, I would do without promising" (519, ch. 49). Her comment, of course, applies as well to her naive idealism about her marriage to Casaubon in the first place.

Moreover, Casaubon's rejoinder suggests how the law of coverture encouraged male egocentricity: "You would use your own judgment: I ask you to obey mine" (519, ch. 49). Thus, in contrasting Dorothea's conception of marriage as a union defined by a voluntary commitment to honor all sacrifices prompted by love and pity with her husband's more legalistic view, Eliot shows how the "dead hand of the law," enforcing the legal subordination of the woman to her husband and depriving her of her moral freedom as an individual, privileges male egotism and counteracts female altruism. By insisting on the "deep difference between devotion to the living and the infinite promise of devotion to the dead" and emphasizing the healthiness of the "need for freedom" that asserts itself imperiously in Dorothea's resistance to her husband's demands, Eliot indicates how the laws of property may corrupt the moral foundation of marriage.

As these two confrontations show, Dorothea is not free to exercise her impulses for the "just administration" of her property until, as a result of Casaubon's death, she acquires her legal majority as a widow. Only then is she able to appoint Mr. Farebrother, release Lydgate from his debt to Bulstrode, and engineer the reappointment of Caleb Garth. Dorothea's demonstrated helplessness in her first marriage and the patent injustice of Casaubon's codicil prohibiting the children of Dorothea and Will from inheriting any of the property she obtained through her marriage with Casaubon shows Eliot's resistance to Spencer's notion that the integration of property and marriage laws was a sign of social progress. While Will eventually achieves his "rightful role of property owner," it is Brooke's—and not Casaubon's—estate that he inherits and this only because Dorothea happens to bear a male heir.

The contrasts Eliot draws in comparing the marriages of Dorothea and her sister provides Eliot with another opportunity to question assumptions like those articulated by Maine and, later, in 1877, by Spencer in *The Principles of Sociology*, that the laws which define marriage in terms of property settlements are a sign of advanced social development. After her marriage and the birth of her son, Celia "naturally felt more able to advise her childless sister" (878, ch. 84). She assumes the responsibility of correcting her sister's "mystical" shortsightedness and strange selflessness by asserting the compelling force of her more conventional view of the obligations of marriage and parenthood. Celia's advice, however, cloaks her secret egotism, for Dorothea's marriage to Will Ladislaw eventually produces a child that is decidedly unwanted by Celia and James Chettam. Moreover, by treating with gentle irony Celia's worship of her son as the "baby Bouddha in Western form," Eliot shows that parenthood is as liable to promote egotism as altruism: "Since Celia's baby was born, she had a new sense of her mental solidity and calm wisdom. It seemed clear that where there was a baby, things were right enough, and that error, in general, was mere lack of that central poising force" (531, ch. 50). Her repeated ironic emphasis on Celia's failure to notice that Dorothea "does not recognize her infant nephew as Bouddha," and so feels the "interest of watching him [to be] exhaustible" (579, ch. 54), indicates Eliot's skepticism about arguments that assume patriarchal concepts of marriage, parenthood, and property laws are indicators of progress.

Thus, when Celia chats pleasantly about how nice it would be if little Arthur were to become a "viscount," she is willfully indulging in maternal egotism. Similarly, when Sir James protests that marriage to Ladislaw will take Dorothea "out of her proper rank into poverty," he reveals not only his personal "prejudice" and "jealousy" but also the more selfish and mercenary motives that he is ashamed to acknowledge, the prospect of more property "for his son and heir," (876, 84) bequeathed to him by a doting and childless aunt. By revealing these motives hidden scrupulously from consciousness, Eliot challenges Spencer's assumption in "Psychology of the Sexes" and elsewhere that the mothers's and father's natural instincts of self-sacrifice for their children are necessarily morally responsible. The parental sacrifices of Celia and Sir James are, indeed, self-serving and shut out the wider, more disinterested kind of altruism and social commitment that is represented by the marriage of Dorothea and Will. In this contrast of sisters, Eliot exposes the illogic which underlies the Victorian separation of men's and women's spheres when Celia urges Dorothea to let James Chettam "think" for her because, as she explains, "men know best about everything except what women know better" (792, ch. 72).

Eliot's treatment of the Garths is also often interpreted as revealing a similarly conservative endorsement of patriarchal values, especially in her handling of the settlement of property following the marriage of Fred Vincy and Mary Garth. U. C. Knoepflmacher writes, for example, that "while Dorothea must leave the community of Middlemarch, Caleb is allowed to stay there. Together with Mary and his new son, this patriarch replenishes the land neglected by Mr. Brooke, Featherstone, and Bulstrode" ("*Middlemarch*" 80). Yet the Garths' property is not "restored," as Knoepflmacher asserts: Fred and Mary come to Stone Court as tenants rather than property owners, and only after the generous intervention of Harriet Bulstrode.

Earlier in the novel, Mary expresses her resistance to patriarchal law when she refuses to assist Peter Featherstone in "doing as he likes" by burning his second will, which would settle his property on Fred Vincy. Eliot does indeed present Featherstone as the archetypal "avunculus" (Knoepflmacher, "*Middlemarch*" 55) as he lies on his deathbed with money spilling out of his casket onto the counterpane and offers Mary the bribe that women typically accept in patriarchal societies. Mary, however, asserts her own right to protect her independence, integrity, and self-esteem, and refuses to "let the close" of his life "soil" the beginning of her own (351, ch. 33).[36] Thus, the marriage of Fred and Mary, like the union of Esther and Felix Holt, does not signal the "just transmission of property" but rather their mutual and voluntary commitment to the ethics of work and self-help, as they follow the example of Caleb Garth.[37]

Moreover, though Mary's marriage thus demonstrates her heritage as her father's favorite daughter, Eliot does not equate Caleb with the other patriarchal authorities in this text, as his submissive relation to his wife indicates. In fact, Mary assumes a stance of resistance not only in relation to Mr. Featherstone but also to another patriarchal authority in this novel, Mr. Farebrother.[38] Mary is quite outspoken in her criticism of the church and uses her "mother's tongue" to complain sharply about clergymen who make "the whole clergy ridiculous." So though Mary wonders over the suppressed emotion in Mr. Farebrother's voice when he counsels her to be direct and open in avowing her love for Fred, she cannot take seriously the "hazy and perhaps illusory" daydream the minister's affection for her seems to promise (561, ch. 52). Thus by choosing a brother-sister rather than a father-daughter relationship in marriage, Mary resists submission to the two traditional sources of patriarchal authority and accepts her place in a marriage which repudiates the legal and sexual ethics of "permanent inequality." Mary is happy to bring forth male children, as a result, perhaps because she recognizes the patriarchal nature of Middlemarch and the prevailing laws defining marriage and property.

Dorothea assumes a similar posture of resistance to traditional patriarchal authority when she marries Will Ladislaw. In accepting Will as her husband, Dorothea rejects Casaubon's express prohibition and acts against the advice of her sister's husband. There is a final obstacle that Dorothea must tear down before she is able to liberate her best soul from its fetters, and that is the custom of reticence about her heart's desires that is the final mark of her heritage, her wealth, her class, and her sex. W. J. Harvey has complained about Eliot's evasive depiction of passion in the scene in which Will and Dorothea make their "childlike" acknowledgment of mutual passion,[39] but the thunderclap that startles them into these confessions is less a sign of Eliot's sentimental indirectness in describing love than it is a recognition of the fact of mortality which can no longer be ameliorated in a post-Darwinian world.

In a world where egotism triumphs so easily over altruism, and where "darkness" often seems to prevail, the satisfaction of the heart's desires rather than the cool gratifications of self-sacrifice provide the best hope of wholeness and the only compensation for loss. By comparing her loss of faith in Ladislaw's love to the mother's loss of her child, Dorothea, in the midnight of her soul, "discovers her passion" and moves beyond the renunciations practiced by Maggie Tulliver and Romola in order to acknowledge more fully the depth of her feeling for Ladislaw and her overmastering desire for a "nearness" which is the best compensation for the failures of justice in her world. The authentic impulse which directs Dorothea's avowal, "Oh I did love him" (844, ch. 80), thus causes her to recognize the force of her passionate desire for Ladislaw, and the pointlessness of the self-denial imposed upon her by the canons of propriety in her class. This recognition impels her to set aside the social taboo which had kept her silent, and so she declares her love to Ladislaw.

In conclusion, Eliot indicates the revolutionary quality of Dorothea and Will's love and marriage by measuring both against the more complacent standards of marriage, parenthood, and justice professed and recommended by her more conventional sister and brother-in-law. So Dorothea, like Esther Lyon, rejects being a "queen" on the terms Celia recommends when she chooses to "live faithfully a hidden" and unhistoric life (896, Finale). Eliot's comment that "no creature whose inward being is so strong that it is not greatly determined by what lies outside it" (896, Finale), shows her recognition of the compromise she made with biological and historical determinism. Yet the marriage of Dorothea and Will remains a celebration of passionate love rather than a sign of the safe transmission of property. Dorothea's renunciation of her marriage portion frees her from the self-interested compromises of James and Celia, and thus her son finally receives a heritage which is more valuable than property alone. The triumph of love and will that Dorothea's marriage to Will Ladislaw celebrates shows, finally, Eliot's faith that by understanding the "mystery which lies under" the physical laws of evolution and by acting on this wisdom, individuals may contribute their best to the "growing good of the world" (896, Finale).

9

Civilization and Degeneration:
Daniel Deronda and Spencer's Later Writing

ON JANUARY 30, 1873, Herbert Spencer published the first number of his *Descriptive Sociology*, a survey of various cultures around the world, presented in tabular form, to illustrate his theories of "social evolution."[1] By September of that year, he considered abandoning the project because he realized that he had "greatly overestimated the amount of desire which existed in the public mind for social facts of an instructive kind" and concluded, in what could be a disparaging reference to his more successful novel-writing friend, that the public "generally preferred" to read literature of an "uninstructive kind" (*Autobiography* 2:268). Nevertheless, having hired a number of young scholars to help him compile the research for his *Descriptive Sociology*, Spencer felt obliged to see the work through to completion, and so he "persisted through the seven following years" (*Autobiography* 2:268) overseeing the compilation of *Descriptive Sociology*, while at the same time completing the numbers for the first part of *The Principles of Sociology*, which began to appear in print in June 1874.

By 1874, Spencer found himself at the uncomfortable center of a storm of controversy about his use in his evolutionary theories of developmental psychology, on the one hand, and of history, on the other. In February of that year, Eliot's long-time friend, Sara Hennell, published a feminist critique of Spencer's *Study of Sociology*. Writing to her shortly afterward, Eliot expressed her somewhat bemused and ambivalent sympathy for Spencer as he felt the fire of hostile criticism from feminists, churchmen, and academics:

> Your letter to the *Examiner* is much milder than I expected, and hardly makes apparent the severe objections you mentioned to me. But I am not sorry that there should be a little boiling of the peas shot at poor Spencer just now, for he is running the gauntlet in rather a fatiguing way between Cambridge men who are criticizing his physics and psychology, and historians who are criticizing the "Sociological Tables" on which he has already spent £500 in the hope that he is doing the world a service. (*GEL* 6:15)

Finding many of her own and Lewes's criticisms of Spencer's approach to psychology and history taken up by others, Eliot perhaps felt more compassion for Spencer, even though she apparently remained skeptical about the "service" he was doing the world in publishing his sociological tables.

The research redacted in Spencer's *Descriptive Sociology* (1873–1881) invited him to reconsider the problems posed by historical and cultural diversity, but *The Principles of Sociology* remains nonetheless marked by three fundamental evasions that characterize Spencer's response to the interpretation of difference. The first can be seen in Spencer's reliance on his paradigm of individual development. In his writing, Spencer usually did not discriminate between examples drawn from ancient Egyptian or Greek culture and those from contemporary non-Western societies, for his developmental view of history and race allowed him simply to group examples of "less developed" societies together with those of "inferior races."[2] In a rare moment in *The Principles of Sociology*, Spencer admitted that he was staggered by the task of interpreting the meaning of the cultural differences suggested by his sociological tables. Recognizing that religion posed some of the most fundamental problems of interpretation, Spencer asked, "Shall we say that the primitive man is less intelligent than the lower animals, less intelligent than birds and reptiles, less intelligent than even insects" because his religious practices suggest that he does not discriminate between animate and inanimate life? (1:142).

Yet, Spencer answered this rhetorical question here and elsewhere in his text by returning to the same comforting conclusion that he reached in *The Principles of Biology*, where he argued that individual development "recapitulated" the development of the race. Throughout *The Principles of Sociology*, Spencer unself-consciously compared the mental processes of children of his own race with that of adults of "lesser races," writing, for example, "Again, we see in the young of our own race a parallel inability to concentrate the attention on anything complex or abstract. The mind of the child, like that of the savage, soon wanders from sheer exhaustion when generalities and involved propositions have to be dealt with" (1:102–3). Though he acknowledged in this passage that he often relied on the evolutionary paradigm of individual development to interpret racial differences, Spencer repeatedly failed to reconsider his premises.

Spencer's unexamined use of historical examples to illustrate the theory of social evolution set forth in *The Principles of Sociology* prompted sharp criticism from British historians in the 1870s. These objections are frequently voiced by modern readers as well:

The great classical systems of sociology all need to place, within the total pattern of history, both contemporary, early industrial society and the ideal society of the future. There are two chief ways of doing this. Liberals like Spencer, who are more aware of the superiority in all fields of contemporary society over all societies of the past, will see history in terms of a temporal continuum between two poles. The ideal society of the future will resemble the past in every way less than the present does, and will be a prolongation of changes already begun. The primitive, the traditional, the militant are the reverse of the ideal. (Peel 198–99)

Unwilling to consider historical examples suggesting that societies in the past were, in some ways, more progressive than those of the present, or to entertain the possibility that the future did not necessarily guarantee an improvement over the present, Spencer assumed that societies developed according to a natural and universal law. Thus, he was able to rank particular societies in an evolutionary hierarchy by noting how closely they corresponded to the standards of English industrial society, which was, for Spencer, the most highly developed culture of its time.

The Principles of Sociology is similarly marked by a second evasion that shows Spencer's effort to silence his doubts about his use of the theory of the conservation of energy to explain the increasingly specialized division of labor in the individual and social body. When the eminent physicist John Tyndall told him that "complete physical equilibrium meant omnipresent death," Spencer responded with alarm: "Regarding, as I have done, equilibrium as the ultimate and highest state of society, I have assumed it to be not only the ultimate but also the highest state of the universe. And your assertion that when equilibrium was reached life must cease, staggered me. . . . I still feel unsettled about the matter" (Russett 128). Though he did not use the term, Spencer came closest to considering the problem of degeneracy in The Principles of Biology (1864–1867), when he argued that "overly" educated women who defied the "supreme end" of their existence by rejecting marriage and motherhood threatened to arrest social progress. To avoid confronting the "spectre of dissolution" in The Principles of Sociology, Spencer turned resolutely away from the subjects of degeneration, retrogression, and extinction, problems Darwin had analyzed provocatively in The Descent of Man (1871).[3]

Finally, while Spencer presented a theory of nationhood in The Principles of Sociology that derived from his evolutionary analysis of gender and racial differences, he failed to address himself to the problem of how nations reproduced themselves.[4] Spencer argued that a fixed sequence of development characterized all societies as they progressed toward nationhood: "The stages of compounding and recompounding have to be passed through in succession. No tribe becomes a nation by simple growth; and no great society is formed by the direct union of the smallest societies" (1:575). Since Spencer regarded marriage practices as a reliable index of cultural development, his study of marriage helped him to identify this progressive sequence; yet he avoided a detailed analysis of the "domestic institutions" in the numbers and first edition of *The Principles of Sociology* (1876). Challenged by Eliot and other feminists who argued that British marriage customs remained in some ways morally objectionable, Spencer characteristically avoided discussing marriage in any detail until he revised this volume in 1877. In this new edition, he argued:

> We are thus furnished with both a relative standard and an absolute standard by which to measure the domestic relations in each stage of social progress. While judging them relatively by their adaptions to the accompanying social requirements, we may be led to regard as needful in their times and places, arrangements that are repugnant to us; we shall, judging them absolutely, in relation to the most developed types of life, individual and national, find good reasons for reprobating them. For this preliminary survey clearly reveals the fact that the domestic relations which are the highest as ethically considered, are also the highest as considered both biologically and sociologically. (1:630)

Repressing the contradictions in his analysis of marriage that feminist critiques had exposed, Spencer maintained that women were required to sacrifice individual development to the biological demands of the race and were expected to surrender their individual freedom, for the good of the nation, by submitting to patriarchal marriage arrangements. This submission Spencer equated with progress.

Because feminist critiques of contemporary sexual practices and marriage customs recognized, on the contrary, the possibility that English society was culturally degenerate, they called into question Spencer's conclusions about the process by which a society and a nation developed. One of the problems in the marriage laws of the 1860s and 1870s that was painfully evident to George Eliot concerned the rights of the wife, in contrast to the mistress, in cases of divorce or abandonment. Feminist activist Annie Besant summarizes these contradictions when she writes: "If you are legally your husband's wife, you can have no legal claim to your children; if legally you are your husband's mistress, your rights as mother are secure."[5] This conflict in the British laws institutionalizing both marriage and illegitimacy underlies the contrast between prolific mistresses and sonless wives that lies at the heart of *Daniel Deronda* (1876) and connects the English and the Jewish plots.

In contrast to Spencer, George Eliot was keenly interested in the challenges that the concept of degeneracy posed for evolutionary theory, and *Daniel Deronda* is, as a result, a novel haunted not only by the past but also by the future (Beer, *Darwin's Plots* 181). The hermeneutical design as well as the plot of this novel inscribes Eliot's most expansive and radical critique of Spencer's use of psychology and history in his *Descriptive Sociology* and in *The Principles of Sociology*. The wonderful epigraph to the first chapter of *Daniel Deronda* suggests that Eliot's response to Spencer's evolutionary theory is central to this novel, for she observes that science, like its "less accurate Grandmother Poetry . . . reckons backwards as well as forwards" (35, ch. 1). In the novel as a whole, Eliot exposes the irony in Spencer's reading of history by questioning the imperial mission that Great Britain assumed in the 1870s and by indicating the need for a moral "conversion" that would restore English Society "to the great river of human history by Hebrew prophetic vision" (Carpenter, *George Eliot* 135).[6]

More specifically, in *Daniel Deronda* Eliot challenged Spencer's evolutionary paradigm of individual development by comparing Gwendolen's and Deronda's relations with their mothers, but this critique prompted her to reconsider her earlier essentialist interpretation of gender differences in her representations of the "maternal emotions." By analyzing the psychology of these two characters whose emotional development has been curiously arrested, Eliot questioned Spencer's fundamental assumptions about the development of both individuals and societies. By identifying the pressure that the future brings to bear upon the present by comparing the courtship periods of these two characters, Eliot disclosed signs of social degeneracy in the marriage customs and educational practices of both British and Jewish culture. Finally, by contrasting English society with a "race" that, in 1870, had no nation and was defined by many nineteenth-century historians as "decadent," Eliot similarly interrogated Spencer's paradigm of race and nationhood.[7]

Daniel Deronda presents a world where evolutionary processes seem somehow to have gone wrong, fostering tragic decay rather than "progress." The first mother and child pair that appears in this novel embodies the degeneracy of mid-Victorian culture, for standing beside the brilliant Gwendolen Harleth at the roulette table at Leubronn is a mother "deeply engaged" in gambling, and at her side is her "melancholy little boy" who has the "blank gaze of a bedizened child" (36, ch. 1). This pair adumbrates Gwendolen's past and suggests her future, a future that she eventually escapes, we learn, with Daniel's help. The mother and child in this gaslit salon also reveal the psychological consequences of the accelerating social change that Eliot described in *Middlemarch* as eroding the "rooted" life and domestic values of rural English culture. This is a world where marriages celebrate the triumph of will and ambition rather than mutual passionate love. It is a world where both parents and children share Daniel Deronda's spiritual dislocation and are obsessed by uncertainties about their "origin." Mordecai diagnoses not only Deronda's spiritual condition but that of all of Eliot's educated contemporaries when he observes, "You are not sure of your origin" (558, ch. 40).

Some of the apocalyptic qualities of *Daniel Deronda* can be located in Eliot's willingness to trace the origins of both sexual love and fear back to its sources in the family. Gwendolen's cry, "Haven't children reason to be angry with their parents?" (379, ch. 29) reverberates throughout this novel, and shows how profoundly unsettling was the question of degeneracy when applied to the family. Eliot's treatment of the family in this novel likewise shows how the feminist analysis of prostitution and female sexuality that emerged after the defeat of women's suffrage in 1867 posed new questions about the "charities of mother, daughter, and sister" and prompted Eliot to reconsider her own assumptions about the psychological development of women.

Moreover, *Daniel Deronda* shows how feminist issues in the 1870s redefined the territory of the "wild zone" for Eliot. While Eliot was writing her final novel, Josephine Butler and other feminists spearheaded a campaign for the repeal of the Contagious Diseases Acts, those legislative measures passed in 1864, 1866, and 1869 that granted police the right to arrest any woman suspected of being a prostitute, subject her to a medical examination, and confine her to a hospital if she were found to have venereal disease (Bauer and Ritt 195–96). Through this campaign, Butler helped to create an unlikely coalition between middle-class ladies and Victorian prostitutes, by encouraging her peers to imagine the prostitutes as their sisters and to recognize their shared oppression in a vice-ridden patriarchal and authoritarian state (Walkowitz 91). According to Judith Walkowitz, "Butler's feminism combined two distinct tendencies—advocating sex equality, while celebrating the virtues of a distinctive woman's culture" (117). One of the characteristic features of Butler's view of prostitution was the special emphasis it placed on the mother-daughter bond. Butler undertook rescue work in the "sacred" name of the mother in order to save fallen "daughters": "Butler's defense of motherhood was a political device, aimed at subverting and superseding patriarchal authority: it gave mothers not fathers the right to control sexual access to the daughters. In this way, Butler sanctioned an authority relationship between older middle-class women and young working women that although caring and protective, was also hierarchical and custodial" (Walkowitz 117). Butler's campaign subsequently divided feminists over the volatile issue of female sexuality and the proper agents of its control.

Eliot's letters indicate that she was aware of this new feminist perspective on prostitution and motherhood.[8] In a letter written during this period, Eliot wrote that the Woman Question seemed to "overhang abysses of which even prostitution is not the worst" (*GEL* 5:58). Another letter suggests that the issues raised by Butler's campaign altered Eliot's view of "race" and its reproduction. In a letter commending Mrs. Nassau Senior for her work with Victorian prostitutes, Eliot observed that the prostitute may be a "better mother or sister of the race" than her ostensibly more virtuous sister because she had a "more human sort of passion in her" (*GEL* 6:46–47).

Eliot's treatment of Tessa in *Romola*, of course, indicates her long-standing sympathy for women who were sexually victimized by men, and this campaign may have increased Eliot's appreciation for the heroic potential of female solidarity. In another letter from this period, Eliot alludes to the Greek sources that she used to chart the "wild zone" in *Silas Marner* and *Felix Holt*: "The influence of one woman's life on the lot of other women is getting greater with the quickening spread of all influences. One likes to think, though, that two thousand years ago Euripides made Iphigenia count it a reason for facing her sacrifice bravely that thereby she might help some Greek women" (*GEL* 5:372). However, Eliot's objections to women's suffrage, her reading of evolutionary psychology and anthropology, as well as her own reaction to being cast in the mother's role made it more difficult for her to accept the idea of female solidarity based on the maternal emotions, and on women's capacities for egotism and altruism in particular. As she grew older, Eliot found herself assigned to play the mother's part not only by George Henry Lewes and his sons but also by a growing circle of younger women whom Eliot recognized as her "spiritual daughters," a group which included Elma Stuart, Mrs. Pattison, Alice Helps, and Edith Simcox.[9] In 1869, for example, Eliot wrote that getting older "brings some new satisfactions, and among these I find the growth of a maternal feeling toward both men and women who are much younger than myself" (*GEL* 5:5).

While Eliot enjoyed the tributes and affection that these women lavished upon her, she felt ambivalence, too, especially over being chosen as the object of Edith Simcox's particularly ardent attention. Shortly after G. H. Lewes's death, Eliot wrote asking that Simcox stop addressing her as "Mother." Simcox summarizes the rest of Eliot's letter: "She knew it was her fault, she had begun, she was apt to be rash and commit herself in one mood to what was irksome in another. Not with her own mother, but her associations otherwise with the name were as of a task, and it was a fact that her feeling for me was not at all a mother's—any other name she did not mind; she had much more respect and admiration for me now than when she knew me first" (Haight, *George Eliot* 533). The recognition of the sensual and erotic dimensions of women's love for each other that Simcox's attentions pressed upon Eliot finds expression in her representation of Gwendolen's bond with her mother. Similarly, Eliot's deepening awareness of the social consequences of prostitution and illegitimacy in Victorian society is dramatized in her presentation of Grandcourt's liaison with Lydia Glasher and Gwendolen's response to it.

The representation of Gwendolen's mother, Mrs. Davilow, turns the Victorian cult of the madonna upside down, revealing Eliot's reexamination of the biological and moral components of the "maternal sensations and emotions." Though Mrs. Davilow is a paragon of self-effacing maternal humility, she fails to protect Gwendolen from "what is called the knowledge of the world" (378, ch. 29), for "indeed she wished that she herself had not had any of it thrust upon her" (378, ch. 29). Unlike the mothers that Butler described, Mrs. Davilow tells Gwendolen that "if there is anything horrible to be done, I should like it to be left to the men" (85, ch. 6), and she willingly surrenders her moral authority over her daughter to patriarchal authorities in the family and the church. By describing how she teaches Gwendolen to accept her "natural" place in the process of sexual selection and to exploit her physical advantages for material gain through marriage, Eliot reveals one of the ways that cultural degeneracy is reproduced in this society.

Eliot dramatizes the implications of Mrs. Davilow's abdication of her maternal authority over her daughter when Gwendolen assumes the mother's role in the tableau vivant from *The Winter's Tale*, while her mother plays the part of the servant. In representing this role reversal, Eliot recalls her differences with Spencer concerning the force of biological and moral law and her valorization of the feminine "art which does mend nature."[10] But this scene also reveals Eliot's reassessment of the charities of mother, daughter, and sister, for when Mrs. Davilow commands, "Music, awake her, strike," Gwendolen displays the hysterical dread that exposes her resistance to heterosexual love and desire.[11] Later, Eliot again suggests Gwendolen's arrested sexual development when Mrs. Davilow finds her daughter "struck down" and sobbing after Rex Gascoigne declares his love for her. In Gwendolen's assertion of her resistance to love, "I shall never love anybody. I can't love people. I hate them. . . . I can't bear any one to be very near me but you" (115, ch. 7), Eliot acknowledges one of the "myriad modes of mutual attraction" that escapes heterosexuality entirely. By thus disclosing Gwendolen's arrested sexual development and later the frigidity that is born of her dread, Eliot challenges the assumptions that Spencer and Darwin made about the natural development of the sexual instincts which predetermined woman's place in the family.

Moreover, as she traces the process by which Gwendolen is induced to overcome the inexplicable fear and dread that prompts her to refuse the marriage proposals of Rex Gascoigne and Henleigh Grandcourt, Eliot exposes the social as well as psychological forces working to promote degeneracy in English life. In *Daniel Deronda*, Eliot again fo-

cuses on the two social institutions charged with directing and preserving the moral life of the nation: the family and the church, institutions
which were conspicuous by their absence in the first edition of Spencer's
Principles of Sociology (1876). In revealing Gwendolen's ambitions for an
upwardly mobile marriage, Eliot suggests the pressure that the future
brings to bear upon the lives of women in her society and dramatizes
how "sexual selection" operates to defeat the moral values that Eliot
identified with the "maternal principle": love, altruism, cooperation, and
female solidarity.[12]

Like Rosamond Vincy, Gwendolen sees marriage as offering her the
opportunity for a "social promotion," and she channels all her energy
and ambition into enhancing her advantages in the marriage market.
Because of the accidents of heredity, Gwendolen possesses a kind of
beauty that allows her to feel "well equipped for the mastery of life" (69,
ch. 4). Gwendolen sees courtship in terms of power rather than love and
would prefer to be perpetually courted rather than submit to marriage.
For Gwendolen, to be "very much sued or hopelessly sighed for as a
bride was indeed an indispensable and agreeable guarantee of womanly
power; but to become a wife and wear all the domestic fetters of that
condition, was on the whole a vexacious necessity" (68, ch. 4).[13] Love is
obviously not one of Gwendolen's criteria for the perfect marriage; her
husband simply must have the requisite "battlement, veranda, stable,
etc., no grins and no glass in his eye" (176, ch. 13).

Eliot notes how Gwendolen's anticipated place in the marriage market puts its mark on her education by observing that she has been
trained according to Spencer's prescription; she has been taught the
skills of self-display with "no disturbing reference to the advancement of
learning or the balance of the constitution" (69, ch. 4). Similarly, because her education accepts female competition in the courtship process as a given, it has intensified Gwendolen's sense of rivalry with her
sisters and female acquaintances. Gwendolen's destructive competitive-
ness finds expression in her murder of canary birds, her vehement rejection of her half-sisters, and her hostility to female friends. Catherine Arrowpoint, for example, makes Gwendolen feel an "unwonted feeling of
jealousy" not only because she envies the heiress her fortune but also
because she recognizes that her rival possesses "a certain mental superiority which could not be explained away" and a "thoroughness in musical accomplishments" which makes Gwendolen feel "in awe of her standard" (82, ch. 6). Without a sense of solidarity with other women which
inspires "theoretical or practically reforming women," Gwendolen's
quest for "freedom" simply expresses her "very common egoistic ambition" (83, ch. 6). By thus displaying the destructiveness of female competition, Eliot indicates how Spencer's paradigm of individual and social

development counteracts the development of the charities of mother, daughter, and sister.

Gwendolen is not presented as the only example of moral decadence in her world, however, for Eliot suggests that decadence is even more widespread in the class Gwendolen hopes to join through marriage. The animal vitality of the dogs and horses in Grandcourt's society contrasts sadly with the languid purposelessness of the men and women; the roving archery matches and foxhunts suggest its sadism, and its balls, musicals, and impromptu amateur theatricals disclose its artificiality and mediocrity.[14]

Eliot alludes to Spencer's theory of sexual selection and suggests how it operates to undermine the moral value of both courtship and marriage in this society when she describes Gwendolen's triumph over Juliet Fenn in her contest to attract the attention of Henleigh Grandcourt, the first "real man" Gwendolen sees (147, ch. 11). Eliot dramatizes the consequences of Spencer's scientific normalizing of the "rule sublime" which requires that "wives must be what men will choose" (132, ch. 10) when she describes Gwendolen's sense of superiority over the less attractive Juliet Fenn. Referring to those features Spencer identified as marks of ugliness—an "underhung jaw" and a "receding brow"—Eliot's narrator observes parenthetically: "Surely, considering the importance which is given to such an accident in female offspring, marriageable men, or what the new English calls 'intending bridegrooms,' should look at themselves dispassionately in the glass, since the natural selection of a mate prettier than themselves is not certain to bar the effect of their own ugliness" (149, ch. 11). By thus suggesting that ugly men who are capable of imagining the more abstract claims of their "offspring" should retire altogether from the contest to attract beautiful women in order to prevent their own blemishes from being reproduced in their daughters, Eliot compresses Spencer's theory of sexual selection into a *reductio ad absurdum.* For Eliot, there was a more appalling moral ugliness evident everywhere in the "English half" of the novel which is located in the "market's pulse" and in the egocentricity of "men's tastes," an egocentricity Spencer redefined as "natural" in his theory of sexual selection.

When courtship is practiced in these terms, marriage becomes little more than polite prostitution. Eliot uses Gwendolen's conversation with Klesmer to expose this decadence and to suggest alternative ends for the paradigms of individual and social development than those Spencer formulated. Gwendolen has overestimated her talents for music and acting because she has accepted the false artistic standards that prevail in her society, where "everything from low arithmetic to high art, is of the amateur kind politely supposed to fall short of perfection only because gentlemen and ladies are not obliged to do more than they like" (307, ch. 23). By declaring instead that a "genius" for singing or acting "at first is little more than a great capacity for receiving discipline" (300, ch. 23), Klesmer counters assumptions like Spencer's and Darwin's that a woman's talent for music, like her beauty, is simply a gift of nature, useful to her in sexual selection but otherwise of no benefit to the world outside her home.[15] In Gwendolen and the Princess, Eliot shows the tragic wastefulness of marriage imagined and contracted on the narrow terms of biological determinism.

Eliot discloses a similar corrupting complicity in the national church, that other moral institution she highlights in the English half of this novel. When Gwendolen's uncle, the Rector of Pennicote, urges her to overcome her inexplicable resistance to Grandcourt's proposal of marriage, Mr. Gascoigne articulates a "worldly" morality that undermines the ethical authority of the church itself.[16] In his appeals to Gwendolen, Eliot exposes a social conservativism that Spencer later defined as typical of "ecclesiastical institutions," but Gascoigne's traditionalism finds particularly destructive expression in his *ex cathedra* interpretations of gender arrangements. Gascoigne echoes Spencer in arguing that "marriage is the only true and satisfactory sphere of a woman" and urges marriage upon Gwendolen as a "duty." Taking a "practical" view of his niece's marriage, Gascoigne points out its material advantages. Seeing it as "a sort of public affair" and anticipating that it "might even strengthen the Establishment," he encourages Gwendolen to ignore her dread and accept Grandcourt's offer when it comes, telling her, "If Providence offers you power and position—especially when unclogged by any conditions that are repugnant to you—your course is one of responsibility" (179, ch. 13).

Gascoigne knows about Grandcourt's philandering, and his willingness to blink at it reveals the same hypocrisy about sexual double standards that apparently allowed many Anglican clergy in these years to support the Contagious Diseases Acts, a position that Victorian feminists saw as tantamount to condoning prostitution (Walkowitz 80). Gascoigne regards Grandcourt's "entangling dissipations" with Lydia Glasher as simply an embarrassing fact which should have been swept into "private rubbish heaps"—until Grandcourt's will discloses the financial and moral threats that his illegitimate family poses to "respectable people" like Gascoigne himself (826, ch. 64). While he has countenanced male "folly," he vehemently objects to the recognition of Lydia's son as heir because he feels that "female morality is likely to suffer from this marked advantage and preeminence being given to illegitimate offspring" (826, ch. 64).

Eliot shows that the sexual double standard revealed in Gascoigne's judgments about Lydia prevails more generally in Grandcourt's society.

Lydia Glasher has been ostracized as a moral degenerate, while Grandcourt's sexual adventures are politely overlooked. Indicating how motherhood is used as a test of a woman's morality, Eliot notes that Lydia "was understood to have forsaken her child along with her husband" and so was presumed to have "sunk lower" (383, ch. 30). Grandcourt, who has also denied his obligation as father, is regarded as eligible and "as seaworthy as ever" (386, ch. 30).[17]

Gwendolen, however, does not enter into her marriage in innocence about Grandcourt's past, and in representing how she overcomes the "dread and terror" inspired by Lydia Glasher's example and appeals, Eliot moves beyond her analysis of female victimization in *Romola* and *Felix Holt*. When Lydia tells Gwendolen about Grandcourt's illegitimate children, the "shock of another woman's calamity" (342, ch. 27), along with her own pride and jealousy, reinforces Gwendolen's impulse to resist Grandcourt's initial advances. When economic necessity prompts Gwendolen to set her sense of sisterhood aside and to accept Grandcourt's hand, her dread is intensified because she feels that she has betrayed both Lydia and the motherright that underlies her appeal that her children's claims be recognized.[18] This secret knowledge engenders a terrible disillusionment, as Eliot indicates, when Gwendolen wonders, if "other men's lives were of the same kind—full of secrets which made the ignorant suppositions of the women they wanted to marry a farce at which they were laughing up their sleeves" (343, ch. 27). Such cynicism about the moral basis of marriage unravels the whole fabric of a society.

What draws Grandcourt and Gwendolen together, then, is not love but rather their "piteous equality in the need to dominate" (346, ch. 27). By dramatizing the consequences of this murderous union defined by "negative" passions (348, ch. 27), Eliot reveals once again the radical flaw in Spencer's theory of sexual selection, which privileges the male will for dominance and assumes that female beauty coincides with a natural feminine submissiveness. Grandcourt is, in some ways, the perfect Spencerian hero, the husband theoretically most "fit" to survive, since he possesses the tenacious will that allows him to "be master of a woman who would like to master him" (365, ch. 28). Yet, though Gwendolen eventually submits and marries him, Grandcourt's single-minded impulse to dominate his wife ultimately kills him.[19]

In describing the conversation between Grandcourt and Gwendolen just before his drowning and in picturing them moving along the quay like creatures who were "fulfilling a supernatural destiny" (745, ch. 54), Eliot emphasizes Grandcourt's will for dominance. Because "his soul was garrisoned against presentiments and fears," Eliot's narrator explains, Grandcourt "had the courage that belongs to domination, and he was at that moment perfectly satisfied that he held his wife with bit and bridle" (744, ch. 54). Such proud confidence in the strength of his mastery, however, defeats him, for Gwendolen, paralyzed when her "own wishes" materialize before her eyes, cannot act to save him. In this way, Gwendolen's childlessness becomes her triumph because the line of Grandcourt's legitimate heirs ends with her (Beer, *Darwin's Plots* 229). Such are the destructive consequences, Eliot shows, when Spencer's idea of sexual selection is literally enacted. Moreover, because the murderous conflict that ends Gwendolen's marriage is not seen through the distancing lens of history, the damage to Gwendolen and other beautiful and "delicate vessels"—and to the children they may bear—appears as a far more immediate threat to the life of the race and the nation than in any of Eliot's earlier novels (160, ch. 11).[20]

While Spencer generally avoided discussing the problem of individual or cultural degeneracy in the first edition of *The Principles of Sociology*, he was later to admit that changes in the family could lead to social disintegration and that increasing militarism could cause the "rebarbarization" of a nation. By 1891, in a number for *The Principles of Ethics*, for example, Spencer warned against the dangers of both socialism and feminism: the "deliberate abolition of that cardinal distinction between the ethics of the family and the ethics of the State ... must eventuate in decay and [the] disappearance of the species or variety in which it takes place."[21]

Spencer's later concern about changes in the structure of the family reflects an unacknowledged contradiction in his analysis of altruism and egotism in the family and the state that had emerged while he was revising the second volume of *The Principles of Psychology*. In that volume he wrote: "While the external activities of each society have tended to maintain an unsympathetic nature, its internal activities have demanded sympathy and have tended to make the nature more sympathetic."[22] As long as war prevailed, he admitted, "men cannot be kept unsympathetic toward external enemies without being kept unsympathetic toward internal enemies, to those, that is, who stand to them as opponents" (2:570). So, he concluded, the moral evolution of the race has "all along" been "negatively restrained by the predatory activities—partly those necessitated by the destruction of inferior creatures but chiefly those necessitated by the antagonisms of societies." Thus, he argued, "only when the struggle for existence has ceased to go on under the form of war, can those highest social sentiments attain their full development" (2:577). From this position, Spencer would declare in *The Principles of Ethics* that women had to submit to traditional gender arrangements and had to defer their demands for equal political rights until all wars were abolished (1:165).

By admitting the social destructiveness of aggression, war, and the economic competition of laissez-faire capitalism, and by recognizing the social benefits of the sympathy nurtured in the family, Spencer came perilously close to identifying women rather than men with the forces of "moral"—as opposed to material—progress. For a moment, then, in his analysis of the forces shaping human evolution, Spencer seemed to confirm Eliot's view that women have "an art which does mend nature" and so contribute more to the moral evolution of the race than men do. By this concession, Spencer undermined all his arguments that sought to confine women to the domestic sphere, for their liberation from it would clearly help to advance the moral progress of society as a whole. Spencer could only defend the traditional separation of men's and women's spheres, then, by an appeal to the authority of natural law, which ensured that men were intellectually and morally superior to women. He concludes by begging the question: "The human race, though a gregarious race, has ever been," and "still is a predatory race" (2:570).

Having long recognized this contradiction in Spencer's analysis of the place of sexuality and gender in human development, Eliot, in *Daniel Deronda*, contrasts Gwendolen's and Deronda's sexual development in order to show how culture intervenes in the establishment of gender differences. Like Gwendolen, Deronda shows a dread of sexuality, and Eliot traces the source of his fear back to his unknown mother.[23] Deronda's anxiety is more distanced and rationalized than Gwendolen's, in part because of his reading of science. The first time he sees Gwendolen, Deronda ponders the Spencerian question, "Was she beautiful or not beautiful?" (35, ch. 1). But in this episode and elsewhere in the novel, Eliot shows how gendered subjectivity complicates the response to such a question. Literature assists Deronda in resisting the "dynamic quality" and sexual coercion of Gwendolen's gaze by suggesting to him that she is a modern "Lamia" and so allowing him to conclude that her "evil genius" must be "dominant" (35, ch. 1). Evolutionary science provides another intellectual defense by prompting Deronda to imagine that Gwendolen must be a "specimen of a lower order" (38, ch. 1). While Deronda does come in time to see Gwendolen as more human, he never reevaluates the sense of moral superiority that overrides his sexual response to her beauty.

Deronda's initial judgmental assessment of Mirah shows a similar dread of female sexuality. When he first sees her, wetting her cloak as a prelude to her attempt at suicide, he thinks of all "the girl-tragedies that are going on in the world, hidden, unheeded, as if they were but tragedies of the copse or hedgerow, where the helpless drag wounded wings forsakenly" (228, ch. 17) and concludes that Mirah is a "fallen woman." In describing the safe haven where he will take her, Deronda stresses the "goodness" of the women who will shelter her: "I will put you in perfect safety at once; with a lady, a good woman; I am sure she will be kind. . . . Life may still become sweet to you. There are good people—there are good women who will take care of you" (232, ch. 17). But Deronda seems to protest too much, especially when, because of his "embarrassment" and shame, he brings Mirah not to his own home but to the over-cozy house of Mrs. Meyrick, who subsequently guards both Mirah and himself from his own repressed desires.

Deronda's suspicions about Mirah's history reflect the assumptions Victorians commonly made about the "public women" of the theater, and when he asks, "Do you belong to the theater?" he assumes her connection with it.[24] Eliot's overemphasis on Mirah's innocence, sweetness, and vulnerability throughout the novel shows her effort to ensure that her readers do not share Daniel's initial assumption that because Mirah is a professional singer, her morals are somehow compromised. Mirah's story, in fact, discloses an "abyss" more horrifying than Victorian prostitution, because her story suggests that, even in the sacrosanct precincts of the patriarchal family, the daughter is not adequately protected from being economically or sexually exploited by her father, especially when the mother does not defend her.

While Deronda feels that Mirah's separation from her mother and brother is as "heart-stirring" as anything that "befell Orestes" (245, ch. 19), he nonetheless allows his own fears to impede his search for her family. Deronda's active literary sensibility seizes upon her quest, for "something in his own experience caused Mirah's search after her mother to lay hold with peculiar force on his imagination" (245, ch. 19). As he reflects on Mirah's "longing" for reunion with her mother, though, Deronda's dread reasserts itself: "Very disagreeable images urged themselves of what it might be to find out this middle-aged Jewess and her son. . . . He saw himself guided by some official scout into a dingy street; he entered through a dim doorway, and saw a hawk-eyed woman, rough-headed, and unwashed, cheapening a hungry girl's last bit of finery" (246–47, ch. 19). These same threatening images evoking prostitution and the sad "fate of women" also inhibit his more successful quest for his own mother.

Eliot locates the sources of the sympathy and compassion that Deronda feels for Mirah in his unconventional education, in his sensitivity to romance, and in his relation to his unknown mother and to the "wild zone" of maternal emotions. Unlike Rex Gascoigne and Hans Meyrick, who have been educated in English universities at their sisters' expense, Deronda has refused the privilege of studying at an English university, where degrees are meant simply to "soften manners," and has instead been educated abroad.[25] In contrasting the earnest self-improvement of

Meyrick's sisters with Meyrick's own dilettantism, Eliot shows the corrupting impact of Spencer's educational theories not only on the education of Englishwomen but Englishmen as well. Meyrick explicitly interprets the moral lessons of the classics in light of contemporary science and philosophy and assesses his "romantic sentiments" for Mirah in a whimsically Spencerian fashion, as he explains to Daniel: "I go to science and philosophy for my romance. Nature designed Mirah to fall in love with me. The amalgamation of the race demands it—the affinity of contrasts assures it. I am the utmost contrast to Mirah, a bleached Christian who can't sing two notes in turn. Who has a chance against me?" (519, ch. 37). Deronda, by contrast, rids himself of this "merely English attitude in studies" that, to Eliot, prohibits the development of genuine knowledge and imaginative sympathy, qualities that provide the most comprehensive foundation for wisdom and morality.[26]

Deronda's moral education, like Gwendolen's, also suggests the failure of the Anglican church to provide any compelling moral guidance, and in contrasting it with Deronda's experience of Judaism, Eliot hints that the Church of England had lost touch with its origins and with the history that it shared with Judaism. While she was writing *Daniel Deronda*, Eliot wrote: "All great religions of the world, historically considered, are rightly the objects of deep reverence and sympathy—they are the record of spiritual struggles which are types of our own. This is to me preeminently true of Hebrewism and Christianity" (*GEL* 5:447). Yet Christianity seems moribund in Deronda's world; the only church that Eliot describes in *Daniel Deronda* is at Monk's Topping, where "each finely arched chapel was turned into a stall" (473, ch. 35). Though Deronda's sense of history awakens his reverence for this ancient church, none of his contemporaries notice the desecration that suggests how far removed the national church is from its origins in another stable at Bethlehem (Carpenter, "Apocalypse" 66).

In fact, throughout *Daniel Deronda* Eliot dramatizes the spiritual alienation that threatens contemporary England by contrasting it with the "National Tragedy" experienced by the Jews. Eliot includes the following passage from Leopold Zunz:

> If there are ranks in suffering, Israel takes precedence of all the nations—if the duration of sorrows and the patience with which they are borne ennoble, the Jews are among the aristocracy of every land—if a literature is called rich in the possession of a few classic tragedies, what shall we say to a National Tragedy lasting for fifteen hundred years, in which the poets and the actors were also the heroes? (575, ch. 42)

Nevertheless, while Eliot's view of nationhood allowed her to define the Princess as a cultural hero of the Jews because she is just such an "actor," who succeeds in blending "emotion" with "thoughts," her feminism prevented her from expressing an unqualified admiration of this culture.

One of the most electrifying moments in all George Eliot's fiction occurs when Daniel Deronda's search for knowledge leads him back to the mother, and thus he discovers that he was, in fact, born a Jew. His meeting with his mother in Genoa differs dramatically from the "ideal" reunions he imagined for Mirah or for himself. In their first meeting, Deronda is inclined to see his mother in poetic terms as an otherworldly spirit, a "Melusinia," a "mysterious Fate" (688, ch. 51), but she quickly shatters all his illusions about her responsiveness to the "maternal sensations and emotions" (Eliot, *Essays* 53). He is chilled when he realizes that she, "it seemed had borne him unwillingly, had willingly made herself a stranger to him, and—perhaps—was now making herself known unwillingly" (690, ch. 51).

By allowing the Princess to speak frankly about her resistance to marriage and motherhood as part of her "passionate self-defense," Eliot permits her to voice a monstrous truth about those "sensations and emotions unknown to man" that Eliot herself evaded in her earlier excursions into the "wild zone." Though the Princess, like Eliot's other female heroes, displays heroic proportions of beauty, intelligence, talent, and moral insight, she lacks the love that Eliot identified earlier as the biological essence of the charities of mother, daughter, and sister. The Princess tells her son:

> "Every woman is supposed to have the same set of motives, or else to be a monster. I am not a monster, but I have not felt exactly what other women feel—or say they feel, for fear of being thought unlike others. When you reproach me in your heart for sending you away from me, you mean that I ought to say I felt about you as other women say they feel about their children. I did *not* feel that. I was glad to be freed from you." (691, ch. 51)

In characterizing her suffering as "unknown to men," the Princess claims the same authority that Eliot herself asserted in her defense of women's unique artistic vision (Eliot, *Essays* 53). The Princess tells Deronda he cannot understand her experience of oppression, that sexual difference places a profound barrier between men and women:

> "You may try—but you can never imagine what it is to have a man's force of genius in you, and yet to suffer the slavery of being a girl. To have a pattern cut out—'this is the Jewish woman; this is what you must be; this is what you are wanted for; a woman's heart must be of such a size and no larger, else it must be pressed small, like Chinese feet; her happiness is to be made as cakes are, by a fixed receipt.' That was what my father wanted. He wished I had been a

son; he cared for me as a makeshift link. His heart was set on his Judaism. He hated that Jewish women should be thought of by the Christian world as a sort of ware to make public singers and actresses of." (694, ch. 51).

Though the Princess protests against the "bondage" she experienced as a Jewish woman, her rhetoric asserts the commonality of women's suffering in all patriarchal cultures. She points to the "slavery" of girl-hood, the emotional confinement women face when heart and soul are squeezed and crippled like "Chinese feet," and the alienation from the body that adult women experience when they are regarded as "ware" to be admired or used as a "makeshift link" in the reproductive processes of evolution.[27]

In her portrayal of the tension between feminist self-assertion and guilt in the Princess Halm-Eberstein's life, Eliot presents her final and most brilliant compromise between feminism and Spencerian evolution-ism. The Princess poses fundamental questions about the extent to which women can escape from the biological determinism Spencer pos-ited and from the gender arrangements that are based upon it. In Der-onda's second meeting with his mother, she shows him her picture and asks: "Had I not a rightful claim to be something more than a mere daughter and mother? The voice and the genius matched the face. Whatever else was wrong, acknowledge that I had a right to be an artist, though my father's will was against it. My nature gave me a charter" (728, ch. 53). In conceding that her nature did indeed give her a "charter" to follow the "higher" path of the artist, Daniel confirms Eliot's emancipa-tionist defense of women's right to use their beauty, musical talent, and skill in acting—or as Darwin called it, "imitation"—for other purposes besides the attraction and gratification of future husbands.

In fact, by making the Princess a great opera singer rather than, for example, a writer, Eliot aims directly at Spencer's theory of sexual selec-tion, for she endows the Princess with those three qualities that he and Darwin singled out as of the greatest use to women in sexual selection. But the Princess's "rare perfection of physiognomy, voice, and gesture," directed by her "forcible nature," distinguish her as a great performer rather than a perfect mate. Moreover, the Princess identifies the trait that Spencer assumed was inherent in all women when she declares, "Love is a talent; I lacked it" (730, ch. 53); thus she refutes by her exam-ple Spencer's assumptions about women's biological instinct for love. In the Princess, then, Eliot presents her most articulate defense of a woman's right to reject the role Spencer would impose upon all women and to assert, instead, her prerogative to contribute to the larger society through her art—a defense which, of course, is colored by Eliot's own self-justification.[28]

As in her earlier novels, Eliot challenged Spencer's assumptions that gender roles are determined by biology alone by showing how patriarchal culture operates to impose traditional roles even upon women who actively resist them. By detailing the terrible difficulties the Princess overcomes in order to become a great singer, Eliot illuminates the plight of the woman artist under attack by evolutionary theory and suggests how women may benefit from the charities of mother, daughter, and sister in developing all their talents.

Moreover, the Princess's response to Jewish culture brings to light specific problems in Spencer's analysis of gender and nationhood, for Eliot shows how the Princess resists the patriarchal prescriptions of her moral duties as defined by Jewish law and lays claim to an artistic vision that allows her to look beyond these cultural limits. In describing how the Princess's father, Daniel Charisi, uses his interpretation of religious law to block her artistic ambitions, Eliot returns to the problem of obedience and resistance that she explored in *The Mill on the Floss* and *Romola.* Though her father allowed her to cultivate her talents in singing and acting the Princess explains that he "did not guard against the consequences, because he felt sure he could hinder them if he liked . . . he knew my inclination. That was nothing to him: he meant that I should obey his will" (696, ch. 51).[29] Thus, her father assumes the same self-defeating authority that Spencerian educators claimed when they prevented women from developing their talents and deciding for themselves how they would use them for the larger good.

Similarly, in noting the oppression suffered by the Jews in gentile cultures, Eliot both questions Spencer's hierarchy of "race" and demonstrates how racial discrimination multiplies the problems of obedience and resistance. As the Princess describes it, her father exercises tyranny within the family and imposes upon her his strict interpretation of the "law" defining the acceptable roles for Jewish women as a compensation for the powerlessness he experienced outside the domestic walls. Men like him, the Princess says, "would rule the world if they could; but not ruling the world, they throw all the weight of their will on the necks and souls of women" (694, ch. 51). Though her father set his will in opposition to hers, nature "thwarted" him, the Princess explains, since he "had no other child than his daughter, and she was like himself" (694, ch. 51).

Eliot justifies the Princess's resistance to her father's narrow interpretation of her duties to her culture by describing how her great gift for "living a myriad lives in one" allows her to keep alive the "tragic yet glorious" emotions that are part of the "binding history" of the Jews. As William Baker reminds us, Eliot knew that Judah al-Charisi was an important thirteenth-century Jewish composer of songs ("George Eliot's Readings" 268–69). In taking the name of Alcharisi, the Princess accepts her role as

a "transmitter" of her culture. In this way, Eliot refutes the pronounce-
ments of nineteenth-century historians who argued that Jewish culture
was "sterile" and suggests the emotions needed to animate the "historical
and mystical idea" that united the Jewish people in all countries from
Biblical times. The Princess also assumes a position that corresponds to
Eliot's own pose of disinterestedness, for she practices an art that transcends "partiality," absorbing the "thought of other nations" in order, as
Mordecai says, to give "back the thought as a new wealth to the world"
(585, ch. 42).

Eliot was not willing, however, to free women entirely from all obligations to serve the nation, and by discriminating the Princess's magisterial
self-assertion from the "common egotism" of Gwendolen Harleth, Eliot
demonstrates the limits she would impose on women's self-determina-
tion. For Eliot, women were morally justified in rejecting their biological
duties to the "race" only if they devoted themselves to some larger cause.
Because the Princess chooses a "larger life" that allows her to contribute
to the growing good of the world, an artistic life that allows her to be
"carried along on a great current" (693, ch. 51), she is justified in rejecting her father's insistence on her obligation to use her body rather than
her talents for the perpetuation of the Jewish "race."

In the Princess's confession, however, Eliot also tries to move beyond
her earlier essentialist analysis of the "maternal emotions," by acknowledging the destructive guilt produced by the Princess's monumental
egotism and secret resistance to her duties as daughter, wife, and
mother. Now that her career as a diva has ended, the Princess feels regret over "all the woman lacking" in herself.[30] She tells Deronda that
sometimes she lives in an "agony of pain" when "all the life I have chosen
to live, all thoughts, all will, forsook me and left me alone in spots of
memory. . . . Then a great horror comes over me: what do I know of life
or death? and what my father called 'right' may be a power that is laying
hold of me—that is clutching me now. . . . I have hidden what was his"
(699, ch. 51). Despite her gifts and "forcible nature," the Princess was
only prepared to rebel secretly against the customs she herself rejected;
but by choosing secrecy rather than outward resistance, she failed to take
a position that could alleviate the suffering of other women of her culture as well as herself. Instead, she relied on her "strength in conceal-
ment" (695, ch. 51) and chose to "deceive" rather than confront her
father when he was dying. By retreating into silence and failing to warn
him that she would "contradict his trust," the Princess thus failed to act
on the moral courage that otherwise characterized her life.

Eliot contrasts the Princess's secret defiance with Catherine Arrowpoint's more explicit resistance to her parents' definition of the duties
she owes to her family, to her class, and to the "nation" (290, ch. 22), in

order to valorize the latter's choice to protest publicly the "superannuated customs and false ambitions" of her culture (290, ch. 22). Catherine
counters her parents' objections to her marriage to Klesmer by observing that "people can easily take the sacred word of duty as a name for
what they desire any one else to do" (289, ch. 22). Eliot endorses Catherine's right to define her duty in her own terms by presenting her marriage to Klesmer as one of the happiest marriages represented in this
text. The fundamental difference between these two daughters who assert their right to reject "customs" they neither love nor respect, then, is
the mode of resistance they choose. While Eliot is prepared to endorse
the open rebellion of Catherine Arrowpoint, as she earlier valorized the
resistance of Maggie Tulliver, Romola Di Bardi, Esther Lyon, and
Dorothea Brooke, the Princess's secret defiance looks like "shame," as
Deronda notes, and it fosters a guilt that is ultimately self-destructive.[31]

The Princess's retrospective reassessment of her obligations to her
family and her race also demonstrates the pressure that the past exerts
on the present and suggests the constraining conservative force of evolutionary biology on Eliot's feminism. Eliot successfully defended the Princess's right to choose her own place in her culture and to define her duty
to it, but she found it more difficult to justify the Princess's repudiation
of her obligations to her husband and her child. The Princess's marriages are compromised by a similar secret defiance, for she, like Gwendolen, entered marriages that promised her dominance and control
rather than mutual submission and altruistic love. "I was never willingly
subject to any man," she tells Deronda, "Men have been subject to me"
(730, ch. 53). In Deronda's rejoinder, "Perhaps the man who was subject
was the happier of the two" (730, ch. 53), Eliot registers her ongoing
resistance to Spencer's normalization of male dominance in marriage.

Likewise, Eliot's reading of developmental psychology made it impossible for her to see the Princess as able to free herself from her bonds to
Deronda simply by allowing Sir Hugo to adopt him. Because Eliot traced
the origins of heterosexual love back to the mother, and because she
insisted on the primacy of the mother-child bond, she found it particularly difficult to imagine how women could responsibly combine the
roles of artist and mother. Though Eliot herself chose the roles of artist
and wife, she elected not to have children. The Princess articulates the
irreconcilable conflict between the demands of an all-consuming career
like her own and the obligations of motherhood; both require the rigorous discipline and control of personal egotism, that quality which assured the Princess's success as a great performer. By dramatizing the
incompatibility of the social and moral roles of the artist and mother,
Eliot acknowledges the troublesome problems that most feminists of the
1870s evaded, by recommending, in response to the arguments of con-

servatives like Spencer, that professional women remain single and celibate (Bauer and Ritt, 266).

Likewise, Eliot's analysis of "moral" law prevented her from justifying the Princess's effort to free herself from her moral obligations to her son simply by settling his father's fortune on him. Parents cannot free themselves from their responsibilities in this way, as Daniel angrily reminds his mother: "You cannot wish me to believe that your affection would not have been worth having" (688, ch. 51). Though the Princess regards her genius as "male," her effort to adopt the same legalistic attitudes about parental responsiblity remain as morally bankrupt as the attitudes of men like Arthur Donnithorne, John Wakem, Godfrey Cass, Tito Melema, Matthew Jermyn, and Henleigh Grandcourt, who father illegitimate children and keep their paternity a secret.

The results of Eliot's meditation on the Princess's biological and moral duties to her child and race are revealed when she shows how her wish to "choose" Daniel's birthright for him is ironically defeated. She tells him, "I chose for you what I would have chosen for myself. How could I know that you would have the spirit of my father in you? How could I know that you would love what I hated? —If you really love to be a Jew" (690, ch. 51). But Daniel responds by showing her that she had not correctly estimated the effects either of the past or of the future:

> No wonder if such facts come to reveal themselves in spite of concealments. The effects prepared by generations are likely to triumph over a contrivance which would bend them all to the satisfaction of self. Your will was strong, but my grandfather's trust which you accepted and did not fulfil—what you call his yoke—is the expression of something stronger, with deeper, farther-spreading roots, knit into the foundations of sacredness for all men. You renounced me—you still banish me—as a son. . . . But that stronger Something has determined that I shall be all the more the grandson whom also you willed to annihilate. (727, ch. 53).

Deronda's response indicates how much more emphasis Eliot, in contrast to Spencer, placed on the effects "prepared by generations" (727, ch. 53) in shaping the present and the future.

Thus, the contrasting positions that Daniel Deronda and his mother take in assessing their responsibilities to their race ultimately illustrate the asymmetry of biological roles. If *Daniel Deronda* examines the question, "Can one escape from one's cultural inheritance—from its genealogical imperative?" as Gillian Beer argues (*Darwin's Plots* 218), it shows as well Eliot's effort to explore an analogous question, pressed home by Spencer's misogynistic conclusions about women's place in society: Can one escape from the constraints of one's gender? Daniel's story shows that it is possible, finally, to evade cultural imperatives, since he "chooses his cultural identity with the Jews. Descent here marries with will" (Beer, *Darwin's Plots* 218). But the problems posed by reproduction cannot be so neatly resolved by this emphasis on choice. Some exceptional women may choose not to bear children, but Eliot recognized that extinction threatened any nation where women generally refused to sacrifice other ego-gratifications to become mothers for the good of the race.

Spencer's views on race and nationality were used by many of his contemporaries to justify British imperialism, and his writings of the 1870s perhaps provide an even more important context for *Daniel Deronda* than Darwin's analysis of race in *The Descent of Man*.[32] In 1878, ill health prompted Spencer to set aside his work on the second volume of *The Principles of Sociology* and write the "Data of Ethics," published the following year and later included in *The Principles of Ethics*. In his *Autobiography*, he cites a letter noting George Eliot's response to it: "Mrs. Lewes, in writing to me about the *Data of Ethics*, expressed her anxiety that I should forthwith finish the *Ethics*, rather than return to the *Sociology*; but, though it would be important to do this, I feel that there is still greater importance in forthwith dealing with Social Evolution under its political aspect, even if under no other" (*Autobiography* 2:329). Unable to credit the criticism of his sociology that may have prompted Eliot's advice to continue writing *The Principles of Ethics*—or to consider that his sociology was ethics in disguise—Spencer assumed, that Eliot had accepted the "general view" of evolutionary theory set forth in his later works. Spencer's reasons for returning to his previous work illustrate his concern about increasing British militancy, especially abroad, which prompted him not only to complete the second and third volumes he projected for *The Principles of Sociology* but also, most uncharacteristically, to try to organize a political protest against imperial policies. He writes:

> I have been so frequently thinking of the question of Militancy *v.* Industrialism, and the profound antagonism between the two which comes out more and more at every step in my Sociological inquiries, and I have been so strongly impressed with the re-barbarization that is going on in consequence of the return to militant activities, that I have come to the conclusion that it is worth while to try and do something towards organizing an antagonistic agitation. We have, lying diffused throughout English society, various bodies and classes very decidedly opposed to it, which I think merely want bringing together to produce a powerful agency, which may do eventually a good deal in a civilizing direction. (*Autobiography* 2:329).

Though Spencer quickly abandoned his effort to organize this political campaign because, as he said, it violated "the principle of specialization of functions" which defined him as a successful philosopher rather than a politician, he remained opposed to British efforts to consolidate their

Empire overseas by military force. Nevertheless, Spencer was extraordinarily blind to the ways his analysis of the "inferior races" had lent itself to the justification of the British colonial expansion that he himself so vehemently opposed (Peel 234).

Eliot was far more perspicacious about how Spencer's theories about race and nationality could be used to justify the most oppressive imperialistic policies, as we see in both *The Spanish Gypsy* and *Daniel Deronda*. In a letter dated 11 February 1875, to Mrs. Henry Ponsonby, Eliot identified two themes in Spencer's sociology which became the focus of her own treatment of race and nationality as she was writing Book 1 of *Daniel Deronda*:

> Mr. Spencer is very anxious to vindicate himself from neglect of the logical necessity that the evolution of the abstraction 'society' is dependent on the modified actions of the units; indeed he is very sensitive on the point of being supposed to teach an enervating fatalism.
>
> Consider what the human mind *en masse* would have been if there had been no such combination of elements in it as has produced poets. All the philosophers and *savants* would not have sufficed to supply that deficiency. And how can the life of nations be understood without the inward light of poetry—that is, of emotion blending with thoughts. (*GEL* 6:124).

In this way, Eliot affirms again her appreciation for the power of inward over outward law.

Eliot recapitulates her critique of Spencer's emphasis on the outward signs of race and nationality most dramatically in her presentation of Deronda's conversations with the "Philosophers' Club." The entire dialogue at the *Hand and Banner* reveals Eliot's rejection of the developmental paradigm which Spencer saw as transforming a tribe into a nation, as well as her refutation of contemporary theories that Jewish culture was degenerate, theories that gained new scientific authority from Spencer's analysis of race. Both Daniel's and Mordecai's arguments against the "law of development" and their assessments of Jewish history express the basis of Eliot's objections to Spencer's fundamental assumptions repeated in *The Principles of Sociology* about gender and racial hierarchies and his corollary belief that a single, fixed, and progressive sequence necessarily defined the process that transforms a "tribe" into a "nation" (*Sociology*, 1:575).

From the opening words of this debate, Eliot uses Spencerian idioms playfully to summarize many of her objections to his theories over the last twenty years. As soon as Deronda enters the room, one of the men asks, "Is he a Great Unknown?"—a question which recalls, of course, one of Spencer's most famous terms in *First Principles*. Lilly inadvertently reveals the individualist bias of Spencer's sociology when he explains how the "aggregate units" of society should be evaluated: "In relation to society numbers are qualities . . . the numbers are an index to the qualities" (585, ch. 42). Later he similarly burlesques Spencer's evasive treatment of cultural and historical differences. But when Pash refers to Spencer's "law of progress," Buchan voices Eliot's most telling criticism of Spencerian sociology:

> "Ye're all agreed that societies change—not always and everywhere—but on the whole and in the long-run. Now, with all deference, I would beg t' observe that we have got to examine the nature of changes before we have a warrant to call them progress, which word is supposed to include a bettering, though I apprehend it to be ill chosen for that purpose, since mere motion onward may carry us to a bog or a precipice. (584, ch. 42)

Buchan's Scottish accent hardly disguises Eliot's own long-standing argument with Spencer over his use of the term "progress."

The debate between Lilly and Deronda about "development" reveals why the problems of interpretation posed by the past and the future remained central to Eliot's critique of Spencer's sociology in *Daniel Deronda*. Lilly invokes Spencer's biological and psychological theories when he insists on the validity of the law of "development": "Change and progress are merged in the idea of development. The laws of development are being discovered, and changes taking place according to them are necessarily progressive; that is to say, if we have any notion of progress or improvement opposed to them, the notion is a mistake" (585, ch. 42). Deronda intervenes, though, to identify the circular reasoning in Lilly's—and Spencer's—analysis of social change and articulates Eliot's final defense against the "ennervating fatalism" of Spencer's biological and racial determinism:

> I really can't see how you arrive at that sort of certitude about changes by calling them development. . . . There will still remain the degrees of inevitableness in relation to our own will and acts, and the degrees of wisdom in hastening or retarding; there will still remain the danger of mistaking a tendency which should be resisted for an inevitable law that we must adjust ourselves to—which seems to me, as bad a superstition or false god as any that has been set up without the ceremonies of philosophising. (585, ch. 42)

Thus, Deronda and Mordecai express Eliot's sense of the importance of conscious resistance in directing change both in the individual and in society and expose Spencer's failure to account for all the motives hidden in the mysteries of the human soul.

Similarly, the racism implicit in Spencer's sociology finds an echo in Lilly's comments about the Jews, whom he views as the "type of obstinate adherence to the superannuated. They may show good abilities when they take up liberal ideas, but as a race they have no development in them" (590, ch. 42). Mordecai's response stands as a defense not only of the Jews but also of any other race branded by Spencer as "less developed" than the English: "Let their history be known and examined; let the seed be sifted, let its beginnings be traced to the weed of the wilderness—the more glorious will be the energy that transformed it" (590, ch. 42). Deronda's example, nonetheless, shows the complexities involved in establishing the "beginnings" of an individual life, and Eliot's great cautionary epigraph about the "make believe of a beginning" reminds us of the infinitely more complex task of defining the "origins" of a race or nation.

While Mordecai articulates Eliot's reasons for insisting on the value of collective history, Daniel expresses her recognition of the individual's need for the freedom to interpret his or her own personal past and the obligations which arise from it. Mordecai sees his relation to Judaism in terms of kinship, so that the past becomes a "parent" (587, ch. 42), though, in his case, the "authority of ideology" replaces the authority of the father when he is forced to recognize, after his reunion with Mirah, the incorrigible selfishness of his father by blood (Welsh, *George Eliot* 302–37). Like his sister, Mordecai represses the bitterness and anger aroused by their biological father's betrayal by recalling the "blessed" memory of their mother, who remains for them a symbol of Unity and Eternal Goodness.[33]

Deronda, on the other hand, has a more complicated relation to both the "past" and to his "parents," and, in this dialogue at the *Hand and Banner*, he is conscious of the coercive quality of Mordecai's ideology. He resists Mordecai's ideological imperatives by asserting his right to use all the "wide instruction and sympathy" that his cosmopolitan education has given him: "What we can't hinder must not make our rule for what we ought to choose. I think our duty is faithful tradition where we can attain it. And so you would insist for any one but yourself. Don't ask me to deny my spiritual parentage, when I am finding the clue of my life in the recognition of my natural parentage" (821, ch. 63). Daniel will not submit to Mordecai's vision, to the imperiousness which insists: "You must hope my hopes—see the vision I point to—behold the glory where I behold it" (502, ch. 42).

Moreover, he is forced, as Mordecai is not, to acknowledge the authoritarianism and misogyny that his mother identifies as part of the Jewish tradition. Thus, when Daniel meets his grandfather's surrogate, Joseph Kalonymos, he defends his right to resist patriarchal authority when reason and sympathy require it:

I shall call myself a Jew. . . . But I will not say that I shall profess to believe exactly as my fathers have believed. Our fathers themselves changed the horizon of their belief and learned of other races. But I think I can maintain my grandfather's notion of separateness with communication. I hold that my first duty is to my own people, and if there is anything to be done toward restoring or perfecting their common life, I shall make that my vocation. (792, ch. 60)

By seeing his relation to Judaism as a chosen "vocation" rather an imposed "duty," Daniel escapes from the tyranny his mother suffered.

If *Daniel Deronda* dramatizes how "ideology" comes to take the place of "fathers," as Alexander Welsh argues, it is in part because Eliot wished to avoid the mindless perpetuation of patriarchal authority that Spencer worked so hard to protect in *The Study of Sociology* and in subsequent works. While Spencer would confine women to family life and contain the ethics of love within the domestic sphere until all wars ceased, Eliot saw the dissemination of sympathy and altruism as the best means to combat the "re-barbarization" that both she and Spencer perceived in Britain's more aggressive imperialist policies. In particularizing the choices by which Deronda embraces Judaism and escapes from the guilt that paralyzes his mother, Eliot discloses the dynamics of power which Spencer ignores in his analysis of both the family and the nation as "aggregate groups." In her treatment of Daniel's marriage and her use of the metaphor of marriage to describe Daniel's final relation to the race and nation he chooses to serve, Eliot repudiates biological functionalism. While Spencer defined marriage as an institution formalizing the biological laws of sexual selection, Eliot continued to insist on the moral function of marriage, the quality which made it, in her view, a uniquely human institution.

Many readers have seen Daniel's marriage to Mirah as a sign of Eliot's sentimental retreat from the more egalitarian marriage of Dorothea Casaubon and Will Ladislaw, or even as Eliot's final endorsement of patriarchal authority in marriage.[34] But when we recognize that in marrying Mirah, Daniel is also choosing *not* to marry Gwendolen, another dimension of the significance of this marriage becomes apparent. Deronda assumes a position of moral superiority, like Felix Holt's relation to Esther, in his friendship with Gwendolen: he has disapproved of her gambling and has restored her jewels to her against her will; he has listened to her guilty secrets and has counseled her to take her fear as a "safeguard" (738, ch 54). Gwendolen, in return, has regarded Daniel with awe and has allowed him to act as a "redeeming influence" on her life. Though Gwendolen's compassionate acknowledgment of the claims of Lydia Glasher serves as a moral touchstone, showing Daniel that she has reached a "common plane of understanding with him on some of the difficulties of life," he nonetheless reveals his dauntless sense of his moral superiority over her when he assumes that a "woman is rarely able to judge" such cases with any "justice or generosity, for according to precedent, Gwendolen's view of her position might easily have been no other than that her husband's marriage with her was his entrance on the path of virtue, while Mrs. Glasher represented forsaken sin" (489, ch. 36). Thus, though Daniel admits Gwendolen's moral capacities as an individual, he fails to free himself completely from a Spencerian assessment of her intellectual and moral weaknesses as a woman.

Because she does not marry the man she loves, Gwendolen is saved from the moral subjection that mutual love enhances, as Eliot makes clear when she describes the infantilizing effect that Gwendolen's love for Daniel has on her:

> Mighty Love had laid his hand upon her; but what had he demanded of her? acceptance of rebuke—the hard task of self-change—confession—endurance. If she cried towards him, what then? She cried as the child cries whose little feet have fallen backward—cried to be taken up by the hand, lest she should lose herself. (842, ch. 65).

Gwendolen must undertake the task of "self-change" alone, since Deronda rejects the appeal of this traditionally paternalistic and Spencerian relation, in which male altruism shelters and protects female dependency.

Finally, Gwendolen achieves a tragic splendor in her solitude when she learns that Daniel will marry another woman:

> She was for the first time feeling the pressure of a vast mysterious movement, for the first time being dislodged from her supremacy in her own world, and getting a sense that her horizon was but a dipping onward of an existence with which her own was revolving. . . . She could not spontaneously think of him as rightfully belonging to others more than to her. But here had come a shock which went deeper than personal jealousy—something vaguely spiritual and vaguely tremendous that thrust her away, and yet quelled all anger into self-humiliation. (876, ch. 69)

Remaining in England alone, without the private consolations of religion or erotic love, Gwendolen achieves the tragic consciousness of time and loss which, Eliot suggests, all her compatriots—male and female—must achieve if they are to avert the "national tragedy" that seems to be threatening English society.[35]

For Gwendolen, the recovery of the "treasure of human affections" ends where it began, in the "wild zone" with her mother. Like Persephone after her sojourn in the darker world, Gwendolen comes back to her mother at Offendene and finds her home to be a "paradise" (830, ch. 64). But even in the healing reunion of mother and daughter, Eliot expresses her new and more complex view of the moral force of mother-love, for she reveals not only its regenerating spiritual power but also its daemonic force. In Gwendolen's consoling words to her mother, "Don't be unhappy. I shall live. I shall be better" (879, ch. 69), and in the night-mares Gwendolen suffers, Eliot pays her final tribute to the ancient, timeless force that moved the Delphic women and still persists in this modern mother and daughter:

> When the Maenads outworn with their torch-lit wanderings lay down to sleep in the market place, the matrons came and stood silent round them to keep guard over their slumbers; then when they waked, ministered to them tenderly and saw them safely to their own borders. (236, ch. 17)

For Eliot, there remains a remnant of the charities of mother, daughter, and sister that is "knit into the foundations of sacredness for all men" (727, ch. 53). In both Gwendolen's and Daniel's case, this mysterious power allows each to find wholeness through their reunion with the mother.

Likewise, after his meeting with his mother, Daniel is able to find a unity in his life through his definition of his vocation and his decision to marry Mirah. Daniel at first regards his visit to his mother as a "disap-pointed pilgrimage to a shrine where there were no longer the symbols of sacredness" (723, ch. 53), but his meeting with her suddenly frees him to admit he is in love with a Jewish woman, as his mother guesses. In depicting this seemingly magical transformation which makes Daniel feel that he is an "older man," released from "all his boyish yearnings and anxieties about his mother" (731, ch. 53), Eliot recognizes the dynamics of erotic love "wherein *love* precedeth *lovable*" (786, ch. 60). In her treat-ment of the love between mother and child in this novel, Eliot focuses on the child's response to the mother and portrays this love as a force which is potentially liberating.

In Daniel's marriage to Mirah, Eliot stretches the limits of plausibility by allowing Daniel to find a woman who answers so perfectly to his dou-ble desires for a lover who will allow him to discover the "larger self" created by passionate love and a partner who will justify his decision to channel his energy in the cause of "partiality" by working to establish a homeland for the Jewish people.[36] The Princess shrewdly observes that Mirah is made for Deronda, because he would never have let himself be "merged in a wife" as his father was (729, ch. 53), and Daniel's reasons for marrying Mirah prompt us to agree. Mirah clearly does not have the Princess's large nature or Gwendolen's willfulness; she does not have a strong voice or a nature that would tolerate the contradictions that make

Deronda's mother into a heroic figure. As Deronda observes, "Mirah has not a nature that would bear dividing against itself; and even if love won her consent to marry a man who was not of her race and religion, she would never be happy in acting against that strong native bias which would still reign in her conscience as remorse" (427, ch. 32). Magically, then, Deronda's sudden recovery of his lost Jewish heritage establishes his claim upon her affections and releases them both from guilt.

Mirah's Jewishness gives her a moral authority that Gwendolen lacks, and this trait suggests Eliot's effort to tip the balance more in Mirah's favor so that her marriage to Deronda appears to reflect the ideal coincidence of physical and moral laws. In coming to acknowledge her love for Deronda, Mirah recognizes the same "selfish" quality that Dorothea recognized in avowing her love for Ladislaw. In the "Psyche mold" of Mirah's frame, Eliot locates that "fervid quality of emotion sometimes rashly supposed to require the bulk of Cleopatra" (801, ch. 61). Finally, Mirah has the "thoroughness and tenacity that give to the first selection of passionate feeling the character of life-long faithfulness" (801, ch. 61). Thus, in accepting Daniel's love, Mirah consents to a marriage that once again celebrates the triumph of mutual egalitarian love.

This marriage, then, ultimately asserts the "unity" that Eliot saw as the link between biological and moral law, a unity that forms the basis of the "fundamental religion of the whole world" (802, ch. 61). Her novel shows, finally, that " 'The Omnipresent . . . is occupied in making marriages,' " which display "all the wondrous combinations of the universe whose issue makes our good and evil" (812, ch. 62). Thus, in designing this conclusion, Eliot presents her final triumphant rejection of the divisive analysis of biological, social, and moral laws presented in Spencer's later works. In this final vision of "Divine Unity," and in the marriage of Daniel and Mirah, Eliot transcends the limits of gender, creed, race, and nationality to disclose the "mystery that lies under" the processes of creation.

Epilogue

GEORGE ELIOT died on December 22, 1880, and Herbert Spencer survived her by more than twenty years. This study would not be complete without a brief outline of the development of his ideas about gender in his writing from 1880 until his own death in 1903. Spencer chatted with Eliot four days before she died, and he later recalled their last conversation in his *Autobiography*:

> During our last interview, which was on the very day she was taken ill, conversation brought evidence that she was veering a good deal away from Comte, and recognized the fundamental divergence from the Comtist conception of society, of views of mine which she accepted. She had been re-reading, with Mr. Cross, the *Data of Ethics* and *Study of Sociology* (the last, indeed, for the third time), and was in general sympathy with their views. So that the influence might have been more manifest in further works if she had lived to write them. (*Autobiography* 2:364)

Spencer, however, fails to provide any details which would allow us to corroborate his sense that Eliot had, at last, capitulated to his views, and especially to the reconstruction of gender relations set forth in these works. In light of Eliot's continued, though tactful and indirect, criticism of his later work in *Felix Holt, Middlemarch,* and *Daniel Deronda,* Spencer's deductions seem to overestimate the persuasive power of his argument. A third reading of *The Study of Sociology* was not likely to have induced Eliot to abandon her criticism of Spencer's most conservative conclusions about gender arrangements.

By 1880, Spencer had passed the zenith of his influence and reputation as the great synthetic philosopher and popularizer of evolutionary thought, and Eliot's critique of Spencer's work throughout her life anticipated objections later voiced by many of her contemporaries. In the 1870s, as we have seen, Spencer was already under attack from historians and psychologists for his work in *Descriptive Sociology* (1873–1881) and *The Principles of Sociology* (1877–1896). By the 1880s, the criticism of Spencer's sociology was even more widespread:

> Confronted with Spencer's conception of sociology, many British intellectuals of the 1880s felt themselves drowning in their own thought world. Comte and Le Play were the straws they clutched at. Modern British sociology was built, more than anything else, as a defense against Spencer. It is in this sense that his influence was decisive.[1]

Similarly, Spencer began to lose his position of influence among sociologists in these years because his "colossal achievement" was bound to
"an impossible political philosophy for a developed industrial society"
(Peel 238).

Moreover, by the mid-1880s, Spencer's reading of biology was undermined by Weismann's analysis of natural selection and by Mendel's experiments with genetics. From 1886–1889, Spencer attempted an "un-
successful rearguard action in defense of the inheritance of acquired
characteristics" (Peel 146), that principle which was, as we have seen,
so central to his analyses of race and gender hierarchies. Finally, in
1888, T. H. Huxley published "The Struggle for Existence in Human
Society," which questioned Spencer's conclusions about the ethical "implications of evolution," and which, as Peel notes, put Spencer in a
"white rage" by exposing his isolation as a "peace-loving Lamarckian in
a relentlessly Darwinian age" (151).

In his *Autobiography*, Spencer noted that his early work had led him
in concentric circles. After writing *The Proper Sphere of Government* in
1842, he realized that the "conceptions set forth in this pamphlet were
crude and incomplete." He was therefore prompted "in the interval between 1842 and 1848 ... to enter on new fields of thought and inquiry" and to undertake "various readings in politics and ethics, joined
with some excursions into biology and psychology," research which was
summarized in his first book, *Social Statics*, published in 1850. After
completing this book, which brought "him round in the latter chapter
to his original topic" (*Autobiography* 2:238), he found himself beginning the circuit again: "In the subsequent seven years, less from intention than from unconscious proclivity, this process was repeated. . . .
This extension of the range of inquiry, leading to more general conclusions, ended in those most general conclusions set forth in the pro-
gramme of the *Synthetic Philosophy* written out in the first days of 1858"
(*Autobiography* 2:274). There is an even larger circle that Spencer trav-
ersed in his writing, however, for if we look at the tendency of his career as a whole, we can see him circling back to ethics again when,
near the end of his life, he began to write his *Principles of Ethics*.

John W. Burrow points out that "the place that Spencer gives his
Principles of Ethics at the end of a series of enormous volumes, the final
consummation, as it were, of the project cryptically foreshadowed in
his first book, *Social Statics*, is an indication of the change which had
come over advanced ethical and political thought in the mid-nine-
teenth-century"[2] In the introductory section of the penultimate volume
of *Synthetic Philosophy*, Spencer recognized the challenge that an evolutionary analysis, in both the natural and social sciences, posed for the
study of ethics. While some social theorists felt that the study of ethics

had consequently become obsolete, Spencer argued the reverse. He held that the study of ethics could be transformed into a "developed science," comprehending and synthesizing research from all fields of the natural and social sciences. He explains:

> Ethics has a physical aspect, since it treats of human activities which, in common with all expenditures of energy, conform to the law of the persistence of energy; moral principles must conform to physical necessities. It has a biological aspect; since it concerns certain effects, inner and outer, individual and social, of the vital changes going on in the highest type of animal. It has a psychological aspect; for its subject matter is an aggregate of actions that are prompted by feelings and guided by intelligence. And it has a sociological aspect; for these actions, some of them directly and all of them indirectly, affect associated beings. (*Ethics* 1:62)

More specifically than any of Spencer's other works, *The Principles of Ethics* sets forth his ideal of the future; it is here, as Burrow observes, that Spencer imagines man as "perfectly adapted to the social state" (*Evolution and Society* 223). After all these long years of study, what is the quality that Spencer reveals as "shining forth in the ideal man?" What is the prize "inside this last envelope?" Burrow concludes, "Inside the last envelope there is written nothing but natural sympathy and the economic division of labor, for these seem, according to Spencer, to constitute the only social relations recognized in the perfect 'Industrial Society'" (223). In Spencer's surprising emphasis on the social value of sympathy and altruism in *The Principles of Ethics*,[3] then, we can see the final evidence of George Eliot's influence upon his thought.

In his preface to this work Spencer partly acknowledges the circling that characterized his career as a synthetic philosopher by noting that "the ethical doctrine set forth is fundamentally a corrected and elaborated version of the doctrine set forth in *Social Statics*" (*Ethics* 1:IV). One of the major "corrections" that Spencer made in revising *Social Statics* for inclusion in *The Principles of Ethics*, of course, involved erasing or qualifying most of the evidence of his support for feminist reforms in 1850. Thus, Spencer cut his chapter on "The Rights of Women" almost by half and struggled to reconcile his more liberal position in 1850 with his view of proper gender relations in the 1880s. Confronted by the written proof of his earlier support for woman's emancipation, but released from the peculiar anxiety of influence exerted by George Eliot, Spencer admits that women should not be "artifically disadvantaged" (2:157) and so in theory should be allowed to enter "the occupations, professions, or other careers which they may wish to adopt" (2:157). Yet, elsewhere in *The Principles of Ethics*, Spencer effectively undermined this position by warning of the physically and mentally "injurious" effects of "celibate" life for women and of the dangers that higher education posed both to women's health and to "race maintenance" (1:520).

Moreover, Spencer's assumptions about the necessary "division of labor" in society generally, and in marriage in particular, prompted him to conclude his chapter on women's rights by consigning women to a subordinate position in marriage and in political life. In marriage, he declared, women surrender "the right to physical integrity, the rights of ownership of property earned or bequeathed, the rights to free belief and free speech," according to the "understood or expressed terms" of the marriage contract (2:160). Similarly, he contends that because man is "more judicially minded than woman, the balance of authority should incline to the side of the husband" in marriage (2:160). Finally, he concludes that women have no claim to political rights, to suffrage, or to participation in the direction of "public affairs," since they do not perform the duties required of male citizens, who furnish "contingents to the army and navy" (2:165). Thus, he reveals the negative side of the anxiety of influence that characterized his relation to George Eliot during his long retreat from the feminist causes he endorsed in the 1850s.

Nonetheless, Spencer's discussion of gender arrangements in *The Principles of Ethics* does reflect a more sympathetic understanding of woman's domestic conditions in the past and is more fully informed by the written and unwritten histories of women's lives that Eliot illuminated, for example, in *Romola* and subsequent works. Spencer begins his chapter on "Marital Beneficence," for example, by noting that "in the history of humanity, the saddest part concerns the treatment of women; and had we the unwritten history we should find this part still sadder" (335).

Spencer's emphasis on the social value of sympathy and altruism not only in this passage but throughout *The Principles of Ethics* is indeed surprising, and this appreciation suggests the more positive influence that George Eliot exerted on Spencer's final description of the society of the future. In defining the "highest altruism" as that "which ministers not to the egoistic satisfactions of others only, but also to their altruistic satisfactions" (*Ethics* 1:251), Spencer seems to acknowledge the damaging social and moral consequences of his earlier emphasis on "instinct" and egotism, consequences that Eliot had dramatized in all of her fiction. Finally, Spencer notes that the capacity for sympathy confers both pleasure and pain on those who possess it in its most developed forms:

Those in whom the sympathies have become keen are of necessity proportionally pained on witnessing sufferings borne by others, not in those cases where they are the causes of sufferings, but where the sufferings are caused in any other way ... and therefore life is made tolerable even to the higher among us at the present time, by a certain perpetual searing of the sympathies, which keeps them down at such levels of sensitiveness that there remains a balance of pleasure in life. (*Ethics* 1:298)

Certainly, we cannot read Spencer's words here without hearing the echo of one of the most famous passages in *Middlemarch*:

That element of tragedy which lies in the very fact of frequency, has not yet wrought itself into the coarse emotion of mankind; and perhaps our frames could hardly bear much of it. If we had a keen vision and feeling of all ordinary human life, it would be like hearing the grass grow and the squirrel's heart beat, and we should die of that roar which lies on the other side of silence. As it is, the quickest of us walk about well wadded with stupidity. (226, ch. 20)

Spencer concludes his passage on sympathy with an eloquent catalogue of the sufferings of the less fortunate throughout the world: the "Negro tortured by Arab slave buyers," the Hindu farmers "half starved and heavily taxed," the Russian peasants in the midst of famine (2:431). In this new and deeper appreciation for the social value of such compassion, we can see Spencer's final tribute to the woman who inhabited the center of the concentric circles that determined his life and thought.

Notes

Chapter 1

1. For example, see Henry James's review of John Cross's *George Eliot's Life* from *Atlantic Monthly* 40 (May 1885): 688–78, conveniently reprinted by David Carroll in *George Eliot: The Critical Heritage* (see especially 498). F. R. Leavis in *The Great Tradition* (28–125) and W. J. Harvey in "Idea and Image in the Novels of George Eliot" provide perhaps the best examples of more recent works that display this critical approach.

2. Many critics focus on the influence that contemporary philosophy exerted on Eliot but do not analyze the ways she criticized and synthesized these ideas in making them her own. See, for example, Neil Roberts, *George Eliot*; K. K. Collins, "Questions of Method" and "George Henry Lewes, Revisited"; and William Myers, *The Teaching of George Eliot*. Hock Guan Tjoa in *George Henry Lewes* treats Eliot as a mouthpiece for Lewes. To a lesser degree, Ruby Redinger in *George Eliot* and Laura Comer Emery in *George Eliot's Creative Conflict*, in describing Eliot's emotional dependencies, also overstate her intellectual passivity.

3. George Eliot, *The George Eliot Letters*, ed. Gordon S. Haight, 1:xlvi. (Hereafter *GEL*).

4. The best example is Gillian Beer, *Darwin's Plots*. See also Suzanne Graver, *George Eliot and Community*.

5. Robert M. Young, "The Historiographic and Ideological Contexts of Nineteenth-century Debate on Man's Place in Nature" 366.

6. On the differences between Spencer's thought and Darwin's, see Robert L. Carneiro, "Structure, Function, and Equilibrium in the Evolutionism of Herbert Spencer"; Derek Freeman, "The Evolutionary Theories of Charles Darwin and Herbert Spencer"; J.D.Y. Peel, *Herbert Spencer*; Ernst Mayr, *The Growth of Biological Thought*; and Cynthia Eagle Russett, *Sexual Science*. More recent critics and intellectual historians who have used the final editions of Spencer's work have, however inadvertently, helped to bury further the evidence of Spencer's inconsistencies by failing to note the implications of these erasures and silences. Studies by feminist critics like Lorna Duffin ("Prisoners of Progress") have also overlooked Spencer's surprising endorsement of feminism in his early years and have thus helped to perpetuate the image of Spencer as a consistently sexist evolutionary theorist.

7. My approach to Eliot and Spencer in this study is indebted in part to the theories of Harold Bloom and their application by Sandra M. Gilbert and Susan Gubar in "Patriarchal Poetry and Women Readers" and *The Madwoman in the Attic*.

8. Herbert Spencer, *An Autobiography* 2:363–64.

9. On Spencer's response to Comte, see S. Eisen's excellent study, "Herbert Spencer and the Spectre of Comte."

10. Robert Carneiro ("Structure") and J.D.Y. Peel (*Herbert Spencer*) do not comment on the significant differences between Spencer's first and subse-

quent editions. Janet Sayers's *Biological Politics* is the first study, to my knowledge, to note Spencer's early feminism. All subsequent references, unless otherwise noted, are to Spencer's first editions of *Social Statics* (1851), *The Principles of Psychology* (1855), and *First Principles* (1862).

11. Michel Foucault, *The History of Sexuality* 1:147.

12. See especially Judith Newton, "History as Usual?"; Frances Bartkowski, "Epistemic Drift in Foucault"; and Biddy Martin, "Feminism, Criticism, and Foucault."

13. Elaine Showalter, "Feminist Criticism in the Wilderness."

14. George Eliot, *The Essays of George Eliot*, ed. Thomas Pinney, 53. (Hereafter Eliot, *Essays*).

15. W. J. Harvey, "Idea and Image in the Novels of George Eliot" 162, citing Eliot's *Adam Bede* 83–84.

16. It is impossible to acknowledge all the feminist scholars whose work has influenced this study. I'd like to note especially my appreciation for the work of Elaine Showalter, Catharine Stimpson, and Sandra M. Gilbert and Susan Gubar in literary criticism; Olive Banks, Barbara Taylor, Mary Poovey, Judith Walkowitz, and Judith Newton in cultural history; and Adrienne Rich, Nancy Chodorow, Dorothy Dinnerstein, and Linda Gordon on theories of mothering.

17. Helene Deutch, *The Psychology of Women* 1:292.

18. Early feminist studies by Patricia Meyer Spacks (*The Female Imagination*) and Ellen Moers (*Literary Women*) do not discriminate between nineteenth- and twentieth-century feminism. Though important studies by Lee Edwards ("Women, Energy, and *Middlemarch*") and Margaret Homans (*Bearing the Word* and "Eliot, Wordsworth, and the Scenes of the Sisters' Instruction") are more sophisticated, neither critic discusses Eliot's feminism in its historical context. By contrast, Deirdre David's *Intellectual Women and Victorian Patriarchy* considers Eliot's place as an intellectual in Victorian England, which, it seems to me, marks an important contribution to feminist scholarship on Eliot. Similarly, Mary Poovey's *Uneven Developments* has helped me define feminist issues in the 1850s more specifically.

19. I have listed in my bibliography several historians of science whose work has been especially helpful in preparing this study; see Thomas Kuhn, Ernst Mayr, Stephen Jay Gould, Carolyn Merchant, Sandra Harding, and Evelyn Fox Keller. On Eliot's reception of evolutionary science, see George Levine, Gillian Beer, Sally Shuttleworth, U. C. Knoepflmacher, Suzanne Graver, and Diana Postlethwaithe. Margaret Homans, in *Bearing the Word*, has argued that episodes between mothers and daughters in women's writing often reveal how the daughter learns to speak "two languages at once" (13). While I share Homans's estimation of the centrality of gender and motherhood in the writing of women writers, I do not share her Lacanian definition of "feminine" language. The voice I would amplify in this analysis is not "presymbolic."

20. Avrom Fleishman, *Fiction and the Ways of Knowing* 139.

Chapter 2

1. For discussions of relevant features of "natural history" in early nineteenth-century English thought and how they helped open the way for the the-

ories of Spencer and Darwin, see George Levine, *Darwin and the Novelists*; Cynthia Eagle Russett, *Sexual Science*; Sally Shuttleworth, *George Eliot and Nineteenth-Century Science*; and Suzanne Graver, *George Eliot and Community*.

2. Spencer's contribution to the theory of evolution has been vigorously debated, from his own day to ours, by historians, sociologists, and anthropologists. Because of her association with Spencer, Eliot accepted many of the fundamental premises of evolutionary theory that he articulated before the publication of Darwin's *On the Origin of Species*. For Lewes's and Eliot's criticism of Spencer's thought see K. K. Collins, "George Henry Lewes Revisited" and "Questions of Method"; K. M. Newton, "George Eliot, George Henry Lewes, and Darwinism"; and George Levine, "George Eliot's Hypothesis of Reality." On Thomas Huxley's role in the debate, see William Irwine, *Apes, Angels, and Victorians* 33–36, and J.D.Y. Peel, *Herbert Spencer* 146–65. Gretna Jones's *Social Darwinism and English Thought* assesses the objections to Spencer's theories raised by Huxley, Leslie Stephen, and D. G. Ritchie (62). Finally, for the best analyses of the more recent manifestations of this controversy, see Marvin Harris, *The Rise of Anthropology*; Derek Freeman, "The Evolutionary Theories of Charles Darwin and Herbert Spencer"; and Robert L. Carneiro, "Structure, Function, and Equilibrium in the Evolutionism of Herbert Spencer."

3. For discussions of Eliot's reception of Darwinism, see the important studies by George Levine, *Darwin and the Novelists*; Gillian Beer, *Darwin's Plots*; Bernard J. Paris, *Experiments in Life*; and K. M. Newton, "George Eliot, George Henry Lewes, and Darwinism." For an excellent shorter study, see John Goode, "*Adam Bede*."

4. Herbert Spencer, "A Theory of Population Deduced from the General Law of Animal Fertility" 485–87. Hereafter cited as "Theory".

5. Herbert Spencer, *The Principles of Biology*, vol. 1 (1864), and vol. 2 (1867). Hereafter *Biology*. This work was originally published in numbers beginning in January 1863. I cite the first edition of the republished volumes for the reader's convenience.

6. Michael Timko, "The Victorianism of Victorian Literature" 615.

7. Ruby Redinger, *George Eliot* 43. See also Gordon S. Haight, *George Eliot* 21.

8. For one of the first analyses of this issue, see Nina Auerbach, "Artists and Mothers."

9. Eric Trudgill, in *Madonnas and Magdalens* (78–90), and Alexander Welsh, in *The City of Dickens*, argue persuasively concerning the "generalized" and idealized quality of mothers depicted in the novels of the period. Both critics, however, ignore the role of the novelists' gender in determining the representation of mothers in these texts.

10. The analyses of motherhood in Nancy Chodorow's *The Reproduction of Mothering* and Adrienne Rich's *Of Woman Born* have been particularly important in shaping my own view of Eliot's representation of maternity.

11. See J.D.Y. Peel, *Herbert Spencer* 83.

12. Herbert Spencer, "The Developmental Hypothesis," was republished in *Essays: Scientific, Political, and Speculative* (1:371); I cite from this collection for the reader's convenience. (Hereafter cited *Essays: Scientific*).

13. Herbert Spencer, "Theory" 468–501.

14. Derek Freeman argues that Spencer's theory of the progressive "development" from "homogeneous to heterogeneous" forms reveals Spencer's assumption that these changes are promoted by a "single" cause (215).

15. Herbert Spencer, "Progress: Its Law and Cause," in *Essays: Scientific* (1:10).

16. James Smith, as quoted in Barbara Taylor, *Eve and the New Jerusalem* 168.

17. Herbert Spencer, *Social Statics: Abridged and Revised, with The Man Versus the State* (1892) 73–79.

18. For a useful discussion of Barbara Bodichon's and Emily Davies's roles in promoting feminist educational reforms, see Carol Bauer and Lawrence Ritt, eds., *Free and Ennobled* 136–65. For a more general discussion of women's education, see François Basch, *Relative Creatures* 103–40 and Joan N. Burstyn, *Victorian Education and the Ideal of Womanhood*.

19. See Herbert Spencer, "The Moral Discipline of Children," *British Quarterly Review* (1858): 364–90; and "Physical Training," *British Quarterly Review* (1858–1859): 363–97. The versions of these essays as they first appeared in these journals are cited throughout. Spencer's essays on education from the *British Quarterly Review* and "What Knowledge is of Most Worth," *Westminster Review* (1859): 1–41, are reprinted substantially unchanged in Herbert Spencer, *Education: Intellectual, Moral, and Physical* (1909).

20. I cite from Herbert Spencer, "Personal Beauty," as reprinted in Herbert Spencer, *Essays: Moral, Political, and Aesthetic* (154). Gillian Beer (*Darwin's Plots*) notes the role of beauty in Darwin's theory of sexual selection and discusses Eliot's response in *Daniel Deronda*. Because she fails to note the importance of beauty in Spencer's early writing, Beer misrepresents both the development of evolutionary thought as it applies to women and Spencer's influence on Charles Darwin in *The Descent of Man* (1871). Gretna Jones argues persuasively in *Social Darwinism and English Thought* that Spencer influenced Darwin's view of sexual selection.

21. Deirdre David, in *Intellectual Women and Victorian Patriarchy*, offers a useful survey of Eliot's equivocal support for feminist causes. However, by beginning with Eliot's views on the Woman Question in 1876 and working backwards, David obscures much of Eliot's earlier support for women's education and other emancipationist causes.

22. Herbert Spencer, "The Genesis of Science," as reprinted in Herbert Spencer, *Essays: Scientific* (2:10).

23. Sandra M. Gilbert makes this point most convincingly in "Patriarchal Poetry and Women Readers." "Milton's bogey" is, of course, a term she borrowed from Virginia Woolf.

24. Charlotte Brontë, *Shirley*, ed. Andrew and Judith Hook (Harmondsworth: Penguin, 1974), 314–15. For an important discussion of this passage, see Sandra M. Gilbert and Susan Gubar, *The Madwoman in the Attic* 187–95.

Chapter 3

1. For a discussion of Eliot's use of myth see K. K. Collins, "Questions of Method"; Joseph Weisenfarth, *George Eliot's Mythmaking* and "George Eliot's

Notes for *Adam Bede*." See also Dianne F. Sadoff, "Nature's Language" and Jay Clayton, "Visionary Power and Narrative Form." For an analysis of the sexual dimensions of such mythmaking, see Sherry Ortner, "Is Female to Male as Nature is to Culture?"

2. See U. C. Knoepflmacher, "George Eliot, Feuerbach and the Question of Criticism"; Bernard Paris, *Experiments in Life*, 165–89; John Goode, *"Adam Bede"*; and Karen Mann, *The Language That Makes George Eliot's Fiction* 98–99.

3. U. C. Knoepflmacher presents the most comprehensive discussion of Eliot's use of Milton in *The Early Novels of George Eliot* (90–126). Several important feminist studies of Milton's *Paradise Lost* have shaped my approach: Sandra M. Gilbert, "Patriarchal Poetry and Women Readers"; Sandra M. Gilbert and Susan Gubar, *The Madwoman in the Attic* 3–104; Marcia Landy, "Kinship and the Role of Women in *Paradise Lost*"; Barbara K. Lewalski, "Milton on Women—Yet Once More"; Jackie Di Salvo, "Blake Encountering Milton." These discussions help explain Eliot's oddly oblique comments about Milton in her review of a contemporary edition of his works (*Essays* 154–57).

4. George Eliot, *Adam Bede*, ed. Stephen Gill. Both page and chapter citations appear for the reader's convenience.

5. For a discussion of female mortality rates in childbirth, see Adrienne Rich, *Of Woman Born* 128–85. Nancy Chodorow's *The Reproduction of Mothering* and Dorothy Dinnerstein's *The Mermaid and the Minotaur* provide some of the terms for my analysis here.

6. The most notorious examples of Eliot's fluctuating level of sympathy for Hetty appear in passages comparing her beauty to that of "kittens" and "small downy ducks." The evolutionary significance of these passages has been frequently noted. John Goode argues, for example, that Hetty is an evolutionary throwback because she possesses such a primitive moral consciousness (*"Adam Bede"* 27–29). I contend that the narrator's passionate sympathy in describing Hetty's confused wanderings, when she clings to life "only as the hunted, wounded brute clings to it" (435, ch. 37), counters purely scientific views of Hetty's impersonal beauty.

7. Reverend Irwine and Dinah Morris express two religious ideologies incorporating radically different theories about nature. Irwine's "pagan" perspective is an important point of contrast between him and the rest of the characters in the novel, including Dinah. See Christopher Herbert, "Preachers and the Schemes of Nature in *Adam Bede*" and Barry Qualls, *The Secular Pilgrims of Victorian Fiction* 143–44. For a discussion of Wordsworth's influence on *Adam Bede*, see Jay Clayton, "Visionary Power and Narrative Form" and W. J. Harvey, "Idea and Image in the Novels of George Eliot."

8. All citations are to Merritt Y. Hughes's edition of *Paradise Lost* (New York: Odyssey Press, 1982).

9. Eliot's description of Hetty also echoes the critical description of Milton's Eve in Charlotte Brontë's *Shirley*. Shirley complains, "Milton tried to see the first woman, but Cary, he saw her not. . . . It was his cook he saw; or it was Mrs. Gill, as I have seen her making custards in the heat of the summer, in the cool dairy, with rose trees and nasturtiums about the latticed window preparing a cold collation for the rectors,—preserves and dulcet creams" (315). Though

Sandra M. Gilbert and Susan Gubar identify Milton as the most powerful pre-
cursor poet, in *The Madwoman in the Attic* they do not discuss in any detail
Eliot's use of Milton in *Adam Bede*.

10. See Stephen Gill's commentary on this passage (*Adam Bede* 601). Eliot's
appreciation of Spencer's essay "The Genesis of Science" indicates her understanding of the fundamental role that language and myth play in the observation and assessment of nature and the place of men and women in it. See also
K. K. Collins, "Questions of Method" and Joseph Weisenfarth, *George Eliot's
Mythmaking* 1–35.

11. The narrator's comparison of Hetty with a "star-browed calf" (128, ch. 7)
can be seen, in retrospect, to lend her a classical dignity during her agonized
journey and her postpartum madness. The comparisons of Hetty and Pandora
indicate the difficulty of imagining a creation myth that does not depict
women as the tragic victims of their sex, a problem which Spencer apparently
confronted but resolved traditionally when he abandoned his earlier more feminist assessment of women's potential.

12. George Levine argues that this scene reveals Eliot's acceptance of the
Darwinian view that "nobody is 'disinterested' . . . there is no pure scientist"
(*Darwin* 225).

13. Jackie Di Salvo presents a brilliant analysis of Milton's use of "domestic
romance" in "Blake Encountering Milton." See Barbara Taylor's *Eve and the
New Jerusalem* for a full discussion of Utopian feminist rhetoric in the period
from Wollstonecraft to Eliot.

14. Bartle does not recognize the complementing relations of Mother,
Daughter, and Sister which find expression in Eliot's depiction of the egalitarian terms of Adam and Dinah's marriage.

15. Ever since Henry James described the golden haze that suffuses the
world of Hayslope, nostalgic critics have argued that *Adam Bede* depicts the
timeless world of pastoral romance. See for example, Murray Krieger, *The Classic Vision* 197–220; Maurice Hussey, "Structure and Imagery in *Adam Bede*";
George R. Creeger, "An Interpretation of *Adam Bede*"; R. A. Foakes, "*Adam Bede*
Reconsidered"; Ian Gregor, "The Two Worlds of *Adam Bede*"; and U. C.
Knoepflmacher, *The Early Novels of George Eliot* 90–126. I would contend, however, that the rituals surrounding haymaking and harvests should not disguise
Eliot's critique of Milton's formula. Eliot not only rejected the timeless pastoral values epitomized in Milton's epic but uses Dinah to redefine womanhood as represented by Milton's Eve. From this perspective, we can begin to reassess facile arguments about Dinah as a "substitute Eve."

16. Eric Trudgill, *Madonnas and Magdalens* 51. Carol Bauer and Lawrence
Ritt provide a review of the conservative objections to feminist educational reforms in *Free and Ennobled* 1–51, 236–65.

17. See David Leon Higdon, "The Iconographic Backgrounds of *Adam Bede*,
Chapter 15" 159. For another perspective, see Nina Auerbach, "The Rise of the
Fallen Woman."

18. Adrienne Rich, "*Jane Eyre*: The Temptations of a Motherless Woman."
Eliot returns to this problem in *The Mill on the Floss*.

19. Alan Mintz, in *George Eliot and the Novel of Vocation*, does not consider the problems of vocation posed by Dinah in his analysis of *Adam Bede* (61).

20. U. C. Knoepflmacher, *The Early Novels of George Eliot* 91; Murray Krieger, *The Classic Vision* 205; R. A. Foakes, "*Adam Bede Reconsidered*" 75; Ellen Moers, *Literary Women* 295. In contrast, see John Goode, "*Adam Bede*" 25; and Bruce K. Martin, "Rescue and Marriage in *Adam Bede*."

21. Virginia Woolf, *The Common Reader: First Series* 176.

22. Gordon Haight and several other critics remind us that Eliot was especially sensitive about her physical appearance because Herbert Spencer rejected her precisely on these grounds, saying that she did not possess the beauty requisite in the woman who would become his wife (*George Eliot* 116–17).

23. Bram Dijkstra discusses how the mirror was used as a figure displaying woman's sexual lawlessness in late Victorian culture in *Idols of Perversity* (132–69).

24. Sandra M. Gilbert and Susan Gubar discuss how Milton's patriarchal language inhibited women writers who tried to depict their own vision of female sexuality. Though Gilbert and Gubar do not discuss Dinah, her condition in *Adam Bede* reflects that wordless state that they describe as the lot of all women in *The Madwoman in the Attic* (3–104). Margaret Homans offers another definition of female language in *Bearing the Word* (13–20). It is useful to compare Dinah's silence to that of Elizabeth Gaskell's heroine in *Ruth* and Brontë's *Shirley*.

25. Gillian Beer discusses the evolutionary implications of the Victorian fascination with "monsters" in *Darwin's Plots* (141–45). Of course, woman as monster is also an important theme in Gilbert and Gubar's *The Madwoman in the Attic* and in Nina Auerbach's *Woman and the Demon*.

26. Ludwig Feuerbach, *The Essence of Christianity* 72.

27. John Goode, "*Adam Bede*" 34. Reva Stump contends that Eliot does not register convincingly enough the discrepancy between Dinah's sense of herself and Adam's view of her as angel in *Movement and Vision in George Eliot's Novels* (65). Stump's argument does not acknowledge that Eliot was herself trapped by a kind of role-playing not unlike that of her heroine because of her decision to narrate *Adam Bede* using a male persona.

28. Joseph Weisenfarth provides this date for the Methodist Conference's decision in "George Eliot's Notes for *Adam Bede*." For more information on nineteenth-century feminists' views on women and work, see J. A. and Olive Banks, *Feminism and Family Planning in Victorian England* 48–49. Katherine Ellis also analyzes these labor divisions in her essay, "*Paradise Lost*."

Chapter 4

1. George Eliot, *The Mill on the Floss*, ed. A. S. Bryant. Parenthetical citations refer to page, chapter, and book of this edition. For an interesting analysis of Eliot's use of her pseudonym, see Alexander Welsh, *George Eliot and Blackmail* 125–31. Sandra M. Gilbert and Susan Gubar argue convincingly that Eliot's

"The Lifted Veil" reflects her response to the exposure of her pseudonym (*Madwoman* 443–77).

2. Gordon S. Haight conclusively dates Eliot's reading of Darwin (*George Eliot* 319). Several recent studies discuss Eliot's response to Darwin: see especially Gillian Beer, *Darwin's Plots* 149–235; Sally Shuttleworth, *George Eliot and Nineteenth-Century Science* 53; and Suzanne Graver, *George Eliot and Community* 199. Both Margaret Homans ("Eliot") and Mary Jacobus ("Men of Maxims") take a different approach; they illustrate Eliot's interest in origins by exploring her debts to Wordsworth. Homans argues that "A 'mother tongue' in Wordsworth might signify feminized Nature's fostering of imaginative growth, but the nature for which Eliot's narrator expresses her enduring love is not at all Wordsworth's maternal nature but rather the nature of objects" ("Eliot" 239).

3. Herbert Spencer, "Physical Training," *British Quarterly Review* (April 1859): 362–97.

4. See Robert Colby, *Fiction with a Purpose* 234–36. Reva Stump (*Movement*) provides a discussion of animal images in her chapter on *The Mill on the Floss*.

5. Herbert Spencer, "What Knowledge is of Most Worth," *Westminster Review* (July 1859): 1–41.

6. I would like to thank Shoshana Knapp for sharing with me her unpublished essay on the relationship between Spencer's theories of education and *The Mill on the Floss*. For discussions of how Eliot's support for women's education finds expression in this novel, see Barbara Hardy, "*The Mill on the Floss*" 47; Elaine Showalter, *A Literature of Their Own* 40–41; A. W. Bellringer, "Education in *The Mill on the Floss*"; and Suzanne Graver, *George Eliot and Community* 199–200.

7. Spencer used sheep to illustrate his theories about how "mixed" breeds often produce hybrids that die out in a generation or two when the traits of both races are "imperfectly coordinated." See Herbert Spencer, "Personal Beauty," in Herbert Spencer, *Essays: Moral, Political, and Aesthetic* (159–60). (Hereafter *Essays: Moral*).

8. Eliot certainly knew of Spencer's early attempt to rationalize human sex differences in his essay "A Theory of Population," which appeared in the *Westminster Review* during her editorship. In this essay, Spencer defines a "law of maintenance" whereby the "power to maintain individual life" varies inversely with the "power to propagate the species" (476), and this in turn may cause, Spencer speculates, an "early arrest" in the development of the "nervous system" and brain functions of fertile women (496).

9. Because many Freudian and psychoanalytic feminist critics do not see Eliot's treatment of Mrs. Tulliver as a response to Wordsworthian sentimentality about motherhood, they overstate her hostility toward Maggie's mother and toward women more generally. See especially Laura Comer Emery, *George Eliot's Creative Conflict*; Nina Auerbach, "The Power of Hunger"; and Patricia Meyer Spacks, *The Female Imagination* 51–59. Sandra M. Gilbert and Susan Gubar present a more balanced assessment in *The Madwoman in the Attic* (491–94). For feminist critiques of the mother's role in education in Eliot's own time, see Mary Wollstonecraft's *A Vindication of the Rights of Woman* 150–52 and

Emily Davies, "Thoughts on Some Questions Relating to Women," in Carol Bauer and Lawrence Ritt, eds., *Free and Ennobled* (126–29).

10. For a discussion of Spencer's anti-Wordsworthian view of children, see Cynthia Eagle Russett, *Sexual Science* 72. On his view of the "struggle for survival," see Robert Carneiro, "Structure, Function, and Equilibrium" 77.

11. For useful analyses of the role of religion in determining Maggie's sense of autonomy, see John Hagan, "A Reinterpretation of *The Mill on the Floss*"; and Sara Moore Putzell, "The Search for a Higher Rule." Eliot can be seen as part of a long line of women authors who demonstrate the inhibiting influences of orthodox religion on a daughter's life. *Jane Eyre* provides the classic example in the character of Helen Burns. See also Patricia Thomson, *George Sand and the Victorians* 162–63, for a brief discussion of the influence of George Sand's on writing *The Mill on the Floss*.

12. For an interesting discussion of this scene, see Nina Auerbach, "The Power of Hunger."

13. This is one reason, perhaps, why so many critics read this novel autobiographically and are disappointed by Maggie's tragic fate. I would argue that the exposure of Eliot's pseudonym prompted her to reevaluate her authority as a woman writer and to see herself as subject, like her heroine, to male censorship and control.

14. Richard Jenkyns singles out Herbert Spencer's *Education: Intellectual, Moral, and Physical* (1860) as a particularly influential work criticizing the role of classical languages and literatures in English education. See Richard Jenkyns, *The Victorians and Ancient Greece* 277.

15. Herbert Spencer argued that language study tends, "if anything, further to increase the already due respect for authority" in "What Knowledge is of Most Worth" (40). Mary Jacobus analyzes Eliot's use of metaphor in this episode to show how "science calls culture" into question in "Men of Maxims and *The Mill on the Floss*." The reverse is also true, since this passage emphasizes how "metaphor"—and language itself—is the common source of all knowledge. This episode, then, with its numerous allusions to Spencer's theories of education, also indicts the unconsciousness misogyny that infected his theories at their very point of origin—in language.

16. See Gerhard Joseph, "The *Antigone* as Cultural Touchstone." David Molstadt also discusses Eliot's allusions to Antigone and Creon in "*The Mill on the Floss* and *Antigone*" (529). Sara Moore Putzell comments on the significance of these parallels in "An Antagonism of Valid Claims." For a more general discussion of Maggie's experiences in the Red Deeps as sexual initiation, see Elaine Showalter, *A Literature of Their Own* 128; Sandra M. Gilbert and Susan Gubar, *The Madwoman in the Attic* 493; Ellen Moers, *Literary Women* 385–86; and Nancy K. Miller, "Emphasis Added."

17. This resolution is often read as a sign of Eliot's endorsement of patriarchal order. But in this scene, Eliot allows Maggie to identify a crucial distinction between the obedience commanded by "unmanly" domination and the submission compelled by the "higher laws" of love and filial piety. Earlier in the novel, Eliot compares Tom and Maggie to Hector and Hecuba and suggests that Tom's understanding of the "outward" law and Maggie's of the "in-

ward" is determined by their experiences in a gendered world (405, bk. 5, ch. 2). Eliot's conclusion, "So it has been since the days of Hecuba, and of Hector" is often read by critics as expressing Eliot's conservative desire to exclude women from those "fierce struggles with things divine and human" in the world outside the home. See, for example, Henry Auster, *Local Habitations* 146 and William Myers, *The Teaching of George Eliot* 50–51. These readings, however, ignore Philip's function in the novel, which is to unsettle the traditional opposition that Tom and Maggie represent. Thomas L. Jeffers, in "Myth and Morals in *The Mill on the Floss*," argues that the rigid separation between the public and private spheres is one of the causes of Maggie's tragedy.

18. Most of Eliot's readers see Maggie's relation to Stephen as the crux of the novel, and most post-Freudian critics see Maggie's final rejection of Stephen Guest as a perverse renunciation not only of sexual desire but as a masochistic denial of beauty, poetry, music, and art as well. For the most influential examples of psychoanalytic readings of Maggie's renunciation, see Bernard Paris, *A Psychological Approach to Fiction* 165–89; Sara Moore Putzell, "An Antagonism of Valid Claims"; Nina Auerbach, "The Power of Hunger"; and Michael Steig, "Anality in *The Mill on the Floss*." Elizabeth Ermarth sees Maggie's renunciation as the culmination of a "long suicide" prompted by infantilizing love for family, religious asceticism, and nostalgic longing for the irrecoverable past in "Maggie Tulliver's Long Suicide." Other critics argue that Maggie's choice reveals the essence of Eliot's conservatism; it is a demonstration of her antifeminism, expressed in her belief in the value of submission to duty, to a religion of self-denial, and to the patriarchal traditions of the past. See George Levine, "Intelligence as Deception;" Sara Moore Putzell, "The Search for a Higher Rule"; Thomas Pinney, "The Authority of the Past in George Eliot's Novels"; and Sandra M. Gilbert and Susan Gubar, *The Madwoman in the Attic* 465–68, 492–96.

Maggie's religious self-denial also echoes Spencer's ideas about female sexuality in "Physical Training," where he illustrated the "uncontrollable vehemence of long denied-desire" by citing the example of a nun who "suddenly lapses from the extremest austerities into an almost demonic wickedness" ("Physical Training" 366). Eliot brings this religiously inspired suppression of "long-denied desire" closer to home by describing Maggie's more familiar domestic asceticism. In this way, Eliot reveals the contradictions in Spencer's sexist educational plan for women by insisting that for both sexes, genuine morality and religious submission must be based not on intellectual deprivation but on a full "knowledge of the irreversible laws within and without."

19. Sara Moore Putzell, in "An Antagonism of Valid Claims," demonstrates the function of Book 4 in defining the relation between the Dodsons and the people of St. Ogg's. See also the comments by N. N. Feltes in "Community and the Limits of Liability in Two Mid-Victorian Novels" and by Henry Auster in *Local Habitations* (144–66). Though he does not discuss Eliot in particular, Maurice Mandelbaum analyzes the relation between Spencer's determinism, theories of "progress," and Victorian Liberalism in *History, Man, and Reason* (193–236).

20. In *Women, Power, and Subversion*, Judith Lowder Newton explains how social change for women is "repressive" in terms of power: "The shift from an

agrarian to an industrial capitalist society . . . intensifies the traditional inequalities in economic function, status, and power between men and women of the middle-class" (126).

21. Sally Shuttleworth argues brilliantly that Maggie's divided consciousness at this point in the novel similarly reflects Eliot's reading of organicist theories of psychology; see *George Eliot and Nineteenth-Century Science* 69–77.

22. Eric Trudgill cites this review in *Madonnas and Magdalens* (227). See also David R. Carroll, ed., *George Eliot* 150, 118.

23. Many post-Freudian critics argue that Eliot's references to her heroine's "higher" and "lower" sensibilities reveal her prudishness. Bernard Paris offers perhaps the best example of this argument (*Psychological Approach* 165–89).

24. Neil Roberts, *George Eliot* 93; Sally Shuttleworth, *George Eliot and Nineteenth-Century Science* 62–68.

25. For the best example of this view, see Nina Auerbach, "The Power of Hunger."

26. On these formal problems, see Barbara Hardy, *"The Mill on the Floss"* 41.

Chapter 5

1. George Eliot, *Silas Marner*, ed. Q. E. Leavis. All parenthetical citations refer to this edition and include page and chapter references.

2. All citations in this chapter refer to the single-volume first edition of Herbert Spencer's *Principles of Psychology* (1855). Spencer was composing this text in 1853–1854, when his relation with Eliot was most intense.

3. For another perspective on Eliot's use of associationist psychology, see Sally Shuttleworth, *George Eliot and Nineteenth-Century Science* 78–95; William Myers, *The Teaching of George Eliot* 42–48; and Fred C. Thomson, "The Theme of Alienation in *Silas Marner*."

4. For an interesting discussion of the ritual of drawing lots, see Joseph Weisenfarth, "Demythologizing *Silas Marner*" and David Carroll, "*Silas Marner*."

5. Eliot's treatment of the power of superstition in Raveloe warns us not to idealize its religious life. Despite their thorough treatment of the religious elements of life in both Lantern Yard and Raveloe, Q. D. Leavis, (*Silas Marner*, Introduction 23–31) and David Carroll ("*Silas Marner*") seem to idealize the latter community. Silas's knowledge of a cure that was scientifically verified by the medical profession in 1785, his ability to read—in contrast to Dolly's illiteracy—and his final comprehension of the "Invisible" as a Power that transcends the narrow definitions of divinity and law that prevail in both communities mark him as intellectually and morally more sophisticated than Dolly Winthrop.

6. This apparent timelessness has prompted many critics to see Raveloe as an ideal Wordsworthian community expressing Eliot's nostalgia for a more natural, more traditional, more hierarchically ordered society. While Eliot identified Wordsworth as an ideal reader for *Silas Marner* (*GEL* 3:382), she takes a more Malthusian view of motherhood that offsets her appreciation for the "natural piety" of Dolly Winthrop and the regenerated Silas. Q. D. Leavis outlines Eliot's debt to Wordsworth in her introduction to *Silas Marner*. See also Lillian

Haddakin, "*Silas Marner.*" Margaret Homans ("Eliot") offers the most comprehensive discussion of the gender politics of Eliot's reading of Wordsworth but does not discuss *Silas Marner* in detail. Robert Colby, in *Fiction with a Purpose* (213–55) and Donald Stone, in the *Romantic Impulse in Victorian Fiction* (174) also make interesting arguments.

7. Eliot may have known about the studies in the 1860s that led to the discovery of the cause of puerperal fever, the disease that killed many Victorian women who gave birth in city hospitals or who were attended by male physicians. See Adrienne Rich, *Of Woman Born* 151–55.

8. See Q. D. Leavis's introduction to *Silas Marner* 7–43; David Carroll, "*Silas Marner*" 184; Henry Auster, *Local Habitations* 177–206, especially 192; Jerome Thale, *The Novels of George Eliot* 65–66.

9. See Sandra M. Gilbert, "Life's Empty Pack" and Joseph Weisenfarth, "Demythologizing *Silas Marner.*"

10. For a fascinating discussion of the role of secrecy and blackmail in this novel, see Alexander Welsh, *George Eliot and Blackmail* 149–50, 163–68.

11. Eliot's feeling about such secret liaisons is suggested by her comments about her own decision to live openly with G. H. Lewes and by her criticism of women who "obtain what they desire and are still invited to dinner" (*GEL* 2:213). Godfrey is freer to indulge in secret affairs without censure than she was, but by making Molly his wife rather than, for example, a prostitute, Eliot indicates that Godfrey apparently believes he is morally obligated to "own" both wife and child. Bruce K. Martin's discussion in "Similarity within Dissimilarity" of Godfrey's role in this novel is notable for his special pleading on Godfrey's behalf. I would argue that Eliot regards Godfrey's "moral cowardice," like that of Arthur Donnithorne and Tito Melema, as one of the most serious of all character flaws because it is an avoidable—and hence remediable— source of tragedy in this novel and consequently the most needful of correction. On the "spiritual barrenness" that prevails at Red House, see Henry Auster, *Local Habitations* 184–88.

12. Compare *Social Statics* (1851), 336–47 with *The Principles of Psychology* (1855), 601–2.

13. For other Victorian versions of this scene, see Charles Dickens, *David Copperfield* and *Dombey and Son*. See also Alexander Welsh's *The City of Dickens* for a brilliant discussion of Dickens's pastoralism.

14. Sally Shuttleworth discusses this scene as showing the "fetishism of commodities" in *George Eliot and Nineteenth-Century Science* (85).

15. Several commentators, notably Ian Milner (in *Structure* 40–45), David Carroll (in "*Silas Marner*"), and Joseph Weisenfarth (in "Demythologizing *Silas Marner*") have noted the role of Chance in the novel and in the artificial accidents that attend Molly Farren Cass's melodramatic death and create the situation in which Silas initially confuses Eppie with his lost gold. Sandra M. Gilbert analyzes Eliot's repeated use of the maternal metaphors which cluster around this climactic episode in "Life's Empty Pack."

16. Sandra M. Gilbert has persuasively described some of the psychological and artistic reasons which may have prompted Eliot to leave untold so much of

the mother's story in *Silas Marner*. She kindly shared an earlier version of "Life's Empty Pack" with me. See also Sally Shuttleworth, *George Eliot and Nineteenth-Century Science* 92.

17. For an excellent discussion of women's legal status in mid-Victorian England, see Mary Poovey, *Uneven Developments* 51–88.

18. Sandra M. Gilbert argues in "Life's Empty Pack," that this scene reveals Eliot's acquiescence to patriarchal law. Elizabeth Ermarth's "Incarnations" provides a useful analysis of Eliot's view of law. Richard Conway, in "*Silas Marner and Felix Holt*," argues, by contrast, that Eliot's feminism informs *Silas Marner*.

19. Compare Spencer's citation with William Shakespeare, *The Winter's Tale* (4.4.90–91) in *The Complete Works of Shakespeare*, ed. Hardin Craig and David Bevington (Glenview Ill: Scott, Foresman, 1973).

20. Many of Eliot's critics have noted the difficulty of adequately defining the form of *Silas Marner*, and this problem, I would argue, results from Eliot's ambiguous treatment of mothers and daughters in this text. Joseph Weisenfarth argues that Eliot's novel reflects the structure of Greek comedy in "Demythologizing *Silas Marner*" (234–35).

21. Ian Milner discusses Eliot's references to Shakespeare's pastoral (*Structure* 40–45). See also Q. D. Leavis's introduction to *Silas Marner* 7–43, and Eliot's letters, *GEL* 3:228, 374, 397.

22. Ian Milner discusses another aspect of the garden metaphors in *Silas Marner* (*Structure* 40–45). John Holloway also comments on the structure of this novel in *The Victorian Sage* (115).

Chapter 6

1. Herbert Spencer, *Principles of Biology* (1864–1867). Hereafter *Biology*. I cite the first edition of this two-volume work for the reader's convenience. The numbers for this work were available to the Leweses and other subscribers beginning in January 1863.

2. Robert Carneiro discusses the importance of the concept of "function" in Spencer's *Principles of Sociology*, but he does not note the implications of this theory for Spencer's analysis of women in "Structure, Function, and Equilibrium in the Evolutionism of Herbert Spencer" 83–94.

3. I refer to Harriet Martineau's popular translation of Auguste Comte's *Positivist Philosophy* (hereafter *Positivist*). For useful discussions of the relation between the ideas of Spencer and Comte, see Maurice Mandelbaum, *History, Man and Reason* and S. Eisen, "Herbert Spencer and the Spectre of Comte."

4. George Eliot, *Romola*, ed. Andrew Sanders. All parenthetical citations refer to this edition. "Moral evolution" is a term from Auguste Comte's *A General View of Positivism*, trans. John Henry Bridges (300). See Sally Shuttleworth's discussion of Eliot's appeal to the authority of history in *George Eliot and Nineteenth-Century Science* (63–64, 96–97). On the impact of Comte on Eliot's thought more generally, see Martha S. Vogeler, "George Eliot and the Positivists" and Nancy L. Paxton, "Feminism and Positivism in George Eliot's *Romola*."

Suzanne Graver has argued in *George Eliot and Community* (45–53) that Eliot's use of history shows her reliance on a model of "social dynamics" which was equated with the "science of progress." By thus asserting that Comte, Mill, Lewes, and Eliot shared Spencer's view of the place of history in the study of "social dynamics," Graver, along with William Myers (*Teaching*), and J. B. Bullen ("George Eliot's *Romola* as Positivist Allegory") obscure fundamental differences between Spencer's and Eliot's views of history. In fact, Spencer's use of Comte's term "social statics" was, according to Spencer, entirely coincidental. While we may dispute Spencer's claim to originality in coining this term, it is clear that his understanding of history differs from Comte's. See also Mary Wilson Carpenter's interesting study of the role of the apocalyptic tradition in shaping *Romola* (*George Eliot* 61–103).

5. Spencer's dismissal of the value of history was evident as early as 1854 in his essay "The Art of Education," where he redefined history as "descriptive sociology."

Sally Shuttleworth argues that the "opposing" models of time that structure *The Mill on the Floss* reveal Eliot's objection to the simple applications of uniformitarian principles to the analysis of human society. In her notebooks of this period, Eliot asks, "Is the interpretation of man's past life on earth according to the methods of Sir Charles Lyell in geology, namely, on the principle that all changes were produced by agencies still at work, thoroughly adequate & scientific? Or must we allow especially in the earlier periods, for something incalculable by us from the data of our present experience? Even within comparatively near times & in kindred communities how many conceptions & fashions of life have existed to which our understanding & sympathy has no clue!" (quoted in Shuttleworth, *George Eliot* 63). When these remarks are seen in the context of Spencer's evolutionary analysis of human and social development, they also indicate Eliot's criticism of his assumption that simple physical laws can adequately assess human behavior in historically determined societies.

6. Victorian feminists found Comte's philosophy useful, first of all, because he recommended that women be given an education identical to that which was to be universally provided for men, an education that included mathematics, astronomy, physics, chemistry, and biology. Comte's curriculum included the Positivist "social sciences": history, art, literature, and religion—the traditional subjects of women's education—in a more systematic and comprehensive way than Spencer proposed (*General* 267). Harriet Martineau, who in 1853 translated into English Comte's *Cours de philosophie positive* remained a Positivist and feminist throughout her life. Harriet Taylor and John Stuart Mill were also deeply impressed by Comte's philosophy, and the latter, in his *Auguste Comte and Positivism* (appearing originally as essays in the *Westminster Review* in 1865), praised Comte particularly for his stance on the education of women (76). Eliot was not alone, then, among Victorian intellectuals in finding that Comte's philosophy provided a rigorous and powerful defense of women's education that was consistent with both her agnostic rationalism and her feminism.

Comte similarly offered legitimacy for feminist efforts to recover the lost history of women. By recognizing their role in the family and the church, Comte made women more visible to social theorists accustomed to treating them as the legal wards of their fathers or husbands. His model of social polity lent important credibility to Eliot's and other feminists' analyses of women's historical role in society.

7. Both Mrs. Jameson and Mrs. Peter Taylor converted to Catholicism (Trudgill, *Madonnas* 262). English Positivists were divided in their support of Comte's later work, as William M. Simon reports in *European Positivism in the Nineteenth Century*.

8. See especially J. B. Bullen, "George Eliot's *Romola* as Positivist Allegory." Gordon S. Haight takes the opposite position by describing Eliot's ambivalent feminism and asserting that she could not be seriously interested in Comte's "cult of the Vierge Mère" (*George Eliot* 396). For a thorough analysis of Eliot's personal relations with the English Positivists, see Martha Vogeler, "George Eliot and the Positivists." Felicia Bonaparte also mentions Comte briefly in *Will and Destiny* and *The Triptych and the Cross*.

9. For a discussion of Eliot's resistance to Comte's authoritarianism, see Martha Vogeler, "George Eliot and the Positivists" and Gordon S. Haight's introduction to Eliot's letters (*GEL* 1:LXII).

10. For another reading of this episode, see Margaret Homans, *Bearing the Word* 198–201. Sally Shuttleworth also raises this point in order to talk about the damage to Baldasarre's identity caused by his amnesia (*George Eliot* 112).

11. K. K. Collins, in "Questions of Method," suggests that as early as 1865, Eliot may have known about Bachofen's theory that the *Oresteia* dramatized the transfer of power from the matriarchal to the patriarchal order. I have been able to discover no direct evidence that Eliot read Bachofen, though her interest in motherhood and her familiarity with German both suggest that she might have. Joseph Weisenfarth has kindly informed me that Eliot certainly knew of Bachofen's work no later than September 1870, because she read and took notes on John Lubbock's *The Origins of Civilization and the Primitive Condition*, which summarizes Bachofen's argument. While Bachofen raised fundamental questions about the historical permanence of the patriarchal family and social order, Comte also admits the possibility that a matriarchal order may have predated the "normal" patriarchal order by showing that the institution of marriage evolved though time. While Comte argued that in monogamous marriage, women held a subordinate position by nature, his depiction of the fetichist view of nature, his description of woman's "natural authority" as mother, and his identification of the family as the first component of social order all suggest the possibility of a matriarchal organization of the family in prehistoric times (*Positivist* 504, 547, 573).

12. For a more complete discussion of this problem, see Nancy L. Paxton, "George Eliot and the City."

13. One of the best discussions of feminist resistance to the Contagious Diseases Acts is Judith R. Walkowitz's *Prostitution and Victorian Society*.

14. J. S. Mill, *The Subjection of Women* 12.

15. Barbara Bodichon's analysis of the marriage laws is conveniently reprinted in Janet Horowitz Murray, *Strong-Minded Women and Other Lost Voices from Nineteenth-Century England* (118–20). See also Mary Poovey, *Uneven Develop-*

ments 51–88. Carole Robinson, on the other hand, argues that Romola is more conventionally submissive in *"Romola*: A Reading of the Novel."

16. Sally Shuttleworth's analysis brought this annotation to my attention (*George Eliot* 105).

17. Andrew Sanders summarizes the political significance of Savonarola's resistance in "A Note on the Political Background of *Romola*" included in George Eliot, *Romola*, ed. Andrew Sanders (677). See also Mary Wilson Carpenter, *George Eliot and the Landscape of Time* 70–71.

18. In her campaign to open the profession of nursing to middle-class women, Florence Nightengale advised only single women to take up this work. Janet Horowitz Murray reprints several of Florence Nightingale's remarks about nursing in *Strong-Minded Women* (297–305); see also Elaine Showalter, "Florence Nightingale's Complaint."

19. While Comte's analysis of moral law remained useful in discrediting the "vulgar notions" of function that find expression in, for example, Spencer's *Principles of Biology* (1864–1867), Eliot was not willing to surrender to Comte's authoritarianism, especially as it expressed itself in his views on Catholicism. See Martha Vogeler, "George Eliot and the Positivists" 423.

Nearly a century later, Simone de Beauvoir recognized the dangers that Positivism posed for feminism:

> Thus, the paternalism that claims woman for hearth and home defines her as sentiment, inwardness, immanence and transcendence; when one offers the existent no aim, or prevents him from attaining any, or robs him of his victory, then his transcendence falls vainly in the past—that is to say, falls back into immanence. This is the lot assigned to woman in the patriarchiate; but it is in no way a vocation, any more than slavery is the vocation of the slave. The development of this mythology is clearly seen in Auguste Comte. To identify woman with altruism is to guarantee to men absolute rights in her devotion; it is to impose on women a categorical imperative. (*The Second Sex* [New York: Vintage, 1974], 287–88)

20. Margaret Homans argues that Romola remains in the position assigned to her by phallocentric culture in *Bearing the Word* (189–217). Because Homans sees all language as male, she ignores, it seems to me, what Romola learns in reading both classical and Christian texts and in participating in her culture as a model of both pagan and Christian virtues.

21. Most critics agree with J. B. Bullen in seeing Romola as an overly idealized madonna figure at the end of this novel ("George Eliot's *Romola*" 425–35). The best discussion is George Levine's *"Romola* as Fable." See also Joseph Weisenfarth's excellent critical summary in *George Eliot's Mythmaking* (146–69).

22. For a discussion of this comment, see Sally Shuttleworth (*George Eliot* 105).

23. Feminist critics, too, see Romola as overly idealized. According to Sally Shuttleworth this episode converts Romola into a "fully fledged Madonna," the perfect object of "private adoration" (*George Eliot* 104). Margaret Homans likewise sees Romola as enacting the part of the Madonna by caring for little Benedetto, but she does not explain why Romola leaves him behind rather

than return to Florence to play the role of madonna (*Bearing* 206–7). See also Deirdre David, *Intellectual Women and Victorian Patriarchy* 193–94.

Chapter 7

1. On the impact of the Reform Bill on Eliot's novel, see Catherine Gallagher, *The Industrial Reformation of English Fiction* 219–63. For a useful analysis of the feminist elements in *Felix Holt*, see Richard Conway, "*Silas Marner* and *Felix Holt*" and Bonnie Zimmerman, "*Felix Holt* and the True Power of Womanhood." Zimmerman argues that Eliot's feminism was qualified by her acceptance of the moral principles expressed in a female conduct book written by Louis Aimé Martin and translated into English as *Woman's Mission*. I would argue rather that it was Comte's theories (echoed by Martin) that more profoundly influenced Eliot's thought in the 1860s and 1870s.

2. George Eliot, *Felix Holt*, ed. Peter Coveney. All parenthetical citations refer to this text.

3. This analysis lent scientific credibility to traditional medical views of women; in 1874, Dr. Henry Maudsley echoed Spencer in writing more directly about the debilitating effects of menstruation upon women's mental and physical capacities. See Janet Horowitz Murray, *Strong-Minded Women* 221.

4. Throughout this study I have compared Spencer's single-volume *The Principles of Psychology* (1855) with the expanded and substantially revised edition, published first in numbers beginning in 1868, and reissued in two volumes in 1870 and 1872. Because the 1870–1872 edition of *The Principles of Psychology* is hard to find, I cite, unless otherwise noted, from the definitive *The Principles of Psychology* (1890), which adds only minor corrections. In the earliest version of *The Principles of Psychology* (1855), Spencer mentions "savages" occasionally (see, for example, p. 411, 418, 419, 421). The effects of his evolutionary analysis are evident in his much more extensive references to "savages" in *The Principles of Psychology* (1870–1872). In this edition, see 1:282; and 2:505, 522, 527, 528, 529, 530, 538. These passages appear substantially unchanged in the 1890 edition.

5. John Lubbock, *Pre-historic Times* and *The Origin of Civilization of the Primitive Condition*. Spencer mentions his meeting with McLennan and with the X Club in his *Autobiography* (2:66; 115–18).

6. Elizabeth Fee, "The Sexual Politics of Victorian Social Anthropology" 88.

7. J. J. Bachofen, *Myth, Religion, and Mother Right*. For Eliot's reception of Bachofen's theory, see K. K. Collins, "Questions of Method"; Elizabeth Fee, "The Sexual Politics of Victorian Social Anthropology"; and Joseph Weisenfarth, *George Eliot's Mythmaking*. Collins argues that Eliot may have read Bachofen as early as 1865, though she does not mention his theory in her notebooks until 1870. Comte was also interested in tracing the growth and development of the family, and since he saw it as constituting the original social unit, he writes in ways similar to Bachofen about the archaic quality of the mother's power. In her own readings of Greek drama, Eliot stressed the power of the wife and mother rather than her debility. See George Eliot, "Love in the Drama," *The Leader* 6 (25 August 1855): 820–21.

8. Herbert Spencer, *Principles of Sociology* (1877–1896), 3 vol. in 5. (Hereafter *Sociology*). This second edition is cited, unless otherwise noted, because it includes the extra number about marriage.

9. Mary Poovey, *Uneven Developments* 11. Eliot is notorious for her condescending treatment of the workingmen in *Felix Holt*. The conservativism she reveals in this novel has not been adequately reconciled with the feminist sympathies evident in her letters of the period and in her treatment of Mrs. Transome and Esther in this work. For relevant discussions of Eliot's conservative politics and its relation to her feminism, see Linda Bamber, "Self-Defeating Politics in George Eliot's *Felix Holt*"; Michael Woolf, "The Uses of Context"; Robin Sheets, "*Felix Holt*, Language, the Bible, and the Problematic of Meaning"; and Arnold Kettle, "Felix Holt, the Radical." See also also David Craig, "Fiction and the Rising Industrial Classes"; Walter Francis Wright, "George Eliot as Industrial Reformer"; and Sally Shuttleworth, *George Eliot and Nineteenth-Century Science* 115–41.

10. Several critics who have discussed Mrs. Transome in the light of classical tragedy have seen her "rebellion" against her marital and maternal obligations as a terrible act of hubris and her suffering at her son's hands as the inevitable consequence of an egotism as gigantic as that of Oedipus or Clytemnestra. See especially W.F.T. Myers, "Politics and Personality in *Felix Holt*." On parallels between Mrs. Transome and the heroic women of Greek tragedy, see Fred C. Thomson, "The Genesis of *Felix Holt*" and "*Felix Holt* as Classic Tragedy"; Michael Edwards, "George Eliot and Negative Form"; Vernon Rendall, "George Eliot and the Classics." On parallels between Mrs. Transome and Medea, see Richard Jenkyns, *The Victorians and Ancient Greece* 125–27.

11. W.F.T. Myers sees this famous description of Mrs. Transome's "bondage" as the just punishment Eliot metes out to a woman who has foolishly rebelled against the traditional restraints of marriage and motherhood ("Politics" 10–12). Likewise, he argues that Eliot shows her criticism of female pride, ambition, and will when she dramatizes Mrs. Transome's regret over her "loveless" relation with her husband and her recognition that she "would have given a great deal . . . if her feeble husband had not always lived in dread of her temper, so that he might have been fond of her now" (*Felix Holt* 445, ch. 35). Similar readings which emphasize Eliot's Tory sympathies disregard her horror over the "death in life of old paralytic vice" (*Felix Holt* 83, Introduction), so evident in the aristocrats protrayed in this novel.

12. On the Contagious Diseases Acts, See Judith R. Walkowitz, *Prostitution and Victorian Society* 90–112. See also Carol Bauer and Lawrence Ritt, eds., *Free and Ennobled* 195–205.

13. For a discussion of the impact of sensationalizing journalistic coverage of the "white slave trade" later in the century, see Judith R. Walkowitz, *Prostitution and Victorian Society* 246–52.

14. Many of Eliot's readers, then and now, have argued that *Felix Holt* reveals her endorsement of Comte's value system. See especially W.F.T. Myers, "Politics and Personality in *Felix Holt*" and Fred C. Thomson, "Politics and Society in *Felix Holt*." Frank E. Manual provides an excellent discussion of Comte's perspective on industrialism in *The Prophets of Paris* (288, 313). Eliot clearly dif-

fered from Comte in her appreciation of the intrinsic value of work and in her concern over the dehumanizing effects of industrial labor. Her remarks about the English proletariat in "The Natural History of German Life" (*Essays* 266–99) demonstrate one of the ways that her commitment to determinism qualified her response to Comte. Eliot's differences with Comte over social hierarchy are evident in her famous exchange with Frederic Harrison in July 1866. Harrison wrote suggesting a plot for a new novel in which the hero would be a capitalist, "a transformed French nobleman with just the best sentiments of feudalism surviving and none of its vices," who would submit voluntarily to the "moral ascendancy" displayed by a "man of the new world with complete scientific and moral cultivation" (*GEL* 4:287–88). Eliot, in response, declined to write any novel that lapsed "from the picture to the diagram," and she pointed out the fundamental difference between a Utopian vision like the one described in Comte's *System of Positive Polity* and the kind of realistic fiction she wished to write (*GEL* 2:300–301). James F. Scott, in "George Eliot, Positivism, and the Social Vision of *Middlemarch*," argues that *Middlemarch* reflects Eliot's first response to Comte's *System of Positive Polity*, but he misrepresents the chronology of Eliot's reading of Comte.

15. Mrs. Transome's adultery can be compared with Tito's, which serves to keep the "fountains of kindness" open. See chapter 6 for a fuller discussion of Tito's relation to Tessa.

16. Eliot's position on marriage cannot be properly called antifeminist: Mary Wollstonecraft, J. S. Mill, and most other Victorian feminists saw marriage as a fundamental social institution, though one which required legal reform. See Olive Banks, *Faces of Feminism*, 48–59.

17. John Ruskin in "On Queen's Gardens" consigns women to the home and garden but makes them "answerable" for the suffering, injustice, and guilt in "the world outside their gates." See E. T. Cook and Alexander Wedderburn, eds., *The Works of John Ruskin* (London: George Allen, 1903), vol. 18, 139. See also Kate Millet's influential reading of this essay in *Sexual Politics* (88–108).

18. Several critics have emphasized Eliot's conservativism, but such readings often fail to explain why Eliot protrays Mr. Transome and his son as so biologically and morally unfit. See, for example, Fred C. Thomson, "Politics and Society in *Felix Holt*." Thomson's analysis of the conservative politics of the novel is typical of the arguments of most critics of *Felix Holt*. Peter Coveney, by contrast, in his excellent introduction to the Penguin edition of *Felix Holt* (7–65), describes Eliot's view of Radicalism as "severe."

19. Most critics have read this reference to the mindless destruction of a priceless tradition as an expression of Eliot's conservative criticism of English Radicalism and her fear of the destructive effects of legislation which would extend working-class power and values. Raymond Williams's treatment of Eliot's "conservative" politics in *Culture and Society* (102–9) and *The Country and the City* (174–80) has been especially influential. Eliot's essay on "Servants' Logic" (*Essays* 391–96) reveals her social snobbery at its worst.

20. On Eliot's use of evolutionary metaphors in characterizing the Tory Establishment in Treby Magna, see K. M. Newton, "George Eliot, George Henry Lewes, and Darwinism." Sally Shuttleworth makes an important point by not-

ing that these descriptions suggesting degeneracy indicate that political reform is needless (*George Eliot* 125–26).

21. There remains, of course, a certain conservatism in Eliot's stance on suffrage and political activism, for both women and men, which finds expression here. This is not incompatible, though, with the "emancipationist" stance Gerda Lerner has described as typical of one group of feminists in *The Majority Finds Its Past* (48–62).

22. Barbara Bodichon, "Objections to the Enfranchisement of Women Considered" 4–5.

23. Michael Woolf, in particular, discusses this issue thoughtfully in "The Uses of Context."

24. See Catharine Gallagher's useful discussion of Eliot's reading of J. S. Mill's *Political Economy* in *The Industrial Reformation of English Fiction* (229–37).

25. Many readers see Esther and Felix's marriage as irrelevant to an understanding of the politics of public life in *Felix Holt*. While W.F.T. Myers, by contrast, recognizes marriage as the crux of the novel, he argues that Eliot reveals her political and sexual conservativism in her description of this marriage. Myers, however, assumes that women face only two alternatives: they may choose either to rebel or to submit to their husbands in marriage ("Politics" 5–33). The evolutionary point of view that Eliot took on social change, as well as her feminism, allowed her to imagine more than these two alternatives. In fact, Spencer wrestled with the paradigms that Myers uncritically adopts and avoided discussing marriage in *The Principles of Sociology* until he could defend his assumption that the traditional patriarchal marriage was the final form of this institution and that it was exempt from the dynamics of social evolution described in this work.

26. See Herbert Spencer, *The Principles of Ethics* 2:160–65. Hereafter cited as *Ethics*.

27. On other feminist arguments, see, for example, Carol Bauer and Lawrence Ritt, eds., *Free and Ennobled* 187–95, 206–35.

28. Florence Sandler also discusses Esther's testimony at the trial as an expression of her heroism in "The Unity of *Felix Holt*."

29. Eliot's letters indicate that the legal complications of her plot may have forced her to soften her treatment of Sir Maximus, because he was the only character with enough political power to intervene in the workings of justice and save Felix from deportation (*GEL* 4:257–58).

Chapter 8

1. Herbert Spencer's "Psychology of the Sexes" first appeared in England in *Contemporary Review* in 1872 and was published a few months later in America. I cite from the latter because it is more readily available: See *Popular Science Monthly* 4 (Nov. 1873): 30–38 (hereafter cited as "Psychology"). This essay was later reprinted in Spencer's *Study of Sociology*, published in England in November 1873 and a few months later in America. I cite from the first American edition *Study of Sociology* (hereafter *Study*). Lorna Duffin discusses Spencer's sex-

ism generally but does not analyze the historical development of his ideas in "Prisoners of Progress." Janet Sayers also notes some of Spencer's editorial changes in *Biological Politics* (32–38).

2. Charles Darwin, *The Descent of Man* (2:316–17). (Hereafter *Descent*). Gillian Beer cites this passage in "Beyond Determinism" (83).

3. For an analysis of how Darwin "fell into the trap of progressive developmentalism," see Gretna Jones, *Social Darwinism and English Thought* 17.

4. Charles Darwin, *The Expression of the Emotions in Man and Animals* (1872).

5. Gillian Beer, *Darwin's Plots* 149–50. Beer also cites Eliot's 1874 letter (*GEL* 6:81) but argues that the facetious style indicates that Eliot was not serious in making this criticism.

6. For a general discussion of Spencer's influence on *Middlemarch*, see Richard Ellmann, "Dorothea's Two Husbands" and N. N. Feltes, "George Eliot's Pier-Glass." For an interesting discussion of scientific metaphors in *Middlemarch*, see Hilda M. Hulme, "*Middlemarch* as Science-Fiction." Sally Shuttleworth, however, provides a much more comprehensive and insightful discussion of the subject in *George Eliot and Nineteenth-Century Science* (142–74).

7. N. N. Feltes, "George Eliot's Pier-Glass" 403.

8. Sally Shuttleworth in *George Eliot* and Gillian Beer in *Darwin's Plots* reach similar conclusions about the importance of science in Eliot's fiction. Other important studies include J. Hillis Miller, "Optic and Semiotic in *Middlemarch*"; George Levine, "George Eliot's Hypothesis of Reality"; and Michael York Mason, "*Middlemarch* and Science."

9. On Eliot and history, see J. Hillis Miller, "Narrative and History"; Brian Swann, "*Middlemarch*" and "*Middlemarch* and Myth"; and Michael York Mason, "*Middlemarch* and History." Sandra M. Gilbert and Susan Gubar also discuss Casaubon's ethnocentric view of culture in relation to his misogyny (*Madwoman* 502–8). Eliot had similar reservations about Comte's use of history. On this subject see Martha Vogeler, "George Eliot and the Positivists" and U. C. Knoepflmacher, *Religious Humanism and the Victorian Novel* 3–115.

10. Herbert Spencer, *Descriptive Sociology* (1873–1881). Hereafter *Descriptive*.

11. William Myers, *The Teaching of George Eliot* 14.

12. Most commentators have read this reference to the "inflexible" relation of marriage as revealing an essential conservativism which would confine women to marriage and deny the fulfillment of their less traditional ambitions. Lee Edwards's "Women, Energy, and *Middlemarch*" is perhaps the best known example. Edwards restates this argument in her excellent study *Psyche as Hero*. See also Kathleen Blake, "*Middlemarch* and the Woman Question." Alan Mintz presents an argument that conspicuously neglects the issue of vocation as it relates to women, in *George Eliot and the Novel of Vocation*. Like Spencer, Mintz implies that women's vocational quest is solved as soon as she accepts her reproductive role. For a corrective, see Susan M. Greenstein, "The Question of Vocation."

13. Sally Shuttleworth analyzes this generalizing aspect of language elegantly in *George Eliot and Nineteenth-Century Science* (142–49).

14. See Eric Trudgill's discussion of the "girl of the period" in *Madonnas and Magdalens* (179–85, 268–71) and Bonnie Zimmerman's "Gwendolen Harleth

and 'The Girl of the Period.' " See also Elaine Showalter's discussion of generational differences in *A Literature of Their Own* (182–239).

15. See especially Jenni Calder, *Women and Marriage in Victorian Fiction* 140–
41, 153; and Lee Edwards, "Women, Energy, and *Middlemarch*." See also Kathleen Blake, "*Middlemarch* and the Woman Question" 306; and Sandra M.
Gilbert and Susan Gubar, *The Madwoman in the Attic* 514–16.

16. See, for example, *GEL* 4:162.

17. In "Radiant as a Diamond," Bonnie Zimmerman demonstrates the association of jewels with female sexuality. They also symbolize, I would argue, the social and economic privilege that has allowed Dorothea and Celia to receive an
education which is wider and less provincial than that of Rosamond Vincy and
Mary Garth.

18. See Carol Christ, "Aggression and Providential Death in George Eliot's
Fiction" and Sandra M. Gilbert and Susan Gubar, *The Madwoman in the Attic*
513. For another reading of the parallels between Dorothea and Lydgate, see
Alexander Welsh, *George Eliot and Blackmail* 230.

19. For a useful discussion of altruism and egotism in this novel, see John
Halperin, *Egoism and Self-Discovery in the Victorian Novel* 143–62.

20. Charles Darwin, like Spencer, argued at this time that well-educated
women should, for the good of the race, have more children than their less educated sisters. See Gillian Beer, "Beyond Determinism" 85 and Suzanne
Graver, *George Eliot and Community* 175.

21. See K. M. Newton, "George Eliot, George Henry Lewes, and Darwinism"
and Suzanne Graver, *George Eliot and Community* 62, 152–53.

22. George Henry Lewes, *The Study of Psychology: Its Object, Scope and Method*
(1879), 71–72. See also, K. M. Newton, "George Eliot, George Henry Lewes,
and Darwinism" 287–88.

23. The association of Rosamond and Casaubon with images of the sea and
the swamp is such a critical cliché it hardly needs further rehearsing. Fred, on
the other hand, is characterized by images of the forest when Farebrother comments that he is becoming an "old stalk" and "younger growths" are pushing
him aside (557, ch. 52), when he is compared to a "sprig" by Mrs. Garth (619,
ch. 57), and, of course, when he is repeatedly associated with fox hunting,
horses, and dogs.

24. K. M. Newton cites this motto from *The Study of Psychology* ("George
Eliot" 287–88). Compare it to Comte's motto, "Love is our Principle, Order
our Basis, Progress our End" (*General* 413).

25. Herbert Spencer, *The Principles of Ethics* (1898). The most dramatic examples of Spencer's repudiation of feminism appear in the first volume of *Principles of Sociology* in a section called "Data of Sociology," pt. 3, ch. 1–12. In the
1892 edition of *Social Statics* Spencer refers his readers to *The Principles of Ethics*,
pt. 4, ch. 20, 24, first published in number form in 1891, for a clarification and
defense of his inconsistency on the Woman Question.

26. U. C. Knoepflmacher presents one of the most persuasive critical arguments about Mary's relation to her father and about the "rooted" Wordsworthian values that this family represents in "*Middlemarch*: An Avuncular
View" (80). Deborah Heller Roazen, in "*Middlemarch* and the Wordsworthian

Imagination," and Gordon S. Haight, in "George Eliot," both describe *Middlemarch* as an "anti-romance."

27. Mrs. Garth's submissiveness, of course, recalls Milton's Eve, but I would argue that Milton is a far less inhibiting presence in *Middlemarch* than Sandra M. Gilbert and Susan Gubar perceive him to be (*Madwoman* 499–535).

28. For discussions of ethical reasoning similar to Mary's, see especially Carol Gilligan, *In a Different Voice* 149–50, 159–74.

29. Lee Edwards argues, for example, in "Women, Energy, and *Middlemarch*," that Ladislaw's rejection of Rosamond's love and Dorothea's later assertion that the awful "nearness" of marriage "drinks up all our power of giving or getting any blessedness" in adulterous love (855, ch. 81) reveals Eliot's repressive view of female sexuality.

30. For further discussion of the mother's temporary power over her children, see Carol Gilligan, *In a Different Voice* 168.

31. See Sally Shuttleworth, *George Eliot and Nineteenth-Century Science* 161–74 and U. C. Knoepflmacher, "*Middlemarch*: An Avuncular View" 80. Sandra M. Gilbert and Susan Gubar take a more qualified view of Dorothea's altruism in this episode (*Madwoman* 506–32).

32. For another interpretation of this passage, see Margaret Homans, *Bearing the Word* 187–88.

33. For all citations, I have compared Herbert Spencer's first volume of the English edition of *The Principles of Sociology* (1876) with the revised first volume of *The Principles of Sociology* (1877–1896).

34. Suzanne Graver cites this note in *George Eliot and Community* (216).

35. For another view see Suzanne Graver, *George Eliot and Community* (167).

36. See Sandra M. Gilbert and Susan Gubar on this episode (*Madwoman* 513).

37. Cynthia Eagle Russett points out in *Sexual Science* (145) that Victorian anthropologists failed to notice that the "numbers of gainfully employed women were expanding by the year." This oversight compromised their conclusions about women's leisure as a sign of progress.

38. M. J. Svaglic argues in "Religion in the Novels of George Eliot" that though Mary Garth takes an anti-authoritarian position, it is not anti-Christian.

39. For a discussion of Eliot's sentimentalized use of metaphors which confuse "childish" and "child-like," see W. J. Harvey, "Idea and Image in the Novels of George Eliot."

Chapter 9

1. Herbert Spencer, *Descriptive Sociology* (1873–1881).

2. For examples of Herbert Spencer's ahistorical use of Greek and Egyptian culture see especially, *Sociology* (1877–1896) 1:147–303, 321. Unless otherwise noted, I refer the reader to this edition because it includes the additional chapters on marriage. Apart from this addition, there are no substantial differences between the 1876 and the 1877–1896 editions.

3. For an interesting discussion of Darwin's treatment of degeneration, see Gillian Beer, *Darwin's Plots* 123–48.

4. For more on the context for the theme of nationhood in *Daniel Deronda*, see the discussions of Jewish culture and theories of race in Gillian Beer, *Darwin's Plots* (202–6); William Baker, "George Eliot's Readings in Nineteenth-Century Jewish Historians"; and Avrom Fleishman, *Fiction and the Ways of Knowing* (95–109). Many critics have sensed a division in *Daniel Deronda*, either between Deronda's and Gwendolen's stories, or between the Jewish and English plots. See Carole Robinson, "The Severe Angel"; Cynthia Chase, "The Decomposition of the Elephants"; William Baker, "George Eliot's Readings of Nineteenth-Century Jewish Historians"; and Barbara Hardy, *The Novels of George Eliot* 108–14.

5. Annie Besant, *Annie Besant: An Autobiography* (Madras: Theosophical Publishing, 1939), 219.

6. Mary Wilson Carpenter, *George Eliot* 135. In another context, Carpenter has argued convincingly that the "narrative structure" in *Daniel Deronda* also "functions as part of an interpretation of interpretation, for its most responsive reading depends on the sophisticated hermeneutical awareness created by contemporary controversy concerning. . . . the Book of Daniel" and the "philosophy of history" contained in it (Carpenter, "Apocalypse" 56).

7. William Baker, "George Eliot's Readings" 263; Mary Wilson Carpenter, "The Apocalypse of the Old Testament" 63–64; Alexander Welsh, *George Eliot and Blackmail* 308–14.

8. Other correspondence describing Eliot's position on the Contagious Diseases Acts may have been censored or destroyed since the issue was deeply shocking for most men and women of the time. Nina Auerbach also discusses Eliot's sympathies for prostitutes in "The Rise of the Fallen Woman."

9. On Eliot's "spiritual daughters," see Gordon S. Haight, *George Eliot* 451–52. I am grateful to Bonnie Zimmerman for allowing me to read her unpublished essay on Eliot's relationship with Edith Simcox.

10. Compare Eliot's allusion to *The Winter's Tale*, in *GEL* 4:364 with Herbert Spencer's reference in *First Principles* 92.

11. For other discussions of Gwendolen's dread, see Barbara Hardy, *The Novels of George Eliot* 130 and Gillian Beer, *Darwin's Plots* 221–22.

12. Gillian Beer argues that Eliot's critique of "sexual selection" is part of the "polemic" of *Daniel Deronda* (*Darwin's Plots* 182).

13. Modern readers have interpreted Eliot's characterization of Gwendolen as revealing her rejection of the educational goals of the "new women" of the 1870s. See Bonnie Zimmerman, "Gwendolen Harleth and 'The Girl of the Period'" and Jennie Calder, *Women and Marriage in Victorian Fiction* 158. But, again, Eliot's effort to counter Spencer's increasingly more influential theories of education shapes her description of Gwendolen's life in the schoolroom and afterwards. Take, for example, her observation that Gwendolen's "quick mind had taken readily that strong starch of unexplained rules and disconnected facts which saves ignorance from any painful sense of limpness" (69, ch. 4).

14. Shirley Frank Levenson discusses the role of art in characterizing Gwendolen's society in "The Use of Music in *Daniel Deronda*." Brian Swann only finds "natural genius" in the men in this novel, so he sees Gwendolen's aspirations as a mark of her moral stupidity and inadequately assesses the role of the Prin-

cess ("George Eliot and the Play"). Spencer and Darwin did not agree about the precise function of women's musical talents in sexual selection. See Spencer's *Autobiography* 2:279 for a discussion of his disagreements with Darwin.

15. For other discussions of Darwin's influence on this novel, see U.C. Knoepflmacher, *Religious Humanism in the Victorian Novel* 125–47; Robert Preyer, "Beyond the Liberal Imagination"; and Gillian Beer, *Darwin's Plots* 194.

16. Most readers see Mr. Gascoigne as a "kindly man"; see, for example, John P. Kearney, "Time and Beauty in *Daniel Deronda*" 290. In a later volume of *The Principles of Sociology*, Spencer described the doubly "conservative" force of ecclesiastical institutions as follows: "In several ways they maintain and strengthen social bonds, and so conserve the social aggregate; and they do this in large measure by conserving beliefs, sentiments, and usages which evolved during earlier stages of the society" (*Sociology* 5: 102–3).

17. Eliot's metaphors that link sailing and sexuality, suggest a parallel between Lydia and the prostitutes harassed by the Contagious Diseases Acts, for this legislation was originally defended as a means to keep the British navy strong by protecting its sailors on leave in home ports from contracting venereal diseases. See Judith R. Walkowitz, *Prostitution and Victorian Society* 75.

18. See Gillian Beer's interesting discussion of the role of inheritance through the mother (*Darwin's Plots* 220–35). I was fortunate to hear Gillian Beer present "Fear and Potency in *Daniel Deronda*" at the George Eliot Centennial Conference: The Artist in a Changing Society (Rutgers University, New Brunswick, N.J., Nov 21–23, 1980). She has since developed this analysis more fully in *Darwin's Plots* (21–35, 228–29).

19. For discussions of Eliot's reading of relevant contemporary anthropology and sociology, see Gillian Beer, *Darwin's Plots* 181–209, 221–35; and Alexander Welsh, *George Eliot and Blackmail* 295–96.

20. I contend that this famous passage comparing Gwendolen to a "delicate vessel" is heavily ironic. For an alternate reading, see Nina Auerbach, "Artists and Mothers."

21. I cite from the first edition of the complete two-volume set of Spencer's *The Principles of Ethics* (1898), 2: 42; this section first appeared in print in 1891.

22. For the reader's convenience, I cite from the 1890 edition of Spencer's *The Principles of Psychology* 2:570; this edition includes only minor corrections of the 1870–1872 edition of this text. Numbers for this second volume appeared in print beginning in March 1871.

23. Alexander Welsh makes a similar argument about Deronda's guilt in *George Eliot and Blackmail* (299). For other views, see Carole Robinson, "The Severe Angel" and Jerome B. Schneewind, "Moral Problems and Moral Philosophy in the Victorian Period."

24. Christopher Kent, "Image and Reality" 109. Kent argues that Victorians generally regarded life behind the scenes in the theater as filled with a "moral infection" that few young women could escape. Deronda, at first, seems to make this assumption about Mirah.

25. Eliot's endorsement of Emily Davies's plan for preparing women to take the same university examinations as men is a significant sign of Eliot's commitment to higher education for women, especially in light of her criticism of the

competitive "cram" system that defeats Deronda, a man of "feminine" sensitiveness and altruistic generosity.

26. Diana Postlethwaite's discussion of the influence of Spinoza on Eliot, Spencer, and Lewes is interesting in this regard. See also her discussion of Eliot's emphasis on "Unity" and its significance for the conclusion of *Daniel Deronda* (*Making It Whole* 164–231).

27. Describing Eliot's girlhood in Coventry, John W. Cross suggests the parallel between Eliot and the Princess by alluding to this speech from *Daniel Deronda* (*George Eliot's Life* 17). Nina Auerbach also comments on Eliot's personal investments in her characterization of the Princess but does not place them in the context of evolutionary thought ("Artists and Mothers").

28. For other discussions of this conflict between artistic creation and reproduction, see Sandra M. Gilbert and Susan Gubar, *The Madwoman in the Attic* 455; Shirley Frank Levenson, "The Use of Music in *Daniel Deronda*" 326; and Nina Auerbach, "Artists and Mothers."

29. Spencer ignored the negative effects of both "domestic slavery" and actual slavery. See, for example, his comments in *Sociology* 3:456.

30. It is especially difficult, I think, for readers who live in an age and culture where birth control is more easily available to appreciate Eliot's reasons for making the Princess a mother as well as an artist, especially in light of the fact that Eliot herself practiced birth control. It is important to see that in dramatizing the Princess's maternity and its impact on her life, Eliot refuses to recommend what many late nineteenth-century feminists were urging upon women as the most "moral" solution to the problems posed by their fertility; that is, to abstain from sex altogether. See, for example, Annie Besant, *Annie Besant: An Autobiography* 242–43, for her position on birth control after 1890.

31. It has not been sufficiently noted that the Princess feels guilty because she secretly contradicts her father's wishes. This aspect of her guilt is overlooked, for example, by Sandra M. Gilbert and Susan Gubar, *The Madwoman in the Attic* 455; Shirley Frank Levenson, "The Use of Music in *Daniel Deronda*" 326; and Nina Auerbach, "Artists and Mothers."

32. Gillian Beer argues that Eliot is more Darwinian in her assessment of race and social change, but this may be because Spencer's inconsistencies on the issue of race prevent modern readers from taking his analysis seriously. In *The Principles of Ethics*, for example, Spencer expresses his disapproval of imperialism by commenting on the "unscrupulous greed of conquest cloaked by the pretense of spreading the blessing of British rule and British religion" (1:217). Spencer also comments about the "lesser development" of sympathy in the Negro, "who jeers at a liberated companion because he has no master to take care of him" (2:28).

33. Likewise, Mirah's answers to the Meyricks' questions about Jewish traditions emphasize her affectionate attachment, which precludes intellectual criticism of its misogyny.

34. See Jenni Calder, *Women and Marriage in Victorian Fiction* 158; Nina Auerbach, "Artists and Mothers"; and Brian Swann, "George Eliot and the Play."

35. Barbara Hardy (*Novels* 151–54), discusses the open-ended quality of *Daniel Deronda* in terms of epic and tragic modes. See also K. M. Newton, "George Eliot, George Henry Lewes, and Darwinism."

36. Perhaps the most interesting and influential analyses of Eliot's manipulation of the plot are Carol Christ's "Aggression and Providential Death in George Eliot's Fiction" and Cynthia Chase's "The Decomposition of the Elephants."

Epilogue

1. P. Abrams, *The Origins of British Sociology* 67.
2. John W. Burrow, *Evolution and Society* 216.
3. While I discuss Spencer's comments in *The Principles of Ethics* 1:IV in particular, his discussion of sympathy throughout this text reveals significant changes in his views.

Bibliography

Primary Sources

Bachofen, J. J. *Myth, Religion, and Mother Right*. Trans. Ralph Manheim. Princeton: Princeton Univ. Press, 1967.

Bodichon, Barbara. "Objections to the Enfranchisement of Women Considered." London: Warrington Crescent, 1866.

Comte, Auguste. *A General View of Positivism*. Trans. John Henry Bridges. London: Trübner, 1865. Rpt. Dubuque, Iowa: Brown Reprints, 1971.

————. *Positivist Philosophy*. Trans. Harriet Martineau. New York: Blanchard, 1858.

————. *System of Positive Polity, or Treatise on Sociology Instituting the Religion of Humanity*. Trans. John Henry Bridges, et al. 4 vols. (n.p.) 1875–1877. Rpt. New York: Burt Franklin, 1973.

Cross, John W. *George Eliot's Life as Related in Her Letters and Journals*. 2 vols. New York: Sproul, 1899.

Darwin, Charles. *The Descent of Man and Selection in Relation to Sex*. 2 vols. London: John Murray, 1871.

————. *The Expression of the Emotions in Man and Animals*. London: John Murray, 1872.

————. *On the Origin of Species by Means of Natural Selection, or Preservation of Favoured Races in the Struggle for Life*. London: John Murray, 1859.

Eliot, George. *Adam Bede*. Ed. Stephen Gill. Harmondsworth: Penguin Books, 1980.

————. "The Art of the Ancients." *The Leader* 6 (17 March 1855): 257–58. *English Literary Periodicals*, University Microfilms, Reel 530.

————. "Belles Lettres and Art." *Westminster Review* 66 (1856): 602–9.

————. *Daniel Deronda*. Ed. Barbara Hardy. Harmondsworth: Penguin Books, 1967.

————. *The Essays of George Eliot*. Ed. Thomas Pinney. New York: Columbia Univ. Press, 1963.

————. *Felix Holt*. Ed. Peter Coveney. Harmondsworth: Penguin Books, 1972.

————. *George Eliot: A Writer's Notebook, 1854–1879*. Ed. Joseph Weisenfarth. Charlottesville: Univ. of Virginia Press, 1981.

————. *George Eliot Letters*. Ed. Gordon S. Haight. 9 vols. New Haven: Yale Univ. Press, 1954–1978.

————. "Love in the Drama." *The Leader* 6 (25 August 1855): 820–21. *English Literary Periodicals*, University Microfilms, Reel 534.

————. *Middlemarch*. Ed. W. J. Harvey. Harmondsworth: Penguin Books, 1965.

————. *The Mill on the Floss*. Ed. A. S. Bryatt. Harmondsworth: Penguin Books, 1979.

————. *Romola*. Ed. Andrew Sanders. Harmondsworth: Penguin Books, 1980.

————. *Scenes of Clerical Life*. Ed. David Lodge. Harmondsworth: Penguin Books, 1973.

————. *Silas Marner*. Ed. Q. D. Leavis. Harmondsworth: Penguin Books, 1967.

Feuerbach, Ludwig. *The Essence of Christianity*. Trans. George Eliot. London (n.p.), 1854. Rpt. New York: Harper and Row, Torchbooks, 1957.

Lewes, George Henry. *The Study of Psychology: Its Object, Scope, and Method*. London (n.p.), 1879.

Lubbock, John. *The Origin of Civilization and the Primitive Condition*. London: Longmans, 1870.

————. *Pre-historic Times, as Illustrated by Ancient Remains, with the Manners and Customs of Modern Savages*. London: Williams and Norgate, 1865.

Maine, Sir Henry James Summer. *Ancient Law: Its Connection to the Early History of Society and Its Relation to Modern Ideas*. London: Murray, 1870.

————. *Early History of Institutions*. London: Murray, 1875.

McLennan, John Ferguson. *The Patriarchal Theory*. London: Macmillan, 1885.

Mill, J. S. *Auguste Comte and Positivism*. London: Trübner, 1865. Rpt. Ann Arbor: Univ. of Michigan Press, 1961.

————. *The Subjection of Women*. London: Longmans, 1869. Rpt. Cambridge: Massachusetts Institute of Technology Press, 1970.

Paris, Bernard J. "George Eliot's Unpublished Poetry." *Studies in Philology* 56 (1959): 539–58.

Spencer, Herbert. "The Art of Education." *North British Review* (Feb.–Aug. 1854): 137–71.

————. *An Autobiography*. 2 vols. London: Williams and Norgate, 1904.

————. *Descriptive Sociology, or Groups of Sociological Facts, Classified and Arranged by Herbert Spencer*. New York: Appleton, 1873–1881.

————. "The Developmental Hypothesis." Herbert Spencer, *Essays: Scientific, Political, and Speculative*. 3 vols. New York: Appleton, 1910. 1:1–7.

————. *Education: Intellectual, Moral, and Physical*. New York: Appleton, 1909.

————. *Essays: Moral, Political and Aesthetic*. New York: Appleton, 1865.

————. *Essays: Scientific, Political, and Speculative*. 3 vols. New York: Appleton, 1910.

————. *First Principles*. New York: Appleton, 1862.

————. "The Genesis of Science." Herbert Spencer, *Essays: Scientific, Political, and Speculative*. New York: Appleton, 1910. 2:1–73.

————. "The Moral Discipline of Children." *British Quarterly Review* (April 1858–July 1859): 364–90.

————. "Personal Beauty." Herbert Spencer, *Essays: Moral, Political and Aesthetic*. New York: Appleton, 1865. 149–62.

————. "Physical Training." *British Quarterly Review* (April 1859): 362–97.

————. *The Principles of Biology*. London: Williams and Norgate, 1864–1867.

————. *The Principles of Ethics*. 2 vols. New York: Appleton, 1898.

————. *The Principles of Psychology*. London: Longmans, 1855.

————. *The Principles of Psychology*. 2 vols. London: Williams and Norgate, 1870–1872.

————. *The Principles of Psychology*. 2 vols. New York: Appleton, 1890.

————. *The Principles of Sociology*. London: Williams and Norgate, 1876.

————. *The Principles of Sociology*. 3 vol. in 5. London: Williams and Norgate, 1877–1896.

————. *The Principles of Sociology*. New York: Appleton, 1885.

————. "Progress: Its Law and Cause." Herbert Spencer, *Essays: Scientific, Political, and Speculative*. New York: Appleton, 1910. 1: 8–62.

————. "Psychology of the Sexes." *Popular Science Monthly* 4 (1873): 30–38.

————. *Social Statics*. London: Chapman, 1851.

————. *Social Statics: Abridged and Revised, with The Man Versus the State*. New York: Appleton, 1892.

————. *The Study of Sociology*. New York: Appleton, 1874.

————. "A Theory of Population Deduced from the General Law of Animal Fertility." *Westminster Review* 62 (1852): 468–501.

————. *The Synthetic Philosophy of Herbert Spencer*. 12 vols. London: Williams and Norgate, 1904. Rpt. Osnabrück: Otto Zeller, 1966.

————. "What Knowledge is of Most Worth." *Westminster Review* 72 (July 1859): 1–41.

Wollstonecraft, Mary. *A Vindication of the Rights of Woman*. Rpt. ed. Carol H. Poston. New York: Norton, 1975.

Secondary Sources

Abrams, P. *The Origins of British Sociology, 1834–1914*. Chicago: Univ. of Chicago Press, 1968.

Auerbach, Nina. "Artists and Mothers: A False Alliance." *Women and Literature* 6 (1978): 3–15.

————. "The Power of Hunger: Demonism and Maggie Tulliver." *Nineteenth-Century Fiction* 30(1975): 150–71.

————. "The Rise of the Fallen Woman." *Nineteenth-Century Fiction* 35(1980): 29–52.

————. *Woman and the Demon: The Life of a Victorian Myth*. Cambridge: Harvard Univ. Press, 1982.

Auster, Henry. *Local Habitations: Regionalism in the Early Novels of George Eliot*. Cambridge: Harvard Univ. Press, 1970.

Baker, William. *The George Eliot–George Henry Lewes Library: An Annotated Catalogue of Their Books at Dr. William's Library, London*. New York: Garland, 1977.

————. "George Eliot's Readings in Nineteenth-Century Jewish Historians: A Note on the Background of *Daniel Deronda*." *Victorian Studies* 15 (1972): 463–74.

————. *Some George Eliot Notebooks: An Edition of the Carl H. Pforzheimer Library's George Eliot Holograph Notebooks*. Salzburg: Salzburg Univ. Press, 1976.

Bamber, Linda. "Self-Defeating Politics in George Eliot's *Felix Holt*." *Victorian Studies* 18 (1975): 419–35.

Banks, J. A. and Olive Banks. *Feminism and Family Planning in Victorian England*. New York: Schocken Books, 1964.

Banks, Olive. *Becoming a Feminist: The Social Origins of First Wave Feminism*. Athens: University of Georgia Press, 1986.

————. *Faces of Feminism: A Study of Feminism as a Social Movement*. New York: St. Martins Press, 1981.

Bartkowski, Frances. "Epistemic Drift in Foucault." In Irene Diamond and Lee

Quinby, eds. *Feminism and Foucault: Reflections on Resistance*. Boston: Northeast University Press, 1988. 43–58.

Basch, François. *Relative Creatures: Victorian Women in Society and the Novel*. Trans. Anthony Rudolf. New York: Schocken Books, 1974.

Bauer, Carol and Lawrence Ritt, eds. *Free and Ennobled: Source Readings in the Development of Victorian Feminism*. New York: Pergamon Press, 1979.

Beaty, Jerome. *"Middlemarch" from Notebook to Novel: A Study of George Eliot's Creative Method*. Illinois Studies in Language and Literature, Vol. 47. Urbana: Univ. of Illinois Press, 1960.

Beer, Gillian. "Beyond Determinism: George Eliot and Virginia Woolf." In Mary Jacobus, ed. *Women Writers and Writing about Women*. New York: Barnes and Noble, 1979. 80–99.

————. *Darwin's Plots: Evolutionary Narrative in Darwin, George Eliot, and Nineteenth-Century Fiction*. London: Routledge and Kegan Paul, 1983.

————. "Fear and Potency in *Daniel Deronda*." George Eliot Centennial Conference: The Artist in a Changing Society. Rutgers University, New Brunswick, N.J., 22 Nov. 1980.

Bellringer, A. W. "Education in *The Mill on the Floss*." *Review of English Literature* 6 (1966): 52–61.

Blake, Kathleen. "*Middlemarch* and the Woman Question." *Nineteenth-Century Fiction* 37 (1976): 285–312.

Bonaparte, Felicia. *The Triptych and the Cross: The Central Myths of George Eliot's Poetic Imagination*. New York: New York Univ. Press, 1979.

————. *Will and Destiny: Morality and Tragedy in George Eliot's Novels*. New York: New York Univ. Press, 1975.

Bowler, Peter J. "The Changing Meaning of Evolution." *Journal of the History of Ideas* 36 (1975): 95–114.

————. *Evolution: The History of an Idea*. Berkeley: Univ. of California Press, 1984.

————. "Herbert Spencer and 'Evolution': An Additional Note." *Journal of the History of Ideas* 36 (1975): 367.

Buckley, Jerome, ed. *The Worlds of Victorian Fiction*. Cambridge: Harvard Univ. Press, 1975.

Bullen, J. B. "George Eliot's *Romola* as Positivist Allegory." *Review of English Studies* 26 (1975): 425–35.

Burrow, John W. "Evolution and Anthropology in the 1860s: The Anthropological Society of London, 1863–71." *Victorian Studies* 7 (1963): 137–54.

————. *Evolution and Society: A Study in Victorian Social Theory*. Cambridge: At the University Press, 1966.

Burstyn, Joan N. *Victorian Education and the Ideal of Womanhood*. Totowa, N.J.: Barnes and Noble, 1980.

Calder, Jenni. *Women and Marriage in Victorian Fiction*. New York: Oxford Univ. Press, 1976.

Carneiro, Robert L. "Structure, Function, and Equilibrium in the Evolutionism of Herbert Spencer." *Journal of Anthropological Research* 29 (1968): 77–95.

Carpenter, Mary Wilson. "The Apocalypse of the Old Testament: *Daniel Deronda* and the Interpretation of Interpretation." *PMLA* 99 (1984): 56–71.

————. *George Eliot and the Landscape of Time: Narrative Form and Protestant Apocalyptic History*. Chapel Hill: Univ. of North Carolina Press, 1986.

Carroll, David R. *"Felix Holt*: Society as Protagonist." In George R. Creeger, ed. *George Eliot: A Collection of Critical Essays*. Englewood Cliffs: Prentice Hall, 1970. 124–40.

————. *"Silas Marner*: Reversing the Oracles of Religion." In Eric Rothstein and Thomas K. Dunseath, eds. *Literary Monographs*. Madison: Univ. of Wisconsin Press, 1967. 1:167–200.

————, ed. *George Eliot: The Critical Heritage*. New York: Barnes and Noble, 1971.

Chase, Cynthia. "The Decomposition of the Elephants: Double-Reading *Daniel Deronda*." *PMLA* 93 (1978): 215–27.

Chodorow, Nancy. *The Reproduction of Mothering: Psychoanalysis and the Sociology of Gender*. Berkeley: Univ. of California Press, 1978.

Christ, Carol. "Aggression and Providential Death in George Eliot's Fiction." *Novel* 9 (1976): 130–40.

Clayton, Jay. "Visionary Power and Narrative Form." *ELH* (1979): 645–72.

Colby, Robert. *Fiction with a Purpose: Major and Minor Nineteenth-Century Novels*. Bloomington: Indiana Univ. Press, 1967.

Collins, K. K. "George Henry Lewes Revisited: George Eliot and the Moral Sense." *Victorian Studies* 21 (1978): 464–83.

————. "Questions of Method: Some Unpublished Late Essays." *Nineteenth-Century Fiction* 35 (1980): 385–405.

Conway, Richard. *"Silas Marner* and *Felix Holt*: From Fairy Tale to Feminism." *Studies in the Novel* 10 (1978): 295–304.

Craig, David. "Fiction and the Rising Industrial Classes." *Essays in Criticism* 17 (1967): 64–73.

Creeger, George R. "An Interpretation of *Adam Bede*." *ELH* 23 (1966): 218–38.

David, Deirdre. *Intellectual Women and Victorian Patriarchy: Harriet Martineau, Elizabeth Barrett Browning, George Eliot*. Ithaca: Cornell Univ. Press, 1987.

Deutch, Helene. *The Psychology of Women: A Psychoanalytical Interpretation*. 2 vols. New York: Grune and Stratton, 1944.

Dijkstra, Bram. *Idols of Perversity: Fantasies of Feminine Evil in Fin-de-Siècle Culture*. New York: Oxford Univ. Press, 1986.

Dinnerstein, Dorothy. *The Mermaid and the Minotaur: Sexual Arrangements and Human Malaise*. New York: Harper and Row, 1976.

Di Salvo, Jackie. "Blake Encountering Milton: Politics and the Family in *Paradise Lost* and *The Four Zoas*." In Anthony Wittreich, ed. *Milton and the Line of Vision*. Madison: Univ. of Wisconsin Press, 1975. 143–84.

Duffin, Lorna. "Prisoners of Progress: Women and Evolution." In Lorna Duffin and Sara Delamont, *The Nineteenth-Century Woman: Her Culture and Physical World*. New York: Barnes and Noble, 1978. 57–91.

Edwards, Lee. *Psyche as Hero: Female Heroism and Fictional Form*. Middletown, Conn.: Wesleyan Press, 1984.

————. "Women, Energy, and *Middlemarch*." *Massachusetts Review* 13 (1972): 223–38.

Edwards, Michael. "George Eliot and Negative Form." *Critical Quarterly* (1975): 171–79.

Eisen, S. "Herbert Spencer and the Spectre of Comte." *Journal of British Studies* 7 (1967): 48–67.

Eisley, Loren. *Darwin's Century: Evolution and the Men Who Discovered It*. Garden City: Anchor Books, 1961.

Ellis, Katherine. "*Paradise Lost*: The Limits of Domesticity in the Nineteenth-Century Novel." *Feminist Studies* 2 (1975): 55–63.

Ellmann, Richard. "Dorothea's Two Husbands." In George Eliot, *Middlemarch*. Ed. Bert G. Hornback. New York: Norton, 1977. 750–65.

Emery, Laura Comer. *George Eliot's Creative Conflict: The Other Side of Silence*. Berkeley: Univ. of California Press, 1976.

Ermarth, Elizabeth. "Incarnations: George Eliot's Conception of 'Undeviating Law.' " *Nineteenth-Century Fiction* 29 (1974): 273–86.

———. "Maggie Tulliver's Long Suicide." *Studies in English Literature, 1500–1900* 14 (1974): 587–601.

———. *Realism and Consensus in the English Novel*. Princeton: Princeton Univ. Press, 1984.

Fee, Elizabeth. "The Sexual Politics of Victorian Social Anthropology." In Mary S. Hartman and Lois Banner, eds. *Clio's Consciousness Raised: New Perspectives on the History of Women*. New York: Harper and Row, Torchbooks, 1974. 86–102.

Feltes, N. N. "Community and the Limits of Liability in Two Mid-Victorian Novels." *Victorian Studies* 17 (1974): 355–69.

———. "George Eliot's 'Pier-Glass': The Development of a Metaphor." *Modern Philology* 67 (1969): 69–71.

Fernando, Lloyd. *"New Women" in the Late Victorian Novel*. University Park: Penn State Univ. Press, 1977.

Fisch, Harold. "Daniel Deronda or Gwendolen Harleth." *Nineteenth-Century Fiction* 19 (1965): 345–56.

Fleishman, Avrom. *The English Historical Novel: Walter Scott to Virginia Woolf*. Baltimore: Johns Hopkins Press, 1971.

———. *Fiction and the Ways of Knowing: Essays on British Novels*. Austin: Univ. of Texas Press, 1978.

Foakes, R. A. "*Adam Bede* Reconsidered." *English* 12 (1959): 173–76.

Foucault, Michel. *The History of Sexuality: An Introduction*. Vol. 1. Trans. Robert Hurley. New York: Vintage, 1980.

Freeman, Derek. "The Evolutionary Theories of Charles Darwin and Herbert Spencer." *Current Anthropology* 15 (1974): 211–37.

Gallagher, Catherine. *The Industrial Reformation of English Fiction, 1832–1867: Social Discourse and Narrative Form*. Chicago: Univ. of Chicago Press, 1985.

Gandesbery, Jean Johnson. "Versions of the Mother in the Novels of Jane Austen and George Eliot." Ph.D. Diss. Univ. of California at Davis, 1976.

Gilbert, Sandra M. "Life's Empty Pack: *Silas Marner* as a Literary Daughteronomy." *Critical Inquiry* 11 (1985): 355–84.

———. "Patriarchal Poetry and Women Readers: Reflections on Milton's Bogey." *PMLA* 93 (1978): 358–82.

Gilbert, Sandra M. and Susan Gubar. *The Madwoman in the Attic: Nineteenth-Century Literature by Women*. New Haven: Yale Univ. Press, 1979.

Gilligan, Carol. *In a Different Voice: Psychological Theory and Women's Development.* Cambridge: Harvard Univ. Press, 1982.

Gilman, Sander. *Difference and Pathology: Stereotypes of Sexuality, Race, and Madness.* Ithaca: Cornell Univ. Press, 1985.

Goode, John. *"Adam Bede."* In Barbara Hardy, ed. *Critical Essays on George Eliot.* London: Routledge and Kegan Paul, 1970. 19–41.

Gordon, Linda. *Woman's Body and Woman's Right: A Social History of Birth Control in America.* Harmondsworth: Penguin, 1977.

Gould, Stephen Jay. *Ontogeny and Phylogeny.* Cambridge: Harvard Univ. Press, 1977.

Graver, Suzanne. *George Eliot and Community: A Study in Social Theory and Fictional Form.* Berkeley: Univ. of Calif. Press, 1984.

Greenstein, Susan M. "The Question of Vocation: From *Romola* to *Middlemarch*." *Nineteenth-Century Fiction* 35 (1981): 487–505.

Gregor, Ian. "The Two Worlds of *Adam Bede*." In Ian Gregor and Brian Nicholas, eds. *The Moral and the Story.* London: Farber and Farber, 1962. 13–32.

Haddakin, Lillian. *"Silas Marner."* In Barbara Hardy, ed. *Critical Essays on George Eliot.* London: Routledge and Kegan Paul, 1970. 59–77.

Hagan, John. "A Reinterpretation of *The Mill on the Floss*." *PMLA* 87 (1972): 53–63.

Haight, Gordon S. "George Eliot." In Ian Adam, ed. *This Particular Web: Essays on "Middlemarch."* Toronto: Univ. of Toronto Press, 1975. 22–42.

————. *George Eliot: A Biography.* New York: Oxford Univ. Press, 1968.

Halperin, John. *Egoism and Self-Discovery in the Victorian Novel: Studies in the Ordeal of Knowledge in the Nineteenth Century.* New York: Burt Franklin, 1974.

Harding, Sandra and Jean F. O'Barr, eds. *The Science Question in Feminism.* Ithaca: Cornell Univ. Press, 1986.

Hardy, Barbara. *"The Mill on the Floss."* In Barbara Hardy, ed. *Critical Essays on George Eliot.* New York: Barnes and Noble, 1970. 42–58.

————. *The Novels of George Eliot: A Study of Form.* New York: Oxford Univ. Press, 1959.

Harris, Marvin. *The Rise of Anthropology: A History of Theories of Culture.* New York: Harper and Row, 1968.

Harvey, W. J. *The Art of George Eliot.* London: Chatto and Windus, 1961.

Harvey, W. J. "Idea and Image in the Novels of George Eliot." In Barbara Hardy, ed. *Critical Essays on George Eliot.* London: Routledge and Kegan Paul, 1970. 151–98.

Heilman, Robert. B. "Return to Raveloe: Thirty-Five Years After." *English Journal* 46 (1957): 1–10.

Henkin, Leo J. *Darwinism in the English Novel, 1860–1910: The Impact of Evolution on Victorian Thought.* New York: Russel and Russel, 1940.

Herbert, Christopher. "Preachers and the Schemes of Nature in *Adam Bede*." *Nineteenth-Century Fiction* 29 (1975): 412–27.

Higdon, David Leon. "The Iconographic Backgrounds of *Adam Bede*, Chapter 15." *Nineteenth-Century Fiction* 27 (1972): 155–70.

Holloway, John. *The Victorian Sage: Studies in Argument*. New York: Norton, 1953.

Homans, Margaret. *Bearing the Word: Language and Female Experience in Nineteenth-Century Women's Writing*. Chicago: Univ. of Chicago Press, 1986.

———. "Eliot, Wordsworth, and the Scenes of the Sisters' Instruction." *Critical Inquiry* 8 (1981): 223–41.

Hulme, Hilda M. "*Middlemarch* as Science-Fiction: Notes on Language and Imagery." *Novel* 2 (1968): 36–45.

Hussey, Maurice. "Structure and Imagery in *Adam Bede*." *Nineteenth-Century Fiction* 10 (1955): 115–29.

Irwine, William. *Apes, Angels, and Victorians: The Story of Darwin, Huxley, and Evolution*. New York: Time Books, 1955.

Jacobus, Mary. "Men of Maxims and *The Mill on the Floss*." *Critical Inquiry* 8 (1981): 206–22.

Jeffers, Thomas L. "Myth and Morals in *The Mill on the Floss*." *Midwest Quarterly* 20 (1979): 332–46.

Jenkyns, Richard. *The Victorians and Ancient Greece*. Cambridge: Harvard Univ. Press, 1980.

Jones, Gretna. *Social Darwinism and English Thought*. Brighton, Sussex: Harvester Press, 1980.

Joseph, Gerhard. "The *Antigone* as Cultural Touchstone: Matthew Arnold, Hegel, George Eliot, Virginia Woolf, and Margaret Drabble." *PMLA* 96 (1981): 22–35.

Kaminsky, Alice. "George Eliot, George Henry Lewes, and the Novel." *PMLA* 70 (1955): 977–1013.

Kearney, John P. "Time and Beauty in *Daniel Deronda*: 'Was She Beautiful or Not Beautiful?' " *Nineteenth-Century Fiction* 26 (1971): 286–306.

Keller, Evelyn Fox. *Reflections on Gender and Science*. New Haven: Yale Univ. Press, 1985.

Kennedy, James G. *Herbert Spencer*. Boston: Twayne, 1978.

Kent, Christopher. "Image and Reality: The Actress and Society. In Martha Vicinus, ed. *The Widening Sphere: Changing Roles of Victorian Women*. Bloomington: Indiana Univ. Press, 1977. 94–116.

Kettle, Arnold. "Felix Holt, the Radical." In Barbara Hardy, ed. *Critical Essays on George Eliot*. London: Routledge and Kegan Paul, 1970. 99–115.

Knoepflmacher, U. C. *The Early Novels of George Eliot: The Limits of Realism*. Berkeley: Univ. of California Press, 1968.

———. "George Eliot, Feuerbach and the Question of Criticism." *Victorian Studies* 7 (1964): 306–9.

———. "*Middlemarch*: An Avuncular View." *Nineteenth-Century Fiction* 30 (1975): 53–81.

———. *Religious Humanism and the Victorian Novel: George Eliot, Walter Pater, and Samuel Butler*. Princeton: Princeton Univ. Press, 1965.

———. "Unveiling Men: Power and Masculinity in George Eliot's Fiction." In Janet Todd, ed. *Men by Women*. London: Holmes and Meier, 1981. 130–46.

Krieger, Murray. *The Classic Vision: The Retreat from Extremity in Modern Literature*. Baltimore: Johns Hopkins Press, 1971.

Kuhn, Thomas S. *The Structure of Scientific Revolutions*. Chicago: Univ. of Chicago Press, 1970.

Landy, Marcia. "Kinship and the Role of Women in *Paradise Lost*." *Milton Studies* 5 (1972): 3–18.

Leavis, F. R. *The Great Tradition: George Eliot, Henry James, and Joseph Conrad*. New York: Doubleday, 1954.

Lerner, Gerda. *The Majority Finds Its Past: Placing Women in History*. New York: Oxford Univ. Press, 1979.

Lerner, Laurence. *The Truthtellers: Jane Austen, George Eliot, and D. H. Lawrence*. New York: Schocken Books, 1967.

Levenson, Shirley Frank. "The Use of Music in *Daniel Deronda*." *Nineteenth-Century Fiction* 24 (1969): 317–34.

Levine, George. *An Annotated Critical Bibliography of George Eliot*. New York: St. Martin's Press, 1988.

――――. *Darwin and the Novelists: Patterns of Science in Victorian Fiction*. Cambridge: Harvard Univ. Press, 1988.

――――. "Determinism and Responsibility in the Novels of George Eliot." *PMLA* 77 (1962): 268–79.

――――. "George Eliot's Hypothesis of Reality." *Nineteenth-Century Fiction* 25 (1980): 1–28.

――――. "Intelligence as Deception: *The Mill on the Floss*." *PMLA* 80 (1965): 402–9.

――――. "Realism, or In Praise of Lying: Some Nineteenth-Century Novels." *College English* 31 (1970): 355–65.

――――. *The Realistic Imagination: English Fiction from Frankenstein to Lady Chatterley*. Chicago: Univ. of Chicago Press, 1981.

――――. "*Romola* as Fable." In Barbara Hardy, ed. *Critical Essays on George Eliot*. London: Routledge and Kegan Paul, 1970. 78–98.

Lewalski, Barbara K. "Milton on Women—Yet Once More." *Milton Studies* 6 (1974): 3–20.

Mandelbaum, Maurice. *History, Man, and Reason: A Study of Nineteenth-Century Thought*. Baltimore: Johns Hopkins Press, 1971.

Mann, Karen. *The Language That Makes George Eliot's Fiction*. Baltimore: Johns Hopkins Press, 1983.

Mansell, Darrel. "George Eliot's Conception of Tragedy." *Nineteenth-Century Fiction* 22 (1967): 155–71.

Manual, Frank E. *The Prophets of Paris: Turgot, Condorcet, Saint-Simon, Fourier, and Comte*. Cambridge: Harvard Univ. Press, 1962.

Martin, Biddy. "Feminism, Criticism, and Foucault." In Irene Diamond and Lee Quinby, eds. *Feminism and Foucault: Reflections on Resistance*. Boston: Northeast Univ. Press, 1988. 3–19.

Martin, Bruce K. "Rescue and Marriage in *Adam Bede*." *Studies in English Literature, 1500–1900* 12 (1972): 745–63.

――――. "Similarity within Dissimilarity: The Dual Structure of *Silas Marner*." *Texas Studies in Language and Literature* 14 (1972): 479–89.

Mason, Michael York. "*Middlemarch* and History." *Nineteenth-Century Fiction* 25 (1971): 417–31.

————. "*Middlemarch* and Science: Problems of Life and Mind." *Review of English Studies* 22 (1971): 154–65.

Mayr, Ernst. *The Growth of Biological Thought: Diversity, Evolution, and Inheritance.* Cambridge: Belknap Press, 1982.

Merchant, Carolyn. *The Death of Nature: Women, Ecology, and the Scientific Revolution.* San Francisco: Harper and Row, 1980.

Miller, J. Hillis. "Narrative and History." *ELH* 41 (1974): 455–73.

————. "Optic and Semiotic in *Middlemarch.*" In Jerome Buckley, *The Worlds of Victorian Fiction.* Cambridge: Harvard Univ. Press, 1975. 125–45.

Miller, Nancy K. "Emphasis Added: Plots and Plausibilities in Women's Fiction." *PMLA* 96 (1981): 36–48.

Millett, Kate. *Sexual Politics.* Garden City: Doubleday, 1970.

Milner, Ian. *The Structure of Values in George Eliot.* Prague: Universita Karlova, 1968.

Mintz, Alan L. *George Eliot and the Novel of Vocation.* Cambridge: Harvard Univ. Press, 1978.

Moers, Ellen. *Literary Women: The Great Writers.* Garden City: Anchor Books, 1977.

Molstad, David. "*The Mill on the Floss* and *Antigone.*" *PMLA* 85 (1970): 527–31.

Murray, Janet Horowitz. *Strong-Minded Women and Other Lost Voices from Nineteenth-Century England.* New York: Pantheon, 1982.

Myers, W.F.T. "Politics and Personality in *Felix Holt.*" *Renaissance and Modern Studies* 10 (1966): 5–33.

Myers, William. *The Teaching of George Eliot.* Leicester: Leicester Univ. Press, 1984.

Newton, Judith Lowder. "History as Usual? Feminism and the 'New Historicism.'" *Cultural Critique* (Spring 1988): 87–121.

————. *Women, Power, and Subversion: Social Strategies in British Fiction, 1778–1860.* Athens: Univ. of Georgia Press, 1981.

Newton, K. M. "George Eliot, George Henry Lewes, and Darwinism." *Durham University Journal* 66 (1974): 278–93.

————. *George Eliot, Romantic Humanist: A Study of the Philosophical Structure of Her Novels.* New York: Barnes and Noble, 1981.

Ortner, Sherry. "Is Female to Male as Nature is to Culture?" *Feminist Studies* 1 (1972): 5–31.

Paris, Bernard J. *Experiments in Life: George Eliot's Quest for Values.* Detroit: Wayne State Univ. Press, 1965.

————. *A Psychological Approach to Fiction: Studies in Thackeray, Stendhal, George Eliot, Dostoevsky, and Conrad.* Bloomington: Indiana Univ. Press, 1974.

Paxton, Nancy L. "Feminism and Positivism in George Eliot's *Romola.*" In Rhoda Nathan, ed. *Nineteenth-Century Women Writers.* Westport, Conn.: Greenwood, 1986. 143–50.

————. "George Eliot and the City: The Imprisonment of Culture." In Susan Merrill Squier, ed. *Women Writers and the City: Essays in Feminist Literary Criticism.* Knoxville: Univ. of Tennessee Press, 1984. 71–96.

Peel, J.D.Y. *Herbert Spencer: The Evolution of a Sociologist.* London: Heinemann, 1971.

Perrin, Robert G. "Herbert Spencer's Four Theories of Social Evolution." *American Journal of Sociology* 81 (1976): 139–59.

Pinney, Thomas. "The Authority of the Past in George Eliot's Novels." *Nineteenth-Century Fiction* 21 (1966): 131–47.

———. "George Eliot's Reading of Wordsworth: The Record." *Victorian Newsletter* 24 (1973): 20–22.

Poovey, Mary. *Uneven Developments: The Ideological Work of Gender in Mid-Victorian England.* Chicago: Univ. of Chicago Press, 1988.

Postlethwaite, Diana. *Making It Whole: A Victorian Circle and the Shape of Their World.* Columbus: Ohio State Univ. Press, 1984.

Poston, Lawrence Stanford. "Setting and Theme in *Romola*." *Nineteenth-Century Fiction* 20 (1966): 355–66.

Preyer, Robert. "Beyond the Liberal Imagination: Vision and Unreality in *Daniel Deronda*." *Victorian Studies* 4 (1960): 33–54.

Putzell, Sara Moore. "An Antagonism of Valid Claims: The Dynamics of *The Mill on the Floss*." *Studies in the Novel* 7 (1975): 227–44.

———. "The Search for a Higher Rule: Spiritual Progress in the Novels of George Eliot." *Journal of the American Academy of Religion* 47 (1978): 389–407.

Qualls, Barry. *The Secular Pilgrims of Victorian Fiction: The Novel as a Book of Life.* Cambridge: Cambridge Univ. Press, 1982.

Redinger, Ruby V. *George Eliot: The Emergent Self.* New York: Knopf, 1975.

Rendell, Vernon. "George Eliot and the Classics." *Notes and Queries* 192 (1947): 544–46, 564–65; 193 (1948): 148–49, 272–74.

Rich, Adrienne. "*Jane Eyre*: The Temptations of a Motherless Woman." In Adrienne Rich, *On Lies, Secrets, and Silence: Selected Prose, 1966–1978.* New York: Norton, 1979. 89–106.

———. *Of Woman Born: Motherhood as Experience and Institution.* New York: Norton, 1976.

Roazen, Deborah Heller. "George Eliot and Wordsworth: 'The Natural History of German Life' and Peasant Psychology." *Research Studies: Washington State University* 41 (1973): 166–78.

———. "*Middlemarch* and the Wordsworthian Imagination." *English Studies* 58 (1977): 411–25.

Roberts, Neil. *George Eliot: Her Beliefs and Her Art.* Pittsburgh: Univ. of Pittsburgh Press, 1975.

Robinson, Carole. "*Romola*: A Reading of the Novel." *Victorian Studies* 6 (1962): 29–42.

———. "The Severe Angel: A Study of *Daniel Deronda*." *ELH* 31 (1964): 278–300.

Rose, Phyllis. *Parallel Lives: Five Victorian Marriages.* New York: Knopf, 1983.

Russett, Cynthia Eagle. *Sexual Science: The Victorian Construction of Womanhood.* Cambridge: Harvard Univ. Press, 1989.

Sadoff, Dianne F. *Monsters of Affection: Dickens, Eliot, and Brontë on Fatherhood.* Baltimore: Johns Hopkins Press, 1982.

———. "Nature's Language: Metaphor in the Text of *Adam Bede*." *Genre* 11 (1978): 411–26.

Sandler, Florence. "The Unity of *Felix Holt*." In Anne Smith, ed., *George Eliot: A*

Centenary Tribute and Unpublished Fragment. Totowa, N.Y.: Barnes and Noble, 1980. 137–52.

Sayers, Janet. *Biological Politics: Feminist and Anti-Feminist Perspectives.* London: Tavistock, 1982.

Schneewind, Jerome B. "Moral Problems and Moral Philosophy in the Victorian Period." *Victorian Studies* 9 (1965): 29–46.

Scott, James F. "George Eliot, Positivism, and the Social Vision of *Middlemarch.*" *Victorian Studies* 16 (1972–1973): 59–76.

Sheets, Robin. "*Felix Holt:* Language, the Bible, and the Problematic of Meaning." *Nineteenth-Century Fiction* 37 (1982): 146–69.

Showalter, Elaine. "Feminist Criticism in the Wilderness." *Critical Inquiry* 8 (1981): 179–205.

——. "Florence Nightingale's Complaint: Women, Religion and Suggestions of Thought." *Signs* 6 (1981): 395–412.

——. "The Greening of Sister George." *Nineteenth-Century Fiction* 35 (1980): 292–311.

——. *A Literature of Their Own: British Women Novelists from Brontë to Lessing.* Princeton: Princeton Univ. Press, 1977.

Shuttleworth, Sally. *George Eliot and Nineteenth-Century Science: The Make-Believe of a Beginning.* New York: Cambridge Univ. Press, 1984.

Simon, Walter. "Herbert Spencer and the 'Social Organism.' " *Journal of the History of Ideas* 21 (1961): 294–99.

Simon, William M. *European Positivism in the Nineteenth Century: An Essay in Intellectual History.* Ithaca: Cornell Univ. Press, 1963.

Smith, Anne, ed. *George Eliot: Centenary Essays and an Unpublished Fragment.* Totowa: Barnes and Noble, 1980.

Spacks, Patricia Meyer. *The Female Imagination.* New York: Avon Books, 1976.

Stang, Richard. *The Theory of the Novel in England, 1850–1870.* New York: Columbia Univ. Press, 1959.

Steig, Michael. "Anality in *The Mill on the Floss.*" *Novel* 5 (1971): 42–53.

Stimpson, Catharine, and Ethel Spector Person, eds. *Women: Sex and Sexuality.* Chicago: Univ. of Chicago Press, 1980.

Stone, Donald. *The Romantic Impulse in Victorian Fiction.* Cambridge: Harvard Univ. Press, 1980.

Strachey, Ray. "*The Cause*": A Short History of the Women's Movement in Great Britain.* London: G. Bell, 1928.

Stump, Reva. *Movement and Vision in George Eliot's Novels.* Seattle: Univ. of Washington Press, 1959.

Svaglic, M. J. "Religion in the Novels of George Eliot." *Journal of English and Germanic Philology* 53 (1954): 145–59.

Swann, Brian. "George Eliot and the Play: Symbol and the Metaphor of the Drama in *Daniel Deronda.*" *Dalhousie Review* 52 (1972): 191–202.

——. "*Middlemarch* and Myth." *Nineteenth-Century Fiction* 28 (1973): 210–20.

——. "*Middlemarch:* Realism and Symbolic Form." *ELH* 39 (1972): 279–308.

——. "*Silas Marner* and the New Mythus." *Criticism* 18 (1976): 101–21.

Taylor, Barbara. *Eve and the New Jerusalem: Socialism and Feminism in the Nineteenth Century.* London: Virago, 1983.

Thale, Jerome. *The Novels of George Eliot*. New York: Columbia Univ. Press, 1959.

Thomson, Fred C. *"Felix Holt* as Classic Tragedy." *Nineteenth-Century Fiction* 16 (1961): 47–58.

———. "The Genesis of *Felix Holt.*" *PMLA* 124 (1959): 4–5, 76–84.

———. "Politics and Society in *Felix Holt.*" In Charles Edge and Howard Harper, eds. *The Classic British Novel*. Athens: Univ. of Georgia Press, 1972. 103–20.

———. "The Theme of Alienation in *Silas Marner.*" *Nineteenth-Century Fiction* 20 (1965): 69–84.

Thomson, Patricia. *George Sand and the Victorians: Her Influence and Reputation in Nineteenth-Century England*. New York: Columbia Univ. Press, 1977.

Timko, Michael. "The Victorianism of Victorian Literature." *New Literary History* 6 (1975): 607–22.

Tjoa, Hock Guan. *George Henry Lewes: A Victorian Mind*. Cambridge: Harvard Univ. Press, 1977.

Trudgill, Eric. *Madonnas and Magdalens: The Origins and Development of Victorian Sexual Attitudes*. New York: Holmes and Meier, 1976.

Vicinus, Martha, ed. *Suffer and Be Still: Women in the Victorian Age*. Bloomington: Indiana Univ. Press, 1972.

———. *A Widening Sphere: Changing Roles of Victorian Women*. Bloomington: Indiana Univ. Press, 1977.

Vogeler, Martha S. "George Eliot and the Positivists." *Nineteenth-Century Fiction* 35 (1980): 406–31.

Walkowitz, Judith R. *Prostitution and Victorian Society: Women, Class, and the State*. Cambridge: Cambridge Univ. Press, 1980.

Weisenfarth, Joseph. *"Adam Bede* and Myth." *Papers on Language and Literature* 8 (1972): 39–52.

———. "Demythologizing *Silas Marner.*" *ELH* 37 (1970): 226–44.

———. *George Eliot's Mythmaking*. Heidelberg: Winter, 1977.

———. "George Eliot's Notes for *Adam Bede.*" *Nineteenth-Century Fiction* 32 (1977): 127–65.

Wellek, René. "The Concept of Evolution in Literary History." In M. Halle, ed. *For Roman Jakobson*. The Hague: Mouton, 1956.

Welsh, Alexander. *The City of Dickens*. Oxford Univ. Press, 1971.

———. *George Eliot and Blackmail*. Cambridge: Harvard Univ. Press, 1985.

Willey, Basil. *Nineteenth-Century Studies: Coleridge to Matthew Arnold*. New York: Columbia Univ. Press, 1949.

Williams, Raymond. *The Country and the City*. New York: Oxford Univ. Press, 1973.

———. *Culture and Society, 1780–1950*. London: Chatto and Windus, 1958.

Wilt, Judith. *Ghosts of the Gothic: Austen, Eliot, and D. H. Lawrence*. Princeton: Princeton Univ. Press, 1980.

Wiltshire, David. *The Social and Political Thought of Herbert Spencer*. Oxford Univ. Press, 1978.

Wolff, Michael. "The Uses of Context: Aspects of the 1860s." *Victorian Studies* 9 (1966 supp.): 47–63.

Woolf, Virginia. *The Common Reader: First Series*. New York: Harcourt, Brace, and
    World, 1953.
Wright, Walter Francis. "George Eliot as Industrial Reformer." *PMLA* 56
    (1941): 1107–15.
Young, Robert M. "The Historiographic and Ideological Contexts of Nine-
    teenth-Century Debate on Man's Place in Nature." In M. Teich and R. M.
    Young, eds. *Changing Perspectives in the History of Science: Essays in Honor of Jo-*
    seph Needham. London: Heinemann, 1973. 344–438.
Zimmerman, Bonnie. *"Felix Holt* and the True Power of Womanhood." *ELH* 46
    (1979): 432–51.
———. "Gwendolen Harleth and 'The Girl of the Period.' " In Anne Smith,
    ed. *George Eliot: Centenary Essays and an Unpublished Fragment*. Totowa: Barnes
    and Noble, 1980. 81–94.
———. "The Mother's History in George Eliot's Life, Literature, and Political
    Ideology." In Cathy N. Davidson and E. M. Broner, eds. *The Lost Tradition:*
    Mothers and Daughters in Literature. New York: Frederick Ungar, 1980. 81–94.
———. "Radiant as a Diamond: George Eliot, Jewelry, and the Female Role."
    Criticism 19 (1977): 212–22.

Index